THE ECONOMIC ROLE OF JEWS IN MEDIEVAL POLAND

The Contribution of Yitzhak Schipper

Jacob Litman

UNIVERSITY PRESS OF AMERICA

LANHAM • NEW YORK • LONDON

University Press of America,™ Inc.

4720 Boston Way
Lanham, MD 20706

3 Henrietta Street
London WC2E 8LU England

Printed in the United States of America

ISBN (Perfect): 0-8191-4245-X
ISBN (Cloth): 0-8191-4244-1

All University Press of America books are produced on acid-free paper which exceeds the minimum standards set by the National Historical Publications and Records Commission.

To the Memory
of my parents
Yehuda Me'ir and Hannah (neé Zalcman)
who, tormented and victimized
by German Nazi brutes in the
liquidation of the Warsaw Ghetto,
continue to sustain me with
their spiritual legacy.

Table of Contents

Preface

Yitzhak (Ignacy) Schipper occupied an eminent place and played a distinctive role among the leaders of the Jewish community of Poland in the first half of the twentieth century. He was writer, speaker, teacher, statesman, and—above all—a historian of his people. From his early youth until his death in the concentration camp of Maidanek, two distinct but interrelated and complementary features characterized his productive life. These were: (1) an active involvement in sociopolitical and cultural affairs directly affecting the Polish Jewish community of his time, and (2) an intense interest and preoccupation with Jewish history, particularly with the socioeconomic aspects of Jewish history in Poland.

In World War II the millenial history of Polish Jewry came to an unforseen and tragic end, destroyed by the brutal twentieth-century totalitarian state of Nazi Germany. Because Polish Jewry, the victim of this modern barbarism, is no more, the contributions of Schipper to the understanding of the history of that community, written mainly in Yiddish and Polish, assume a special significance not only for the Jews in the United States but also for the general English reader interested in the sentiments and attitudes of that doomed generation of Polish Jewry. For Schipper was, in more than one sense, a true representative of that generation. His way of thinking as a historian and his entire career as an activist in Jewish life reflect to a considerable degree the milieu, the ideas, and the hopes of the people among whom he lived and to whom he dedicated his extraordinary abilities and a lifetime of scholarly work.

Schipper considered himself a historian who, by definition,

must be involved in the urgent problems of his own world and who must seek in history phenomena pertinent to contemporary issues. Thus, his purpose and approach were related to the existential problems of Polish Jewry in his time: racial and political anti-Semitism threatening from without, assimilationism threatening from within, and the need to strengthen the historical unity and defenses of the Jewish communities in Poland through a re-identification and emancipation expressed in modern, nationalistic terms. Although he was not a Marxist in a doctrinal sense, Schipper's thinking centered around the beliefs that: (a) economic factors constitute a basic key for the understanding of history and (b) a re-examination of Jewish history in terms of economic struggles is indispensable for the Jewish masses of his generation in their efforts to secure social, economic, and national rights.

Schipper's historical studies represent a pioneering contribution. He introduced a new orientation in modern Jewish historiography, and pointed toward hitherto unexplored directions. An analysis and critical evaluation of his contributions to the understanding of the economic history of Jews in medieval Poland is presented in this book, focusing on those aspects of Schipper's investigations which are significant in terms of his specific findings and characteristic in terms of his approach.

Initially, this study was submitted as a doctoral dissertation at New York University in 1968, and in this connection, I acknowledge my indebtedness to Professor Abraham I. Katsh, chairman of the sponsoring committee, who encouraged me to proceed with it. I am equally obliged to the other two members of the committee, Professor David Rudavsky and Professor Emanuel Stein, for their interest, advice, and emendations. Whenever I consulted with either one of them, I had the distinct feeling of being in the presence of dedicated teachers and true gentlemen. I must also express my thanks to the National Foundation for Jewish Culture and the Memorial Foundation for Jewish Culture for the grants which made it possible for me, at that juncture, to devote myself to the research and the writing.

* * *

In preparing the original manuscript for publication sixteen years later, the question of updating it became a matter of foremost consideration. In my efforts to fulfill this essential condition, however, it became clear that, besides certain comprehensive works representing Jewish economic histories in a wider sense, nothing of real significance came out that would directly impinge on the substantive aspects of the manuscript except for the very valuable and timely book by D.B. Weinryb, *The Jews of Poland* (Philadelphia: 1976). This work and certain other pertinent publications (such as the recently published *Khazarian Documents of the Tenth Century* by N. Golb and O. Pritsak which Schipper would have welcomed and utilized in support of his theory on the origin of Jews in Poland) were consulted and, to the extent applicable, incorporated in the present text.

The preferred spelling of the surname Schipper also posed a question in view of the fact that, other than an orthography employing a double *p*, the usage of one *p* is not uncommon. Indeed, the name appears as Schiper, Ignacy (Yiẓḥak) in the *Encyclopaedia Judaica* (Jerusalem: 1972). My conclusion that the spelling with a double *p* is both proper and preferable is predicated on the facts that (a) the name is indisputably German in origin and form, (b) all Schipper's writings in German and Polish from 1902 through 1920 appeared with the German spelling of the name, (c) the elimination of one *p* from the German spelling, as it appeared in his Polish writings published in the 20's and 30's, seems to have been a halfhearted way of Polonizing the name since a complete Polonization would have called for the additional changes required to transliterate the German Schipper to the Polish Szyper, and (d) amazingly—although not unexpectedly, perhaps—Schipper's last work in Polish (*Siedemset lat gminy żydowskiej w Płocku*), published in 1938, appeared with his name spelled again with a double *p*. Hence, in this book the name is Schipper except when transliterated from Yiddish or Hebrew in which case it is Shiper.

With respect to Schipper's first name, which can take on five forms—Ignaz (in German), Ignacy (in Polish), Itskhok (Romanized from Yiddish), Yiẓḥak or Iṣḥaq (Romanized from Hebrew), and Yitzhak, prevalent today in American periodicals and the press, I have decided to use the conventional Yitzhak in the title as well as in two opening sentences of the book and simplify the matter by utilizing the initial *I.* in all other instances throughout the text.

The Romanization of Arabic, Hebrew, Yiddish, and Russian names or titles has also been simplified. In the case of Arabic or Hebrew it has been done by eliminating diacritical marks where tolerable (e.g. *ts*, instead of ṣ or ẓ for the *tsadi*) and discarding macrons, breather signs for an *aleph* and *ayin* at the beginning or end of the word, letter doubling for the *dagesh forte*, and the Hebrew *he* at the end of the word. The Romanization system of YIVO Institute for Jewish Research has been followed in the case of Yiddish except that the *ḥet* in words or names of Hebrew origin is indicated and names of places, nationalities, journals, periodicals and anthologies are capitalized. As for Russian, the simplification relates primarily to the Cyrillic letters Й or Ь (the latter only in the middle of the word) being both transliterated with the Roman *Y*, and the Cyrillic И or Ы being both transliterated with the Roman *I*.

During long months of research, I found the people on the staffs of the Jewish Division of the New York Public Library and the Public Library of my Township of Union, New Jersey to be most courteous and helpful. Ms. Dina Abramowicz, the librarian of the YIVO Institute for Jewish Research, was also always ready to assist me in locating relevant items scattered in various periodicals that are not easily obtainable. To all these people and to Dr. Alfred Miller, of blessed memory, who resided at the time in Jerusalem and who provided me with photostatic copies of Schipper's articles in the library of the Hebrew University, I am truly beholden.

Words of appreciation are also due to Mrs. Miriam Wachtel who ably assisted me in editing and checking the original manuscript as well as to Mmes. Minnie Fine and Elizabeth Duda for their efficiency in typing it.

In all technical matters relating to the production of the book,

I am indebted to Mr. George W. Cooke of Publication Arts and to the University Press of America for their professional expertise, meticulous attention, and cooperative manner. Any inaccuracy or oversight, however, is to be attributed to me since, ultimately, I am solely responsible for the entire text, including all quoted passages translated from German, Polish, Russian, Yiddish, and Hebrew.

All in all, this publication could not have been realized at the present time without the understanding and support shown by the officers of the United Synagogue of America with whom I am associated professionally. My sincere thanks are hereby tendered to all of them, especially to Mr. Norman Glikin who graciously volunteered to facilitate matters.

It must be said, in conclusion, that I cannot thank enough my wife and children for their understanding and patience.

J.L.

Ignatz Schipper (1884-1943). Photograph courtesy of the YIVO Institute for Jewish Research.

1

The Times and the Man

A comprehensive appreciation of the position which Jews occupied in the economy of medieval Poland is inconceivable without reference to the studies on the subject by Yitzhak (Ignacy) Schipper, who was a perceptive historian and an esteemed figure in the Jewish community of Poland before the Nazi onslaught of 1939. Schipper was born on the ninth of November, 1884 in Tarnów, a town in Poland's province of Cracow. In this place of his upbringing, which in many respects represented a microcosm of the Jewish historical macrocosm in Poland, Schipper began his investigations into the past and before long developed a philosophy about the role of the historian as a scholar whose prime motive for searching into bygone times must be the questions and challenges of his own contemporary world. Accordingly, besides the factual evidence and documentation, written history should be studied and understood in terms of the author's own times, his own background, his situation, associations, outlook, and attitude. It follows therefore that a description of these biographical aspects, as they relate to Schipper, are in order at the very beginning of this book.

Tarnów remained Schipper's principal place of residence for

about half of his lifetime, until 1919. Even today, a visitor to Tarnów can readily recognize its medieval origin. The marketplace is rectangularly enclosed by old stone structures and displays a mixture of Gothic and Renaissance architecture. The Town Hall, one of the oldest of those structures and the focal point of the medieval quarter, retains, in spite of a number of inevitable restorations, its original Gothic style to which, in the course of time, Italian architects and sculptors added Renaissance elements.[1] Off the marketplace there is a labyrinth of narrow, winding streets and passages where the dwellings with their tiny courts, dark corridors, heavy iron doors, hanging street lanterns, and cramped little stores and shops close together reflect the desire of the medieval burgher to remain safe within the confines of the city walls. Parts of the old defensive walls are visible within the system of the old buildings, especially on streets running along the old moat.[2] The Collegiate Church, presently the Cathedral, can trace its origin back to the first wooden church of Tarnów built by Spicymierz,[3] voivode (military commander) of Cracow and one of the earliest owners of the town during the first half of the fourteenth century. Surrounding the church are old collegiate stone buildings, one of which, the Mikołajewski house built in 1523, housed the oldest school in Tarnów. Although the original old Gothic style of the Cathedral is no longer visible from the outside because of numerous conflagrations which several times ruined greater parts of the town,[4] the inner sanctuary contains some of the oldest sacred art objects in the history of Poland. Its monuments of the Renaissance period represent many of the counts, and members of their families, to whom Tarnów belonged during the Middle Ages.[5]

The visitor will also notice the church and monastery of the Bernardines, built by John Amor Tarnowski in 1468. Erected outside the town proper, the church and monastery were built with the stones and bricks of the old deteriorating castle of the Tarnowski counts, traces of which still remain. The monastery constituted a separate fortified settlement and an underground passage leads from it to the new castle. The archives maintained by the Bernardine monks include priceless Latin documents pertaining to the history of Tarnów[6] and its environs, as well as to the history of the entire Polish kingdom. The curious might also wander to the hill of St. Martin on which, it is believed, a pre-Christian settlement of Slavs had their pagan sanctuary.

Under Austrian Rule

Until 1772 Tarnów was a private town in the Polish kingdom. Although its municipal administration nominally enjoyed the Magdeburg Charter, it was dependent on the Polish lords who owned the town. The history of the Jews in Tarnów until the end of the eighteenth century was the subject of a special study by Schipper,[7] who as a youth was fascinated by the historicity of his native town and spent much time investigating its past.

With the annexation of southern Poland by Austria following the first partition in 1772, Tarnów became a city in the Galician province of the Austrian Empire. The history of its Jewish population reflects closely Jewish life in Galicia generally under the changing conditions and policies of the Hapsburg emperors and their respective governments.[8]

First came the government of Maria Theresa which, in its relation to Jews, was interested in only one thing: more money.[9] This was followed by the "humanitarian" policies of Joseph II, the enlightened absolute monarch who was determined to emancipate the Jews through decrees and compulsory Germanization. But Joseph II's reforms,[10] which did not take into account the specific conditions and needs of the Jews, were resisted by the Jews in Tarnów as much as by Jews in all Galicia. Steeped in religious traditions, the Jewish masses were still strongly committed to a cultural and social separatism.[11] Nonetheless, the ideas of the Enlightenment had repercussions in the *Kulturkampf* that eventually ensued within Galician Jewish society.

By the end of the eighteenth century Tarnów experienced a period of development owing to the new "Emperor's Road," built in 1784-1785, and the incorporation of four nearby villages into the municipality. Tarnów became one of the bigger cities in Galicia, but the Jews did not share in its period of boom. Already impoverished by a great conflagration in 1792 which burned down the entire Jewish section, the Jews suffered a further deterioration of their situation under the reactionary regime of Metternich. It reinstituted and enforced ghetto regulations, renewed economic restrictions, imposed heavy taxes with additional levies on kosher meat and candles, and issued a number of contradictory laws which local civil servants interpreted as they wished. In the years immediately preceding the March Revolution of 1848, the Jews in the Tarnów district were even accused of having committed ritual murders.[12]

The Revolution of 1848 brought about a fraternization between the Polish democratic, liberal elements and a rather thin layer of the Jewish population, namely, certain urban Jews who were well-educated, progressive and politically active. But the Bach reaction negated the March Constitution of 1849, which had granted equal rights to Jews, and actually instituted new restrictions. Jewish affairs were once again put under the jurisdiction of the Catholic hierarchy which chose to cooperate with the Jewish orthodoxy rather than the new Jewish intelligentsia of whom it was suspicious.[13]

The first significant changes came after the Austrian defeat on the Italian front in 1859. Although the government was not yet willing to institute fundamental reforms with regard to its Jewish population, it realized that it must do something for purely practical reasons as well as financial considerations. The protests expressed in the press of Western Europe, which became rather loud and embarrassing, also had to be answered. Thus, a number of decrees were issued that eliminated the existing marriage limitations, the prohibition on hiring Christian servants, the strictures concerning testimony of Jews in courts, the residence restrictions in villages, the entrance requirements into certain trades and industries, etc.

The Constitution of 1861 removed all previously imposed restrictions and the general situation improved considerably, but equal rights were extended to Jews gradually and not everywhere to the same extent. Jewish participation in municipal councils was implemented relatively quickly, but not always in proportion to the size of the Jewish population, especially in the large cities.[14]

In Tarnów the 1866 municipal elections brought into the city council nine Jewish councilmen and four alternates. For the first time the town hall included a Jewish assessor. In the next municipal elections, held in 1870, thirteen Jewish councilmen and eight alternates were elected. The subsequent elections produced more or less the same results. As a rule, the well-to-do, assimilated Jews ran for municipal office, and many of those elected often became "permanent" members of the municipal government. The elections were basically contests between the richer Jewish families of Tarnów, the role of the common people being minimal. There was no Jewish policy, no collective political activity. The efforts of the Jewish councilmen were by and large relegated to individual interventions, the results of which depended on the personal ambitions of each officeholder. Generally, their accomplishments could not be described as important or as consciously aiming to protect the interests of the total Jewish community and improve its situation.[15]

Having finally left the ghetto confines, the Jews of Tarnów began to play a more active role in the city's economy as its merchants, tailors, and hat manufacturers. Jews began to avail themselves, in ever increasing numbers, of the public education which was now open to them and which produced a considerable number of Jewish intelligentsia, doctors and lawyers who, although assimilationist, often participated in Jewish communal affairs. And yet, in 1867, one year after the Jews of Tarnów were officially praised by the Catholic bishop for their exemplary assistance in extinguishing a great fire that erupted in the Cathedral, an anti-Jewish riot took place in the city which only the nearby military garrison was able to quell.[16]

The general tendency of the rapidly growing class of educated Jews was toward either German or Polish cultural assimilation. The German trend was somewhat stronger in Eastern Galicia where, besides Poles and Jews, there were Ukrainians who made up the bulk of the peasantry in the area. For centuries they had successfully resisted the pressures of Polonization and conversion to Roman Catholicism; now influenced by the general spirit of romantic nationalism, the Ukrainians began stressing their national character (the Ukrainian language, culture, and folklore and the Greek Orthodox creed).[17] The trend toward Polish assimilation among the educated Jews was more pronounced in Western Galicia where the Ukrainians constituted an almost invisible minority, and where Jews were attracted by Polish emigrés from Congress Poland who brought to Galicia the revolutionary romanticism of the Polish uprisings.

When the Austrian Constitution of 1867 instituted parliamentary rule in the autonomous provinces, the Ukrainians and the Poles became engaged in a bitter struggle over the national character of Eastern Galicia. The Jews found it difficult to remain neutral in this struggle.[18] When the Austrian government, having finally abandoned all attempts to Germanize Galicia, took a position favorable to the Poles, Jewish cooperation with the latter became inevitable. The Poles became the dominant political force and the Polish orientation among Galician Jewry prevailed.[19]

Paradoxical as it may seem, the Hasidic *zaddikim*[20] who had complete power over the uneducated Jewish multitudes in Galicia worked closely with the assimilated Jewish intelligentsia. This rather strange cooperation between the ultraorthodox separatists and the assimilated and freethinking Jews, mostly careerists, came about after 1867, the year in which the Austrian government reluctantly abandoned its Germanic-centralist orientation and agreed to transfer the administration of Galicia to the Poles. The Jewish assimilationists, who saw themselves as Polish patriots and votaries of the Polish national cause, assumed the role of spokesmen on behalf of the Jewish community vis-à-vis Polish officialdom. To strengthen their position, they found it quite opportune to support the Hasidic rebbes who were intent on monopolizing the inner spheres of Jewish life. Thus, the various Hasidic courts became supporters of Polish nationalism. They voted for candidates of the Polish parliamentary club, even when some of those candidates were known anti-Semites. Politically, the vital interests of the Jews became subservient to the interests of the Poles.[21]

It soon became clear that the Poles were interested only in themselves, and the heightened nationalistic feelings produced a new wave of anti-Semitism. As the latest "scientific" theories about the inferiority and dangerous depravity of Jews began to penetrate the Galician hinterland from abroad,[22] the historically rooted hostility to Jews emerged again. Now, besides the traditionally anti-Semitic elements of the Polish society, the chauvinistic agitation against Jews captured also the Polish civil servants, government officials, free professionals, and university students. They joined the National Democratic Party, organized by the Polish middle class, and called on the Polish population to boycott the Jews.[23] The renewed do-away-with Jews propaganda brought a surge of anti-Jewish riots that had to be quelled by the military, as was the case in Tarnów, and led to an organized economic assault against Jews. This was encouraged by the Galician government which proceeded to eliminate Jews from certain trades by establishing monopolies and imposing all kinds of restrictions. The economic boycott became so deliberate, through the instituted *kółka rolnicze* (cooperative stores in the countryside),[24] and so virulent, with its incessant reminder to Christians to "buy from your own kind," that beginning with the eighties an ever-growing pauperization of the Jewish population set in. By the turn of the century it took on alarming proportions, and many Jews began to leave Galicia.[25] Thus, the political and civil rights which Jews in Galicia obtained in the second half of the nineteenth century brought nothing but a further deterioration of conditions due to the widening economic boycott and the discriminatory policies of the provincial Polish government. The growing menace of anti-Semitism dashed even the hopes of some leading assimilationists as they began to realize that the Poles could not be trusted in their attitude towards Jews.[26] Out of the general disappointment two new movements took root in Jewish life: Zionism and socialism. The first was troubled about the future; the second, about the lack of true democratic representation of the Jewish masses.

Tarnów at the Turn of the Century

The new political, social, and cultural orientations of Galician Jewry in the eighties, the decade often described as the incubation period of modern Jewish movements and organizations, were not only reflected in Tarnów but in certain respects given their first impetus in that city. Tarnów was in the forefront of impending changes and responses.

The city was for many decades a bulwark of orthodoxy and Hasidism. The religious segment of its Jewish population represented a considerable social and cultural force. One could meet here followers of various Hasidic dynasties (sects), each with its own *kloyz* (place of worship). Of the Hasidic *kloyzn*, the greatest and best known was that of the Sanzer Hasidim, that is, the followers of the *zaddick*, Rabbi Ḥayyim Halberstam, who lived in Tarnów. Popularly known as the *Great Kloyz*, it was the fortress of ultraorthodoxy, open twenty-four hours a day for prayer and study. Before dawn, the melancholy chants of students pouring over an intricate Talmudic passage could be heard. Latecomers to morning services were unable to find a seat, and in the evening it was full of worshippers and students, conversationalists, disputants, pilpulists, psalm reciters, etc.[27]

Besides the various Hasidic groups, there existed dozens of smaller shuls or minyanim[28] (congregations) organized by "private" smaller groups. The small places of worship often served as a sort of rallying point for religious as well as social, occupational, and even political purposes. There were also the old shul, about five hundred years old, and the new synagogue, a magnificent copper-domed structure, built in Byzantine style, in which services were conducted by a professional cantor accompanied by a well-trained choir.

Mention must also be made of the *besmedresh* (house of study) which was always crowded with worshippers, students, Jews who would come in the evening to listen to a *magid* (wandering preacher), and individuals with some time on their hands. In the winter tea was served continually for anyone who wished to warm up.[29]

Although in the second half of the nineteenth century, and particularly during its last two or three decades, the Jewish community of Tarnów included progressive groups and a large secular segment, the deeply rooted religious and traditional mores pervaded its life. Manifested in many different ways, it was best seen on the Sabbath and holidays when all Jewish stores and shops were closed and the economic life of the town virtually came to a stop. Even the trolley was half empty. The Hasidic way of life—its spirit, customs, habits, folklore, and ceremonies—was not confined to its own safeholds, but was very much a part of public life. The Hasidic rebbes who resided in Tarnów exercised an influence not only on their followers but indirectly on many Jews in all walks of life. Their personalities and prestige could not easily be disregarded.[30] The extent of the orthodox influence and traditional way of life is described by Joshua Landau, one of the founders of the Jewish Socialist Party in Tarnów,[31] in these words:

> Religious subservience and obscurity dominated the Jewish homes. The Jewish clergy and the kehilla people put their stamp on all of Jewish public life. Many times our important meetings came to naught because most of our members were at the time engaged in . . . worship. Not always could our meetings begin on time. Members used to convert our local into a minyan and conduct the *Minḥa-Ma'ariv* (afternoon-evening) services. Thus we had to work with an element which, on one hand, was illiterate and religiously conditioned and, on the other, afraid to lose their jobs and livelihood at a time when there was much poverty and hunger on the Jewish street.[32]

While other elements of the Jewish community began to organize political parties, the religious segment was primarily involved in communal affairs, maintaining or participating in a number of local social institutions: school and yeshivas, a Talmud Torah for poor children, the Jewish hospital, the *Bikur Ḥolim* society, etc. The group that centered around the *Great Kloyz*, especially, never affiliated with any political party, maintaining that it did not befit a truly religious Jew to associate with organizations which bore a modern and secular character.[33]

In Tarnów the ripening nationalist counterforce came to the fore immediately following the wave of pogroms in Russia in 1883. Jewish refugees from Russia, and the publication of Leo Pinsker's *Autoemancipation* reinforced the growing national reawakening among Tarnów Jews. The Zionist slogans received a resounding and enthusiastic echo in town, particularly among some of the assimilated Jewish youth. Busy with their own local politics and ambitions, the community leaders and politicians did not respond at once. The greater problems of Galician Jewry did not seem to matter so much to them. However, the growing anti-Jewish propaganda in the eighties and the anti-Jewish riot that took place in Tarnów itself, coupled with the economic shifts, changed the general climate of opinion and brought a definite transformation within the Tarnów kehilla leadership.[34]

A leading role in organizing the first Zionist group in Tarnów was played by Abraham Saltz, a student at the university of Vienna. Together with four other students from Tarnów he joined the *Kadima* (Forward), the first organization of Jewish nationalist students that was founded in Vienna by Peretz Smolenskin in 1883.[35] Saltz regularly mailed to his native town the first Jewish nationalist weekly, *Autoemancipation*, published in Vienna, together with other brochures and material for dissemination among youth. And it was he and his friends who, after a brief period of recruiting people on an individual basis, undertook to win over the local Association of Jewish Mercantile Youth as well as a group of the older and intellectually inclined Gymnasium students who maintained their own *Selbstbildung Kreis* (Circle for Self-Education). When Saltz returned to Tarnów in 1887, he found a base for further Zionist activities.The very first project, a "Maccabean Festival,"[36] became a turning point in the growth of the Zionist idea in Tarnów and beyond.[37] It led immediately to the organization of *Ha-Teḥiya* (The Revival) to which youth from both orthodox and enlightened circles came in numbers to participate in cultural gatherings and discussions.

The organization served as an example to other towns and cities, including Lwów, which formed similar units. Tarnów became a center of the new Zion movement, and similar groups organized in other localities turned there for advice and instructions.[38]

But it was not until 1893 that the various Zion groups could convene in Lwów for the First Conference of Delegates of Jewish Nationalists in Galicia. The conference officially established the Zionist Party of Galicia, and Abraham Saltz of Tarnów, the chairman of the conference, was elected president of its Central Executive Committee. The party adopted the following objectives: the renaissance of Jewish peoplehood; dissemination of national culture through knowledge of Jewish history, the Hebrew language, and Hebrew literature; fight against assimilation; and the creation of Jewish settlements in Palestine.

At the second conference of the party, held in Lwów a year later, it was decided that: (1) the party would conduct an independent Jewish policy in parliamentary, provincial, and municipal elections and (2) a Galician Union of Jewish Colonization in Palestine would be established under the leadership of Abraham Saltz. In consonance with the latter decision, a colonization society, *Ahavat Tsiyon*, was established in Tarnów. It obtained its official charter from the Austrian government in 1896, and its temporary executive committee consisted of members of the party's Central Committee who resided in Tarnów. The existence of *Ahavat Tsiyon* gave additional prestige to the Tarnów Jewish community and intensified immensely its growing Jewish nationalist spirit and Zionist agitation.[39]

To realize the establishment of its first colony, Abraham Saltz was in touch with all major Jewish bodies and philanthropic foundations in Europe. He enlisted the support of twenty orthodox rabbis of various towns, including the zaddick of Tshortkev. He traveled to Paris to confer with Baron Edmond Rothschild and concluded with him the memorable transaction according to which *Ahavat Tsiyon* obtained ten thousand dunam of land in the Galilee for one hundred thousand French francs. A festive banquet was held in Tarnów in June of 1898 when the administrator of the newly established colony *Maḥanayim* left for Palestine together with the first group of pioneers, which included sixteen from Tarnów.

Although the *Maḥanayim* colony was at best an initial experiment that was unsuccessful,[40] the mere fact of its existence left a distinct mark on the contemporary generation of Tarnów Jews. It was an enterprise that showed the high degree of commitment to the Zionist ideal on the part of Galician Jewry and of the Jews of Tarnów in particular.[41]

The *Ahavat Tsiyon* eventually became a local committee of the World Zionist Organization. It remained one of the strongest Zionist mainstays in Galicia and exerted a great influence on the Tarnów Jewish community in spite of bitter opposition from the ultraorthodox Hasidic circles and radical Jewish socialists.

In the eighties the social structure of the Jewish community in Tarnów already included, besides the traditional class of merchants and the relatively new class of a professional intelligentsia, thousands of ill-paid Jewish wage earners. Their dire poverty was conspicuously reflected in the two sections of the city in which these laborers and poor artisans concentrated. One was the old medieval Jewish ghetto near the marketplace with its dark, narrow streets and passages teeming with a conglomeration of paupers of all sorts: day laborers, market hawkers, matchmakers, funeral weepers, sextons, and all kinds of voluntary "assistants." The other was the so-called *Grabówka* where the conditions were even more deplorable. It was in these two sections that a passer-by could hear the humming of the first revolutionary songs. In the *Grabówka*, especially, there was political ferment among the poor workers who caught on to the slogans of the socialists proclaiming the class struggle and the inevitable proletarian revolution. The Jewish Socialist Party (Zh.P.S.) found many supporters among the poor and downtrodden who lived here in dilapidated dwellings, dingy cellars, dusty attics, wooden or clay huts, etc.[42]

But not all Jewish laborers[43] joined the ranks of the radical Zh.P.S. The Zionists, too, attracted some workers, especially young commercial clerks. A very small number of clerks and shop workers organized within the local Zionist group of Tarnów a section of their own which in 1904 became a separate entity known as the *Poale Zion*.[44] This new organization immediately drew a considerable number of Jewish working youth and students of the local Gymnasium. Besides political and fund-raising activities, it embarked on an intensive educational program for the working youth that included instruction in Yiddish, Polish, arithmetic, Jewish history, discussions, library evenings, etc., all organized and ably conducted by the Gymnasium students within its fold.[45] The organization grew fast and its mark on the life of the Jewish community in Tarnów was unmistakable.

By the beginning of 1905 *Poale Zion* not only offered classes for the uneducated as well as courses and lectures for adults, but also maintained a growing library, an employment bureau, and a travel bureau.[46] It took its own stand and reacted independently in relation to all major questions affecting the Zionist movement. Its pronouncements were often resolute and effective. It denounced the pogroms in Russia in 1905 more vigorously than any other Jewish group, demonstrating its socialist and progressive approach to social, political, and economic questions. That it became recognized as a serious political factor, equal in importance to the other major parties in Tarnów, is attested by its participation and vigorous pre-election activities in 1906. The voice of the Tarnów *Poale Zion* concerning the need for a separate Jewish nationalist representation in the Austrian parliament was quite loud in that campaign.

The establishment of a national *Poale Zion* party in Austria strengthened the position of the *Poale Zion* group in Tarnów. However, in 1906, at the Third *Poale Zion* Conference, a decision was made to deepen further its labor-class orientation by separating from the Zionist organization. This caused a great deal of confusion in Tarnów, where many were active in both organizations. The increased emphasis on labor-class awareness and proletarian interest caused some active members in the Tarnów *Poale Zion*, especially the intelligentsia among them, to leave its ranks. As a result of this, a serious inner crisis developed.[47]

By the turn of the century the numerous meetings, special events, and festive occasions organized by the various Zionist groups in Tarnów endowed its Jewish life with a new, vigorous spirit of Jewish nationalist awareness, with greater enthusiasm and commitment for Jewish causes in general and Zionist projects in particular. But the Zionist idea which progressively pervaded larger sections of the Jewish population in Tarnów was still meeting a great deal of strong and stubborn opposition.

The main and hardest struggle of the Zionists was with the local assimilationist trend, deeply rooted among the wealthy and educated. For among the tough, extreme, and uncompromising orthodoxy, there were many yeshiva youths who were impressed with Zionist romanticism and who eagerly listened to the dream of *ge'ula* (redemption). As for the Jewish left, it was nationalist in character and in some political respects worked hand in hand with the Zionist democratic element. However, some of the sophisticated and westernized Jewish intellectuals, gathered in the local Adam Mickiewicz Literary Association, kept belittling sarcastically the Zionist idea as an unrealistic dream. They believed more in the national aspirations of the Poles, the ideas and ideals of which were beautifully expressed by the neoromantic contemporary Polish poets and literati.[48]

The Initial Steps

One of the centers of the Polish national sentiment in Tarnów was the Gymnasium, and Schipper was among the numerous Jewish students who attended this school. Around the time of Schipper's birth, Tarnów had a population of 40,000, of whom over forty per cent were Jews. The Jewish society of Tarnów, as shown in the preceding pages, underwent a considerable metamorphosis in the second half of the nineteenth century. It lost its traditional uniformity and became an economically, socially, and culturally diversified community with divergent ideologies and orientations. This was reflected, to some extent, in Schipper's own immediate family. His father, Moyshe Schipper, came from one of the better Jewish families in town, a family guided by traditional ideals of learning, piety, decency, tact, and discretion. Nevertheless, Moyshe Schipper married out of his social class; his wife, Hannah, was the daughter of a baker. And, rather than remain within the circle of his own relations, Moyshe Schipper chose to become part of his wife's environment—that is, part of the working, uneducated, but homely and simple folk. Thus, as a child Schipper grew up in surroundings that could not claim much erudition or refinement but that made up for it abundantly with its warmth and the naturally prevailing hearty and sincere attitude to people that was so characteristic of Schipper throughout his life.[49] He attended the traditional *ḥeder*.[50] However, sensitive to the dominant cultural trends of his time, Schipper sought to acquire a broader education. He apparently prevailed upon his parents to enroll him in the Gymnasium where the world of Polish culture opened its doors to Schipper, whose proclivity for literature and history was indeed exceptional. Naturally, the poetry and writings of the Polish national neoromantics, expressing both a longing for social justice and yearning for national freedom, had a profound influence on young Schipper, as it had on so many other Jewish students. A relatively high degree of idealism and intellectual intercourse seems to have existed among the students of the school, encouraged no doubt by the teachers. It is known, for instance, that Schipper's natural aptitude and interest in history was well nurtured and directed by his history teacher, Joseph Leniek, who encouraged him to undertake certain local research projects and instructed him on the nature of historical methods.[51]

There were also the inevitable influences of friends, a number of whom happened to be of very high intellectual calibre. For a while, one of Schipper's close friends was Karl Sobelson (Radek), the intellectually alert and intense Jewish youth who vigorously led the illegal socialist students' group *Promień* (Beam) and who years later became a prominent figure in the Communist Party of the Soviet Union.[52]

Swayed by his unusually articulate friend, Schipper—himself a dynamic, enthusiastic, and zestful youth—joined the ranks of *Promień* and became for a while one of its active and fervent spokesmen. Although he may not have been a convinced Marxist or believer in dialectical materialism, the ideals of social justice and economic fair play were very close to his heart. He even attempted to imitate the Italian, Ada Negri, writing songs about social injustice and the poverty of the masses.[53]

The dream of a better society and a more equitable social order animated Schipper all his life, but he decided quite early that his first obligation was to his own abused people. It is quite possible that, among other reasons, this realization came to Schipper from his contact with individual orthodox yeshiva students. The "progressive" Gymnasium students, convinced of their noble mission, tried to enlighten and redeem the orthodox students from religious fanaticism, but the influence became to an extent reciprocal. While the yeshiva *boḥurim* (students) got a taste of Polish culture and learned to recite the poems of Wyspiański, the "enlightened" Gymnasium students absorbed from the "backward" yeshiva youths something of the Jewish ethos, the Yiddish folklore, and the loyalty one should feel to one's own heritage.[54] In addition, the alert and critical Schipper must also have detected a callous note in the radical views of his friend Karl, who insisted that in a socialist Poland, a country in which all would enjoy equal rights, the Jewish question would *ipso facto* disappear. He got the impression that to the assimilated and cosmopolitan Karl Sobelson the disappearance of the Jewish question was tantamount to the disappearance of the Jewish people as a distinct historical and cultural entity. This kind of solution for the Jewish people young Schipper could not accept. In his heart he felt a greater commitment to his own people than to the socialist theories or the Polish national cause. This is quite evident from the fact that his first attempts in historical research in libraries and local archives dealt specifically with Jewish history and Jewish questions. The keen interest in Jewish history and his unquestionable predilection for this subject remained with Schipper throughout his life. In fact, it became the badge of his career as a historian.

Schipper's realization that his first duty was to his own people was undoubtedly related to the fact that the assimilationist trend in the Gymnasium was vigorously counteracted by Jewish nationalist ideas which grew increasingly stronger as Jewish students became disgusted with the hypocrisy of the Poles. Max Binenstock, somewhat older than Schipper, organized at the Gymnasium the clandestine Circle for Judaism. Its main objective was to bring Jewish students a modern, progressive version of Jewish knowledge. The emphasis of its program was on Jewish history and literature, and the Zionist idea. Max Binenstock befriended Schipper and brought him into the Circle, and he soon became one of its most active members. Abraham Chomet, another student and member of the Circle, emphasized the fact that the relationship between the two secret clubs operating in the Gymnasium, the socialist *Promień* and the Zionist Circle for Judaism, was very friendly and reflected the general atmosphere of intellectual intercourse and exhange of ideas as well as the idealism and commitments that prevailed among the students.[55] The members of the Circle, though poor and often penniless, were always in a good mood and in high spirits, particularly when they gathered in the room of one of the girls which the group mockingly dubbed the "salon." Schipper wrote, "the poorer we were, the more ideas we had, more humor, more romance, more lectures, more Zionist fire."[56] Max, called by his friends affectionately and facetiously "Our Lawgiver Moses with the Staff" (because of his first Jewish name and the second part of his last name, "stock"), traveled to Vienna to the convention of Zionist students. He went in borrowed shoes and slacks and, having met there with Theodore Herzl himself, returned to the group infused with ideas that were heatedly discussed until the early morning hours for days and weeks. There was great excitement, enthusiasm, dedication, and quite a bit of fun, and the work of Schipper in the years to come was rooted in the spiritual atmosphere of the "salon."[57] The students of the Circle established their own library, which eventually became the People's Library of Tarnów with 10,000 volumes. To purchase library books, one of the group organized a choir that earned money in assisting at services in the synagogue. Some members, among them Schipper, wrote for the monthly *Moriah*, founded by the Zionist Youth Convention held in Lwów in 1902.

Eventually, those who graduated and became university students organized the first academic association of Zionists called *Bar Kokhba*, in which Schipper and Max Binenstock played leading roles.

Involvements in Political and Cultural Actions

The Zionist Gymnasium and university students constituted in Tarnów a group that exerted an extraordinary influence on the entire Jewish population. *Bar Kokhba* manifested in all its activities a proud nationalist orientation. It combated local assimilationism; it opposed and protested the pro-Austrian position of the Tarnów rabbi and demanded of him and the kehilla that substantial help be extended to Jewish refugees from Russia in the crucial period 1904-1905; it engaged in hot debates on Jewish issues with the Jewish socialists, debates which often turned into fist fights and disturbances. *Bar Kokhba* included the best element of the young Jewish intellectuals who later became leading figures of the Zionist movement in Galicia and Poland. Of the eighteen names enumerated by Abraham Chomet as members of *Bar Kokhba* in 1905, seven already held doctoral degrees.[58] By that time Schipper, who was graduated from the Gymnasium in 1903, completed two years of study in jurisprudence at the University of Cracow and was getting ready to transfer to the University of Vienna to study law, philosophy, and social economics.

At the same time, he became increasingly involved in the cultural and political activities of the Zionists in Tarnów. That his position and influence in Zionist circles grew is attested by the fact that in 1904 Schipper was one of the two main speakers at the most important and solemn event of that year: the mourning convocation called to honor the memory of the founder of the World Zionist Organization, Theodore Herzl. In 1905-1906 Schipper was already among the members of the Tarnów Committee of the Zionist Organization, the representative body of all local Zionist groups which had sprung up among the various classes of the Jewish community.[59] One of these groups was the local *Poale Zion.*

Although the exact time of Schipper's formal affiliation with the *Poale Zion* has been a disputed question, it is quite certain that Schipper was among the educated young people who, attracted by its sociopolitical character and educational aims, gravitated toward that group in its early stage of existence. While it may be true that Schipper's official career as a leading figure of *Poale Zion* on a national level did not begin before 1910,[60] the year when he formally greeted in the party organ, *Der Yidisher Arbeter*, the Fifth Party Day of the *Poale Zion* in Austria,[61] his sympathies and activities in the local branch must have commenced much earlier. Thus, Abraham Chomet, a friend and eye-witness of Schipper's life and activities in Tarnów, notes that following the 1906 Conference in Lwów when, due to the growing emphasis on class consciousness and proletarian interests, many of the Jewish intelligentsia left the ranks of *Poale Zion*, the inner crisis in the Tarnów branch was overcome, thanks to the efforts of Schipper and others who remained and continued their active participation in it.[62] This, then, would indicate that Schipper was affiliated with the *Poale Zion* group in Tarnów as early as 1906. It also points to the fact that at that time, at least, he was not among the vacillating intellectuals who shunned radical positions and who therefore went over to the camp of the middle class Zionists.[63] The 1907 Tarnów elections are of interest in this connection because the twenty-four-year-old Schipper was on the common list of candidates. He was affiliated with the group of independent community-minded people, ideologically oriented towards socialist circles, who united with young Zionists against the Jewish assimilatory politicians and the perpetual kehilla clans. This block, although not successful in its first attempt in the municipal elections, shattered the established Jewish plutocracy during the kehilla elections that took place the same year.[64]

As the *Poale Zion* of Galicia asserted itself more and more as a Zionist party of independent political and social actions, Schipper became increasingly involved in its affairs. In 1908 he expressed his unequivocal support of Yiddish as a national language of the Jewish people. He published two articles on the history and revival of Yiddish language and literature as a powerful cultural force uniting millions of Jews in Russia and Galicia.[65] His views reflected the position of *Poale Zion* and other spokesmen of Jewish nationalism in the Diaspora.[66] In 1909 he became part of the central leadership of *Poale Zion* in Galicia and was placed in charge of its department of culture. This area was of particular interest to Schipper because it involved educational programs and projects for students and the working youth and brought him into direct contact with them. At that time, in addition to the existing *Poale Zion* Youth Association, another party adjunct was formed. It consisted of student groups called *Ḥerut* (Freedom), whose central office in Lwów began publishing its own periodical, *Nasze Hasło* (Our Motto) in 1909. Schipper became its editor in 1910, one of the busiest years of his early political career. A number of problems, tasks, and events claimed the attention and time of Schipper who was already a practicing lawyer in Tarnów. For a while he was the editor of the party's chief and widely respected organ, *Der Yidisher Arbeter*.[67] In Tarnów itself he was actively involved in the party's efforts (including strikes) to organize the local *belfers* (teacher assistants). The party's purpose was to improve the *belfers'* material situation as well as that of the commercial clerks and workers in private offices whose union operated under the umbrella of the Tarnów *Poale Zion*.

One of the most memorable events of that year was the First of May celebration in which Zerubavel, the leading figure of the World *Poale Zion* Party, participated. Schipper was among the speakers at the festive afternoon meeting held in the *Poale Zion* house and again at the evening gathering which was devoted to a literary program.[68]

An extensive political and educational campaign was launched that year in connection with the population census conducted by the government. Since the authorities did not recognize Yiddish and explicitly prohibited the declaration of Yiddish as a national language of the Jewish population, the *Poale Zion* together with other Zionist groups mobilized Jews to counteract this prohibition.[69] Numerous popular meetings were organized to enlighten the Jewish populace on its right to declare Yiddish as its mother tongue. Schipper was among the main spokesmen in that campaign. Together with his party associate, Daniel Leibel, writer and well-known expert on Jewish literature, he traveled and delivered many speeches at mass rallies to promote the cause of Yiddish.[70]

While Zionist groups were engaged in this political action, other educational activities were not neglected. A Zionist committee to deal with educational questions, the first of its kind, met in Lwów in November, 1910 to evaluate educational accomplishments and to plan for the future. It decided to set up a

National Commission composed of two departments, one for administrative matters and one for educational problems proper, and Schipper was asked to serve in the latter.[71] Two months earlier at an annual general meeting, Schipper was elected to the new Executive Committee of the Tarnów *Poale Zion* which consisted of ten members.[72] The rising reputation and popularity of Schipper as a man of thought and action are well reflected in Chomet's testimony regarding the ever-expanding political and cultural doings of the Tarnów *Poale Zion* in the years preceding World War I:

> The *Poale Zion* in Tarnów attained a great deal of prestige, primarily due to the cultural activities conducted by Schipper, well known already as a historian, and Daniel Leibel, the Yiddish littérateur, both of whom dedicated their unusual talents and intellectual abilities to a whole generation of youth which grew up under their guidance and supervision.[73]

Schipper and Leibel were the permanent lecturers of the literary meetings held every Sabbath, and both were chiefly responsible for the growing interest in the expanding program of courses, classes, and literary evenings. The library became the largest in town; the dramatic club gave the best performances of Jewish drama and one-act shows; and many cultural events were offered by the *Poale Zion* in Tarnów.[74] Schipper, in particular, generated much enthusiasm amongst the youth and young adults with his natural, folksy friendliness, cheerful disposition, and nimble wit. He undoubtedly represented an unusual combination of scholarship and dedication.[75] He was a man alert to the needs and problems of the simple, working folk as well as erudite in the intricacies of scholarly theories and the intellectual trends of his time, especially those that affected his own people. In the latter respect, Schipper was already known far beyond Tarnów as a young, promising historian, writer, and polemicist.

In Polemics with Other Historians

In 1902, while still a seventh-grade Gymnasium student, Schipper bravely addressed himself, on the basis of his own critical investigations, to the controversial topic in vogue: the early legislation of Polish rulers concerning Jews, especially the *Privilegia* granted by Casimir the Great (1333-1370).[76] This topic occupied Jewish and non-Jewish historians before and during Schipper's lifetime,[77] and Schipper himself returned to it in later years several times to modify and, eventually, to assert his position in the light of further research and study. His penchant for history took much of his time in Cracow as well as in Vienna.[78] (When he was older, Schipper referred to his "weakness" for poking around in archives and collecting historical notes.) He worked assiduously for countless days in Polish and German archives and libraries searching for documents and acquiring a wealth of data and information which, to a great extent, constituted the underpinning of his later historical works.[79] Thus, in 1905 he submitted to *Moriah* two articles dealing with the Jews under the first Polish rulers of the Piast dynasty and under Casimir the Great. A year later, he published another article in the same journal on the genesis of Jewish usury in the Middle Ages. In all of these he again discussed the history and circumstances of the legal position of Jews in thirteenth and fourteenth century Poland.[80]

The polemic concerning the legal charters, more commonly known as *Privilegia*, granted to Jews by the Polish rulers Boleslas the Pious of Kalisz in 1264 and Casimir the Great in 1334, 1364, and 1367,[81] reflected different approaches and interpretations and centered around three basic aspects:

(1) The theory popularized mostly by Jewish historians of the assimilationist school (Nussbaum, Kraushar, Sternberg, and others)[82] that the charters reflect a remarkable magnanimity and disinterested hospitality on the part of the early Polish rulers towards the Jews at a time when in other Western countries they were exposed to suffering and persecutions;

(2) The question of the historicity and authenticity of the so-called Boleslas-Casimir *Privilegium* of 1367, raised mainly by Hube and Kutrzeba; and

(3) The substantive aspects of the charters as they relate to the Jewish social and economic position.

In his first articles, mentioned above, Schipper deals with all three aspects of the controversy, but his main thrust is against the contentions of the assimilationist historians.[83] He still agrees here with the explanation offered by Ludwik Gumplowicz that the 1264 *Privilegium* represented the formal recognition of the Jews as a special group of people, a sort of "financial association" with rights to conduct business and legal guarantees for the safety of life and property.[84]

As for the questionable authenticity of the Boleslas-Casimir document of 1367, Schipper does not yet take a definitive position, although he presents Bloch's arguments rejecting Hube's thesis that the document, in view of its completely different, much more extensive and favorable text, could not have originated with or been given by Casimir the Great.[85] Schipper concludes that "Bloch's assumptions as to the genesis of that *Privilegium*, though they are very probable and explain the inconsistencies of this charter, still do not have the power of irrefutable truth."[86] But three things appear to Schipper quite certain: that the Polish charters can be traced back to those granted in Western Europe, that their immediate model was the *Privilegium* granted by Frederick II to Jews in Austria in 1244, and that the political and economic motives underlying the Polish charters were the same as those of their prototypes in the West. However, against the background of arbitrary exploitation that had already existed in the countries of the Holy Roman Empire, the charters granted to Jews in the thirteenth century in Central Europe (in Austria by Frederick II in 1244, in Bohemia by Ottokar II in 1254 and 1268, in Silesia by Bolko in 1295 and by Henry of Glogau in 1299) were most significant in that they recognized the importance of Jews as an economic factor in territories that had not yet undergone the process of colonization. In Poland, especially, the charters were more propitious not only for economic reasons but also for specific political reasons.

Schipper, however, makes the point that, apart from the fact that the charters were neither permanent nor automatically valid in all parts of the kingdom, the guarantees of personal safety, property, etc., which the assimilationist historians regarded as magnanimous, would have been among the obvious rights of every Christian. In relation to the Jews they were considered "favors" granted by the rulers; for here too, just as in other countries of medieval Europe, the Jew, as a non-Christian and stranger, needed the explicit protection of princes and kings and he could obtain this protection only under certain conditions and for a definite price.[87] Thus, Schipper refuted the obsequious theories of the assimilationist historians.

In his critical survey of literature relating to the history of Jews in Poland,[88] Schipper takes up more resolutely the question of the authenticity of the 1367 Boleslas-Casimir *Privilegium*, designated by Schipper as BIII (in distinction to BI—the Kalisz *Privilegium* of 1264 confirmed by Casimir the Great in 1334 and 1364, and BII—the *Privilegium* of Casimir the Great of 1367 confirmed by Ladislas Jagiello in 1387). To clarify matters, it should be stated that Casimir the Great, guided by the principles of law and order, which were sorely lacking before his time, and recognizing the role of the Jews in the growth of the country, in 1334 confirmed the Kalisz *Privilegium* as binding in all territories of his realm and officially proclaimed the Jews as the direct subjects of the king rather than the individual princes. As a result of anti-Jewish excesses, pillages, and murders in the wake of general misfortunes (the bubonic plague, fire in Breslau, etc.) for which Jews were blamed, the king again renewed the General *Privilegium* in Great Poland and Little Poland and, following the conquest of Ruthenia, he confirmed it for that territory as well in 1367 at the request of Jews from Lwów, Cracow, and Sandomierz. But in the same year of 1367 he apparently granted a new charter (BIII) to the Jews of Great Poland, substantially different from the previous charters, although it followed the previous master text. BIII undoubtedly reflected a higher stage of economic and social development and gave more leeway to Jews to carry out their economic activities, but the document lacked the date and signatures of the court officials.

Since the original copies of these charters were not preserved, historians like Hube and Kutrzeba believed that Casimir the Great never granted BIII to the Jews of Great Poland but that the latter composed it themselves and presented it in 1453 to Casimir Jagielonczyk for his approval, contending that it was issued by Casimir the Great back in 1367.[89]

In his refutation of Hube and Kutrzeba's arguments, Schipper proceeds to correct, first of all, the erroneous conclusion of Hube that in 1364 Casimir the Great confirmed the Kalisz *Privilegium* for the Jews of Great Poland only, citing as evidence the document as published by Bershadski.[90] He then supplements Bloch's contentions, which he considers to be incomplete and not strong enough, with a number of important points in support of the fact that BIII was not only a new, independent charter but a piece of legislation sorely needed in Great Poland in view of (1) the spreading anti-Jewish sentiments at the time and the pogrom in Poznań in 1367; (2) the fact that Jewish credit operations, conducted here on a greater scale, were regulated in two discordant ways: according to the 1347 Code adopted by the *szlachta* (nobility) of Great Poland at its assembly in Piotrków, which prohibited loans on promissory notes, and according to the *Privilegia* of 1334 and 1364, which gave creditors more freedom, including the right of lending against mortgages; and (3) the new practice of entering loan transactions into public records as a new form of security, which required legal sanction and formulation.[91]

As an argument against the authenticity of BIII, Kutrzeba had used a letter written by Cardinal Oleśnicki (who was known for his anti-Jewish sentiments) in which he vehemently tried to dissuade Casimir IV (Jagielonczyk) from confirming the charter, referring to it as "*falsissima . . . privilegia.*" In his refutation, Schipper proves that "*falsissima*" also conveys the meaning "original." Then, because BIII speaks of court records[92] as having been started during the time of Casimir the Great, while the oldest of these records dates from 1374 in Little Poland and 1386 in Great Poland, Kutrzeba took this as another proof that the document was spurious. In Schipper's rejection of this thesis he argues that Article 32 of BIII concerning the entry of Jewish claims in official records applied not only to the land records but to municipal records as well, the extant city records of Cracow showing a number of entries relating to Jewish loans against real estate security in 1366. He also goes on to show that the extant land records of 1374 and 1386 are not necessarily the oldest ones. And so Schipper concludes in defense of the accused Jews of Great Poland with these words:

> Neither the argumentation of Hube nor that of Kutrzeba can convince that BIII represents a document falsified by Jews and that Casimir the Great had nothing to do with its formation. None of the important arguments brought by these investigators would withstand a critical analysis in support of their thesis.[93]

An adjunct to the main controversy developed between Schipper and Bałaban around the question whether the *Privilegium* of Casimir the Great, granted to the Jews of Lwów (and Ruthenia) in 1367, *i.e.* BII, was granted again to the same Jews by Ladislas Jagiello in 1387. Wisłocki, who published a document which he found in the Ossolineum library, concluded that it represented BII and that it was confirmed by Jagiello, despite the fact that this document, too, lacked the formal concluding passages and official stamp. However, this drawback of Wisłocki's document and an analysis of its text led Bałaban to present six points, among them the testimony of Oleśnicki referred to above, to show that Jagiello did not confirm BII and that the document found by Wisłocki represents a private copy rather than an official document.[94] Thus, Bałaban shared the views of Gumplowicz, Nussbaum, Hube, Kutrzeba, and others in this matter. Schipper's answer, published in the Russian *Yevreyskaya Starina*, besides refuting point by point Bałaban's argumentation, expresses surprise that Bałaban joined the camp of those who take the obviously inimical testimony of Oleśnicki to be more reliable than the public declarations of the king himself, professing his favorable disposition and policy toward Jews. Schipper cites archival evidence in support of the fact that Jagiello did not refuse to confirm BII for the Jews of Ruthenia and Poland. He explains the only serious argument regarding the official shortcomings of Wisłocki's document by admitting that it indeed represents a copy made by the end of the fifteenth century by some cleric who apparently deleted the stereotyped concluding formula.[95]

As late as 1917, in a short review of Schorr's book on the General *Privilegia* of Polish Jewry, a final footnote to the controversy is given by Schipper. He not only reiterates his position but is happy to note that Schorr went yet a step further by pointing to the fact that BIII did not require at all the saction and signatures of the high nobles because the king was the sole patron of the Jews; they were his *servi camerae*, and the charter represented a private royal act of legal validity and force despite the fact that the high men of the nobility and clergy did not endorse it.[96] The missing date on the document presented to Casimir IV for approval in 1453 is to be explained by the fact that since the original document was lost during a conflagration in Poznań, the scribe who prepared the new copy for the king omitted certain formalities.[97]

Although until this day the question of authenticity of the BIII charter has not been resolved, Jewish historians tend to accept the views of Bloch, Schorr, and Schipper. Mahler thinks that precisely the lack of date and signatures of the royal officials points to the authenticity of the document rather than to its questionable provenance. It indicates that while Casimir the Great granted this most favorable of all charters to the Jews, the representatives of the high nobility and clergy refused to sign a document that would give Jews such broad and liberal rights, especially in the area of credit on land mortgages. The document thus reflects the king's determination to withstand the growing centrifugal forces in the country: the Church and the nobility.[98]

The Early Legal Status of Jews in Poland

A comprehensive picture of the legal status and economic position of the Jews in Poland from the second half of the thirteenth century through the fourteenth, as reflected in the royal *Privilegia* and in practice, was presented by Schipper in his second major work,[99] for which the articles and monographs already mentioned and others published between 1906 and 1911 constituted either preliminary or integral essays.[100]

For comparative reasons and in order to demonstrate the "dilettantish treatment" and fallacious conclusions in the "outdated histories" of Polish Jews by Kraushar, Sternberg, Maciejowski, Perles, Nussbaum, Gumplowicz, and others,[101] Schipper utilizes here not only the charters but, to a great extent, a considerable number of archival sources overlooked by the other historians.[102]

Having submitted the basic document of all Polish charters, the Kalisz *Privilegium* of 1264, to a comparative analysis with its immediate antecedents in other countries and having scrutinized its juridical paragraphs in the light of the other sources, Schipper provides here his own conclusions regarding the legal status of Jews. In the first place, he refutes the accepted notion of Gumplowicz that the Jews in Poland constituted within the scheme of social estates in Poland another "national estate," representing an integral part of the nation, subject to national rule and national courts.[103] The regulations of BI, according to Schipper, clearly betray their underlying concept that the Jews were considered as serfs belonging to the royal (or ducal) treasury, although the technical term *servi camerae* is not explicitly mentioned in the document. The Jew was under the exclusive jurisdiction of the king, as patron and protector, which in practice was carried out by the voivode, the first-instance judge in all criminal matters between Jews and Christians.[104] In civil matters or inter-Jewish criminal matters, as in all internal problems, Jewish law was applied and a Jewish judge had the power to decide, although the king had the right to call before him any case involving Jews. The Jews were not subject to municipal laws (German or local); they were subject to special and separate regulations as delineated in the granted charters. But the latter—Schipper is careful to emphasize—degraded the position of Jews to that of servitude to the king according to the pattern provided by the West; for until the middle of the thirteenth century, Jews in Poland constituted a free group of people enjoying the exclusive right of the free to buy and keep slaves.[105] The deterioration of the social position of the Jews from the second half of the thirteenth century, Schipper ascribes to the attitudes planted by the Germans who began settling in Poland at that time and who brought with them concepts inimical to Jews. However, in Poland the transplanted *servi camerae* concept did not lead to the very sad consequences that it brought about in the countries of Western Europe.

In his later works Schipper's view on the entire subject of the sociolegal position of the Jews in Poland during the period under discussion remains unchanged.[106] This view was inextricably linked with the economic role of the Jews, as Schipper understands and propounds it. Here again he differs with the generally accepted view relating the charters to the occupation of moneylending as the dominant, if not altogether exclusive, economic activity of the Jews in the early history of Poland. The discussion on the economic aspects, as reflected in the royal charters as well as in actual life of that period, must be postponed for another chapter, for Schipper found it necessary first to answer two basic questions bearing directly on the economic role and position of the Jews. First, there was the question of the beginning of Jewish capitalism in the early Middle Ages and second, the question of the origins of Jews in Poland.

A Look into the Old History of Tarnów

This chapter, which deals with the initial steps of Schipper as a historian, cannot be concluded without reference to still another study that Schipper completed in 1905 which met the standard of such a scholarly periodical as the *Kwartalnik Historyczny*.[107] This study, on the history of Jews in his native town until the end of the eighteenth century,[108] was significant not only because it was based on firsthand archival sources but mainly because it represented an examination and treatment of a microcosm reflecting a macrocosm, at least inasmuch as the position of the Jews in a town owned by private lords, as distinct from Crown towns, was concerned. From this study, Schipper gained a close look at basic socioeconomic relationships revealing underlying motives and relevances. He drew indeed a number of fundamental inferences which guided his thinking in subsequent investigations and which characterized his interpretations of Jewish history under the specific conditions of Poland. Thus, for instance, he concludes that the history of Jews in Tarnów was, on one hand, the history of their relationship with the Polish magnates, the residents of the castle and owners of the town to whom the Jews "belonged," and, on the other hand, the history of their continuous struggle with the municipality, which always strived to gain from the Tarnów lords a measure of power over the Jews, as well as with the burgesses, organized in their guilds, who continually aimed at pushing out the Jews from their economic positions.[109] In these terms he interprets numerous incidents, among them the vacillating attitude and changing ordinances of Ladislas Dominick, the lord of Tarnów in the first half of the seventeenth century, who in 1633 circumscribed the commercial activities of the Jews and eventually put them under the prejudicial jurisdiction of the municipal government, apparently under the pressure of the Tarnów commonalty. In 1637 he issued a new charter bringing the Jews back under the jurisdiction of the castle and granting them the same rights as those enjoyed by all townspeople. These freedoms were lost in 1643 when Jewish rights were restricted by virtue of the alleged economic losses they caused to their Christian neighbors.[110]

Quite characteristic of Schipper is the point he makes concerning the Tarnów Collegiate Church and the local clergy in general, who obediently followed the instructions given by the bishop of Cracow. On a visit to Tarnów in 1725 he stated that the Jews enjoyed too much freedom and that their "arrogance" should be curtailed. At the same time, Schipper notes, the Collegiate Church was not averse to earning considerable dividends by investing its capital with the local Jewish kehilla, at seven per cent interest, at a time when it would not have been prudent to invest in land and property in view of political uncertainties and disturbances.[111]

Altogether this monograph shows that from the very beginning Schipper was indefatigable not so much in collecting historical facts and data for descriptive purposes alone as in pinpointing and identifying that piece of evidence which is most revealing in terms of providing a dialectical explanation of the motives and reasons behind the mere facts.

Notes

1. Ludomir Rubach, *Tarnów i najbliższa okolica* (Warsaw: 1953), p. 20.

2. *Ibid.*, p. 17.

3. Also known as Spytek of Melsztyn.

4. Jan Leniek, "Tarnów za czasów Leliwitów," in *Dzieje miasta Tarnowa* (Tarnów: 1911), p. 28.

5. Rubach, *op. cit.*, p. 18.

6. Leniek, *op. cit.*, p. 52.

7. See *infra*, pp. 29 f.

8. A. Chomet. "Tsu der geshikhte fun Yidn in Torne," in *Torne*, ed. by A. Chomet (Tel-Aviv: 1954), p. 28.

9. This government doubled the so-called "tolerance tax" and instituted additional fees such as the "wedding tax." It aimed to eliminate altogether the poor Jews who could not bring the state any revenues. See Ph. Friedman, "Dzieje Żydów w Galicji, 1772-1914," in *Żydzi w Polsce Odrodzonej*, ed. by I. Schipper, A. Tartakower, and A. Haftka (Warsaw: 1932-1935), vol. I, p. 381.

10. The measures designed to transform Galician Jews into enlightened and productive citizens included obligatory military service, the requirement to adopt German names and European attire, compulsory education in the "Josephinian" schools especially established for Jews, occupational rehabilitation, etc. See *ibid.*, pp. 382, ff.

11. Chomet, *op. cit.*, p. 29.

12. *Ibid.*, pp. 30 ff.

13. Friedman, *op. cit.*, p. 388. The Jewish intelligentsia in Galicia grew even under the reactionary rule of Metternich since Jewish students were not forced out of the universities. The first indigenous Jewish physicians and lawyers set up offices in Lwów during the decade of 1830-1840. See D. Sadan and H. Ormian (eds.), *Zikhron Mordekhai Zev Braude* (Jerusalem: 1960), p. 300.

14. Although the number of Jewish councilmen constituted an absolute majority in forty-five municipalities, only in ten of those were Jews elected to serve as mayors. In the Sejm of Galicia, which consisted of 150-155 deputies, there were never more than five Jewish deputies. Friedman, *op. cit.*, p. 392.

15. Chomet, *op. cit.*, p. 51.

16. In this riot one Jew died, forty-three were wounded and forty-eight Jewish families robbed. *Ibid.*, p. 50.

17. Jacob Shatzky, "Di Yidn in Poyln fun 1772 biz 1914," in *Di Yidn in Poyln* (New York: 1946), pp. 443 and 447.

18. Shatzky notes that Jews never appreciated correctly the Polish-Ukrainian conflict. Instead of cooperating with the Ukrainians as one subjugated group with another, they not only preferred to side with the stronger but also minimized and ridiculed the ambitions and aspirations of the Ukrainians, the illiterate peasants. Even in the beginning of the twentieth century, when Jews themselves began to recognize their own national aspirations and began to express sympathy for the Ukrainian cause, the logical and practical inferences from that recognition never materialized. *Ibid.*, pp. 463 ff.

19. Most indicative of this orientation is the fact that in 1880 more than 300,000 Jews (almost half of the Jewish population) declared German as their mother tongue. Ten years later, 621,000 Jews declared that Polish was their mother tongue, and only 138,000 chose German. Yiddish was not recognized by the authorities and Jews were not permitted to declare it as their native tongue. See J. Tenenbaum, *Galitsye—mayn alte heym* (Buenos Aires: 1952), p. 98.

20. The leaders of the various groups (or dynasties) that developed among the Hasidim were called zaddikim (also rebbes, in distinction to the officially appointed community Rabbis). Considered by their followers as men of unusual gifts, possessing even supernatural powers through which they could help the individual Hasid, the revered zaddikim held sway over great numbers of Hasidim who followed them blindly. The various Hasidic groups were usually called by the name of the town in which their particular zaddick resided or, as they used to say, held his "court," often a quite elaborate dwelling with assistants and servants as well as pilgrims who came to obtain the zaddick's blessing and to benefit from being in his presence. See I. Zinberg, *Toledot Sifrut Yisrael* (Tel-Aviv: 1959), vol. V, pp. 199 ff; D. Rudavsky, *Emancipation and Adjustment* (New York: 1967), pp. 129-132.

21. N. M. Gelber, *Toledot ha-Tenu'a ha-Tsiyonit be-Galitsya* (Jerusalem: 1958), p. 15.

22. See *infra*, Chap. II, pp. 42 ff.

23. Friedman, *op. cit.*, pp. 394-396.

24. Initially meant to help the farmer in marketing his products, the *kółka rolnicze* broadened their activities to include all possible commercial transactions between city and countryside. In Eastern Galicia the Ukrainian nationalists followed the example of the Poles with the blessings of the provincial government which thus sought to win the cooperation of the Ukrainians politically. *Ibid.*, p. 403; Shatzky, *op. cit.*, pp. 455-458; also J. Kenner, *Kvershnit* (New York: 1947), pp. 58 ff.

25. The terrible economic situation of Jews in Galicia became known to the world when journalists, commissions, and people including Theodore Lessing and Carl Emil Francos visited Galicia and brought the situation to light. Shatzky, *op. cit.*, pp. 460-461.

26. *Ibid.*, p. 467.

27. Y. Geffen, "Dos yiddishe-religyeze Torne," in *Torne, op. cit.*, p. 206.

28. *Shul (Schule):* Judeo-German designation for a synagogue or house of prayer and study. *Minyan:* literally, quorum of ten adult men required for public worship.

29. Geffen, *loc. cit.*

30. Y. Blazer, "A blik ibern religyezn yidntum in Torne," in *Torne, op. cit.*, pp. 217-219.

31. The Jewish Socialist Party was founded in Tarnów in 1904. It came into the open for the first time in 1905, at the May celebration attended by 10,000 workers, as an entity independent of the Polish Socialist Party and the Austrian Social-Democratic Party.

32. J. Landau, "Yidish-sotsyalistishe partay-Zh.P.S.," in *Torne, op. cit.*, p. 636.

33. As time went on, certain religious circles realized the importance of political action and founded, much later, the *Agudat Yisrael* party and the *Ts'irey Agudat Yisrael.* The Zionist element among the religious Jews joined the *Mizraḥi.*

34. In the struggle for leadership in the kehilla, Herman Mertz and his supporters defeated the clique of Dr. Goldhammer, an ambitious, assimilated lawyer with influence in the municipal government who was used by certain rich Jewish families for their own interests. Chomet, *op. cit.*, p. 54.

35. Peretz Smolenskin (1842-1885), outstanding Hebrew writer and journalist, editor of the Hebrew publication *Ha-Shaḥar* in Vienna, leading *Haskala* figure and proponent of Hebrew as the language of the Jews, was an ardent fighter against Jewish obscurantism. One of the first to contend that the Jews are not only a religious group but a nationality, he instructed his numerous readers that the Jews must strive toward national emancipation in a political and moral sense. See J. Klausner, *Historya shel ha-Sifrut ha-Ivrit ha-Ḥadasha* (Jerusalem: 1960), vol. V, pp. 227-231.

36. In their attempts to imbue the youth, and the Jewish society in general, with a national spirit, Zionists stimulated an interest in Jewish history, stressing its heroic events and periods. The public "Maccabean Festivals," organized by the Zionists as a modern way of observing Hanuka, became an important and impressive means of propagating the idea of Jewish peoplehood. Bitterly opposed at first by assimilationists as well as the official leadership of the Jewish community, the "Maccabean Festivals" became very popular among the broad Jewish masses whose awareness of a common Jewish national destiny grew stronger and deeper. Gelber, *op. cit.*, p. 109.

37. A. Chomet, "Di tsiyonistishe bavegung in Torne," in *Torne, op. cit.*, p. 355.

38. *Ibid.*, p. 356.

39. A great event took place in Tarnów in May, 1897 when the Constitutional Meeting of *Ahavat Tsiyon* brought to the city forty-eight delegates from

various parts of Galicia, among them a special representative of Dr. Theodore Herzl. At the First Zionist Congress in Basel, Dr. Herzl brought to the attention of the delegates the fact that the administration of *Ahavat Tsiyon* presented him with a petition signed by ten thousand Jews who expressed their readiness to settle in Palestine at his call. *Ibid.*, p. 358.

40. *Maḥanayim* suffered from financial difficulties and from differences of opinion among its own leadership in Palestine as well as Austria. Dr. Herzl considered the whole project premature, although the *Ahavat Tsiyon* administration in Tarnów saw in it a positive and concrete step.

41. Chomet, "Di tsiyonistishe bavegung in Torne," in *Torne, op. cit.*, p. 362.

42. E. Wurtzel, "Funem yidishn arbeter kamf," in *Torne, op. cit.*, pp. 667 ff; also Landau, *op. cit.*, p. 635.

43. One of the earliest Jewish industries was that of clothing manufacture. In the seventies, this industry was already in the hands of several firms that specialized in manufacturing better garments for the bigger centers of the Austro-Hungarian Empire. One modern plant became known for its fashionable quality goods shipped abroad. Alongside the clothing industry a number of related enterprises developed: underwear, knitwear, hats, shoes, leather, and fur coats, etc. D. Seiden, "Konfektsye-industrye in Torne," *Torne, op. cit.*, p. 235; also, Chomet, "Tsu der geshikhte fun Yidn in Torne," *op. cit.*, p. 64.

44. Initially, its full and rather long name was The Educational Association of Young Jewish Workers and Commercial Apprentices—*Poale Zion*, and its dissociation from the main Zionist group was urged by its young leaders, among them Jacob Kenner, the author of *Kvershnit*, who wanted the Association to identify with the labor class rather than with the Zionist middle class. See Chomet, "Di tsiyonistishe bavegung in Torne," *op. cit.*, p. 461.

45. Kenner, *op. cit.*, pp. 23-27.

46. *Der Yidisher Arbeter*, Lwów, No. 5 (March 12, 1905).

47. Chomet, "Di tsiyonistishe bavegung in Torne," *op. cit.*, pp. 465-468.

48. The outstanding men of letters, representatives of the period known in the history of modern Polish literature as *Młoda Polska* (Young Poland) were Jan Kasprowicz (1860-1926), Kazimierz Tetmajer (1865-1940), Stanisław Przybyszewski (1868-1927), and Stanisław Wyspiański (1869-1907). Their popular literary productivity included poetry, playwriting, and journalism of a socioliterary and didactic character. Related to European modernism, it was strongly neoromantic, nationalistic, and folk-oriented, expressing the belief that Poland's redemption lay under the russet cloak of the Polish peasant. See *Wielka Encyklopedia Powszechna*, Państwowe Wydawnictwo Naukowe, (Warsaw: 1966), pp. 377-378; *Encyklopedja Polska*, vol. XXI (Cracow: 1935), pp. 201-218, 476-477, 198-201, 226-227, 477-478.

49. J. Hirschhaut, "Dr. I. Shiper—zayn lebn un shafn," *Fun Noentn Ovar* (New York: 1955), p. 186.

50. It is quite possible that his father thought of sending him to a yeshiva to study for the rabbinate, in view of the boy's abilities. *Loc. cit.*

51. Jacob Shatzky, "Dr. I. Shiper (1884-1943)," in *Zamlbikher*, No. 6, p. 472; Hirschhaut, *op. cit.*, p. 188.

52. A member of the revolutionary élite of the Communist party, Karl Radek was closely associated with Lenin and Trotsky in the years immediately preceding and following the end of World War I. Besides being a member of the Comintern Presidium and a secretary of the Executive Committee of the Comintern, Radek occupied leading positions in the highest echelons of the propaganda apparatus of the Russian Communist Party, serving at various times as the chief foreign affairs commentator and editor of *Pravda* and *Izvestya*. During the 1936-37 purge trials in Moscow he was sentenced to ten years imprisonment as a Trotskyite deviator. See *The Universal Jewish Encyclopedia*, vol. IX (New York: 1943), p. 64; *New Century Cyclopedia of Names*, C. L. Barnhart, ed. (New York: 1954), p. 3293.

53. Shatzky, "Dr. I. Shiper (1884-1943)," *op. cit.*, p. 471.

54. *Loc. cit.*

55. Chomet, "Di tsiyonistishe bavegung . . . ," *op. cit.*, p. 363.

56. Quoted by Chomet, *ibid.*, p. 364, from Schipper's article "Max" in the Memorial Book published in Lwów, 1924, dedicated to Dr. Max Binenstock, who died in 1923.

57. *Ibid.*, p. 366.

58. *Ibid.*, p. 371.

59. *Ibid.*, p. 374.

60. Sh. Sokol, "I. Shiper," *Yidisher Kemfer* (New York: June 1943).

61. *Der Yidisher Arbeter*, Oct. 24-26, 1910.

62. Chomet, "Di tsiyonistishe bavegung," *op. cit.*, p. 468. At that time a number of refugees from Russia who fled during the pogroms of 1905 became active members in the Tarnów *Poale Zion.* Mostly craftsmen, they represented a more radical element that fully identified with the position of the *Poale Zion* party in Russia led by Dov Borokhov, whose ideas were expressed in *Di klasnmomentn un di natsyonale frage*, published in 1905, and *Undzer platform*, published in 1906, and became the cornerstone of the Marxist ideology of *Poale Zion.*

63. Regarding affiliation with *Poale Zion*, see also Hirschhaut, *op. cit.*, pp. 197 ff.

64. Chomet, "Tsu der geshikhte . . . ," *op. cit.*, p. 62.

65. "Tsum artikl fun H. F. Klayn, 'Di yidishe shprakhlere'," *Kunst un Lebn*, ed. by A. Reisen (Warsaw: 1908); and "Vegn dem yidish renesans," *Literarishe Monatshrift* (Wilno: March 1908). In 1913 he again published an article in the same vein, "A naye tkufe in undzer kamf far yidish," *Der Yidisher Arbeter*, nos. 49-50 (Lwów: Dec. 25) which he dedicated to the chief ideologist of *Poale Zion*, Dov Borokhov.

66. Cf. S. Dubnow, *Nationalism and History* (Philadelphia: 1961), p. 190.

67. Hirschhaut, *loc. cit.* See also Tennenbaum, *op. cit.*, p. 164.

68. *Der Yidisher Arbeter*, no. 7, May 6, 1910; also, Chomet, "Di tsiyonistishe bavegung," *op. cit.*, p. 469.

69. Gelber, *op. cit.*, p. 586.

70. Chomet, *op. cit.*, p. 468.

71. Gelber, *op. cit.*, p. 587.

72. Chomet, op. cit., p. 470.

73. *Ibid.*, pp. 472-473 (paraphrased). Cf. also B. Weinreb, "Daniel Leibel," *Torne, op. cit.*, p. 315.

74. Chomet, *loc. cit.*

75. The extent of his dedication is again attested by Chomet, who recalls that in 1912 or 1913 Schipper gave him his silver watch to use as collateral for a loan needed to pay the rent for the *Poale Zion* quarters. Chomet, "Yidishe visnshaftler, literatn un publitsistn fun Torne," *Torne, op. cit.*, p. 334.

76. Schipper, "Ustawodawstwo Kazimierza Wielkiego w stosunku do Żydów," *Moriah* (Lwów: 1902).

77. Tadeusz Czacki, *Rozprawa o Żydach i Karaitach* (Wilno: 1807); 2nd ed., (Cracow: 1860). Ludwik Gumplowicz, *Prawodawstwo polskie względem Żydów* (Cracow: 1867). Romouald Hube, "Przywilej Żydowski Bolesława i jego potwierdzenia," *Biblioteka Warszawska* (Warsaw: 1880). Philip Bloch, *Die Generalprivilegien der polnischen Judenschaft* (Posen: 1892). Moses Schorr, "Organizacja Żydów w Polsce," *Kwartalnik Historyczny*, XIII (1899). Hilary Nussbaum, *Historya Żydów*, vol. V (Warsaw: 1890). St. Kutrzeba, "Stanowisko prawne Żydów w Polsce w XV wieku," *Przewodnik naukowy i literacki* (1901). Majer Bałaban, "Dwa przyczynki do stosunków Jagiełły z Żydami lwowskymi," *Kwartalnik Historyczny*, XXV (1911), pp. 234-239.

78. I. Schipper, *Yidishe geshikhte*, 4 vols. (Warsaw: 1930), p. ii (hereafter referred to by its subtitle, *Virtschaftsgeshikhte*).

79. *Loc. cit.* See also Hirschhaut, *op. cit.*, p. 189.

80. Schipper, "Żydzi w Polsce za Piastów," *Moriah* (Lwów: 1905); "Żydzi za Kazimierza Wielkiego," *Moriah* (Lwów: 1905), pp. 46-50, 74-79, 104-107;

"Geneza lichwy żydowskiej w średniowieczu," *Moriah* (Lwów: 1906), pp. 178-182, 226-230.

81. See *infra*, pp. 24 f.

82. For more details concerning the assismilationist school of Jewish historians see I. M. Biderman, *Mayer Balaban, the Historian of Polish Jewry* (New York: 1976), pp. 19-36.

83. In another article, written in 1909, Schipper provides a most biting criticism of the books by Kraushar, Sternberg, and Nussbaum, describing them as "obscure and misleading" and stating that Sternberg knows nothing about Jews in medieval Poland besides the charters, which he misinterprets, and some notes from Gallus, Kadłubek, and Długosz (oldest Polish chroniclers) while Nussbaum uses commonplaces, clichés, and excerpts from other manuals. See Schipper, "Przegląd krytyczny literatury, odnoszącej, się do historji Żydów w Polsce średniowieznej," *Wschód* (Lwów): 1905), no. 5.

84. Gumplowicz, *op. cit.*, p. 132 and Schipper, "Żydzi za Kazimierza," *op. cit.*, p. 49.

85. Bloch, *op. cit.*, pp. 86 ff, especially p. 101.

86. Schipper, "Żydzi za Kazimierza," *op. cit.*, p. 52.

87. *Ibid.*, pp. 48, 50, 74 ff. The evolution of the legal status of Jews in the Middle Ages is elaborated upon by Schipper in his subsequent studies and books, which will be discussed later.

88. *Supra*, p. 23, n. 83.

89. Cf. Balaban, "Korot ha-Yehudim bi-Ymey ha-Beynayim," *Bet Yisrael be-Polin*, vol. I, p. 8 (note).

90. S. Bershadski, *Russko-Yevreyskiy Arkhiv* (Petersburg: 1903), No. 1.

91. Schipper, "Przegląd krytyczny," *op. cit., Wschód* No. 12 (1909).

92. Meaning the so-called *Akta grodzkie i ziemskie*, the first-instance records of the territorial communities of the landed gentry in distinction to the municipal records.

93. *Ibid.*, No. 13 (1909).

94. Bałaban, "Dwa przyczynki do stosunków Jagiełły z Żydami lwowskymi," *op. cit.*, pp. 234 ff.

95. Schipper, "Sporniye voprosi epokhi Vladislava Yagello," *Yevreyskaya Starina*, VI (1913), pp. 102-107.

96. As in all medieval states, the political organization of Poland under the Piast dynasty was that of a hereditary monarchy based on a system of Estates, each enjoying their specific rights and privileges. By the end of the Piast period, however, the political process had already set in whereby the Polish *szlachta* (nobility) began to arrogate for itself political and economic powers at the cost

of the Crown as well as all other Estates. This process led to the adoption of the *liberum veto* prerogative and to the emergence of a Republic of Nobles in Poland rather than absolute monarchy as was the case in all European states, except England. But unlike the latter, the political omnipotence of one single class was carried in Poland to an extent unparalleled in any other European country. See R. H. Lord, *The Second Partition of Poland: A Study in Diplomatic History* (Cambridge: 1915), pp. 7 ff. Also, *The Cambridge History of Poland*, W. F. Reddaway, *et al.*, eds., vol. I (Cambridge: 1950), pp. 416-430, 438-440.

97. M. Schorr, *Die Hauptprivilegien der polnischen Judenschaft* (Vienna: 1917), reviewed by Schipper in *Moriah*, XII (1917), pp. 432-433.

98. R. Mahler, "Di Yidn in amolikn Poyln," *Di Yidn in Poyln*, vol. I (New York: 1946), pp. 26-27. Cf. also S. W. Baron, *A Social and Religious History of the Jews*, vol. X, J.P.S. (Philadelphia: 1965), pp. 44-46 as well as B. D. Weinryb, *The Jews in Poland: A Social and Economic History of the Jewish Community in Poland from 1100 to 1800* (Philadelphia: 1976), pp. 33 ff.

99. I. Schipper, *Studya nad stosunkami gospodarczymi Żydów w Polsce podczas średniowiecza* (Lwów: 1911); translated into Yiddish by E. Ringelblum and D. Leibel as *Di virtschafts-geshikhte fun di Yidn in Poyln beysn mitlalter* (Warsaw: 1926), referred to hereafter as *Studya* or *Studies.*

100. I. Schipper, "Przyczynek do dziejów żydowskich własności ziemskich w średniowieczu," *Moriah* (Lwów: 1908), pp. 42-46, 70-75; "Początki ekonomiki żydowskiej. Najwcześniejszy handel żydowski w Polsce (VIII-XII w.)," *Almanach Dra Leona Reicha* (Lwów: 1910), pp. 165-173; "Yevreyskiy kredit v Polshe v XIV vyeke," *Yevreyskaya Starina* (1910), pp. 542-568; "Ranniye stadyi yevreyskoy kolonizatsyi v Polshe," *Yevreyskaya Starina* (1911), pp. 161-179, 348-371.

101. Schipper, *Studya, op. cit.*, pp. 2-3, 45.

102. *Ibid.*, p. 69. The matter of overlooked sources Schipper raised already in his critical review of historical literature in which he says: "By some strange coincidence contemporary investigators of Jewish history in Poland began their studies mainly after the fifteenth century, sometimes unwillingly casting an eye backward into the Middle Ages. . . . The main reason for treating the medieval history of Jews in Poland stingily seems to be the lack of orderly published sources relating to those times. That such sources are not lacking, that there is a hundredfold more information about the life of Jews in medieval Poland than that provided by the famous General *Privilegia* (to which, with small exceptions, the knowledge of historians has been limited thus far) one can easily see if one would browse through the publications of Piekosiński, Helcel, Ulanowski, Krzyżanowski, Czołkowski, Wierzbowski, etc., and look into the official land records (*Akta grodzkie i ziemskie*)." Schipper goes on to say that his main problem in preparing his work was not the limited amount of data but the overwhelming amount of it, noting that from published sources alone he came to

almost 1,200 notes in addition to the hundreds of notes found in the archival records of cities such as Cracow and Lwów, and the court books of Great Poland. "Przegląd historyczny," *op. cit.*, No. 5 (1909).

103. Gumplowicz, *op. cit.*, p. 131.

104. The voivode (in Polish, *wojewoda*) was in the time of the Piasts the representative of the ruler, king or duke, in various capacities, especially in leading the military. In later times his powers were considerably restricted. Setting prices of goods in towns, the judicial matters regarding Jews, leading the military of a given province were among his main functions. His position was also coupled with a seat in the Sejm. See R. Mahler and E. Ringelblum, *Geklibene mekoyrim tsu der geshikhte fun Yidn in Poyln un mizraḥ Eyrope* (Warsaw: 1930), p. 51, n. 1. Also, Weinryb, *The Jews in Poland, op. cit.*, p. 34.

105. Schipper, *Studies, op. cit.*, pp. 45-49. To substantiate his contention that Jews were a free element until the middle of the thirteenth century, Schipper cites also the testimony of the Polish chronicler, Wincenty Kadłubek, according to which offenses against Jews were severely punished under Mieszko III (1173-1202), which is most indicative of the Jews' privileged position. Cf. Baron, *op. cit.*, vol. X, p. 31 and Mahler, "Di Yidn in amolikn Poyln," *op. cit.*, p. 19. Also, Weinryb, *The Jews in Poland, op. cit.*, pp. 35 ff.

106. In Schipper's works see "Początki Żydów na ziemiach ruskich i polskich," *Almanach Żydowski* (Vienna: 1918), pp. 236-265, reprinted in *Bleter far Geshikhte*, XIII (1960), Warsaw, pp. 26-59, used here for reference, see pp. 48 and 58; *Virtshaftsgeshikhte, op. cit.*, vol. II, pp. 105-106; *Dzieje handlu żydowskiego na ziemiach polskich* (Warsaw: 1937), p. 9. Mahler and other younger historians adopted the same view. See Mahler, "Di Yidn in amolikn Poyln," *op. cit.*, pp. 19-22.

107. The *Kwartalnik Historyczny* (Historical Quarterly) was the official publication of the Polish Historical Society and the principal organ of Polish historical science. It was founded by Professor Ludwik Finkel, an eminent scholar at the University of Lwów, who had organized the Historical Society and who brought to Polish historiography the methods of historical research advanced by Ranke in Germany. Cf. Ludwik Finkel and S. Starzyński, *Historya uniwersytetu lwowskiego*, vol. II (Lwów: 1894), pp. 64, 79.

108. Schipper, "Żydzi w Tarnowie do końca XVIII wieku," *Kwartalnik Historyczny*, XIX (1905), pp. 228-237.

109. *Ibid.*, p. 228.

110. *Ibid.*, pp. 229-230.

111. *Ibid.*, pp. 234-235.

2

The Origin and End of Jewish Capital

In 1907 Schipper's name became known among historians through his first substantial and controversial study in German dealing with the origins of Jewish capital in Western Europe, published initially in the *Zeitschrift für Volkswirtschaft, Sozialpolitik und Verwaltung.*[1] This work marked the beginning of Schipper's independent and eminent reputation as a Jewish historian and scholar. It had been written as a dissertation for his doctoral degree in jurisprudence which he obtained that year, at the age of twenty-three, from the University of Vienna. The two years spent in Vienna and its great university must have been most rewarding to Schipper in terms of academic experience and growth. Together with such students as Joseph A. Schumpeter (1883-1950), he attended the seminars of Eugen v. Philippovich, K. Th. v. Inama-Sternegg, prominent economic historian and statistician whom Schipper quoted in his early works, and, above all, the seminars conducted by the respected Eugen v. Böhm-Bawerk, the Austrian statesman and economist who, along with Carl Menger and Friedrich v. Wieser, is regarded as cofounder of the Austrian or Viennese school of economics. Eugen v. Böhm-Bawerk's personality and lectures, described by Schumpeter in superlative terms,[2] must have enriched and stimulated the young Jewish student from Tarnów. The fact that Böhm-Bawerk was, to use the words of Schumpeter, "a theorist, born to see and to explain large relationships; to seize instinctively, but with a firm hand, on the threads of logical necessities" must have been of particular liking to Schipper. Both revealing and important for his socialist outlook already acquired at the Tarnów Gymnasium, must also have been Böhm-Bawerk's critique of the economics of Karl Marx, especially the latter's use of the labor theory of value. The masterfully critical exposition of the Marxist system by his teacher and the antisocialist attitude of the Austrian school in general seem to be directly related to the fact that Schipper in his later years not only modified his political views but consistently tended to keep clear of an identification with Marxist dogmatism until, in 1922, he left the *Poale Zion* altogether to join the centrists among Zionists.[3]

Sombart's Challenge

The study of the genesis of capital among Jews in the Middle Ages was no doubt motivated by Schipper's interest in tracing the earliest economic activities of Jews in Poland. Schipper's research aimed at the proper understanding of the royal charters which—their preoccupation with credit transactions notwithstanding—were grossly misinterpreted, to Schipper's mind, by his predecessors. But more than that, the question was most timely and pertinent in view of the ever-expanding echo of the "scientific" theories of modern anti-Semitism, expounded not by ordinary Jew-haters but by respected men of German scholarship, Heinrich v. Treitschke, Houston Stewart Chamberlain, and Werner Sombart. Treitschke, the celebrated author of a history glorifying the German people, clamored in his articles in the *Preussische Jahrbücher* (1879) that "the Jews are our misfortune." Chamberlain summed up all of history in his notorious *Foundations of the Nineteenth Century* (1899), as a conflict between the superior Aryan race and the inferior Semites, especially the

Homo Judaicus element which constitutes a threat to mankind. Sombart, posing as an objective economist, concluded that the spirit of capitalism is identical with that of the Jewish people; that, in fact, the Jew—anthropologically (racially), psychologically, religiously, and otherwise—represents the very embodiment of the nature and meaning of capitalism. Starting with the premise that the statistical method in economic investigations must be supplemented by the genetic method and stating carefully, but parenthetically, that other factors, besides the Jews, also played an important role in the economic history of the Western world, Sombart proceeded to expound his theory.[4] He felt that economic developments in Europe as well as in European colonial expansions in modern times are inextricably linked with Jewish migrations, the economic activities of Jews, their participation in international trade, their role in colonizing territories, especially in America, the economic methods and devices they contrived, and the like.[5]

In discussing the latter, Sombart postulated that the Jews are responsible not only for the external forms of modern commerce, for the organization or formation of economic instrumentalities and institutions, but also for the inner spirit animating the capitalist social economy, which, he felt, is nothing but a reflection of the Jewish racial psyche. Sombart admitted that proof could not be based on documentation, but he relied on the "testimonies" or "feelings" of non-Jews who, in their direct dealings and experiences with Jews, were in a position to form opinions as to the latter's methods and inherent characteristics, even though these opinions might be one-sided and colored by hatred. The very fact that certain judgments about the Jews remained uniform in various localities raised the credence value of that type of evidence, as far as Sombart was concerned. He therefore presented the complaints, petitions, litigations, interdictions in various countries to show the reaction of non-Jews to the behavior of Jews in the economic sphere: their alleged methods of undermining indigenous merchants, their allegedly negative traits and influence, and like charges. According to that "uniform" testimony, the Jews succeeded in their competition with Christians because of unethical methods. Sombart admitted that these methods were not so much the result of cheating or lying or deliberate intent to injure on the part of the Jews as the result of a characteristic Jewish indifference to the established laws and norms of Christian society which, Sombart contended, were designed to satisfy the needs of both the producer and the merchant according to their social position.

Contrary to existing Christian ethics which scorned profit for its own sake as ungodly, according to Sombart, Jews defied the existing protective regulations enacted by municipalities and guilds forbidding competition, price-cutting, outbidding, and such. Disregarding established commercial morality and the limits set by society, they engaged in more than one economic activity. They looked for every opportunity to outbid, to take away customers, to undermine national industry with imports, to monopolize certain trades, to cut prices by selling stolen, old, damaged, inferior, and illegal goods, all in order to satisfy the greediness inherent in their capitalist nature.[6]

To appear objective, but without any reference to the actual legal and social condition of the Jews as strangers discriminated against, Sombart pointed also to the fact that Jews discovered ways and means to lower costs of production. He conceded that they exercised extreme frugality and were satisfied with smaller profits, that they stimulated the market and increased the turnover of goods through enterprises based on planning, foresight, and the implementation of new ways to increase the clientele (new types of goods, greater variety, modified terms of payment, combining goods with services).[7]

Echoes of Sombart's ideas were heard everywhere in Europe in the years preceding World War I, for reports of public lectures given by Sombart, in his capacity as professor of the Berlin University, often appeared in the European press.[8] Although these lectures were at times tempered with comments on the objective circumstances that account for the Jewish role in the emergence of modern capitalism, which is characterized by a purposefully callous spirit, the distinct impression conveyed was that pecuniary pursuits constitute a basic Jewish trait rooted in the rational, teleological spirit of Judaism and Jewish tradition.[9]

Certain Jewish circles in Germany greeted Sombart's *Die Juden und das Wirtschaftsleben* with much enthusiasm. They saw in it a document confirming not only the significant contributions of Jews to modern economic achievements, but also attesting to the indispensability of Jews for the future growth of the German economy, with which those Jewish groups were eager to identify, Sombart's clearly racist position notwithstanding.[10] In the hinterland, however, there was intuitive apprehension. Men like Schipper sensed the evil intent of the combined racial and economic theories of Sombart, which aimed to prove "scientifically" the affinity of Jewishness with capitalism and the inborn "genius" of Jews for commercialism. But rather than address himself to the racial or—as Reich called them—the anthropo-geographic aspects[11] of Sombart's thesis, Schipper chose to concentrate on the basic question of the source of Jewish funds. He hoped to prove that "the actions of people depend on the circumstances and the relationships in which they find themselves rather than on their abilities and racial characteristics." Schipper believed that in the Middle Ages, in particular, the position of the Jews as a distinct economic group was the result of their unintended and inevitable adjustment to a specific set of circumstances.[12]

Confutation of "Old Capitalism"

Sombart reinforced the popular notion that Jews in the Middle Ages were the natural heirs of the Phoenicians. He postulated that at the fall of the Roman Empire rich Jews had managed to salvage wealth from ancient times in the form of precious metals and jewels, which they hid during the barbarian invasions and put into circulation at the beginning of the Middle Ages.[13] It was that "old capital" that enabled Jews to enter into the extensive West-East trade, ramified monetary transactions, and eventually into credit operations that constituted their main economic activities throughout the Middle Ages.

Putting aside the fact that the "old capital" theory is undocumented and unsubstantiated in any way, Schipper questions whether the Jews could indeed have saved substantial capital following the fall of the Roman Empire. And if they could not have done so, how did the accumulation of funds come about? His answer to the first part of the question is negative on the basis of a brief but comprehensive analysis of the historical and economic situation of the Jewish communities in Palestine, Babylonia, Alexandria, Greece, and Rome before the advent of the Middle Ages. Of all these communities, only the Babylonian could claim substantial wealth, since many of its Jews owned land and estates and many leased public revenues. The once opulent community in Alexandria, known in the first and second centuries for its great merchants, shippers, and financiers, was poor indeed by the beginning of the fifth century, having experienced a period of decline characterized by anti-Jewish policies and excesses and an expulsion in 415.[14] In Greece, Jews were farmers, specialists in agriculture and the silk industry, rather than merchants. Byzantine emperors who monopolized the trade of the major products (silk, wine, oil, corn, etc.) left little if any room for commercial possibilities.[15] As for the Roman Empire in the West, especially in Rome proper, Schipper cites evidence[16] showing that the Jewish *libertini* there were poor artisans, part of the city proletarians, whose numbers were for a long time augmented by new arrivals and who were forced to pay special Jewish taxes (*Fiscus Judaicus*). If Italian Jews had some small possessions, they lost them during the wars and upheavals of the fifth century.

Prior to the barbarian invasions in the West, the Syrians controlled trade between the East and Rome and they were the chief international merchants. But the volume of this trade became insignificant for a long time because the political seat was transferred to Constantinople and because the Germanic tribes that inherited the western part of the Roman Empire could not at once provide markets for Eastern goods. In view of these known historical facts and developments, Sombart's theory that Jews retained wealth from ancient times through the period of invasions and migrations appears to be highly improbable.[17] Characteristic of Schipper's description of the pertinent historical developments is his emphasis on the fact that the Jews did not constitute a special economic class in Rome or in other countries but were engaged in various occupations. He notes that "unlike the Greeks and Romans, the Jews appreciated correctly the value of farming and craftsmanship" and that "more than a hundred of the sages of the Talmud were artisans."[18]

As for the second part of the question, namely: How did the accumulation of liquid capital in Jewish hands come about in the high Middle Ages?, Schipper offers a twofold answer. The first is related to Jewish landownership. The second has to do with the fact that Jews supplanted the Syrians in international trade with the Orient in the wake of the great conquests of Islam.

Jewish Landownership

That Jews in Byzantium as well as in the West were landowners in the earliest stages of the Middle Ages is clearly stated in many primary documents that Schipper cites profusely together with historical studies treating of that subject.[19] Schipper points to the fact that there were whole areas known for their predominant Jewish ownership (*Terra Ebreorum*) in Provence, Lombardy, Spain, and other Roman provinces and that sources from the fourth century mention Jewish *curiae* in Germanic lands and Gaul (Cologne, Narbonne, Lyons) which, predicated on landownership, must have been those of Jewish proprietors. Jews belonged to the class of landowners who cultivated their holdings as free farmers (*coloni*), often with the help of their own slaves,[20] because they enjoyed the status of *Civis Romani.* Although the Edict of 438 by Theodosius II, guided by the interest of Christianity as the ruling religion, limited that status somewhat, its interdictions barring Jews from holding public office, keeping Christian slaves, building new synagogues, and the like remained on paper for a long time, until after the barbarian invasions. At that time the land was divided between the Roman citizens and the victorious Germanic tribes, and the Jews, as Roman citizens, obtained their share of cultivated as well as uncultivated land in various provinces. Jewish landowners became well known as growers of vines and makers of wine as well as oil producers.[21] The very fact that Church edicts of the sixth century (Orlean in 538 and 541, Macon in 581, and Toledo in 589) repeatedly enjoined Jews from keeping Christian slaves provides eloquent evidence that such practices must have been widespread in Gaul and Spain, attesting to the great need of the Jewish landowners for workers.[22]

However, the situation changed when the Germanic peoples accepted Christianity. Under Roman law, the Jews were granted essential rights such as the practice of Judaism and a measure of judicial autonomy. When the distinction between the pagan or Arian tribes vanished as the Roman citizen became part of the new conglomerates, the right of citizenship was gradually supplemented by the Germanic *Stammgesetzen* based on tribal kinship and custom. In the new circumstances the Jew became a stranger, a man outside the established *marche*, in need of a protector.[23] The process of making the Jew a stranger was reinforced by the legislation of the Church. That legislation, repeatedly and consistently, revolved around two main objectives: (1) to prevent Jewish influence and authority over Christians and (2) to relegate Jews to an inferior status befitting a deicide people, a *secta nefaria*.[24] Schipper related these developments, which had their beginnings in the fifth century and continued throughout the Dark Ages, with the slow but continuous reduction of Jewish landholdings. Reduced to the status of unprotected strangers, Jews had no choice but sell their lands and convert them into transferable wealth. This was especially true when it became illegal for Jews to hold slaves on their estates or to own land altogether in certain parts of Europe where the influence of the Church among the rulers became stronger. The process of converting landholdings into money, according to Schipper, began at the latest in the second half of the sixth century, but varied in time and degree in different countries, the only exception being Spain where Egica's decree of 694 forbidding Jews to own land and homes was shortlived due to the Moslem conquest in 711. While Jewish owners of big estates undoubtedly collected land rents for a considerable period of time, it was the involuntary sale of big landholdings that became the main source of liquid capital in Jewish hands. That capital grew because the Jews put it to good use in response to the need for commercial exchange with the East. This development came about because of the Arab conquests which opened up new economic opportunities.[25]

Although the shift to world commerce assumed quite pronounced proportions under the Carolingian rulers, especially in West Francia and the Middle Kingdoms where masses of people became serfs and a general economic stagnation set in, Jews continued to hold land and play a role in agriculture wherever that was possible. Schipper emphasizes the fact that in Spain under the Moors Jewish economic activities were not based on commerce but almost exclusively on landownership. Agriculture was also a significant Jewish occupation in East Germanic and Slavic provinces until the twelfth century and possibly later, long after free landholdings in Jewish hands were a thing of the past in the West.[26] But even in the Frankish states and the Holy Roman Empire where interest in real estate among Jews lessened considerably, in view of their commercial activities which required them to be often on the move and to settle in towns along the commercial routes, references to Jews owning land are frequent.

The landed possessions of Jews in Narbonne, inherited apparently from the days of Moslem rule, received the approbation of Carolingian rulers in the eighth century. Later, the charters received by some Jews of Septimania from Louis the Pious; the privileges conferred by Henry IV on Jews of Speyer and Worms; the decree of Charles the Simple requiring Jews to pay tithes from lands that had belonged to Christians (an ecclesiastical demand officially formulated at the Gerona Council of 1068 and extended ten years later at another Council in Gerona to all land owned by Jews)—all this evidence proves that Jews continued to hold land. It also indicates that the process of divesting Jews of their landholdings was slow and painful. This in spite of pressing demands by the Church and the ongoing process of feudalization, mutually complementary forces. These ecclesiastical and feudal pressures were completely incompatible—politically, religiously, and socially—with the position of the Jew as a landowner. In the hierarchical system of feudalism in which land ownership was a source of political power and social position, a Jew could not be permitted to own land, for this would have given him the rights of a feudal suzerain in territories populated by Christians. Hence, the protestations of the Church[27] and the special royal letters which Jewish landowners needed to confirm their rights as the king's vassals. These letters, Schipper points out, reflect the change in the character of Jewish landownership; for, whereas at an earlier time Jewish property under cultivation was referred to in the sources as *allodium Judaicum* (*i.e.*, Jewish land inheritance free from feudal fee obligations), the charter of Louis the Pious speaks of Jewish land as *res propriae* (*i.e.*, fiefs within the feudal system).

Still later documents from the tenth century reveal that confiscated Jewish land had previously been burdened with feudal fee obligations. In the tenth century royal protection in the form of special letters ceased to exist. As the Christianization of the feudal system progressed, Jewish lands became the property of the Church and clergy. In the eleventh and twelfth centuries foreclosed lands held by individual Jewish moneylenders had to be sold to Christians. Nonetheless, Jews were not completely divorced from agricultural pursuits, for living in a town in those times did not imply complete removal from rural life, and in the newer countries of Jewish settlement on the eastern borders of the Germanic lands, the suppression of landholding by Jews would have been quite impractical and inexpedient for the local rulers, at least for a while.[28]

This, then, was Schipper's two-pronged confutation of Sombart's speculations regarding capital resources retained by Jews from antiquity and his theory of their racial affinity with the "capitalist attitude to life." Schipper collected all possible evidence to prove that whatever funds Jews possessed in the high Middle Ages (800-1200) could not have come from ancient times but must have come from their big landholdings which they were compelled to sell over a long period of time under gradually worsening circumstances. He also showed that as long as possible, and wherever possible, the Jews in the Middle Ages preferred to remain in agriculture or in related industries rather than in commerce, a preference indubitably manifested by their occupations in Spain, Sicily, Greece, Provence, Burgundy, etc.

Schipper's views, however, were not universally accepted as conclusive. They became known as Schipper's theory, debated by historians but by no means rejected offhand, although Oelsner did state rather impulsively that just as Jews could not salvage gold from antiquity, so there could not be a "sudden feudalization forcing Jews at once to sell their landed property, and thus to acquire the necessary capital for money-lending. . . ."[29] Kulisher acknowledged Schipper's able demonstration of considerable Jewish landholdings in the period between the sixth and eighth centuries, but he questioned whether this fact could have had any relationship and significance for the big financial operations that Jews conducted five or six centuries later. Furthermore, the early sale of big estates is inferred rather than documented.[30]

The fact is, however, that Schipper does not speak of any "sudden" feudalization nor of any rapid sale of landed estates. Nor does he project the idea that the considerable sums of money realized at the early stages of the land-selling process were directly related to the extensive credit activities conducted by Jews in the later Middle Ages. A most important economic phase of international trade during which the initial capital resources were greatly augmented intervened between these two periods.

An idea was also projected that Schipper himself became less confident about the validity of his theory as time went on. This was based on the fact that in his *Virtschaftsgeshikhte*, published twenty-four years later, in which the exposition of the Jewish economic position in the early Middle Ages follows most closely that of *Anfänge des Kapitalismus*, the theory of Jewish capital derived from land sales is completely omitted.[31] But one must remember that in 1930 the *Virtshaftsgeshikhte* was not meant to be an answer to Sombart's speculations. There was no need for it in view of the critical literature that already existed. Schipper may have thought that the rapidly growing Jewish agricultural colonies in Palestine were a much more eloquent reply than a book in Yiddish meant primarily for Jewish youth and workers.[32] But the Yiddish translation of *Anfänge des Kapitalismus*, published in 1920, does not contain any revision or modifications of Schipper's original views.

Most pertinent, however, is Baron's opinion in the matter. Rejecting the "old capital" theory as undocumented and confirming Schipper's refutation of Sombart's view on the origins of Jewish capital in the medieval West, Baron proceeds to devote some space to the explanation based mainly on M. Lombard's contention that the Arabs, because of their monetary supremacy due to constant exploitation of gold and silver mines in Islamic countries and central Africa, were able to export substantial surpluses of those metals to the West with Jewish participation in the process of East-West exchange. In the last analysis, however, Baron concludes:

> Be it as it may, the use of Western Jewish "capitalism" did not entirely depend on the importation of gold but may as well have originated with such luxury articles as silk or pepper, both of which often played the role of currency in mercantile exchange far more frequently than alum. Nor did Jews necessarily depend on their own imports. If there were capital accumulations in the hands of Frisian merchants or local grandees, Jewish settlers were able to transform their landholdings, even under pressure, into much liquid capital and then increase it rapidly through usual commercial profits.[33]

International and Internal Trade

The growing role of Jews as international merchants in the medieval world, subjected to a rigid separation between the Christian West and the Islamic East from the second half of the seventh century on, is treated by Schipper in a general but comprehensive way in his *Anfänge*[34] as well as in a special monograph in German.[35] More extensively, with attention to different countries, Schipper treats of the subject in the first volume of his *Virtschaftsgeshikhte.*[36]

In tracing the evolution of this economic activity, Schipper again points out that in the times of the Merovingian rule Jews in Italy, Provence, and Spain were mainly occupied in agriculture. Their participation in commerce, conducted with moneys collected from land rents, was to begin with a side occupation, limited to trade in jewelry and especially in slaves. The need for slaves was a result of the repeated barbarian attacks, the population decrease in the cities and the ruined countryside, and the ensuing need for working hands on the great feudal estates.[37]

A statement of Pope Gregory I attacking Jewish slaveholding as well as repeated prohibitions of the Church Councils in the matter give an indication of the scope of Jewish participation in that *exsecrabile commercium* in slaves. However, Schipper stresses the fact that there was actually no opposition on the part of the Pope to slavery and slave trade as such, as he himself bought Saxon slaves to work on Church lands. The Pope's objection was, in the first place, against Jews keeping Christian slaves, and in the second place, against the possible conversion of slaves to Judaism.[38] Neither minimizing or exaggerating the role of Jews in the slave traffic during the Merovingian and Carolingian periods, nor being in the least defensive about it,[38] Schipper proceeds to show that the pronounced and far-reaching importance of Jews in general and international trade in particular took place during the Carolingian period as a result of the demographic, political, and economic changes that transpired in the Mediterranean world.

Sources from the sixth and seventh centuries reveal that all oriental wares known in the Frankish state at the time of the Merovingian kings were brought by Syrian merchants who penetrated quite deeply into the West.[40] The first definite information regarding Jewish contacts with the Orient came from the beginning of the eighth century, that is, after the Arabs conquered the Near East, North Africa, Sicily, and Spain. By breaking the unity of the Mediterranean area, the Arab conquest created a new set of circumstances most auspicious for the socially and economically displaced Jews in the West to assume the role of international merchants. Competition in the field of commerce disappeared almost completely as the once-dominant Syrians converted to Islam, became fully absorbed in the Arab world, and severed contacts with the Christian countries. Competition on the part of Greek or Slavic merchants was of no consequence. Only the Jews were economically well qualified to fill the vacuum created by the departure of the Syrians and the rather rigid division of the Mediterranean into two separate and completely different religious and cultural spheres. Besides having a certain measure of experience in commerce, they could (1) rely on an unbroken chain of Jewish communities in the West as well as in the East for the necessary contacts, information, advice, help, and protection and (2) use to good advantage their international means of communication—the Hebrew language.[41] Thus, the declining share of Jews in the agriculture of Christian Europe was compensated by their indispensability and growing role in trade. That transformation, Schipper goes on to explain, resulted not only from the separation between the East and West but also from economic developments within Western Europe proper. Here the higher secular as well as ecclesiastical nobility became very much aware of the importance of the Jewish merchant as their appetites for pomp and splendor grew and their needs for luxury items and special wares, obtainable only in Asia Minor and India, became increasingly greater.

Back in the first half of the seventh century even King Dagobert could not do without the Jewish merchant. Under the rule of the Carolingian kings, trade with the Orient conducted by Jews reached considerable proportions, and Charlemagne's appreciation of that trade is a well-known fact. At that time territorial lords attached professional merchants to themselves and the merchants acted as the lord's agents; hence, the phenomenon of Jewish merchants becoming the protegés of feudal suzerains. At first the protection and special privileges (fee and tax exemptions) which the kings and lords extended to Jewish merchants were given them as a reward for the conduct of commercial affairs. In time, however, the Jewish merchants were expected to pay for the protection and concessions granted.[42] Thus Louis the Pious received part of the profits every year or two, while in 877 Charles the Bald received ten percent of the Jews' net profit. And this, undoubtedly, accounts for the further growth and success of Jewish commercial activities.[43]

Jewish merchants sold their precious oriental goods (jewelry, gems, silks, rugs, perfumes, ivory, glass, etc.)[44] mainly to the rich in the feudal system: the landed nobility, the grandees, and the higher clergy. In the tenth century the commercial and social relationships between Jews and the ecclesiastical dignitaries were very favorable in spite of the official position of the Church. Outside the papal domain, Jews transacted a great deal of business with bishops and abbots who had in their possession considerable riches and who were most anxious to obtain the goods brought by Jews from the East. Schipper surmises that Charlemagne ordered strict supervision over ecclesiastical properties and treasuries because Jews may have informed him that they were very generously paid for their deliveries of Oriental wares to the clergy.[45] Indeed, he goes on to say, certain sources reveal that Jews knew how to make the most of the gullibility of the higher clergy. Even more than that, the fact that transactions were made on an individual, private basis rather than on the open market allowed Jews to set their own prices.[46] Schipper also points out that the landed feudal aristocracy, in pursuit of luxury and outer display, was not averse to using serfs as payment for commodities purchased from Jews. Thus, the trade in goods went hand in hand with the traffic in slaves, a commodity in great demand in the Moslem world. Archbishop Agobard complained bitterly in his *De Insolentia Judaeorum* about the sale and shipment of Christian slaves to Spain by Jews with the apparent acquiescence of the kings who, instead of forbidding the practice, extended their protection to the Jewish traffickers.[47] But as denunciations became louder and prohibitions stricter, the Jewish merchants turned to the pagan hinterlands of Central and Eastern Europe to obtain their slaves as well as other articles such as hides and furs.

In support of the fact that Jewish merchants penetrated deep into Eastern Europe and were possibly among the first trail blazers in this vast, virgin expanse, Schipper cites the *Kitab al-Masalik wa'l-Mamalik* (Book of the Roads and Kingdoms). Written by Ibn Khurradadhbih, the Persian postmaster-general of the Caliphate in 846, this book contains a lengthy passage describing the four routes used by Jewish merchants called Radhanites.[48]

Schipper is probably the first Jewish historian to make full use of this remarkable and strikingly cogent piece of contemporary evidence. He deduces from it, as will be shown in the subsequent chapters of this study, far-reaching conclusions,[49] especially with regard to one of the two commercial land routes delineated by Ibn Khurradadhbih which "led from the West through the heart of Europe, via Germany and the Slavic lands to Itil on the Volga, the capital of the Khazars, where the Radhanites maintained their emporia under particularly favorable circumstances, thanks to the cooperation of their Khazar coreligionists."[50] The other land route led from France to Spain, North Africa, Palestine, Syria, Babylonia to India and China, while the two water routes, also commencing in France, made use of the Mediterranean to Egypt and from there via the Red Sea to India, or to Antioch and from there by land and the Euphrates to Baghdad and by the Tigris to the Persian Gulf and further to India and China. That this extensive intercontinental commerce was conducted by sea is well verified in other sources which attest to ships owned by Jews and the fact that their sailing was protected by special royal orders.[51]

The Jewish communities in Italy, especially in South Italy, constituted until the end of the tenth century an important link along this line of communication. This is well documented by sources speaking of direct travel from Jaffa to Gaeta, from Capua to Egypt, from Germany to Jerusalem via Venice, etc.[52]

While stressing the fact that the Radhanites were, according to Ibn Khurradadhbih's narrative, polyglots who could communicate in seven languages, Schipper does not seem to think that they represented Jewish merchants from various lands. Nor is he aware of the fact that the name Radhanites (*radhaniya* in Arabic) may be derived from the Persian term *rahdan*, meaning wayfarer or merchant-traveler. He is rather convinced that all of them hailed from the West in consonance with Heyd's reasoning, based on the fact that all their routes had the same point of departure in Southern France. He is in agreement with the contention of De Simonsen, who found considerable evidence that the term is identical with *nautuae Rhodanic, i.e.*, "sailors of the Rhodanus" (the Latin name for the Rhone River). This is a sobriquet by which the Jewish merchants from Arles in particular, famous for their distant travels to Asia, were known. Other German scholars, among them Aronius and Caro, also believed that the hub of Jewish international trade was centered in the southwestern parts of the Frankish Empire,[53] and that its concomitant development of internal commerce in the forms of regional and local fairs proceeded from these parts to the north and east along the old Roman trade routes and river valleys, principally of Champagne and the Rhineland, where the Jewish merchant figured most prominently and where Jewish settlements multiplied rapidly.[54] Noting the growing prominence and prosperity of the Jews as the leading international and internal merchants in the Carolingian Empire, Schipper cites evidence that even fairs were shifted from the Sabbath to other days for the convenience of Jews. He concludes that although they were protegés and servants of the kings, and in need of charters to safeguard their security and commercial rights, the Jews often enjoyed a status higher than that of other royal servants principally because of their monopoly on Oriental trade, their importance for local commerce, and their ability to pay taxes.[55]

In general, Schipper seems to agree with Roscher's thesis that in the high Middle Ages only the Jews could fill the great need for carrying on a professional trade in goods in the West because they had the initial capital, the knowledge and experience, and could rely on the solidarity of the Jewish communities throughout the split Mediterranean world.[56] Hence, their preeminence in commerce, their monopoly in international trade, but not in the trade of slaves,[57] and the continued growth of their capital resources during that period of time.

The first signs of a gradual decline in the heyday of Jewish international and domestic trade activities appeared in Italy in the tenth century. While one may see evidence of Jewish prominence and success, which nettled the Italian mercantile republics, in the repeated attempts of the Venetian doges (in 932, 945, 992) to impede Jewish trade, by imposing travel restrictions on the Mediterranean or by prodding the emperor into anti-Jewish actions, Schipper saw in the rise of these republics a portent of things to come.[58]

The Road to Decline

In the eleventh century a number of interrelated factors began to converge and to bring about a gradual deterioration of the general position of Jews: (1) the Crusades, (2) the transformation of the erstwhile "royal merchants" into *servi camerae*, the final medieval definition of the status of Jews, and (3) the rise of an indigenous class of burghers.

The Crusades, although not initially motivated by material competition and envy,[59] produced, nevertheless, significant economic repercussions. Not only did the Crusades break the barriers of isolation and bring about a greater degree of international intercourse which stimulated the volume of city, intercity, and international trade but, like all military ventures, they generated a great need for money on the part of the feudal suzerains who organized the expeditions. The latter point is brought out by Schipper, for it had a direct bearing on the gradual deterioration of the status of medieval Jews who ultimately became the fiscal object of the feudal rulers and overlords in the West, to be limitlessly exploited and discarded when no longer exploitable. Parenthetically, it should be noted here that by far the greater part of the four volumes of Schipper's *Virtshaftsgeshikhte* represents a most striking and telling compilation of evidence in support of this cardinal economic fact of Jewish history in England, France, and Germany in the late Middle Ages, the beginnings of which are detectable in the period of the Crusades.

Thus, Schipper points out, until the end of the tenth century, with the single exception of Carl Martel who in 732 engaged mercenaries to fight the Saracens, the Christian rulers fought their battles with the help of their vassals as provided by the feudal system of rights and obligations. However, by the end of the tenth century it became clear that, for military purposes, the system was lacking. Vassals were not obligated to fight longer than six weeks, unless their suzerain was the attacked party, and they could not be easily mobilized because the vassal's consent was needed for any military expedition even though the lord granted his fief or other benefices to the vassals in advance. As the feudal lords realized that in order to conduct their wars successfully they would have to follow the example set by the Venetian doges and hire professional soldiers, money became the most crucial problem. In the eleventh and twelfth centuries, when military expeditions grew in number and the need for money to conduct them became more acute, the Jews seemed to be the obvious choice as a source of capital if assigned the function of *servi camerae* of the king. As the chief feudal suzerain, the king, in turn, could turn over the Jews as his *regale* to his immediate vassals, the great secular and ecclesiastical nobles, in the form of a feudal benefice.[60]

Originally, as a "stranger" the Jew had no rights, but this was tempered by the privileges granted to people outside the feudal society. Then, conditions shifted gradually to define Jews as a special category of serfs, owned by the king for his exclusive benefit. Eventually Jews became an object of financial speculation and rivalries as conflicts developed between the secular and ecclesiastical authorities, between the secular suzerains themselves, and between the state and local authorities. With the growth of cities conflicts involving Jews arose between the overlords and the municipalities. Schipper describes and analyzes all this exhaustively, drawing on all possible sources, to show how the Jew in the Middle Ages became progressively a fiscal pawn, doomed to lose whatever financial resources he may have once accumulated.[61]

In doing this, Schipper is very much intent upon demonstrating and expounding the dialectical evolution of this process as well as upon exposing the hypocritical aspects of the policies of the Christian medieval society in its attitude to Jews. The economic aims and interests of its classes, hidden under the guise of religious and "ethical" differences, were of paramount importance.

In the earlier stages Jews could only be the subject of conflict between the kings who granted the Jews extensive rights and the Church authority which demanded strict adherence to Canon Law designed to keep Christians and Jews apart. But the Church also aspired to share in the temporal authority of the kings and obtain territories and cities in which bishops could independently exercise secular powers. Wherever the Church succeeded, Jews and their possessions were transferred to the jurisdiction of the clergy. This did not necessarily impair the position of the Jew because the Church authorities were just as interested in his capacity, experience, and participation in the economic development of the ecclesiastical demesnes and cities as the secular rulers were in theirs,[62] Canon Law interdictions notwithstanding. Newly established cities, under secular or ecclesiastical jurisdiction, offered attractive conditions to Jews for the same reason; Christian merchants, still dependent on the city overlords, raised no objection. For a while, at least, both elements lived in peace and enjoyed the same rights although the Jewish merchant, who initially may have been more itinerant than his Christian counterpart, also tended to settle and retail directly to consumers. Schipper cites many sources[63] to illustrate the fact that the Jews constituted an essential commercial element playing a significant role in the development of the cities in the West along the Rhine and Main. Jewish merchants of Worms and Mainz, both rich and poor, participated in the fairs of the cities in the Rhineland, especially the fairs of Cologne. The princes and nobles lent Jews money for their trade transactions, and charters granted by Henry IV in such cities as Frankfurt, Hammerstein, Dortmund, Goslar, and Angern exempted Jews from duties on wine, dyes, salt, meat, medicines, and food products.[64]

Soon, however, the Christian merchant began pressing for a measure of independence and self-government. While he eventually became a free burgher, a member of the municipal council with a say in economic questions and a definite degree of political power, the Jewish merchant remained isolated, outside the policy-making body, but more often than not dependent on and affected by the decisions of the city government in which an obligarchy of Christian merchants became the dominant force. These decisions were of necessity dictated by the merchant's guild whose main objective was to maintain a protected monopoly of the local market and perpetuate a safe, noncompetitive economic order. The only element that could upset this closed order, based on the assumptions and rationale of the Christian economic doctrine of the Middle Ages, was Jewish competition. Hence, the need to suppress the Jew and force him to relinquish his position as a merchant. Thus, Schipper concludes, wherever Christian merchants, and burghers in general, attained political power, persecution of Jews became an inevitable matter of fact. The process of eliminating Jews from trade in the cities intensified further when the cities acquired rights that infringed upon the Jewish revenues as being the prerogative of the emperor (or the nobleman) only.[65]

Yet, the process of displacing Jews from their mercantile positions was very gradual. Similar economic developments produced similar anti-Jewish restrictions, with a time lag of several centuries, moving in a wave-like manner from West to East. Displacement of Jews began in the Italian cities around the middle of the tenth century; in South France, in the eleventh century; in Germany, still later—not before the middle of the thirteenth century; and in Eastern Europe, which needed the Jewish merchant the longest, by the end of the fifteenth century. In this connection Schipper agrees with Roscher's contention that adverse policies towards Jews in the Middle Ages were almost in inverse proportion to the general level of economic development,[66] a position that Schipper substantiates throughout his historical writings with convincing evidence.

And so it was that wherever Jews were forced to relinquish their position as merchants, particularly as retailers who did their purchasing and selling of goods and commodities locally, the richer among them turned either to wholesale commerce, or to trade in money and credit. Wholesale commerce was an area in which the guilds could not enforce their will, but which eventually became difficult as heavy duties were imposed by cities through which the Jewish wholesaler had to pass. Many of the wealthier Jews turned therefore to trade in money and credit, the indispensable financial concomitant of a growing national commerce and industry.[67]

Although generally the twelfth century, noted for the rise of commerce and industry in Western Europe, is considered to be the critical period for the freedom of Jewish mercantile activities, Schipper emphasizes the fact that the role and importance of Jews was still considerable. This was especially true in Germany where the nobility did not sympathize with the burghers and their demands. In royal cities such as Regensburg, Jews were granted full freedom to trade, with considerable concessions, in 1182. In addition to trade in gold and silver and monetary exchange, an area in which Jews excelled and which constituted a very important component of general trade due to the absence of uniform currency, retail commerce was still the main occupation of Jews in Germany. Schipper takes exception to the position of Stobbe, to whom he is no doubt indebted for a great deal of information and data, that Jews were forbidden entirely to engage in retail business, even with food products and on market days.[68] Nonetheless, by the end of the twelfth century more and more restrictions were imposed as the Christian class of merchants and artisans grew stronger and became capable politically of forcing the Jews to withdraw from the economic position they had occupied for hundreds of years. In this process, Schipper concludes, "the independent commerce of the Christian burghers was built on the destroyed fortunes of the strangers,"[69] adding that this explains why North Italian cities like Genoa, Pisa, Mantua, Luca, etc., in which commerce attained great proportions, had almost no Jews, according to Benjamin of Tudela.

The Sponge

The subject of Jewish involvement in money dealings and credit operations, which became known as the Jewish monopoly of usury in the Middle Ages, is first treated by Schipper in his article, "The Genesis of Jewish Usury in the Middle Ages,"[70] included with minor changes and revisions in *Anfänge des Kapitalismus*. Years later he dealt with it again extensively in the *Virtshaftsgeshikhte.* A comparison between the two treatments will not reveal any change in the interpretation of the subject but rather a further substantiation of the same position in *Virtshafts-*

geshikhte where the evidence, arranged horizontally and vertically for each individual country, is both massive and weighty.

In analyzing the evolution of Jewish money transactions, Schipper brings out a number of pertinent factors and phases. Noting at first the general view that trade in currencies began not with indigenous populations but among slaves and strangers, he asserted that until the eleventh century the Jews, as strangers among the tribes and peoples of Europe, did not engage in the business of moneylending. While there may have been single instances of individual Jews lending money, it was not in any way a Jewish occupation. Using as evidence the decisions of the Church Councils in Constanz (814), Paris (829), and Worms (829), Schipper emphatically points out that moneylending at that time was rather an exclusive activity of the Christian clergy, who exploited simple folk with very high interest rates. Jewish participation in money dealings, on the other hand, was confined to the verification and change of currency accompanying the commerce in goods and commodities. A merchant engaged in the latter could not operate successfully without a currency expert and a man willing to make the needed money exchange.[71]

The situation changed in the eleventh century when commercial culture in the West reached a level of development in which borrowing money was no longer a matter of misfortune or emergency but a prerequisite for business. The prohibition of the Church found less and less sympathy in the growing cities when it became evident that trade transactions could not be carried out without credit. The Christian burgher, who was short of capital, and the growing cities in general needed the professional moneylender. At the same time the feudal suzerains also required ever greater sums of money to maintain their military strength and position. For commercial as well as security reasons, the Jews tended to maintain reserves of liquid capital, accumulated during the Carolingian period of profitable international trade. By now they had become the suzerain's *servi camerae* and were granted the privilege of engaging in usury since this could only mean greater income for the king's treasury or the coffers of the territorial overlord, both of whom knew how to exploit the fact that

Christians were forbidden to charge interest. Thus, Schipper concludes, the Jews were actually drawn by the force of circumstances of that period into the position of moneylenders. He states:

> Royal and ducal credit privileges granted to Jews and motivated by the strictly selfish interests of the rulers, constituted the strongest factor which pushed the Jews into the business of usury. . . . Whenever the kings and territorial overlords granted credit privileges to Jews, they never asked what benefits their other subjects would derive from the credit operations conducted by their Jewish agents. The rulers were interested only in one thing: having at their disposal a big reservoir of capital which the Jews were supposed to provide.[72]

The fact that before the Lombards and Caursines became the moneylenders in the Middle Ages, Jews had been allowed to charge interest helped them to monopolize the credit business in its initial stages and contributed to the growth of their capital resources, but not for long. As the military campaigns of the Crusades heightened the demand for money among the nobility to maintain their knights and soldiers and armor, they had to mortgage their landed benefices, the mainstay of their wealth, to Jewish creditors. While the ecclesiastical lords could obtain loans from the Italian bankers because such loans were guaranteed by the Church, the secular nobility had to turn to their own Jews. The Jew lent his money with minimal guarantees, despite his lien on the noble's land, for, in the last analysis, the Jewish creditor was not a free agent. Quite the contrary, he depended on the lord for protection and his body and possessions legally belonged to the lord. Ultimately, the Jewish creditor became the fiscal instrumentality of medieval royalty and the ruling aristocracy. He acted as the proverbial sponge that sucked in the wealth of the country, at first that of the nobility, which did not pay any taxes on behalf of the state, and progressively that of the rest of the population, which was compelled to borrow money at high rates of interest to pay heavy taxes, in order that the wealth accumulated in the Jewish sponge might be at will squeezed into the coffers of the rulers.[73]

Schipper agrees with Sombart that in this process the Jew indirectly contributed to the decline of the feudal system because the exacted wealth did not, as a rule, return to the feudal economic unit but became rotating capital put again into orbit. However, the Jews themselves were not in control of this situation. Not only did they lose their capital resources but their entire position in the West became gradually uncertain and remained dangerously insecure throughout the late Middle Ages.

In 1096 Jews attacked by the mob were still protected by Christian burghers who needed Jewish credit and did not wish Jewish money to fall into the hands of the mob. However, a half century later, in 1146, the Christian merchants who no longer depended on Jewish money sided with the impoverished rabble, charging that Jewish usury hampered the economic development of the land and weakened the buying power of the population. Indeed, the productive credit for trade and business was gradually taken over by the Lombards and Caursines who, in their capacity as tax agents of the Curia and the "papal financiers," enjoyed special privileges and spread from Italy to France and Germany.[74]

By the thirteenth century Jewish credit lost its productive character and the Jewish moneylender became the creditor of the poor classes of feudal society. He came face to face with those who could least afford to pay interest and to carry the burden of medieval usury. Thus the clash between the Jewish moneylenders and the poor Christian borrowers became inevitable. The animosity and hatred of Jews derived from the "conflict of interests between the pauper and the capitalist," to use the words of Schipper who, in this connection, again quotes Roscher in concurrence with the latter's conclusion that the "pogroms of Jews, in which the main purpose was the destruction of promissory notes, should be considered as a crisis of a barbarian character, a medieval form of the phenomenon which we call today 'social revolution'."[75]

In describing the heyday of Jewish moneylending in the eleventh and twelfth centuries, Schipper does not hide the fact that Jews derived enormous profits from lending money against land mortgages, which the creditors could use during the period of the loan, and from the excessively high rates of interest vouchsafed by the royal charters. On the contrary, he brings massive evidence to show that Jewish capital had to work exceedingly fast and under particularly favorable conditions in order to satisfy the ever-growing demands of the kings. Until the thirteenth century the king's *servi camerae* were given a free hand in their moneylending transactions, and no limit on interest rates was set by the authorities. When eventually interest rates were fixed in the thirteenth century, they were prohibitively high, betraying the obviously rapacious fiscal motives of the suzerains.

In Provence the rate of interest was set at 300 percent in 1243; in Austria at 173 percent in 1244. In England the rates averaged from 43 to 86 percent. In France the rate of 43 percent set by Philip Augustus in 1206 was later doubled, as shown by Depping. In comparison with these rates, Schipper notes, the interest charged by Jewish moneylenders in the eleventh and twelfth centuries was not high at all.[76] To derive their full share, the kings and overlords made sure that all Jewish credit transactions and contracts were registered and a matter of record. While this system protected the lender to the extent that it provided him with a legal warrant, it also gave the authorities full control over the accumulated capital in the hands of the Jewish moneylenders. In this way the lords knew what proportion of it to demand for themselves or when to confiscate accumulations of capital.

Moreover, as the commercial tempo of the cities gained momentum and chattel securities became more frequent, the royal *Privilegia* provided written guarantees designed to protect the Jewish moneylender against a loss, even if the pledge remained with the borrower. Jews were even allowed to take stolen goods as pledges, and until the beginning of the thirteenth century they could extend loans against the pledge of sacred vessels and vestments of the Church or sell such objects.[77] Citing, furthermore, considerable documentary evidence, based on the *Regesten* by Aronius and *Monumenta Germania* by Pertz, that archbishops, bishops, and the clergy in general were among the clients of Jewish creditors, especially before Pope Gregory VII energetically opposed the practice of simony, Schipper demonstrates that the clergy not only turned to Jews and extended protection to them but actually allowed and even encouraged Jews to exploit, through usury, the Christian populace. Jewish moneylenders were permitted to keep their documents and loan securities in Church sacristies, and on occasion a Jewish creditor was even sent to the Pope to present his case regarding unpaid loans. This kind of cooperation with the Jewish creditor was dictated, besides the practice of simony, by the clergy's need of capital to carry out its great art projects and to satisfy the demands of the *Camera Apostolica.* Many high Church officials also found it advantageous to engage Jews as their agents in commercial dealings, including the sale of Church objects and relics. This led to accusations in which Jews were made the scapegoats for the ruin of certain churches due to the misdeeds of the men in cassocks. Thus, Schipper concludes, the religious motive propagated and stimulated by the Crusades was hardly the decisive factor in the hatred and persecution of Jews. Jewish pogroms in the Middle Ages were of a strictly socioeconomic character. They were the result of a deliberate policy on the part of the state to use Jewish usury for its own benefit. [78]

The End of Jewish Capital

The major part of the four volumes of Schipper's *Virtschafts-geshikhte* is also devoted to a detailed and incisive analysis of the methods used by the rulers of the countries of Western Europe to extort money from all classes of medieval society through their Jewish *servi camerae.* Schipper traces the evolution of that extortion, beginning with the landed nobility and clergy and ending with the poor of the cities. This callous fiscal exploitation began with the granting of charters, incentives, guarantees, and assistance in collecting debts and gradually proceeded toward higher taxation of Jews, a system of controls, manipulatory decrees and ordinances (assessments, partial or full debt amnesties, etc.), expropriations, confiscations, and finally to the expulsions that took place successively in England, France, and German territories when in each of these countries the dried up Jewish sponge became useless. In examining the circumstances that led to the expulsion of Jews from France in 1394, Schipper points to the fact that unbearable taxes levied by the state drove the population to the Jewish moneylenders. In 1380, overburdened with growing debts and avidly desiring to shake off the burden, the populace finally attacked the royal revenue office, as well as the Jews, robbing pledges and burning all evidence of credit claims. In 1382, when the mass of debtors repeated the action, Jews began to leave Paris. The king offered some tax relief to the population but increased the burden of taxes on the Jews. They were expected by the king to contribute more money in order to stop the riots. In the end, his Jewish *servi camerae* went bankrupt, and the king then ordered their expulsion in 1394.[79] The king's policy of fiscal exploitation was the decisive factor in relegating Jews to the single occupation of moneylending. In the south of France where the king's power was weakened by local feudal lords, moneylending was not as typical a Jewish occupation as it was in Northern and Central France.[80]

In England, where the central power of the king was stronger, the policy of dealing with Jews from a strictly fiscal point of view was initiated by Edward the Confessor (1042-1066) and Henry I (1100-1135) and carried out by their successors with a methodical thoroughness. The process of extorting Jewish capital by means of a tight system of controls, requiring an elaborate administrative framework with a deliberate set of rules and regulations, ended here a century earlier than in France. Not long after the fabulous wealth of Aaron of Lincoln was confiscated,[81] the policy of Henry II (1154-1189) and Richard I (1189-1199) of using Jews in order to drain the population—including the barons, the landed gentry, and knights—led in 1189 to pogroms in London, Lincoln, Stamford, etc. A year later, in an attack on the "Jewish Chamber," all credit records were jubilantly destroyed. Afterwards the king inherited the possessions and collected the claims of his Jewish treasury serfs who retreated to the castle and committed suicide there. The concession relating to debts which John I (1199-1216) granted to his vassals in 1215[82] was annulled by him in 1216, and this again strained the relationship between the Jewish creditors and their Christian debtors. John's successor, Henry III (1216-1272) stove off anti-Jewish riots for a time, but pogroms broke out in 1262 and again in 1264 when the economic crisis reached a peak as a result of the demands of continuous warfare. The acute money shortage threw the knights into greater debt for which they mortgaged all their possessions until the only way out was to kill their creditors. The king was forced to limit Jewish credit to eliminate the so-called "rent purchase" agreements and sale of promissory notes in 1269. In 1275 Jewish credit was forbidden altogether. By then it was easy for Edward I (1272-1307) to show his Christian vassals that he was on their side, for he knew that his Jewish *servi camerae* were financially exhausted, having lost all their capital. But it also meant the bankruptcy of the royal fiscal policy and the king's capitulation to the demands of the nobles, knights, and clergy. During the period 1255-1273, the king was still able to extract from the Jews 420,000 pounds (about $60,000,000), an average of 23,300 pounds per year. After 1287, when the Jews could provide only the much smaller sum of 12,000 pounds, he lost interest in them and three years later was ready to oust them from the country.[83]

In Germanic territories the general process of draining capital through Jews and from Jews took on specific forms in view of the characteristic decentralization of political power in Germany. Even before the period of the Black Death, nobles and cities used all kinds of means to obtain suzerainty over Jews in order to gain at least a share of Jewish revenues for partial protection and jurisdiction. The first to get full jurisdiction over Jews in their territories were the Electors, *i.e.*, the princes with the prerogative of electing the king. According to the royal "Golden Bull" of 1356, Jews became property of the Electors' territories, on a par with the Electors' natural wealth. Although Jews remained under royal jurisdiction for a longer time in the *Reichstädte* (royal cities), many cities and territories obtained rights over Jews mainly because of the short-sighted financial policies of the kings. Whenever the latter needed money, they willingly pledged the outstanding fiscal contributions of their

Jewish *servi camerae* as security for loans. Overlords often did the same, and cities gradually obtained greater rights over Jews as a result of the fact that the nobility was often forced to surrender their fiscal claims against Jews of the cities. After the Black Death the process intensified as cities began admitting Jews on the basis of special agreements and the municipalities became the factual owners of Jews, although the king and nobility never gave up their right of sharing the Jews and their revenues.[84]

In the long struggle for the authority over Jews between the kings and the overlords, between the latter and the rising power of the burghers, and between the city patricians and the craftsmen and artisans organized in their guilds, the Jew was relegated to the position of the poor man's moneylender. As the nobility and city patricians no longer required his credit but expected ever greater revenues from him, his customers became the poor artisans and peasants who could neither keep up with the generally rising prices of goods and commodities nor meet rising tax demands. The consumptive credit of the Jews led to the further pauperization of the borrowing masses in spite of the fact that in the fifteenth century interest rates declined[85] and opposition to Jewish moneylending grew stronger.

In analyzing the evolution of the forms of Jewish credit during the period 1350-1500, Schipper demonstrates its gradual deterioration. While in the second half of the fourteenth century territorial overlords still borrowed money from Jewish bankers against pledged revenues from duties on merchandise imported from Italy and France or from taxes, the farming of these revenues was soon taken over by the Fuggers and Welsers, the banking families in whose hands there already existed great concentrations of capital.[86] Real-estate mortgages became rare as prohibitions of Jewish credit against this form of security were instituted. Credit based on promissory notes also became more difficult. Until approximately the end of the fourteenth century, Jews could trade freely with promissory notes since debtors were obliged to repay loans to the bearers of such bills. By that time, however, orders were issued forbidding the transfer and trade in promissory notes. Furthermore, "Jewish Books" were instituted in which all credit transactions had to be registered in order to be recognized by the courts. In a number of provinces the promissory notes had to be stamped by officials: the city, the Jewish judges, or the chancery of bishops, as the case might be. Even loans against pawned objects became restricted since such commodities as wool, grain, cotton goods, certain products made by craftsmen, agricultural implements in rural areas—none of these could be used as pledges.[87]

While the interest of the rich patricians in control of the cities dictated restrictions on Jewish credit, the fight against Jewish moneylending was led by the Church in cooperation with those most affected by usury: the artisans and the peasants. As the cancellations of Jewish claims (*Schuldtilgungen*) by the end of the fourteenth century brought an end to many of the larger Jewish banking houses and a general decline in Jewish capital resources,[88] Christians found it profitable to lend money to Jews for the latter's credit operations, despite the constant agitation and intimidations of the clergy. Eventually, Christians began to disregard the Church prohibitions and enter the credit operations themselves.[89] In the cities Christian capital magnates began extending credit to the nobility and certain city banks began lending to the general population at lower interest rates. Characteristically, the establishment of such banks coincided with the expulsion of Jews.

Describing the waves of persecution, the repeated host-desecration and ritual-murder libels, and the hounding of Jews from province to province and from city to city until their final expulsion, Schipper points to the common denominator of all these anti-Jewish actions: the underlying financial considerations and economic causes. Some were simply extortions on the part of the lords. There even existed prior agreements between the lords as to the division of the Jewish loot.[90] Other instances of anti-Jewish excesses helped the cities to free themselves of the patronage of the lords who shared in the Jewish revenues and who interfered in the internal affairs of these municipalities.[91] But the ferment of the lower classes, exploited in the city by the patricians and in the countryside by the landed gentry, which constituted the main reason for "Jew burnings" in 1348–1350, continued to be a decisive factor in the never-ending persecutions and expulsions of Jews. In this connection Schipper cites many terrible anti-Jewish excesses in the cities of various provinces (Franconia, Swabia, Rheinland, etc.) during the rebellions of artisans and craftsmen and during the revolts of the peasants.[92] In his words:

> The Jewish usurer was supposed to be the instrument for weakening the material situation, and thereby also the political aspirations, of the guilds which were after positions of power in the municipal councils and city halls. In the countryside and territories ruled by the overlords, the Jew found himself in the same situation of being between the hammer and the anvil, for with the help of the Jewish usurer the overlord sucked the material strength of his peasants and city subjects. Consequently, when the hammer of the oppressed classes began to pound, it fell first of all on Jewish heads.[93]

To give an idea of the huge amounts of capital which Jews owned or handled and of which they were completely divested by the end of the Middle Ages in Western Europe, Schipper provides a host of documentation. In England, for instance, after Henry II had taken one-fourth of all Jewish possessions and confiscated the enormous wealth of Aaron of Lincoln in 1185, the Jews paid him a Crusade tax of 60,000 pounds in 1188.[94] The annual tribute of the comparatively small Jewish population in England[95] amounted to one-thirteenth of the king's annual income which, according to Ashley, was 120,000 pounds and which Stobbe compared with approximately fifteen to twenty million dollars.[96] Although there is a dearth of documents for France, the situation in that country must have been similar to that in England, as indicated by the fact that when Philip Augustus allowed the Jews to return to France in 1198, they were able to remit the sum of 150,000 silver marks to the royal treasury. And the pecuniary capacity of the Jews in Germany can be deduced from the fact that in the beginning of the thirteenth century the Jews of Cologne alone, under duress, gave to Archbishop Dietrich enough money to build almost all the buildings of the

Godesberg fort, according to documents cited by Aronius. Sources from 1385, 1390, and 1391 showing the annulments of Jewish claims ordered by Emperor Wenceslas indicate the magnitude of Jewish credit operations. The city of Nuremberg, for example, concluded twenty-nine agreements with her Jewish "pact-burghers" in 1385, according to which the latter agreed to transfer to the city their credit claims in the amount of 80,986 gulden (approximately $320,000), a sum greater than all revenues of that city for that year.[97] The same sources indicate the imposing capital accumulations of Jews in Germany in the second half of the fourteenth century, a period characterized by the rise of great Jewish banks in German cities like Nuremberg, Regensburg, Ulm, Frankfurt-am-Main, Strassbourg, etc. Rabbi Jacob of Ulm, for instance, was in a position in 1376 to induce a Count Palatine and his army to help him collect his claims from nobles. In 1390, after the proclaimed annulment of claims, he was still able to hire a certain knight to attack the city of Nuremberg because it took away Jewish houses. In Regensburg the annuled nine promissory notes of Rabbi Kalman in the amount of 13,000 gulden represented thirteen percent of all notes of Jews in that city, while the rescinded notes of the Zorline family in Frankfurt constituted three-fifths of all nullified notes in the amount of 17,848 gulden.[98]

By the end of the fifteenth century there may have been traces of Jewish capital in Germany, but that capital was no longer in Jewish hands nor, for that matter, were there many Jews left in that country. The Jewish center shifted further to the East.

Notes

1. Schipper, *Anfänge des Kapitalismus bei den abendländischen Juden im früheren Mittelalter (bis zum Ausgang des XII Jahrhunderts)*, (Wien: 1907), 66 pp., reprinted from *Zeitschrift für Volkswirtschaft, Sozialpolitik und Verwaltung* (Wien: 1906), vol. 15; Yiddish translation by H. Maimon as *Onhoyb fun kapitalizm bay Yidn in Mayrev-Eyrope*, (Warsaw: 1920), 88 pp., utilized in this study and referred to in the following as *Onhoyb.*

2. "Schumpeter on Böhm-Bawerk," in *The Development of Economic Thought*, ed. by H. W. Spiegel (New York: 1966), p. 369 ff. See also J. Schumpeter, *Ten Great Economists* (New York: 1965), pp. x, 143 ff. Schumpeter describes Böhm-Bawerk as a scientist and public servant "of high standards of duty which impressed itself on subordinates as well as on disciples. . . . His life was a completed whole, the expression of a personality at one with itself, never losing itself, everywhere proving its superiority by its own weight and without affectation—a work of art, its severe lines gilded by an infinite, tender, reserved and highly personal charm." *Ibid.*, pp. 145-146. Böhm-Bawerk's seminars Schumpeter describes as "an activity which will remain unforgettable to all of us . . . no words can express what he has been to us . . . his advice, his encouragement, his critical guidance. . . ." *Ibid.*, pp. 150, 143.

3. It may be in place to note here that, although he occupied a leading position in the *Poale Zion* for over a decade, Schipper was very much part of the inner ideological strife between the radical and moderate elements which continued ever since the Hague Conference of the World *Poale Zion* in 1907 and came to a boiling point in 1920, the year the party split into two separate entities. The crucial problem that brought about the split was the party's relationship to the Third Socialist International, dominated by the Comintern. At the Fifth World Conference of *Poale Zion* held in Vienna in 1920, Schipper, together with his friend Chomet, represented the right wing of the party in Poland which, rejecting any association with the Third International, made unsuccessful attempts to ally the *Poale Zion* with the Second International. Back in Warsaw where, at the party council of November 1920, it became clear that the Polish *Poale Zion* decided on a course to the left, Schipper became the leader of the opposition that declared its allegiance to the so-called *Aḥdut Avoda*, the Palestinian leading faction of the right wing, proclaimed as a separate party in Vienna. The new party of the right was faced with the very difficult task of organizing its groups in cities and towns, but Kenner admits that the constituent groups, especially in the provinces, were successfully established thanks to the help and leadership provided by Schipper. However, Schipper's association with the new *Poale Zion* Right was not of long duration. In 1922 he moved still further to the right. See Chomet, *op. cit.*, p. 480 and Kenner, *op. cit.*, pp. 175, 279.

4. W. Sombart, "Der Anteil der Juden am Aufbau der modernen Volkswirtschaft," *Neue Rundschau* XXI (1910), pp. 145-173, 585-615; Polish translation, *Żydzi a spółczesna gospodarka społeczna* by A. W. and Z. K. (Warsaw: 1911), used in this study for reference. Major parts of this study were included by Sombart in his main book, *Die Juden und das Wirtschaftsleben* (Leipzig: 1911), the English translation of which, by I. Epstein, as *Jews and Modern Capitalism* (Glencoe, Ill.: 1951) is utilized here.

5. Sombart, "Der Anteil der Juden am Aufbau der modernen Volkswirtschaft" in Polish translation, *op. cit., passim.*

6. *Ibid.*, pp. 55-92. Cf. M. Arkin, *Aspects of Jewish Economic History* (Philadelphia: 1975), pp. 144-148.

7. *Ibid.*, pp. 98 ff.

8. A typical report appeared in *Wschód*, Nos. 48, 51, 52 (Lwów: 1909).

9. *Ibid.*, Nos. 51, 52.

10. See H. Feldstein, *Przyszłość Żydów (z powodu rosprawki Wernera Sombarta)*, (Lwów: 1912), pp. 4, 9-12.

11. N. Reich, "Capitalism and the Jews: A Critical Examination of Sombart's Thesis," *The Menorah Journal*, XVIII (Jan. 1930), pp. 16-17. For other critical evalutations of Sombart's writings see L. Bretano, *Die Anfänge des modernen Kapitalismus* (Munich: 1916), especially pp. 158 ff; H. R. Trevor-Roper, "A Fertile Error," *Commentary*, XII (July 1951), pp. 89-91; Also E. E. Hirschler, "Medieval Economic Competition," *Journal of Economic History*, XIV (1954), p. 52.

12. Schipper, *Onhoyb, op. cit.*, p. 84. In quite another connection he briefly rejects the racial theory ascribing to Jews inborn commercial abilities, stating his conviction that if there is such a thing as "race, (it) does not exist at the beginning but rather at the end of the historical process." *Studies, op. cit.*, p. 5.

13. W. Sombart, *Der Moderne Kapitalismus* (Munich-Leipzig), vol. I, p. 270.

14. Schipper's evidence concerning Palestine, Babylonia, and Alexandria is based mainly on Graetz, Philo, and Midrashic materials.

15. Based on *Gaonic Responsa* and reports of Benjamin of Tudela.

16. The weight of his evidence from Latin literature is in the satires of Juvenal and the epigrams of Martial. He also utilizes Vogelstein and Rieger's *Geschichte der Juden in Rom*, vols. I-II (Berlin: 1895), rejecting L. Herzfeld's suggestion in *Handelgeschichte der Juden des Alterthums* (Brunswick: 1879) that Jews "on the other side of the Tiber" engaged in petty trade.

17. Schipper, *Onhoyb, op. cit.*, pp. 5-14. See also *Virshaftsgeshikhte, op. cit.*, vol. I, pp. 14-18.

18. *Ibid.*, p. 14.

19. See *Onhoyb, op. cit.*, pp. 14-16.

20. Schipper cites here the repeated demands of Pope Gregory I that Jews not be permitted to keep Christian slaves unless given the status of *coloni*. *Ibid.*, p. 15.

21. Cf. C. Roth, "Economic Life and Population Movements," *The World History of the Jewish People*, second series, vol. II (New Brunswick, N.J.: 1966), p. 30.

22. *Loc. cit.* See also *Virtschaftsgeshikhte, op. cit.*, p. 24.

23. *Virtshaftsgeshikhte, op. cit.*, pp. 22-23. Cf. J. Parkes, *A History of the Jewish People* (Baltimore, Md.: 1964), pp. 66-68.

24. *Ibid.*, pp. 78 ff.

25. Schipper, *Onhoyb, op. cit.*, pp. 16-17; also, *Virtshaftsgeshikhte, op. cit.*, pp. 25-26. The premises underlying the legal status of the Jews in the early Middle Ages had already been discussed by Schipper in his *Żydzi za czasów Kazimierza Wielkiego, op. cit.*, pp. 47-48. Cf. J. Parkes, "Christian Influence on the Status of Jews in Europe," *Historia Judaica*, I (1938), pp. 33-34 and his *The Jew in the Medieval Community* (London: 1938), pp. 101 ff. Cf. also Baron, *op. cit.*, vol. IV, pp. 154-156. Baron adds that Jewish religious requirements and considerations—such as rigid abstention from work on the Sabbath and holidays, the need to live together to meet the exigencies of religious observances and to maintain Jewish institutions—also contributed to the process of selling land. *Ibid.*, pp. 156-158.

26. Schipper, *Onhoyb, op. cit.*, pp. 71, 76; and *Virtshaftsgeshikhte, op. cit.*, p. 40.

27. Schipper cites the complaint of Pope Stephen III (758-772) to the Archbishop of Narbonne. *Onhoyb, op. cit.*, p. 72 and *Virtshaftsgeshikhte, op.*, p. 41.

28. See *Onhoyb, op. cit.*, pp. 70-75 and *Virtshaftsgeshikhte, op. cit.*, pp. 39-42. Cf. Parkes, *The Jew in the Medieval Community, op. cit.*, p. 41 ff. and 49. While Parkes uses by and large the same sources as Schipper (*Leges Visigothorum*, XII; Aronius, Bouguet, G. B. Depping, G. Caro, and others), he added an important point that apparently escaped Schipper, namely, that Jewish landownership was limited further by a law forbidding Christians and Jews to be tenants of each other from the time of Louis the Pious or somewhat later. *Ibid.*, p. 42. On the question of Jewish landownership and its gradual decline see also Baron, *op. cit.*, vol. IV, pp. 153-158, 161-164; Roth, *op. cit.*, pp. 31-32; and L. Finkelstein, *Jewish Self-Government in the Middle Ages*, 2nd ed. (New York: 1964), pp. 10-11. The latter points out that the rabbis tried in various ways to keep Jews on the land and stem the tide to commerce. Besides providing tax exemptions for Jewish farmers, the *Ḥerem ha-Yishuv* (ban on moving into a town without community acceptance) was instituted to prevent Jews from coming into towns. *Ibid.*, pp. 12-14.

29. T. Oelsner, "The Place of the Jews in Economic History as Viewed by German Scholars," *Yearbook VII of the Leo Baeck Institute* (1962), p. 200.

30. M. Kulisher, Review of Schipper's "*Anfänge des Kapitalismus bei den abendländishen Juden . . . ,*" *Yevreyskaya Starina*, I (1909), pp. 140-144.

31. Hirschaut, *op. cit.*, p. 191.

32. See the "Foreword" in *Virtshaftsgeshikhte*, especially p. iv.

33. Baron, *op. cit.*, pp. 211-213 and n. 80 on pp. 346-347.

34. Pp. 18-30.

35. Schipper, *Der Anteil der Juden am europäischen Grosshandel mit dem Orient (bis zur begründung der modernen Kolonialwirtschaft)*, (Czernovitz: 1912), a reprint from *Heimkehr*, collective book of the Jewish National Academic Association *Emuna* in Czernovitz, Berlin (1910).

36. Pp. 26-60.

37. Hoffman points out that not only was slavery inherited from the pagan world, but it was rooted among the newly converted Germanic tribes who once used to kill all their war prisoners but now turned prisoners taken in wars with other pagan tribes (Saxons, Normans, Danes, Magyars) into slaves. The trade in slaves developed either because of low supply, in times when there were no wars, or because of oversupply resulting in both the import as well as export of slaves. See M. Hoffman, *Der Geldhandel der deutschen Juden während des Mittelalters bis zum Jahre 1350* (Altenburg: 1910), p. 16.

38. Cf. I. Abrahams, *Jewish Life in the Middle Ages*, Meridian Books ed. (Cleveland: 1961), pp. 98 ff.

39. Although Schipper refers several times to G. B. Depping (*Die Juden in Mittelalter*, Stuttgart: 1834), who identified the Verdun slave dealers as Jews, and is very much indebted to G. Caro ("Die Juden des Mittelalters in ihrer wirtschaftlichen Betätigung," *Monatsblätter für Geschichte des Judentums* [1904] and *Sozial-und Wirtschaftsgeschichte der Juden im Mittelalter*, 2 vols., Leipzig: 1908, 1920), who ascribed to Jews a very considerable share in international slave trade, he does not share the view that Jews were the main carriers of that trade or that in time it became a Jewish monopoly. See *Onhoyb, op. cit*, p. 23. Oelsner in her attempts to minimize the role of Jews does not include Schipper among the historians who exaggerated Jewish participation in the traffic of slaves on unproved suppositions and conjectures. See Oelsner, "The Place . . . ," *op. cit.*, p. 189. Cf. Parkes, *The Jew in the Medieval Community, op. cit.*, pp. 45 ff; Baron, *op. cit.*, vol. IV, pp. 188-193, especially p. 336 n. 59; and M. Hoffman, *op. cit.*, pp. 17-18.

40. Schipper relies here chiefly on the evidence cited by W. Heyd, *Geschichte des Levantehandels im Mittelalter* (Leipzig: 1865), and Scheffer-Boichorst, "Zur Geschichte der Syrer im Abendlande," *Mitteilungen des Institutes für österreichischen Geschichtsforschung*, VI. See *Onhoyb, op. cit.*, p. 20; *Virtshaftsgeshikhte, op. cit.*, p. 27; and *Der Anteil . . . am Grosshandel, op. cit.*, p. 5.

41. Cf. Roth, *op. cit.*, pp. 20 ff. and Baron, *op. cit.*, pp. 171 ff.

42. Cf. M. Weber, *General Economic History* (New York: 1966), p. 152.

43. The only possible limitation, Schipper notes, may have been in trade with grain products and wine, as per *Capitulare de Judaeis* of 814, which apparently was not obeyed since sources dating from a few years later indicate trade

in wine in Narbonne where Jews continued to own vineyards. See *Onhoyb, op. cit.*, p. 22.

44. A much fuller enumeration of the luxury items from the East is given by Roth, *op. cit.*, pp. 25-26.

45. *Virtshaftsgeshikhte, op. cit.*, p. 34.

46. *Onhoyb, op. cit.*, p. 26.

47. *Ibid.*, pp. 24 ff. and *Virtschaftsgeshikhte, op. cit.*, pp. 32 ff. Cf. Parkes, "Christian Influence on the Status of the Jews in Europe," *op. cit.*, pp. 35-36, where it is pointed out to what extent Agobard, from his point of view, had reason to fear Jewish influence in the Court and among the ruling classes. Agobard's attitude to Jews is also discussed by Parkes in his *The Jew in the Medieval Community, op. cit.*, pp. 19-20.

48. Schipper was aware of this passage from its French translation published in 1865-1866 in *Journal Asiatique*, Series V, and the use made of it by Heyd, *op. cit.*

49. The Radhanites and their mercantile travels later became the subject of special investigations and studies and Ibn Khurradadhbih's description, a much-quoted passage used by various historians. See D. Simonsen, "Les Marchands Juifs appelés 'Radanites'," *Revue des Etudes juives*, LIV (1907); J. Jacobs, *The Jewish Contribution to Civilization* (Philadelphia: 1919), pp. 194-204; E. Adler, *Jewish Travellers* (London: 1930), pp. 2-3; L. Rabinowitz, "The Routes of the Radanites," *JQR*, XXXV (1945) and his *Jewish Merchant Adventurers: A Study of Jewish Radanites* (London: 1948); R. S. Lopez and I. W. Raymond, *Medieval Trade in the Mediterranean World* (New York: 1955), pp. 29 ff. See also Baron, *op. cit.*, vol. IV, pp. 180-181 and p. 328 n. 39 and Roth, *op. cit.*, pp. 23 ff. and Arkin, *op. cit.*, pp. 43-44.

50. Schipper, *Der Anteil . . . am Grosshandel, op. cit.*, p. 7.

51. Schipper cites as an example the letter of protection issued by Louis the Pious in 829. See *Onhoyb, op. cit.*, p. 23 and *Virtsshaftsgeshikhte, op. cit.*, p. 32.

52. Schipper cites the sources in *Anteil, op. cit.*, p. 8.

53. See *Virtshaftsgeshikhte, op. cit.*, p. 31. Besides the suggestion of the Persian term *rahdan*, which seems more plausible to Baron who considers attempts to relate the Radhanites to one particular place of origin as untenable, Jacobs suggested the town Rhagae in Persia as the possible base of the Radhanites. See Baron, *op. cit.*, vol. IV, pp. 180-181 and 328; Roth, *op. cit.*, pp. 23 ff.; and L. Rabinowitz, "The Routes of the Radanites," *op. cit.*, p. 254. While the origin of the Radhanites remains a matter of conjecture, the assumption given by Rabinowitz seems most reasonable, namely, that the Radhanites "were an association of merchants from the several countries in which the languages (they used) were the vernacular . . . their own common medium of expression being Hebrew. . . ." Rabinowitz, *op. cit.*, pp. 278-280.

54. Cf. Roth, *op. cit.*, pp. 43 ff.

55. See *Onhoyb, op. cit.*, p. 24; *Virtshaftsgeshikhte, op. cit.*, p. 33.

56. W. Roscher, "The Status of the Jews in the Middle Ages Considered from the Standpoint of Commercial Policy," *Historia Judaica*, VI (1944), pp. 16, 19.

57. In another place Schipper qualifies his statement concerning the monopoly of Jews in international trade by saying that even if the Jews were not the only merchants in the West they appear to have had a definite monopoly on a number of products imported from the Orient for a very long time. *Onhoyb, op. cit.*, p. 21.

The matter of the Jewish mercantile monopoly in the Carolingian period and the view that "Jews" and "merchants" were synonymous terms at that time has been a matter of varying interpretations among scholars. Roth seems to take the position that Jewish identification with commerce in the Dark Ages is justified in view of the increasing references to Jews as merchants in Hebrew as well as Latin documents, especially in the records of the Carolingian chanceries from the eighth century on. Parkes takes a similar position, although his statement that "it was almost impossible for lawyers and writers of the 9th and 10th centuries to think of 'merchants' without at the same time thinking of 'Jew' " is qualified by the phrase that "it is absurd to talk, as do many authors, of any Jewish monopoly of all trade." On the other hand, Hoffman considers the theory that the Jews were the chief carriers of trade between the Orient and the Occident to be an oversimplification of history for, besides Jews, there were also Frisians, Bulgars, Greeks, Syrians, and—especially—Italians who engaged in trade as capably as Jews. Still farther, in deprecating the mercantile position and role of the Jews, are the views expressed by Oelsner in her refutation of Roscher's theory. See Roth, *op. cit.*, pp. 32 ff.; Parkes, *The Jew in the Medieval Community, op. cit.*, p. 44; Hoffman, *op. cit.*, p. 8; T. Oelsner, "Wilhelm Roscher's Theory of the Economic and Social Position of the Jews in the Middle Ages," *YIVO Annual of Jewish Social Studies*, XII (1958-1959). A very comprehensive exposition of the occupational transition of Jews to commerce in the high Middle Ages, corresponding fully with Schipper's views, is provided by R. Mahler in his essay, "When and How Did Jews Become a Commercial People," (Yiddish), *YIVO-Bleter*, VII, pp. 20-35.

58. *Onhoyb, op. cit.*, pp. 29-30, and *Virtshaftsgeshikhte, op. cit.*, p. 38. Cf. Roth, *op. cit.*, pp. 36-37.

59. *Virtshaftsgeshikhte* II, *op. cit.*, p. 42. Cf. M. Hoffman, *op. cit.*, p. 12.

60. *Virtshaftsgeshikhte, op. cit.*, pp. 61-63. The term *regale* as used by Schipper signifies both the king's jurisdiction over the Jews and his claim on the revenues derived from them as a royalty belonging to his private treasury. In tracing the concept of *servitudo camerae*, Schipper notes that although the official documents do not mention it until the beginning of the twelfth century (in the

Anglo-Saxon jurisdiction of that time and in the charter granted to the Jews of Worms in 1157) and the term as such does not appear in the official documents until the beginning of the thirteenth century, the idea had already been known in the ninth century, for in 846 Archbishop Amulo of Lyons had described the Jews as servants and taxpayers of the princes. In the thirteenth century the German *Sachsenspiegel* and *Schwabenspiegel* codes attempted to justify the concept historically by contending that Emperor Vespasian, thankful to Josephus Flavius for curing his son Titus from an illness, decided after the destruction of Jerusalem to accept many Jewish prisoners as his personal bodyguards. Since that time Jews in the Roman Empire were the "servants of the state" and since the German rulers were the legal inheritors of the Roman Empire, the Jews, *ipso facto*, became their private property. *Ibid.*, pp. 66-67. Parkes notes that "in the evolution of the idea of *servitudo camerae*, . . . the conception of 'stranger' was in some aspects linked to the conception of 'villein,' for the villein was also a person who was rightless as far as his personal lord was concerned. But in practice, custom gave the villein more security than the Jew. . . ." See Parkes, *The Jew in the Medieval Community, op. cit.*, pp. 106-107. Cf. Finkelstein, *op. cit.*, p. 47.

61. The aspects and implications of the situation of Jews as the private property of the lords and the ensuing rivalries between the various centers of power in the Christian medieval society for the right to extract money from Jews is succinctly discussed by Parkes, *op. cit.*, pp. 109-119.

62. Schipper cites here as characteristic the complimentary declaration of Ruediger, the Bishop of Speyer, concerning the contribution of Jews in establishing that city. See *Onhoyb, op. cit.*, pp. 32-33 and *Virtschaftsgeshikhte, op. cit.*, pp. 63-65. Cf. B. Blumenkrantz, "Germany, 843-1096," *The World History of the Jewish People, op. cit.*, p. 163.

63. From Hebrew Responsa and to a greater degree from Aronius' *Regesten zur Geschichte der Juden in fränkischen und deutschen Reiche bis 1273* (Berlin: 1903).

64. *Onhoyb, op. cit.*, p. 35; *Virtshaftsgeshikhte, op. cit.*, pp. 43-44.

65. *Onhoyb, op. cit.*, pp. 31, 34; *Virtshaftsgeshikhte, op. cit.*, II, p. 43 ff. Regarding medieval Christian economic thought, the monopolistic contentions of the Christian resident *mercator* and his wish to suppress external interference, see M. Weber, *op. cit.*, pp. 166-168; also, R. H. Tawney, "Religion and the Rise of Capitalism," in *The Development of Economic Thought, op. cit.*, pp. 17-23, 26. Cf. Hirschler, *op. cit.*, who presents some interesting evidence to show that the medieval market was not as stationary and noncompetitive as generally assumed.

66. *Onhoyb, op. cit.*, p. 32.

67. *Ibid.*, pp. 34, 37, 39; *Virtshaftsgeshikhte, op. cit.*, pp. 65, 72. Cf. R. Strauss, "The Jews in the Economic Evolution of Central Europe," *Jewish Social Studies, III* (1944), pp. 21-22.

68. *Onhoyb, op. cit.*, p. 37. Cf. O. Stobbe, *Die Juden in Deutschland während des Mittelalters* (Braunschweig: 1866), p. 104.

69. *Onhoyb, op. cit.*, p. 78. Schipper used here the words of J. Strieder, *Zur Geschichte des modernen Kapitalismus* (Leipzig: 1905), p. 65.

70. *Supra,* Chapter I, p. 36, n. 80.

71. *Onhoyb, op. cit.*, p. 42.

72. See "Geneza lichwy żydowskiej," *op. cit.*, p. 227. Cf. Parkes, "Christian Influence on the Status of the Jews in Europe," *op. cit.*, pp. 36-37.

73. *Onhoyb, op. cit.*, pp. 46-47; *Virtshaftsgeshikhte, op. cit.*, pp. 69 ff. Cf. Baron, *op. cit.*, vol. IV, p. 203.

74. Parkes noted that the Lombards and Caursines were "much more unscrupulous than Jews" in their financial activities and credit operations in Italy and subsequently in all of Europe in the thirteenth century. Initially, they sought charters similar to those issued to Jews but later obtained much better terms and enjoyed a number of advantages, the right to leave the country, the right to sell their privileges, etc. See Parkes, *The Jew in the Medieval Community, op. cit.*, pp. 317-320. Also, M. Beard, *A History of Business* (Ann Arbor: 1962), p. 137 and H. Pirenne, *Economic and Social History of Medieval Europe* (New York: 1937), p. 133.

75. Schipper, "Geneza lichwy żydowskiej," *op. cit.*, p. 230; *Onhoyb, op. cit.*, pp. 48-49; *Virtschaftsgeshikhte, op. cit.*, p. 102, and in vol. II, p. 65.

76. *Onhoyb, op. cit.*, pp. 59 f. To substantiate these facts, Schipper cites Aronius, *op. cit.*, Depping, *op. cit.*, and Goldschmidt, *Geschichte der Juden in England* (Berlin: 1886); cf. Abrahams, *op. cit.*, pp. 241-243.

77. *Onhoyb, op. cit.*, pp. 54-55; *Virtshaftsgeshikhte, op. cit.*, vol. II, p. 54. Schipper also refers to the *takanot* (enactments) issued by the synods of rabbis in 1223 and 1245 forbidding Jews to handle Christian sacramentals. Cf. G. Kisch, "The Jewish Law of Concealment," *Historia Judaica*, vol. I, pp. 3-30; also Finkelstein, *op. cit.*, pp. 188-189.

78. *Onhoyb, op. cit.*, 56-58; *Virtshaftsgeshikhte, op. cit.*, p. 101 in vol. II pp. 52-54. See Edward H. Flannery, *The Anguish of the Jews* (New York-London: 1965), p. 110.

79. *Virtshaftsgeshikhte, op. cit.*, pp. 106-107. Cf. Parkes, *The Jew in the Medieval Community, op. cit.*, pp. 378 ff.

80. *Ibid.*, pp. 92-93. Schipper cites from *Milḥemet Mitsva* by Me'ir G. Simon of Narbonne (second half of the thirteenth century) in which it is stated that under Louis IX Jews could not engage in any other activity but money-lending since all other economic endeavors were forbidden to them.

81. It was put into the special royal chamber called the *scaccarium Aronis*,

while all his outstanding mortgaged loans were listed in a special register, *de debitis Aroni.* Cf. Baron, *op. cit.*, vol. IV, pp. 82, 203 f.

82. *Ibid.*, p. 208. Cf. Parkes, *The Jew in the Medieval Community, op. cit.*, pp. 168-170, 371.

83. *Onhoyb, op. cit.*, p. 51; *Virtshaftsgeshikhte, op. cit.*, pp. 75-79, 83-84. On the basis of per capita tax records Schipper estimates the Jewish population in England by 1290 to have been *ca.* 2,500-3,000. *Ibid.*, p. 84.

84. *Virtshaftsgeshikhte, op. cit.*, vol. III, pp. 5-7. Cf. Parker, *The Jew in the Medieval Community, op. cit.*, p. 121.

85. In Nördlingen, for instance, the interest rate fell from 43⅓% to 27½% during the period 1388-1433 and to 17⅓% in 1447-1453; in Frankfurt-am-Main the prevailing rate of interest in the fourteenth century ranged from 43½% to 32½%, but was 21⅔% in the fifteenth century. Schipper cites many more illustrations and abundant documentary evidence showing how Jewish moneylending was controlled and manipulated. Municipal councils determined at the time of admitting Jewish "pact-burghers" norms of credit operations, taking under consideration the interest of the city and its dwellers and assuring the latter of lower interest rates compared with those charged to outsiders, particularly the nobles. Municipal councils also saw to it that lower interest rates were charged for larger loans while higher rates were applied to small loans. In this way the rich city patricians not only sought better terms for themselves but actually weakened, for their own interest, the economic position of craftsmen and laborers. Some municipalities provided in their agreements with Jews that the latter must lend money to the city at special low interest rates. See *Virtshaftsgeshikhte, op. cit.*, vol. III, pp. 42-44. Cf. Parker, *The Jew in the Medieval Community, op. cit.*, pp. 227-229.

86. Cf. Weber, op. cit., pp. 194-195.

87. *Virtshaftsgeshikhte, op. cit.*, vol. III, pp. 44-46.

88. Using extensively and advantageously such extant fiscal records as Nahum's tax projection for Jewish communities in 1438 and the assessment of Jewish wealth in the margraviate of Meissen prepared by the Emperor's *Schatzmeister* Conrad in 1414-1420, Schipper assembles a number of revealing tables and comparisons showing the decline of Jewish capital. Thus he computes that the wealth of thirteen Jewish communities in 1438 amounted to no more than the sum of promissory notes cancelled in Regensburg alone in 1391. The data assembled from primary sources show not only the marked decline of Jewish means but point unmistakably to the main reason why Jews were successively expelled from German cities and royal territories in the fifteenth century. *Ibid.*, vol. II, pp. 230-231, 238-239; vol. III, pp. 55-63.

89. To substantiate, Schipper uses here illustrations from the German literature of the fifteenth and sixteenth centuries, especially Thomas Murner's *Nar-*

renbeschwerung and Sebastian Brandt's *Narrenschiff* which reveal that Christian usurers were worse than the Jewish ones. *Ibid.*, pp. 47-50. Cf. Hoffman, *op. cit.*, pp. 26 ff.

90. Schipper cites many illustrations of such extortions in various German provinces, especially in Austria. As an example of an agreed-upon pool for robbing Jews, he cites the understanding of the Archbishop of Würzburg and Bamberg with the Margrave of Brandenburg in 1422 and other similar instances. *Virtshaftsgeshikhte, op. cit.*, III, pp. 78-80. Cf. Weber, *op. cit.*, p. 202.

91. The city of Cologne, for instance, did not renew its pact with the Jews in 1424 because the Archbishop demanded that Jewish payments be remitted to him in the future as they had been in the past. In Erfurt a litigation between the Archbishop of Mainz and that city resulted in the permission to expel Jews if the city would compensate the Archbishop with 500 gulden. *Virtshaftsgeshikhte, op. cit.*, III, p. 81.

92. *Ibid.*, III, pp. 81-86.

93. *Ibid.*, p. 82.

94. *Onhoyb, op. cit.*, p. 80.

95. *Supra*, p. 82, n. 83.

96. *Onhoyb, op, cit.*, p. 81; *Virtshaftsgeshikhte, op. cit.*, p. 75.

97. These claims included 7,000 gulden collectible from the city itself, 22,591 from burghers and craftsmen, 72,580 from the landed gentry, 8,000 from the Nuremberg count, 3,813 from Duke Frederick of Bavaria, 1,800 from the Count of Öttingen, 1,800 from the Bishop of Eichstadt. *Virtshaftsgeshikhte, op. cit.*, vol. III, pp. 38-39.

98. For more documented illustrations, see *Virtshaftsgeshikhte*, vol. III, pp. 51-54.

3

Jewish Origins in Poland

Schipper received a further measure of distinction as a result of his treatment of the question of Jewish origins in Poland, a controversial subject that remains unresolved to this day.[1] The problem was not new when he first discussed it in 1911 in his *Studies.*[2] The question had already been raised in 1807 by Czacki, who concluded that "Jews came to us from two directions, that is from Bohemia and from Russia (Kiev)."[3] Following Czacki, Jewish historians like Kraushar, Sternberg, and M. Gumplowicz took essentially the same position.[4] The last, however, introduced the Khazars, who were the subject of many studies and discussions among scholars in the second half of the nineteenth century.[5] Gumplowicz thought that since the Khazars were temporarily in control of Polish territories at that time, the Jews among them were the very first progenitors of Polish Jewry.[6] Inadequately substantiated and rather indiscriminately connected with Lelewel's statement concerning Jewish beginnings according to early Polish chronicles and legendary tradition,[7] the Khazar idea was considered not only conjectural but too farfetched to be taken seriously. Nevertheless, Schipper, although not uncritical of Gumplowicz's treatment and presentation of the idea,[8] adopted it and built it up to a theory of his own, persisting in its defense in almost all his major subsequent writings.[9] It was not merely an academic question in which he wished to take a stand for purely scholarly reasons but a matter of important practical implications. To sustain his thesis, Schipper made a brave effort to muster all supporting data and information available in primary as well as secondary sources.[10]

The Khazar Kingdom

Based on his research and findings, Schipper posits a number of pertinent assumptions regarding the Khazar kingdom:

1. Jewish communities existed from ancient times in parts of the extensive territory of that kingdom. Jews from Armenia and the Caucasian regions came to this part of the world even before the Christian era. They settled at first around the Black Sea and eventually spread in westerly and northwesterly directions over Slavic lands. The second immigration, which lasted without interruption for ten centuries since the beginning of the Common Era, consisted of Greek Jews. This element increased in number, especially in the wake of Church persecutions in the ancient provinces of Byzantium proper at various times, particularly after the persecutions of Leo III in the eighth century. This immigration was further augmented in the eighth century by Persian, Arab, and Egyptian Jews, and in the tenth century by Jews from Babylonia and Palestine.[11]

2. Having been themselves mostly farmers or craftsmen, known for their competence in a number of industries, especially the silk industry, the Jews from Byzantium, who constituted the most numerous Jewish element in Khazaria, were to a great extent responsible for the introduction of agriculture and certain industries to the Khazars who had been originally hunters and herders.[12] But besides their economic contribution, the Greek Jews became a dominant cultural factor among the Khazars and through their influence the Khazars, particularly the Khaqan and the ruling circles, converted to Judaism, as attested by Arabic and Hebrew sources as well as other documents.[13]

3. Following the conversion to Judaism, the Khazar kingdom attained in southeastern Europe a position of political, cultural, and economic consequence. At the height of its development in the eighth and first half of the ninth centuries, the political control and influence of the Khazars reached as far as the Dniester and the subterrains of the South Carpathian mountains where one of its tribes, the Kabars (*Kabaroi*, in Greek), established relationships with the Magyars and penetrated as far as modern Hungary. In the beginning of the ninth century when the Khazars conquered Kiev, they came in touch with the most advanced among the Slavic tribes, the White Croats, mentioned in the Kiev Chronicle and by Constantine Porphyrogenitus. They also controlled lands of such Slavic tribes as the Polians, near Kiev, as well as the Severians, Vyatichis, and Radamichis northwest of Kiev, who were obliged to pay tribute to the Khaqan.[14]

Thus, "reciprocal influences between Slavic elements and the Khazar-Jews are indubitable" and the king of "*Gebalim*," prominantly referred to in the Khazar Correspondence, must have been the ruler of the Slavic lands of Chrobacya (Croats).[15]

4. There are signs and indications that even before the downfall of the Khazar kingdom following the 965 invasion by Svyatoslav, the ruler of the Kievan Russians, the Khazar Jews were active in the extensive territories of Khazaria. Their missionary activities among the Danubian Bulgars, for instance, worried the Patriarch of Constantinople, and there is evidence that they were missionizing in places as distant from one another as Hungary and Caucasia. By the end of the tenth century (986) Khazar Jews were still among the participants in a religious debate held in Kiev in the presence of Vladimir, the Russian ruler, and the characteristically vigilant and hostile attitude toward Jews on the part of the clergy of the young Christian Church in Kievan Russia is more than indicative of strong Jewish influences.[16] All this points not only to the religious influence of Khazar Jews among Slavs but also to the fact that these Jews were rather widely distributed in those parts of Europe which, between the eighth and tenth centuries, were within the Khazar sphere of control or contact.[17]

5. Following the fall of the Khazar kingdom in 969,[18] the Khazar Jews spread in various directions. While some remained in the Volga basin and the Black Sea vicinity, others migrated to the West in two ways: (1) the southern sub-montane territory of the Carpathian ridge to south Slavic lands branching off to Istria and Croatia (Kraina) and (2) from Kharkov to Kiev over the Ruthenian (Red Russia), Polish, and Mazovian lands to Bohemia and as far as Lusatia. The main evidence of these migrations lies in the nomenclature of historical settlements derived from such names as Chazar, Kazar, Kozar, Kabar, etc., found along the indicated directions of migration, and some epigraphic proof (Khazar graves), traceable especially along the Russian path of movement. Schipper displays a remarkable originality in his study of geographic places to prove his theory of Khazar-Jewish migrations to Southwestern and Western Europe, and especially to Poland. He points to a considerable number of equiparant and cognate place names containing the "Khazar" component in its various nuances on the southwestern route, that is, in Transylvania, Istria, Croatia, and Carinthia. He also delineates the links of the northwestern route dotted with Khazar graves in today's Ukraine: *Koganovo* (derived from Khaqan) near Kharkov; *Kozaroviche* near Kiev; *Kozarka* and *Kozari* in the Novgorod province; *Kozarka*, a rivulet falling into Bistritsa; *Kozarovshchizna* in the region of Oshmyany; *Kozarów* in the Polish region of Janów; *Koziari* in the vicinity of Brodnice; *Kozara* in the region of Lwów; *Koziari* near Halicz; *Kozarze* in the region of Cracow; *Kozarze* in Mazovia at the Nureć River; *Kozarek* at the Polish-Prussian border; and similar place names in Bohemia, ending with *Kozarci* in Lusatia. The connecting point between the two main routes of Khazar-Jewish migration appears to be, according to Schipper, the villages *Kaviory* near Cracow and *Kaviary* near Sandomierz. These two places, mentioned by Długosz and in the oldest Polish land documents as having had Jewish cemeteries, must have been founded by the Kabars (*Kabaroi*), the Khazar tribe that penetrated to Hungary and came to Poland through the famous "Greek Route." This particular point in Schipper's reasoning is explained by him in these words:

> . . . one can even determine the time and route by which the Kabars arrived to these regions. It is known from the history of the Khazars that around the middle of the ninth century they had waged a war against the Pechenegs. In connection with these hostilities, the Magyars and with them the Khazar tribe which in Greek sources is called *Kabaroi* emigrated to Hungary. According to Paul Cassel the *Kabaroi* are identical with the Khazar *Ḥaverim* (the latter Hebrew term meaning comrades in arms). From Hungary, these "Kabar-Ḥaverim" emigrated through the so-called "Greek Route," that is, through the valley of Poprad and Dunajec to the Tatra mountains (West Carpathia) and the region of Cracow and Sandomierz. The Khazar settlements in the Slavonic lands come to light in the interesting "Second Khazar Letter" of 1096 which speaks of the Khazars as near neighbors of the Ashkenazim, that is, Jews from Germany. Against the background of the nomenclature of the *Kozar* and Kabar settlements in the various regions of the Slavonic lands, and particularly in Russia and Poland, the fact of a Khazar-Jewish immigration during the time of the Khazar kingdom as well as later, that is, after the fall of that kingdom, becomes quite conspicuous. The latest dates for the establishment of the Khazar-Kabar settlements (in Poland) fall into the eleventh or twelfth century when the memories about the Khazars were still fresh.[19]

Thus, based on the premises concerning Khazaria that (1) the Judeo-Khazar element was mainly agricultural in character, (2) the Khazar kingdom included considerable parts of Slavic land, (3) the fall of the kingdom in 969 stimulated migration, and (4) the Khazar-Jewish migration to the West reached the western boundaries of Slavic lands, Schipper concludes: "We must assume that the Jewish element which until the end of the eleventh century migrated to Polish-Russian lands for the purpose of colonization came from the East."[20]

The Trade Routes

The conclusion above is further reinforced by Schipper's analysis of the commercial relationships which existed at the time in Eastern Europe.

In the realm of commercial activities Schipper distinguishes two phases: (1) the earlier phase of the Baltic-Asian commerce in which Khazaria with its two major emporia, Itil and Samandar, served as a land of transit for international trade between Byzantium, the Arabian Caliphate, and the people of the North and (2) the later phase in which Kiev became "the second Constantinople" and the carriers of international trade, especially the trade in slaves, along the land route north of the Alps were chiefly the Radhanites. The fall of the Khazar kingdom which coincided with the rise of the Italian cities constituted the dividing line between the two phases, and these two factors account for the changes that took place. But in neither phase did the Khazar Jews play a significant role in commercial activities.

Rejecting, as grossly exaggerated, Gumplowicz's hypothesis that between the eighth and tenth centuries Jews were the only possible merchants in the Baltic-Asian trade, Schipper points to the enormous quantity of Arabic coins found in Russia and the Baltic lands and cites a great deal of other proof indicating that the Volga Bulgars, the Burtas, the Russians, and the Scandinavians were chiefly responsible for this trade. In his view, the fact that this trade was directed mostly to the Arabs rather than from the Arabs clearly denies the possibility of Jewish participation in it.[21] And this was so despite the fact that international trade and the revenues derived from it constituted the economic base of the Khazar state, as attested by Ibn Ḥawqal. Schipper notes all the favorable circumstances that contributed to the inevitable growth of commerce in the last two centuries of its existence—the advantageous geographic location of the country and the international trade routes that traversed it, the stable and efficient state organization which provided protection to trade, the existing religious tolerance and the prevailing equality among various tribal groups, the branched-out influences of the Khazars outside its confines, etc. But he nonetheless maintains that Khazar Jewry was only indirectly connected with the transit trade that took place in their country. Occupying an in-between position, they obviously collected considerable revenues in tolls and customs from foreign merchants. The Khazar state served as a secure depot for these foreign traders, but there are no indications whatever that Khazar Jews themselves traveled to other countries in the role of merchants. The Khazar state as such had an agricultural character, and the ruling Khazar Jews appear to have had extensive farms. In the two major cities, Itil and Samandar, which served as entrepôts for other nations, the Jews actually constituted a minority. Moslems were in the majority in Itil and Christians in Samandar. Thus, one may reasonably assume that the Khazar Jews who eventually emigrated to the Russo-Polish lands represented in the main an agricultural element.[22]

In the second phase of commercial relationships, following the destruction of Itil at the hand of the Russians, Khazaria did not altogether lose its strategic importance but the center of international trade shifted to Kiev. Besides the loss of political importance, two other interrelated developments led to this shift. One was that the routes of the Radhanites, which utilized the Mediterranean and led through Mohammedan territories, lost their erstwhile usefulness for the Jewish merchants traveling to the East. This occurred because Italian cities began blocking these routes to Jews by the beginning of the tenth century.[23] (Merchants from Venice, Amalfi, and Bari reached the northern shores of the Black Sea and eventually established Italian colonies there.) The other development was that the persistent need for slaves could be satisfied only in the heathen countries of Central Europe and further east, that is, in the countries called *Esclavonia* (the apparent etymon for "Slav" and "Slavs") referred to by R. Yehuda ha-Kohen of Mainz (eleventh century) and Benjamin of Tudela (twelfth century) as "Canaan" because "the men of that land sell their sons and their daughters to the other peoples."[24]

Both these developments account for the fact that beginning with the second half of the tenth century sources concerning Jewish relationships with the East relate mainly to the route across the Slavic countries of central Europe to Khazaria and/or Kiev which the Radhanites now adopted as their route for carrying on business operations with the East. Of these sources, besides the general testimony of Ibn Khurradadhbih concerning the use of the land route through Slavic lands by the Radhanites, the earliest direct and indubitably indispensable report of Ibrahim ibn Ya'qub (quoted by al-Bakri) is advantageously utilized by Schipper in conjunction with the Khazar Correspondence and a number of other inferential materials. Ibn Khurradadhbih's narrative is pertinent in view of the information it provides that the Radhanites transported eunuchs and slave girls, among other goods, and that Slavic was one of the seven languages they used. But Ibrahim ibn Ya'qub was the first outsider to provide a number of interesting details about the Polish realm of Mieszko I, which he himself visited around 965, and about the wares carried by various merchants, including Jews, who traveled through that country on their way to or from Prague. He is presumed by Schipper to have been one of the Radhanites who reached Cracow through the "Greek Route," the same route by which Jacob ben Eliezer "from the land of Nyemec" (Polish designation for Germany) delivered Ḥasdai ibn Shaprut's letter to Khaqan Joseph, traveling through the land of "*Gebalim*," as suggested by Harkavy.[25]

Between the two anchorage centers of the Radhanites' trade, Prague and Kiev, (or other points in Khazaria, including Hungary) lay the southern parts of Little Poland, the valley of Poprad and Dunajec, Stary Sącz, and Cracow.

The Sources

In seeking to substantiate further the fact that Poland became increasingly a land of commercial transit between the West and the East, Schipper musters evidence not only from standard works on the subject by Jacobs, Heyd, Ernest Babelon, and others whom he utilizes in his earlier *Anfänge des Kapitalismus* and *Studies*, but subsequently finds new evidence from the studies by Szelągowski, Rutkowski, and especially Brutzkus.[26] Above all, he seeks to bring to bear upon the subject all possible Hebrew sources in his *magnum opus*, the *History of Jewish Commerce in Polish Territories* (in Polish), published in Warsaw in 1937.[27] Thus, he refers to the fact that Joseph ben Joshua ha-Kohen, Italian-Jewish historian of the sixteenth century, in his chronicle *Emek ha-Bakha*, described Persian Jews who fled in the eighth century to European countries via Khazaria. In this chronicle, the unvocalized Hebrew *Ssivinia* seems to Schipper to stand for Sl(a)vinia, and the point of arrival which reads *Hal* is taken by him to refer to the Ruthenian town of Halicz. It is near this town that Kozari, one of the oldest Jewish colonization points, can be traced according to the Polish land records.[28] In this way he indicates not only the circumstance that the land of the Khazars represented an important link between Persia and the West, particularly for Jews, but also the possibility of a Jewish settlement in Halicz, or its Ruthenian environs, as early as the eighth century.[29]

The next piece of evidence pointing to the existence of a Jewish community located on the Prague-Kiev route in Little Poland, Schipper finds in Yehuda ben Me'ir ha-Kohen's *Sefer ha-Dinim*.[30] The pertinent passage in this work tells of two Jewish boys from Primit (possibly Primut) in Polni (or Ploni) who were taken prisoners in 1031 and brought to Prague as slaves for sale. In Schipper's view, Yehuda ha-Kohen, who designated Russia as the "Greek Canaan," was referring in the story to the Polish town of Przemyśl (Primit = Primis = Primisl = Przemyśl).[31]

Schipper presents further evidence from Jewish sources to establish the fact that Poland was visited by Jewish merchants from Germany. They came from Cologne, Mainz, and especially Regensburg which in the twelfth century appears to have become a leading center of the Radhanites or the so-called *Holkhey Rusya* (travellers to Russia). The evidence includes:

(1) The testimony given by Eliezer bar Nathan of Mainz (RaBaN), who visited Poland around 1150, in his *Even ha-Ezer*;

(2) Isaac ben Asher ha-Levy of Speyer, who told of partnerships formed by Jewish merchants to buy wares in Russia and pay for them from a common bank, later dividing the wares as well as the profit by lots, as stated in Menaḥem ben Zeraḥ's (end of eleventh century) *Tseda la-Derekh*;

(3) The noted travelogue, *Sibbuv ha-Olam* by Petaḥia of Regensburg (twelfth century) who was in Prague and Kiev and who traveled in the land of *Kedar* (Khazaria) along the Dnieper among the Polovtsi (Qipchags) to the Black Sea and Crimea,

where he met Karaites, and from there via Mosul to Baghdad;

(4) The equally, if not more, famous travelogue of Benjamin of Tudela whose name for the Slavonic territories was *Esclavonia*, a region beginning in Bohemia, where Prague served as a major station of slave traffic, and extending further to the East. It was called Canaan by Jews living there because of its being a source of slaves;[32] and

(5) A number of explicit and generally uncontested indications in the Responsa literature of the eleventh to thirteenth centuries revealing both the commercial as well as the religio-cultural contacts established between German Jews and the Russian Jewish communities. They include the important letter of R. Eliezer b. Isaac of Bohemia (*ca.* 1200) to R. Yehuda b. Samuel he-Ḥasid (the Pious), cited in the Responsa of R. Me'ir of Rothenburg, stating that the Jewish communities in Poland, although pious, are too poor to be able to provide for their religious needs.[33]

The case of early Jewish presence in Poland is further buttressed by external evidence. Most important in that respect are the numerous specimens of coins of the tenth and eleventh centuries from Verdun, Troyes, Cologne, Mainz, Regensburg, etc., found in Poland and the praise given by the chronicler Gallus Anonymus to Queen Judith, wife of the Polish King Ladislas Hermann (1079-1102) for her work in ransoming Christian slaves from Jewish traders. In this pious activity, she probably was not much more successful than Bishop Adelbart of Prague, who resigned from his post because he could not compete with the "cursed gold" of the Jewish slave traders and was unable to redeem even as many Christian slaves as were brought by one of those traders. In addition, Schipper cites indirect but relevant evidence from Aronius attesting to the fact that at Passau, on the Bavarian-Slavic border, customs duties were established in 906 for slaves, as for all other wares carried by Jews from Slavic lands to the West, and that customs tariffs set by Ottokar in 1191 and by Prince Leopold of Austria in 1192 contain many details regarding the import and export trade, including the slave trade by Regensburg Jews doing business with Kiev.[34]

The Inferences

Taking into consideration the geographic location of Poland, situated between Khazaria-Kievan Russia, Hungary-Bohemia, and the Germanic lands, and relying both on the increased interest of medieval Jewish writers in the Slavic lands of Central and Eastern Europe, in the wake of the increased commerce conducted with or through these lands by Western Jews, as well as on the evidence pointing to early Jewish communities on the eastern borders of Poland, Schipper concludes that an influx of Jews to Poland already existed in the ninth and tenth centuries from the East as well as from the West. He states:

> In the oldest times, as far as historical documents go back, Jewish elements already flowed into Polish-Russian lands from two sides: from the East and from the West. Which of the two migration waves is older cannot be determined. However, it can be categorically stated that the movement from the West did not display any colonization tendencies.[35]

The Jews from the West had no reason to settle in Slavic lands until the end of the eleventh century when they began to move to Poland, prompted by the Crusades and the rise of Christian retail merchants in the West. Among the first western Jews to emigrate to Poland were those from Bohemia, as attested by the Czech chronicler Cosmas and clearly indicated in other documents.[36] Prior to the twelfth century Poland represented only a transit land to the Jewish merchants from the West. Although their travels contributed to the establishment of Jewish settlements along the trade routes, as had been the case in various parts of Europe during the Dark Ages,[37] the character of the oldest Jewish settlements in Poland was determined not by the Radhanites but by the Jews who arrived from the East. Otherwise, the fact that the oldest Jewish communities turned up near Poland's eastern borders, according to the extant documents (Przemyśl, 1031; Kiev, 1113; Cheringov, before 1181; Vladimir in Volhynia, before 1171), rather than in its western provinces would seem to be quite inexplicable. The western boundaries of the Khazar kingdom may be a highly debatable question, but the fact is that by the middle of the tenth century it reached as far as the vicinity of Kiev which bordered on Poland and which later belonged to Poland.[38]

It also stands to reason that the first Jewish colonists in Poland were from the East rather than the West. The latter were limited numerically, prior to the German colonization of Poland and the persecutions of the first Crusades, and represented a transient, commercial element bound for Kiev or back home, while the former, consisting of Khazar or Byzantine Jews who were traditionally either farmers or craftsmen, were inclined to settle in the new Polish sites permanently. Furthermore, settlements of German Jews usually called Judendorf, Judenfurt, Judenberg, etc., in Germanic lands had their counterparts in Poland under the Polish names of Żydowo, Żydów, Żydowska Wola, etc. However, these cannot be traced earlier than the first half of the thirteenth century in Silesia and the western province of Poland (Żydowo near Gniezno, 1205; near Kalisz, 1213; near Szamotul, 1257). In provinces further to the East (Kuyavy, White Russia, Red Russia, and Lithuania) such names of Jewish settlements appear still later, that is, in the fourteenth and fifteenth centuries, although, Schipper assumes, "some of those undoubtedly existed already in the thirteenth century."[39]

What is most significant, however, is that these Jewish settlements, judging by the Polish suffixes of their names (*-ów, -owo*), which indicate land possession, must have been essentially agricultural in character like those called Kozari, Kozara, Kozarzów, Kaviory, etc. The first Jewish colonists in these settlements also came from the East rather than the West,[40] although the agricultural economy of the Jewish villages located near commercial centers, such as Gniezno (Gnesen), Kalisz, and Breslau, may have been combined with commerce as was usually the case with such Jewish independent settlements in the West.[41] In any case, "the oldest sources from Silesia, which was under the rule of the Piast princes, show that Silesian Jews lived before the Tartar invasion (1241) from agriculture either as landowners or as peasants."[42] In 1150 Jews owned the village called Mały Tyniec, and in 1200 Sokolników near Breslau (Wrocław) belonged to two

Jews, Hatskel and Joseph, and it is documented that Jewish peasants working on princely lands had to pay a tithe to the Bishop of Breslau according to a written agreement between the latter and Prince Henry I of Silesia.[43] Thus, Schipper concludes, until the Tartar invasions in 1241 the Jewish colonists in Poland, who under the Piast princes constituted a free class with the right to own slaves,[44] were undoubtedly occupied mainly in agriculture although the Piast may have used a few individual Jews from Bohemia as minters and administrators of matters pertaining to currency and finances.[45] Altogether, he notes, "it is no exaggeration to state that the Khazar-Jewish element played a pioneering role in the economic progress of Poland, which in the eleventh century was still primarily a country of hunters and beekeepers."[46] Furthermore,

> . . . the influences of the immigration of this element were reflected also in the organization of the Polish state. This point is brought up by St. Zakrzewski and it is true that similarities existed between the relationship of the Piast princes to the state and the relationship of the Khazars to the Black Sea lands. One can point to a similarity between the Polish *drużyna* (cohort) system, mentioned by Ibrahim ibn Ya'qub, and the organization of the Khazar "king of kings." . . . Together with the Radhanites who visited Polish territory for short periods, the Khazar Jews played a great role in transforming the total organization into a state organism. Not the Norman invaders nor the Pomeranians, but the peaceful Khazar-Jewish element, reared in the strong organizational framework of Khazar absolutism, and the moving Radhanite element, knowledgeable in world relations—they and similar groups carried out the peaceful work of construction. The oldest and newest Polish historiographers have been aware of this, although they do not emphasize that among the foreigners who carried out that task there were, first of all, Khazar Jews and Radhanites.[47]

But the first phase of the Jewish colonization in Russo-Polish lands, together with its achievements, was completely wiped out by the Mongol invasion. Thus the year 1241 became a turning point in the history of Jewish immigration and colonization in

Poland. It was in this year that Khan Batu began his plundering raids on his way to conquer Hungary, reaching as far as Silesia where he was stopped. The first Jewish communities in Poland, especially those on its eastern frontiers, lay ruined as Jews from the East and Little Poland ran for their lives to Silesia, Moravia, Bohemia, and Austria. Schipper notes that the lack of reference to Jewish communities in the territories of Kievan Russia during the reign of the Tartar khans in 1241-1350 contrasts with the growth of Jewish communities in Silesia, Great Poland, and Mazovia. By the end of the thirteenth century and in the first half of the fourteenth, new Jewish settlements appeared in these western provinces, with Silesia showing the strongest growth, from three communities in the twelfth century to sixteen communities in 1300-1350.[48] While Jewish refugees from the eastern provinces may have settled in these new communities following the recession of the Mongolian threat, the second wave of Jewish immigration to Poland, between the middle of the thirteenth and the middle of the fourteenth centuries, came from the West. This can be seen from the fact that Jewish names found in the documents of that period are of German provenance, that is, names common among Jews of Nuremberg, Vienna, Moravia, Silesia, etc.[49] Another fact to be noted is that the General *Privilegium* of Kalisz of 1264 was nominally granted at the initiative of Jews who apparently brought with them this German form of Jewish legislation. This document, together with the Austrian charter of 1244 after which it was patterned, echoes the oldest German lawbook, the *Sachsenspiegel*, and the Jewish charters of Speyer (1090) and Worms (1157).[50]

But this part of the chapter of Jewish origins in Poland consists of well-established and well-known facts. It bears the distinct character of compulsory immigration from the West—impelled by the intensified attacks on Jews in Germany in the first half of the thirteenth century (1218, 1235, 1241). It also reflects the deterioration of the legal and social status of Jews as *servi camerae*, the growth of European cities, and with it the increased political power and determination of burghers to eliminate Jews from commerce.[51] The German expansionist course towards Eastern Europe which carried with it persecuted Ashkenazi Jews to Poland, where they subsequently became the dominant and all-pervasive element of the growing Jewish communities in that country, is hardly a subject of controversy in the annals of the historiography of Polish Jewry. What has remained a controversial subject is the preceding period of approximately three centuries during which Jews from the East had already established settlements in Poland, according to Schipper's theory.

The Critique

Although the Khazar kingdom as such, with all its moot questions, became part and parcel of general Jewish historiography, the Khazar theory as it relates to Jewish origins in Poland continues to be a subject of debate. Certain historians before and after Schipper have maintained that the history of the Jewish community in Poland began with the influx of Ashkenazi Jews which gained momentum after the Mongol invasion. Others accepted, with greater or lesser reservations and emendations, Schipper's thinking as containing certain definite aspects of historical truth, or at least, as a reasonable hypothesis deserving of mention and consideration. The latter category includes the younger historians like Ringelblum and Mahler who worked and, to an extent, identified with Schipper as well as men like Friedman, Brutzkus, Kupfer and Lewicki, and Poliak. Ringelblum, the young martyr of the Warsaw Ghetto who considered himself a disciple of Schipper, limited his position to a concise exposition of his teacher's view, adding only that neither the countries of origin nor the approximate date of arrival of Jews in Poland have been as yet irrefutably determined.[52] Mahler expressed the view that, although direct evidence is lacking, one may assume with a high degree of probability the existence of Jewish settlements in Poland before the end of the eleventh century because of two basic and certain facts: (1) that Polish principalities were located between two countries, on the east and the west, in which Jews lived and (2) that these Jews conducted an active trade and communicated with one another. Moreover, until the middle of the thirteenth century agriculture was either a main or a side occupation of Jews settled in Poland because the cities in that country still had a predominantly agricultural character and because the names of villages cited by Schipper (with the exception of "Kawiory") justify this hypothesis.[53]

Brutzkus expressed surprise at Schipper for having adopted M. Gumplowicz's method of deriving historical conclusions from possible connections between place-names and Khazar Jews. The historical fact of Khazar rule in Kiev and Hungary in the ninth century, Brutzkus thought, cannot serve as sufficient evidence of a Jewish presence in Poland. Also, the established fact of Jewish commercial caravans traveling through Poland in the ninth, tenth, and eleventh centuries cannot be used as definite proof of permanent Jewish settlements in Poland at that time. Sources referring to international trade say nothing about Jewish colonies or stations, although it may be assumed that the passage through that country led to the eventual founding of such colonies.[54] In the last analysis, however, the work of Brutzkus in assembling the evidence, especially the Hebrew sources, depicting the trade routes of the so-called *Holkhey-Rusya*, his suggestion that Jewish settlements sprang up eventually along the trade routes leading through Poland, and above all, his Schipperian interpretation of Yehuda ha-Kohen's passage from *Sefer ha-Dinim*, regarding "Primit" as the Polish Przemyśl, strengthened substantially the trade-route aspects of Schipper's theory.[55] This was further reinforced by Kupfer and Lewicki, whose full and critical examination of the known Hebrew sources relating to Slavic people in Central and Eastern Europe is indispensable for any discussion of the subject.[56] Their research led the authors to the conclusion that the first appearance of Jews in Central and Eastern Europe which goes back as far as the eighth century was related to two facts: (1) the Khazar kingdom and (2) the active participation of Jews in the trade between the West and the East. They postulated that medieval Jewish writers became interested in the Slavs of Central and Eastern Europe because new Jewish communities cropped up along the routes of commercial communication between Prague and Magdeburg in the West and Kiev and Cheringov in the East.[57]

Poliak took a position which went far beyond that taken by Schipper with regard to the extent of Khazar migrations to the West as well as the North. Poliak contended that within evolving Polish-Lithuanian Jewry, the Khazar element constituted, initially at least, by far the greatest part because the immigration of that group lasted several centuries, especially following the deterioration of Khazaria in the eleventh century. Again in the fourteenth and fifteenth centuries, the disintegration of the Golden Horde also brought a surge of Armenians and Tartars to Lithuania and Poland. In these migratory movements one route led to Hungary via Poland and the other to the principalities of Kiev, Cheringov, and Pereyeslav, where Jewish communities had existed even before the Russians took them over. The migratory route led even further north along the Don and Dnieper to the Lithuanian territories above Smolensk.[58]

Among the historians who seriously minimized the role of Jews from the East in the genesis of Polish Jews and who took the position that Khazar Jews had very little or nothing to do with the beginning of the Jewish communities in Poland, one should note Dubnow, Bałaban, Halpern, and Weinryb.

Considering the overall—geographic, political, and religio-cultural—gravitation of Poland towards the West, her closeness and dependence on Germany in particular, Dubnow concluded that "the Slav lands on the banks of the Warta and Vistula . . . were bound to attract the Jews at a very early period (possibly the ninth century) in their capacity as international traders." He noted, however, parenthetically that, while "the *predominating* element came from the West, it is quite possible that there was an admixture of settlers from the Khazar kingdom, from the Crimea, and from the Orient in general, who were afterwards merged with the western element."[59]

More interesting is the shift of position taken by Bałaban, Schipper's slightly older contemporary and his "lifelong rival," who was most cautious and conservative with indirect evidence and not given to sweeping generalizations without a good deal of direct proof.[60] Initially, that is until the mid-twenties, Bałaban agreed in essence with Schipper's exposition of the question.

Although he circumspectly minimized the immigration from the East, stressing the fact that there is no actual evidence of early Jewish settlements in Russo-Polish parts except for Kiev where a Jewish community did exist by the end of the tenth century, he nevertheless acknowledged that Jews arrived in Poland not only from the West but also from the East (including Khazaria and Byzantium) and that a translocation of individual Jewish families or entire groups from Kiev to the vicinities west of Podolia (Red Ruthenia) ought to be assumed. Moreover, he took into account the view of those who hold that Khazar or Russian Jews who settled in such villages as Żydowo, Żydowska Wola, Kozarze, Kawiory, etc., in Red Ruthenia and Little Poland seem to have been land cultivators.[61] Bałaban, however, reformulated his position in a special essay, published in 1931. This essay was meant as a direct critique of Schipper's Khazar theory because of the appearance of the *Virtshaftsgeshikhte* in which, in Bałaban's view, Schipper not only repeated his previous exaggerated hypotheses but actually presented them as axioms.[62]

Agreeing with Schipper as to the general division of the migration phases which includes the basic proposition that Jews "were coming" to Poland from the West as well as from the East in the first phase, until the eleventh century, and in the second phase, until the Mongolian invasion, Bałaban asserted here a number of critically important points:

1. That the data relating to the eastern immigration are indirect and less certain than those pertaining to the movement from the West;

2. That none of the sources confirming Jewish commercial transit through Poland prove that there existed a process of Jewish settling in that country;

3. That just as the generalization cannot be made, on the basis of the sources, that Jews in Silesia in the twelfth century were engaged only in agriculture, since it would appear from the same sources that they were also engaged in commerce and industry, so even less can it be said about the Khazar-Jewish element that it was inclined to settle permanently and that it was engaged exclusively or mainly in agriculture; and

4. That "Kawiory," the name of villages near Cracow and Sandomierz mentioned in the sources as having had Jewish cemeteries, seems to be derived from the German *Kirchhof*, meaning "churchyard," which, on account of its graves, is usually associated with a graveyard, rather than from the Khazar tribe "*Kabbaroi*," while "Kozary" or "Kozarze" may be related to the Polish *koza* (goat).[63] As for such names as "Żydowo," these are not indicative of either a Khazar-Jewish settlement or of an agricultural settlement just as settlements in various parts of the Germanic lands called *Judendorf* do not necessarily imply a community of Jewish farmers.[64]

With regard to Kiev, where the existence of a large and strong Jewish community during the period between the tenth and thirteenth centuries cannot be disputed, Bałaban allowed that:

> A certain part of Kiev Jews probably emigrated to Poland or to the particular Piast principalities, but we are in no position to trace this immigration because we have no sources, whatsoever, for such a task. . . . We can only state that when Casimir the Great took Red Ruthenia he found there two Jewish communities, Lwów and Przemyśl, which indicates an expansion of the Jewish population from the East (Kiev?) to the West.[65]

Halpern seems to be even more restrictive than that. True, Jews played an important role in the foreign trade of Kiev and the *Holkhey Rusya*, mentioned in the German halakhic literature, traveled in caravans by way of Poland at least until the second half of the thirteenth century, but these "Jewish caravans which traveled between Regensburg and Kiev . . . seemingly left no definite traces along the route" because the "first mention of a permanent Jewish settlement in Cracow, the principal Polish station on the caravan route, was in 1304" and information about permanent Jewish settlements from the twelfth century relates only to the western parts of Poland (Greater Poland and Silesia) rather than to its eastern parts.[66]

In his review of Schipper's *History of Jewish Commerce in Polish Territories*, Halpern was mainly critical of the way in which Schipper utilizes the Hebrew sources for his inferences, implying a degree of manipulation and inexactness. These sources, he pointed out, are almost always secondary and presented in a confused form, while such a primary source as the account of Ibrahim ibn Ya'qub is not as decisive as Schipper would make it appear because it does not indicate the degree to which Jews participated in the transit trade of Poland. Nor does the other information referring to Jewish participation in the international trade say anything about Jewish commerce in Poland proper.[67] In other words, we can determine the genesis of Jewish economic activities and Jewish communal life in Poland only on the basis of direct evidence stating clearly and unequivocally the existence of such activities and life. Any other evidence must, of necessity, be speculative and therefore doubtful at best, but more often inadmissable.

Basically, the same approach is taken by Weinryb, who in his thoroughly incisive critique of the Khazar and trade-route theories refutes practically all evidence, indications, and grounds advanced by Schipper as being indirect, unreliable, irrelevant, or altogether valueless. Rejecting or questioning the value of such sources as the entry in Joseph ha-Kohen's *Emek ha-Bakha*, the documents evincing emigration of Byzantine Jews to Khazaria (except for al-Mas'udi's *Muruj adh-Dhahab*), the place-names as indicative of the migration of Khazar Jews to Poland, Yehudah ha-Kohen's story regarding "Primit," the Ḥasdai-Joseph Correspondence, etc., Weinryb points also to the inadequacy and exiguity of such celebrated accounts as that of Ibn Khurradadhbih, Ibrahim ibn Ya'qub, Petaḥia of Regensburg, and Benjamin of Tudela for the case of Poland.[68] Even the bracteates with Hebrew inscriptions are "not necessarily coins minted by Jewish minters for the state." The only factual information relating to Jews from Kievan Russia or Galicia (*i.e.*, Red Ruthenia) is "about a few Jews from there who arrived in western Europe and about some who traveled from the West to those regions."[69] The rest, Weinryb feels, represents an artificial construction motivated by considerations other than historical truth. It is nothing but an attempt to explain the origins of Jews in Poland in which insufficiently documented historical reasoning and inferences are calculated to respond to the existing sociopolitical problems of the society in which the historian lives and to project the political views which he himself holds and wishes to propagate.[70]

The Implications

Thus, according to Weinryb, Schipper's theory of Jewish beginnings in Poland is untenable because it is wanting in solid supporting evidence and also because it is politically motivated and Jewishly biased. Obviously, the question of evidence is highly debatable and will remain so as long as the degree of credibility, attributed to different categories of evidence and to circumstantial clues, depends on the judgment of individual historians and as long as history, its definite facts as well as its inevitable conjectures, is largely a matter of interpretation. Such direct proof of the relatively early presence of Jews in Poland as the extant bracteates with Hebrew inscriptions of the first Polish princes can be viewed as a decisive and irrefutable piece of evidence, or it can be reduced and made irrelevant, as Weinryb has done, by allowing for the assumption cited above. Parenthetically, one wonders whether this isn't also—in the words of Ettinger—"an excessively critical tendentiousness negating the value of sources because they do not tally with the presumptions of the 'anti-apologeticists'."[71]

On the other hand, there can be no doubt that Schipper's research and conclusions regarding the Jewish beginnings in Poland were not merely an academic exercise in historical speculations. That they were also meant to serve nationalist Jewish causes of his time is evident not only in the implied meaning of his conclusions but also in his explicit assertions which, spurning the apologetics of preceding historians, point to counterattack, self-reliance, and positive action. Accordingly, when certain Polish historians decried his *Studies*, following its publication, and one of them, Marylski, angrily denounced Schipper for "attempting to put prehistoric Poland under Jewish feet,"[72] Schipper retorted that "such voices cannot deter us. We return to this problem (*i.e.*, Jewish beginnings in Poland) with the . . . responsibility of opposing the ignorance and impetuousness of a well-known group of Polish publicists and some of their Jewish parrots. . . ."[73] Defending his interpretation of the Khazar type of place-names in Poland as against that given by Marylski, Schipper asserts:

> The mere fact that the names of the settlements derived from "Kozar" and its analogies emerge evenly in Hungary and South Slavonia as well as in Russia, Poland, Bohemia and Lusatia is clear evidence of the naïveté of a certain pseudohistorian (*i.e.*, Marylski) who . . . gets himself involved in such an unfortunate etymological deduction as the derivation of "Kozary" from the Polish *kozy* (goats). If that be so, then the places on the northern mountain slopes of Caucasia which are called "Kasara" and "Kusri" owe their names to . . . the Polish goat.[74]

Schipper showed the Polish anti-Semites of his time that Jews could claim the same rights as the Poles, having lived in Poland at least as long as the latter and having been among the first to bring to Poland a measure of agricultural and commercial civilization. But he was even more interested in providing a historical perspective and guidelines for his own people.

In depicting the Khazar kingdom—its stable and efficient state organization, military strength, religious tolerance and influence, Hebrew as the official language of the state, agricultural character of the country, which wisely exploited its geographic position for international trade (conducted by Moslems and Christians rather than Jews)—Schipper undoubtedly projected Zionist ideas and ideals to his own generation. He hoped to influence thereby its youth and imbue it with a sense of national self-respect, purpose, and responsibility. This is conspicuously evident in his repeated emphasis on agriculture as the natural economic pursuit of Jews whenever and wherever they were not forcibly alienated from the soil. Meant to refute the anti-Semitic propaganda which labeled Jews as a disloyal foreign element and as unproductive economic parasites, it was even more intended to advance the basic premise of the *Poale Zion* ideology that Jewish national emancipation depended on a reformation of the economic structure of Jewish life. This reformation aimed to eliminate the one-sided preoccupation of Jews with trade and intermediary commercial functions and to bring about a return to productive physical labor, as of old. *Poale Zion* ideology specifically included a return to agriculture as the indispensable occupation for normalizing Jewish existence in the Diaspora as well as for renewing a Jewish national home in Palestine.

Schipper's apparent political tendencies and purposes, however, do not necessarily nullify or minimize the historical plausibility of his views concerning the Jewish beginnings in Poland even if one were to judge them to be pure conjecture.[75] It is therefore important to note that historians like Baron and Roth, very cognizant of the fact that the problem of Jewish origins in Eastern and Central Europe cannot be based on precise documentation, concluded nonetheless that the assumption of the early existence of Jewish settlements in Eastern Europe and Central Europe is well within reason. In discussing the account of Ibrahim ibn Ya'qub and the arrival of German Jews in Poland, Baron notes that "it was in Poland, in particular, that this western Jewish wave encountered the equally large influx of Jews from the East, especially Khazaria, both leaving behind many place names like Żydowo . . . Kozari, and Kozarzów," adding furthermore that "apparently entire villages were founded by Jews and Khazars as far West as Greater Poland."[76] Roth's position, although stated in more general terms, is basically the same since it, too, allows for the existence of Jewish settlements in various areas of Eastern Europe as a result of Khazar penetrations in the direction of Central Europe:

> In the same way as Iraqi Jews found their way at this time to Frankish Gaul . . . so they may have found their way to Slavonic Poland and Bohemia, where the Spanish Jewish traveler Ibrahim ibn Ya'qub . . . may well have found an Arabic speaking Jew to serve as his interpreter. . . . It may be presumed even when proof is lacking that they (*i.e.*, Jewish merchants active in these regions in the Dark Ages) established, or at least were in contact with, local Jewish settlements. . . . Certainly, in the 12th/13th century Poland was decimated or worse by the Tartar invaders who swept over the country. . . . But there is no reason to imagine that the

destruction was comprehensive and some Jews at least must have survived to build up their communal lives anew.[77]

Thus, Schipper's basic thesis concerning the antiquity and genesis of Jewish existence in Poland, although questioned and debated by compilers of confirmed facts, remains, to say the least, a conjectural or surmised part of the historiography of Polish Jewry, to be considered and weighed but by no means disregarded as invalid.

Notes

1. See Mahler, "Di Yidn in amolikn Poyln," *op. cit.*, p. 1. Also, E. Ringelblum, "Dzieje zewnętrzne Żydów w dawnej Rzeczypospolitej," *Żydzi w Polsce Odrodzonej*, I. Schipper, A. Tartakower, A. Haftka, eds. (Warsaw: 1932-1935), vol. I, p. 37.

2. Actually three chapters of his *Studies* (Chaps. II, III, and V) in which he deals with the subject were published in 1910 in the *Jewish Almanach* (Lwów), edited by Leon Reich under the title "Początek ekonomiki Żydów w Polsce: Najwcześniejszy handel żydowski w krajach słowiańskich (od VIII do końca XII wieku)," pp. 165-173.

3. He based this conclusion on statements of the Bohemian chronicler, Bishop Cosmas, and the Polish chronicler Długosz. See Czacki, *op. cit.*, p. 66.

4. A. Kraushar, *Historya Żydów w Polsce* (Warsaw: 1865), vol. I, pp. 36-90; Sternberg, *Geschichte der Juden in Polen* (Leipzig: 1878), p. 6 ff.

5. See *The Jewish Encyclopedia*, vol. IV, pp. 1-7, especially pp. 3-4.

6. M. Gumplowicz, *Początki religii żydowskiej w Polsce* (Warsaw: 1903), p. 16.

7. Joachim Lelewel's Polish work in twenty volumes entitled *Poland, Her History and Affairs Surveyed* (Posen: 1853-1876), is based on a very detailed and critical analysis of primary documents and has served as a fount of Polish historical knowledge.

8. See Schipper, "Przegląd krytyczny," *Wschód, op. cit.*, Nos. 5 and 6, in which he said that M. Gumplowicz "played a hazardous game with history, gleamed and flared with bold hypotheses . . . reached fantastic conclusions, based on fantastic evidence," that the Khazars occupied all of Poland, reaching as far as Mecklenburg, in pre-Christian times, that their relationship to the aboriginal Slavic population was that of rulers to subjects, and that since they

were converted to Judaism it follows that Jews were the actual rulers of Poland in those times.

9. These include besides the aforementioned publications (*supra*, Chap. I, p. 38, n. 99 and 100; "Der Anteil . . . am Grosshandel" and the *Virtshafts-geshikhte*) the following: "Agrar-Kolonisation der Juden in Polen," *Jüdische Fragen* (Vienna: 1910), pp. 64-78; *Kultur-geshikhte fun di Yidn in Poyln beysn mitlalter* (Warsaw: 1926); "Dzieje gospodarcze Żydów Korony i Litwy w czasach przedrozbiorowych," *Żydzi w Polsce Odrodzonej, op. cit.*; "Rozwój ludności żydowskiej na ziemiach dawnej Rzeczypospolitej," in *ibid.*; and numerous references in other articles and studies. Schipper provides a comprehensive presentation of his position regarding the entire subject of the Jewish origins in Poland, and the Khazar theory as an integral part of it, in a special monograph published in the *Almanach Żydowski* (Vienna: 1918) entitled "Początki Żydów na ziemiach ruskich i polskich (od najdawniejszych czasów do r. 1350)." A Yiddish translation of this monograph appeared in *Bleter far Geshikhte*, XIII (1960), Warsaw, pp. 26-59, utilized here and referred to in the following as "Początki."

10. Besides the Arab geographers and travelers, Istakhri, Ibn Faḍlan, Ibn Ḥawqal, and Muqaddasi, to whom Schipper refers the reader quite often, as well as the Khazar Correspondence and Schechter's Cambridge Document, Schipper relies heavily on scholars who, up to and during his time, dealt with the subject directly or whose studies and opinions had what he considered a significant bearing on it, especially A. Harkavy, "Khazarskiye Pisma" in *Yevreyskaya Biblioteka*, VII (St. Petersburg: 1879) and "So'obshcheniya o Khazarakh," *ibid.*, VIII (1880); D. Chvolson, *Corpus inscriptionum hebraicum* (St. Petersburg: 1882), *Achtzehn hebräische Grabschriften aus der Krim* (St. Petersburg: 1865), and *Ibn Dosta izvyestiya o Khazarakh* (St. Petersburg: 1869); Hirschfeld, *Das Buch al-Chazari* (Breslau: 1865) and "Mittelalterliche Berichte von Arabern über die Slaven," *Zeitschrift der historischen Gesellschaft für Provinz* (*Posen*, VI); G. Jacob, *Der nord-baltische Handel der Araber im Mittelalter* (Leipzig: 1887); P. Cassel, *Magyarische Alterthümer* (Berlin: 1848); Vambery, *Der Ursprung der Magyaren* (Leipzig: 1882); K. Potkański, *Kraków przed Piastami* (Cracow: 1897); E. Kunik, "Lechcica," *Kwartalnik historyczny* (Lwów: 1898); H. Kutschera, *Die Chazaren* (Vienna: 1909); J. Bergl, *Geschichte der Ungarischen Juden* (Leipzig: 1879); S. Kraus, *Studien zur bizantisch-jüdischen Geschichte* (Vienna: 1914); and others. Cf. *The Jewish Encyclopedia*, vol. IV, pp. 4-7. For the Arabic sources mentioned above and others, see Dunlop, "The Khazars," *The World History of the Jewish People, op. cit., passim*, especially pp. 329-334.

11. See *Studies, op. cit.*, p. 7; "Początki . . . ,"p. 33; *Virtshaftsgeshikhte, op. cit.*, pp. 43 ff; cf. Dubnow, *History of the Jews in Russia and Poland*, vol. I (Philadelphia: 1916), pp. 14-18; also Friedman, "Geshikhte fun Yidn in Ukraine," *Yidn in Ukraine*, vol. I (New York: 1961), pp. 1-2. Regarding persecutions of

Jews in Byzantium see A. Scharf, "Jews in Byzantium," *The World History of the Jewish People, op. cit.*, pp. 53 ff.

12. *Studies, op. cit.*, p. 8; "Początki," *op. cit.*, p. 36; *Virtshaftsgeshikhte, op. cit.*, p. 44. Cf. Scharf, *op. cit.*, p. 66; Baron, *op. cit.*, vol. III, p. 197.

13. Schipper relies here heavily on Krauss, *op. cit.*, pp. 105, 119, 151. Cf. Dunlop, *op. cit.*, p. 340, and Baron, *op. cit.*, vol. III, pp. 198 ff. Brutzkus is of the opinion that the choice of Judaism as the religion of the Khazars, dictated for political reasons, must have been stimulated by Persian Jews who lived in Transcaucasia where a separate Khazar tribe called Yendser also accepted Judaism, forming the Khazar-Jewish kingdom of Daghestan. J. Brutzkus, "The History of Jewish Mountaineers in Daghestan," (Yiddish), *YIVO Studies in History*, II (Wilno: 1937), pp. 27 ff.

14. In describing the territorial expansion of the Khazar kingdom towards Central Europe, Schipper relies heavily on the investigations and studies of Harkavy, Potkańsky, Kunik, Cassel, and Vambery. See "Początki," *op. cit.*, p. 36; *Virtshaftsgeshichte, op. cit.*, II, p. 94; *Studies, op. cit.*, pp. 10-11. Cf. Dunlop, *op. cit.*, pp. 344, 348. As for the White Croats and the other Slave tribes, see *The Cambridge History of Poland*, vol. I (Cambridge: 1950), pp. 10-11, 14.

15. *Studies, loc. cit.* The debatable identity of "*Gebalim*" was the subject of polemics between Schipper and T. E. Modelski, the latter suggesting that "*Gebalim*" or "*giblim*" (mountains) refers to the lands in the Alps. The exchange of views took place in *Yevreyskaya Starina*, vol. IV, pp. 142-148 and vol. V, pp. 100-107. Cf. Baron, *op. cit.*, vol. III, pp. 210, 331 n. 48.

16. To substantiate Jewish missionary activities in various parts of the Khazar kingdom, Schipper cites Kutschera, *op. cit.*, pp. 155-158; J. Caro, *Essays* (Gotha: 1906), p. 118; J. Bergl, *op. cit.*, pp. 20-21; Jacob, *op. cit.*, p. 83; *Regesti i Nadpisi*, Nos. 156, 164; the Cambridge Document, and other corroborating studies. See "Początki," *op. cit.*, pp. 41-43. Cf. S. Ettinger, "Kievan Russia," in *WHJP, op. cit.*, p. 323; also R. Mahler and E. Ringelblum, *op. cit.*, pp. 16-17.

17. Friedman notes that the great number of Jews (six million) in the Roman Empire in the first century is to be explained by the fact that there were many Roman converts, especially among the Roman aristocratic families who lived in the colonies on the Black Sea. Jewish expansion in Eastern Europe had an ideological, missionary character which had its beginning in the first century but reached a high point in the period between the eighth and tenth centuries. In the tenth century this expansion suffered two serious defeats: (a) the fall of the Khazar kingdom and (b) the acceptance of Christianity by the Kievan principality where the Greek-Orthodox Church embarked upon a policy of persecuting Jews in order to diminish strong Jewish influences and thus consolidate its own position. See Friedman, "Geshikhte fun Yidn in Ukraine," *op. cit.*, p. 3.

18. Brutzkus notes that although the Russians destroyed also the separate Jewish-Khazar kingdom in Daghestan, that kingdom regained its independence

and lasted until the invasion of the Tartars in 1237. See Brutzkus, "History of the Jewish Mountaineers," *op. cit.*, p. 35.

19. *Virtshaftsgeshikhte, op. cit.*, II, p. 96. Schipper expresses the same view in other places. See *Studies, op. cit.*, p. 34; "Rozwój ludności żydowskiej," *op. cit.*, p. 22; "Początki," *op. cit.*, pp. 37-40.

20. "Początki," *op. cit.*, p. 31.

21. See *Onhoyb, op. cit.*, pp. 27-28; "Przegląd krytyczny," *Wschód, op. cit.*, Nos. 5, 6; *Studies, op. cit.*, pp. 13-15. Schipper relies here mostly on the evidence provided by Fraehn, *De Chazaris: Experta de Scripteribus Arabicis* (Petersburg: 1821) and Jacob, *op. cit.* Characteristically, in *Onhoyb, loc. cit.*, Schipper gives the Khazar Jews some credit for initiating commercial relationships with Jews in Slavic and Hungarian lands, but in subsequent studies he changed this position, maintaining that the Greek Jews in Khazaria may have been engaged in trade only with Byzantium, from which they had been expelled, and with Asia Minor. See *Virtshaftsgeshikhte, op. cit.*, pp. 35-36; *Der Anteil der Juden am Grosshandel, op. cit.*, p. 10.

22. *Studies, op. cit.*, p. 17; *Der Anteil der Juden am Grosshandel, op. cit.*, pp. 10-11. Cf. Dunlop, *op. cit.*, pp. 342, 352; Halpern, "Jews in Eastern Europe," *op. cit.*, pp. 291-293.

23. See *supra*, Chap. II, pp. 55 f.

24. See *Studies, op. cit.*, pp. 20, 24-26; "Dzieje gospodarcze Żydów Korony i Litwy," *op. cit.*, pp. 113-114; *Dzieje handlu żydowskiego na ziemiach polskich* (Warsaw: 1937), pp. 3, 6-7. Cf. Rabinowitz, "The Route of the Radanites," *op. cit.*, pp. 258 ff; also Mahler and Ringelblum, *op. cit.*, p. 17; Baron, *op. cit.*, vol. III, pp. 214 f. and 335 and vol. IV, p. 172; *The World History of the Jewish People, op. cit.*, pp. 28, 310; Weinryb, *The Jews in Poland, op. cit.*, pp. 22-23.

25. *Onhoyb, op. cit.*, p. 28; *Studies, op. cit.*, pp. 10 ff; "Dzieje gospodarcze Żydów," *op. cit.*, pp. 113-114; *Dzieje handlu żydowskiego, loc. cit.* Schipper draws his information about Ibrahim ibn Ya'qub and his travel reports largely from F. Westberg, *Ibrahim ibn Jakub's Reisebericht über die Slavenlande aus dem Jahre 965* (Petersburg: 1898), which has been superseded by T. Kowalski, *Relacja Ibrahima ibn Jakuba z podróży do krajów słowiańskich w przekazie al-Berkiego* (Cracow: 1946). Regarding the identity and importance of Ibn Ya'qub, see E. Ashtor, "Ibrahim ibn Ya'qub," in *WHJP, op. cit.*, pp. 305-308. Cf. Baron, *op. cit.*, vol. III, pp. 217-218. As for the carrier of Ḥasdai's letter, Schipper persists in calling him Jacob ben Eliezer in several of his writings and as late as 1932 (see his "Początki," *op. cit.*, p. 28 and "Rozwój ludności żydowskiej," *op. cit.*, p. 22) although he is named in *The Jewish Encyclopedia* (vol. IV, p. 3) Isaac b. Eliezer. In his latest book, however, *Dzieje handlu żydowskiego na ziemiach polskich, op. cit.*, published in 1937, the Khazar Correspondence is altogether omitted, possibly because all research concerning the origin and authenticity of the Ḥasdai-Joseph correspondence proved to be inconclusive and put the entire

matter in doubt. See B. D. Weinryb, "The Beginnings of East European Jewry in Legend and Historiography" in *Studies and Essays in Honor of Abraham A. Newman* (Philadelphia: 1962), pp. 490-491 as well as Weinryb, *The Jews of Poland, op. cit.*, p. 21; also, Dunlop, *op. cit.*, pp. 329-340. The authenticity of the Khazar Correspondence has been recently vindicated by N. Golb who, in connection with his discovery of a letter in Hebrew written by Khazarian Jews from Kiev in the first half of the tenth century, scrutinized anew the Cambridge Document and, in producing an improved text and translation, presented evidence attesting to its genuineness and trustworthiness. See Golb, N. and O. Pritsak, *Khazarian Documents of the Tenth Century* (Ithaca and London: 1982).

26. A. Szelągowski, *Najstarsze drogi z Polski na Wschód w okresie bizantyńskim i arabskim* (1909); J. Rutkowski, *Zarys dziejów gospodarczych Polski* (Posen: 1923); J. Brutzkus, "Di ershte yedies vegn Yidn in Poyln," *Historishe Shriftn* (Warsaw: 1929); *idem.*, "Di handls-batsiungen fun di Mayrev-Yidn mitn altn Kiev," *Shriftn far Ekonomik un Statistik* (Berlin: 1928); see Schipper's "Dzieje gospodarcze Żydów," *loc. cit.*

27. These sources had been partially utilized in 1918 in his special monograph on Jewish beginnings in Poland, "Początki," *op. cit.*, pp. 26-30.

28. "Początki," *op. cit.*, p. 26; *Virtshaftsgeshikhte, op. cit.*, II, p. 96 f. One variant of the *Emek ha-Bakha* Mss. notes the European countries as *Rusia, Ashknaz* (Germany), and *Shvisia*, with *Hal* as the point of arrival; the other variant has *Ssvinia*, possibly *Sskonia*, instead of *Shvisia* and *Hiyla* (*Hayla*) instead of *Hal.* The latter led Neufeld to conclude that Joseph ha-Kohen referred here to Saxony and its city of Halle. See the M. Letteris edition of *Emek ha-Bakha*, (Cracow: 1895), p. 19 and S. Neufeld, *Die Halleschen Juden in Mittelalter* (Berlin: 1915).

29. Cf. Friedman, "Geshikhte fun Yidn in Ukraine," *op. cit.*, p. 13; Weinryb, *op. cit.*, pp. 476 f.

30. Written in Mainz in the eleventh century. It is partly preserved in a published fragment of *Abi ha-Ezri* called *Sefer Rabiya* by Eliezer ben Joel ha-Levi of the twelfth and thirteenth centuries and in *Or Zaru'a* by Isaac ben Moses, the latter's pupil, as well as in the Responsa of R. Me'ir of Rothenburg of the thirteenth century.

31. See "Początki," *op. cit.*, p. 29; *Virtshaftsgeshikhte, op. cit.*, II, pp. 96 f; "Dzieje gospodarcze Żydów," *op. cit.*, p. 114; *Dzieje handlu żydowskiego, op. cit.*, pp. 4-5; and Schipper's *Kultur-geshikhte fun Yidn im Poyln beysn mitlalter* (Warsaw: 1926), pp. 15-16. Brutzkus relates the story of the captive boys from Primit to the known fact that the Russian princes Yaroslav and Mscislav took and ruled the city of Przemyśl in 1015-1031 and sold many of its inhabitants as slaves to Constantinople. See Brutzkus, "Di ershte yedies vegn Yidn in Poyln," *Historishe Shriftn*, I (1929) YIVO, pp. 70 ff. Also, Baron, *op. cit.*, vol. III, p. 219. Cf. T. Lewicki, "Hebreishe mekoyrim tsu der geshikhte fun di slavishe felker-

shaftn in der tsayt fun frier mitlalter," *Bleter far Geshikhte*, IX (1956), p. 22 or I. Kupfer and T. Lewicki, *Żródła hebrajskie do dziejów Słowian i niektórych innych ludów środkowej i wschodniej Europy* (Breslau-Warsaw: 1956), pp. 36, 41-44; Weinryb, *op. cit.*, p. 465, 481-482. The first history of Jews in Przemyśl was written by M. Schorr, *Żydzi w Przemyślu do końca XVIII wieku* (Lwów: 1903), but he was unfamiliar with Yehuda ha-Kohen's reference.

32. See *supra*, p. 99 of this chapter.

33. "Początki," *op. cit.*, pp. 50-51; *Der Anteil am Grosshandel, op. cit.*, p. 16; *Virtshaftsgeshikhte, op. cit.*, II, p. 46; "Dzieje gospodarcze Żydów," *op. cit.*, pp. 114-116; *Dzieje handlu żydowskiego, op. cit.*, pp. 7-8. Specific names of rabbis in Kievan Russia who studied in the West and of western rabbis who traveled to the East include R. Moshe of Kiev (twelfth century), who seems to have been a disciple of Rabbenu Tam of Rameru and who maintained a halakhic correspondence with R. Samuel b. Ali, the Baghdad Gaon; Isaac of Cheringov (twelfth-thirteenth centuries) who studied in England; Benjamin of Vladimir (twelfth century) who studied in Cologne; Isaac b. Dorbello (twelfth century) and Eliezer b. Isaac (twelfth century), who left accounts of their visits in Russia, and others. A critical analysis in detail of the Hebrew sources cited by Schipper, as well as those that escaped his attention, is provided by Kupfer and Lewicki, *op. cit., passim.* Cf. also with the evidence from Hebrew sources concerning the beginnings of the Jewish communities in Kievan Russia cited by Friedman in his "Geshikhte fun Yidn in Ukraine," *op. cit.*, pp. 18-20 and by S. Ettinger, "Kievan Russia," *op. cit.*, p. 321.

34. See *Onhoyb, op. cit.*, p. 29; *Studies, op. cit.*, pp. 25 f.; "Początki," *op. cit.*, pp. 27, 29; "Dzieje gospodarcze Żydów," *loc. cit.*; *Dzieje handlu żydowskiego, op. cit.*, pp. 4-6. Data regarding extant West European coins in Poland Schipper based on M. Gumowski's *Wykopaliska monet z X-go i XI-go wieku* (Cracow: 1906). As for the slave trade, cf. S. W. Baron and A. Kahan, *Economic History of the Jews* (New York: 1975), p. 271.

35. "Początki," *op. cit.*, p. 30.

36. Besides Cosmas, Schipper cites Aronius' *Regesten, op. cit.* Nos. 10, 11 and documents published by Bondy-Dvorsky, *Regesten zur Geshichte der Juden in Böhmen, Mähren und Schlesien* (Prague: 1905). "Początki," *loc. cit.*

37. See Roth, "Economic Life and Population Movements," *op. cit.*, pp. 45-46, 48.

38. Cf. S. Kętrzyński, "The Introduction of Christianity and the Early Kings of Poland," *The Cambridge History of Poland, op. cit.*, p. 19 and especially p. 29.

39. "Początki," *op. cit.*, pp. 43-44. "Rozwój ludności żydowskiej," *op. cit.*, pp. 22-23; *Virtshaftsgeshikhte, op. cit.*, II, pp. 95-98; *Studies, op. cit.*, pp. 30, 33, 35. Schipper is careful, however, to note in a few cases that the seemingly Jewish character of the place-name is not related to Jews. *Ibid.*, p. 33, notes 22

and 23. On the Jewish nomenclature of places in Germanic lands and Poland as well as other countries, see Roth, "Economic Life and Population Movements," *op. cit.*, p. 46 and Additional Note B, pp. 390-391.

40. *Studies, op. cit.*, pp. 30, 35.

41. "Początki," *op. cit.*, pp. 44, 47; *Virtshaftsgeshikhte, op. cit.*, II, p. 100.

42. "Dzieje gospodarcze Żydów," *op. cit.*, p. 111.

43. *Ibid.*, p. 112; "Początki," *loc. cit.*; *Studies, op. cit.*, pp. 30-31. Cf. Mahler and Ringelblum, *op. cit.*, pp. 26-27. On the agricultural character of Jewish settlements in the West as well as in Eastern Europe see Roth, *op. cit.*, p. 31 and the Additional Note B, *loc. cit.*

44. *Supra*, Chap. I, p. 28.

45. *Studies, op. cit.*, p. 28; *Virtshaftsgeshikhte, op. cit.*, pp. 101-102. The point is important because a considerable number of extant coins bearing the names "Mieszko, King of Poland" in Hebrew characters constitute direct evidence of Jewish presence in Poland under one of the three Piast rulers, all of whom were named Mieszko. Cf. Mahler and Ringelblum, *op. cit.*, pp. 23-26, where the studies of Polish authorities on Hebrew bracteates found in Poland are referred to. See also Baron, *op. cit.*, vol. III, p. 218.

46. "Początki," *op. cit.* p. 40. It should be noted that the editor of *Bleter far Geshikhte* (in which Schipper's essay on Jewish origins in Poland was reprinted in a Yiddish translation in 1960) makes the following remark: "The newest archeological investigations in Poland deny this hypothesis of Schipper."

47. "Początki," *op. cit.*, p. 41. The Polish historians referred to are St. Zakrzewski, *Zagadnienia historyczne* (Cracow: 1918), p. 212; J. N. Sadowski, *Pamiętnik Akademji Umiejętności* (Cracow: 1876); K. Rakowski, *Wewnętrzne dzieje Polski* (1908), p. 13, *passim.*

48. *Studies, op. cit.*, pp. 62-63, 65; "Początki," *op. cit.*, p. 53; "Rozwój ludności żydowskiej," *op. cit.*, p. 23; *Virtshaftsgeshikhte, op. cit.*, II, pp. 102-103. On the Mongolian invasion of Poland see A. B. Boswell, "Territorial Division and the Mongol Invasion," *The Cambridge History of Poland, op. cit.*, pp. 91 ff.

49. "Początki," *op. cit.*, p. 55; *Virtshaftsgeshikhte, op. cit.*, II, p. 105. Schipper cites here many interesting examples from source materials revealing typical names of Oriental Jews next to Hebrew names with German diminutive endings.

50. "Początki," *op. cit.*, p. 56; *Virtshaftsgeshikhte, op. cit.*, II, p. 106.

51. "Początki," *op. cit.*, pp. 45 f.

52. E. Ringelblum, "Dzieje zewnętrzne Żydów w dawnej Rzeczypospolitej," *Żydzi w Polsce Odrodzonej, op. cit.*, pp. 37-38. As for Ringelblum's estimate of Schipper, see his essay, "Der boyer fun der moderner historiografye," *Bleter far Geshikhte*, II (1958), pp. 5-14.

53. Mahler, "Di Yidn in amolikn Poyln," *op. cit.*, pp. 2-4, 6-7, 12-13. Regarding "Kawiory," the name of two villages mentioned in the sources as having had Jewish cemeteries, Mahler followed the idea suggested by Brutzkus that its etymon is the Hebrew *kevarim* (graves) rather than the Khazar tribe "*Kabbaroi*," See also *infra*, p. 103, point 4. As for Friedman's position, see his "Geshikhte fun di Yidn in Ukraine," *op. cit.*, pp. 12-20.

54. Brutzkus, "Di ershte yedies vegn Yidn in Poyln," *op. cit.*, pp. 55-57, 62-64.

55. *Ibid.*, pp. 57-61, 66-72. See also Brutzkus, "Di handls-batsiungen fun Mayrev-Yidn mit dem altn Kiev," *YIVO Shriftn fun Ekonomik un Statistik*, I (1928), pp. 69-75; and *idem.*, "The Khazar Origin of Ancient Kiev," *Slavonic and East European Review*, XXII, pp. 108-124.

56. Kupfer and Lewicki, *Źródła hebrajskie to dziejów Słowian, op. cit., passim.* See also Harkavy, *Ha-Yehudim u-Sefat ha-Slavim* (Vilna: 1876).

57. Lewicki, "Hebreishe mekoyrim tsu der geshikhte fun di slavishe felkershaftn," *op. cit.*, p. 20.

58. Ab. N. Poliak, *Kazariya: Toledot Mamlakha Yehudit be-Eyropa* (Tel Aviv: 1943), pp. 219, 223-224, 227, 250 ff.

59. Dubnow, *History of the Jews in Russia and Poland, op. cit.*, p. 39.

60. See Biderman, *op. cit.*, pp. 235-238.

61. Bałaban, *Historja i literatura żydowska ze szczególnym uwzględnieniem historji Żydów w Polsce*, vol. II (Lwów: 1924-1925), pp. 323-324; or the Hebrew translation of the same in *Bet Yisrael be-Polin, op. cit.*, p. 1.

62. Bałaban, "Kiedy i skąd przybyli Żydzi do Polski?," *Miesięcznik Żydowski*, I (1931), p. 3.

63. Without the benefit of a fully developed onomatological science of Slavic languages, Schipper's explanation of the place-names Kozari, Kozarze, Kozar, etc. represents a remarkable and admirable attempt at utilizing toponymy for historical investigations. However, the most recent conclusions of Slavic onomatology regarding the morphology and derivation of these names justify Bałaban's rather than Schipper's view. See M. Altbauer, "Meḥkaro shel Yitsḥak Shiper al ha-Yesod ha-Kuzari-Yehudi be-Mizraḥ Eyropa," *I. Shiper*, Sh. Eidelberg, ed. (New York: 1966), pp. 48 ff.

64. Bałaban, "Kiedy i skąd przybyli Żydzi do Polski," *op. cit.*, pp. 5-11, 116.

65. *Ibid.*, p. 117.

66. Halpern, "The Jews in Eastern Europe," *The Jews: Their History, Culture and Religion*, ed. by L. Finkelstein, vol. I (1960), 3rd ed., pp. 294-296.

67. Halpern, "On Schipper's *History of Jewish Commerce in Polish Territories*," (in Hebrew), *Kiryat Sefer*, XV (1938), pp. 207-208.

68. Weinryb, "The Beginnings of East European Jewry in Legend and Historiography," *op. cit.*, pp. 476-497.

69. *Ibid.*, p. 497, n. 2 and n. 3. Weinryb refers here to those individual travelers whose names are mentioned above in this chapter, p. 113, n. 33.

70. *Ibid.*, pp. 449-458, 500. For Weinryb's critical position of the Khazar theory and his view concerning the origin of Jews in Poland see also his *The Jews of Poland, op. cit.*, pp. 19-22 and pp. 27-29 respectively.

71. See Ettinger, "Kievan Russia," *op. cit.*, pp. 319-320 and 442, n. 1.

72. A. Marylski, *Dzieje sprawy żydowskiej w Polsce* (Warsaw: 1912), p. 41; see also pp. 30-36.

73. "Początki," *op. cit.*, p. 25.

74. *Ibid.*, p. 38.

75. In dealing with the subject of the migration of the Khazars to Kievan Russia, Ettinger correctly emphasizes the notion that "one should not underestimate the value of conjectures in connection with the settlement of a minority group in a remote period when historical sources are sparse." See Ettinger, "Kievan Russia," *loc. cit.*

76. Baron, *op. cit.*, vol. III, p. 218. In another connection Baron refers the reader to the debate between J.Staszewski, author of the *Geographic Dictionary: The Origin and Meaning of Geographic Names* (in Polish), and his reviewers L. Papp and L. Kiss which in underscoring "the extreme difficulty of deriving historical conclusions from possible connections of certain geographic names with ethnic groups . . . places question marks before Schipper's long debated theory that the numerous localities in Little Poland and Red Russia bearing such names as Żydów or Kozarzów are necessarily indications of Jewish and Khazar settlements there." See Baron, *op. cit.*, vol. X, p. 314, n. 37.

77. Roth, "The Early Jewish Settlements in Central and Eastern Europe," *op. cit.*, pp. 302-304.

4

The Factual Image of Jewish Moneylending

As has been demonstrated in the preceding chapters of this study, it is Schipper's considered view, remonstratively expressed more than once in his *Studies* and elsewhere, that the histories of the Jews in Poland written before him were lacking in their treatment of the earliest stages of Jewish existence in that country. In the first place, the writers of those histories were either unaware of or by and large deleted the initial three centuries of Jewish presence in Russo-Polish lands. These centuries, prior to the devastation wrought by the Tartar invasion, constituted a period in which the economic role of Khazar Jews in agriculture as well as western Jews in commerce were of considerable importance to the early burgeoning of the Piast principalities. In the second place, the authors of previous histories presented erroneous pictures of the legal and economic situation of the Jews in Poland in the period following the Tartar devastation.

The Royal Charters and the Economic Role of Jews

Motivated by apologetic and ingratiatory tendencies, the Jewish historians of the assimilationist school, in particular, were responsible for these basic distortions. They considered the *Privilegia generalis*, with their predominantly favorable provisions, to be the best and only mirror reflecting the true situation of the Jews. Since they did not scrutinize these official legal blueprints against their historical background and, especially, against the extant records relating to the facts, they arrived at completely false conclusions. Even L. Gumplowicz, whom Schipper singles out next to Kutrzeba as an independent investigator who seriously attempted to gain an objective understanding of the Kalisz *Privilegium*, failed to see that this charter actually degraded the legal position of the Jews in Poland from that which they enjoyed prior to 1264. Moreover, since about half the articles of this basic legal document deal specifically with credit transactions, he relegated the Jews in early Poland to a special class whose only or main economic function was to supply the capital so greatly needed by the young and underdeveloped Polish principalities.[1] This erroneous conclusion was of special interest to Schipper, for besides being directly related to the economic history of Jews in Poland, it tallied with the generally accepted notion of the Jew as a moneylender, as a pecuniary parasite, and Schipper thought that it was high time to expose the fallaciousness of this sterotyped and hostile attitude.

Emphasizing the fact that following the Tartar invasion the historian is faced with a paucity of sources relating to the eastern provinces of Poland and that the characteristic silence about the established trade relationships with Kiev is indicative of an interruption of Jewish life and Jewish economic activities in that part of Europe,[2] Schipper proceeds to show that the Kalisz Charter and the economic relationships of Jews in Poland during the first hundred years or so following the issuance of that *Privilegium* must be understood in the context of the shift in the gravity of Jewish life in Poland from its eastern parts to those bordering on Germany, Bohemia, and Moravia. He points to a number of pertinent developments to illustrate this shift and the consequent mutation in the overall character of the Jewish economic role which assumed a more western pattern but was not as one-sided as the royal charters would seem to indicate. These developments include:

1. The fact that the Piast princes put their monetary matters, including the minting of coins, in the hands of Jews who fled from Bohemia following the pogroms in Prague in 1161 and 1187, among whom, according to the testimony of the Czech chronicler Cosmas, there were very rich mint masters. Undoubtedly, these Jewish minters were responsible for the coins bearing the names of Piast rulers in Hebrew letters which were uncovered in the archeological excavations at Wienica, Głębokie, and Bekerów.[3]

2. The characteristic incipience of new Jewish communities in the western regions of the Piasts (Płock and Warsaw in Mazovia, Kalisz and Poznań in Great Poland, Cracow and Sandomierz in Little Poland),[4] especially in Silesia, at that time still under the rule of Polish princes, where sources note three communities in the twelfth century, eight in the thirteenth century, and nineteen in the first half of the fourteenth century. But, Schipper advisedly notes, while the Silesian sources of the twelfth and beginning of the thirteenth centuries still refer to Jewish landowners and farmers, the subsequent sources speak only of Jewish merchants and moneylenders. The commercial character of the Silesian communities is evidenced also by their location along the trade routes leading from Germany to Poland, Bohemia, and Moravia.[5]

3. The disappearance of the Radhanites' trade with Kiev and its supplantation by a growing trade with Hungary along the "Greek Route" which touched only the western parts of Poland, especially Silesia and Little Poland. This trade, however, did not belong to the western Jews as much as to Jewish merchants from Greece and the Middle East, judging by the fact that the *Pinkas ha-Kahal* (community record) of Kresmir dating back to the fourteenth century cites names of Oriental Jews such as Kolonimos, Aba Mari, Kaleb Yakar, who apparently settled there, and

Silesian documents of the fourteenth century also mention typical names of eastern provenance, such as Kobos (from Jacobos), Sabday, Ilia, etc.[6]

The lively trade from Greece to Poland and Lower Austria via Hungary is attested by the special privilege which Ladislas Łokietek (the Short) granted to Jews of Stary Sącz in 1327, exempting them, as well as non-Jewish merchants, from all duties on wares brought from Hungary or Cracow to the local fair.[7] These wares included wine, olives, wax, metals, and furs, while the Polish export consisted mainly of salt. Another testimony concerning this trade comes from Isserlein of Neustadt near Vienna (1390?-1460) who in his *Leket Yosher* speaks of sugar and rice having been imported to his city from Candia, and of Lwów as an ascending commercial link between the West and Constantinople. Lwów, mentioned already by Judah Crescas, the creator of the Catalonian map (1343), as *ciutat de Leo*, became the recipient of wares coming from Byzantium via Hungary in the second half of the fourteenth century, and Jews from Western Poland in search of these wares began traveling now to this new center. In the second half of the thirteenth century there were undoubtedly Jewish commercial activities going on along the routes leading to Prussian cities (Stettin, Thorn, and Danzig) but this was stopped in 1309 when Seyfridt von Feuchtwagen, the head of the Teutonic Order occupying Prussia, forbade the Jews to come to his realm.[8]

The commercial activities, however, are hardly reflected in the economic clauses of the Kalisz Charter and the subsequent two charters (BII and BIII). These documents contain only one comprehensive clause guaranteeing Jewish merchants complete freedom of movement, the full right to buy and sell and transport all manner of goods as long as they pay the same duties and tolls as those paid by Christian merchants. Significantly, the clause positively permits Jews to trade in food articles although the Church authorities at the Synod of Breslau in 1266 explicitly opposed it for fear that Jews might "sometime poison Christians whom they consider their enemies."[9]

But, Schipper points out, this single clause concerning commerce, as opposed to so many relating to credit, in a general type of document such as a royal *Privilegium* is quite understandable, because in its comprehensive way it provides adequately the necessary conditions and guarantees for a growing and thriving trade. The business of credit, however, which is by its very nature a more complicated economic transaction, would of necessity require more regulations designed to take under consideration the variety of possible circumstances and, above all, the methods of safeguarding loans. To conclude from this, as many historians did, that the majority of Jews who settled in Poland were moneylenders is not only erroneous but also misleading. In the same way, it is incorrect and deceptive to say that because court records reveal Jewish claims on the nobility and the burghers, moneylending must have been the exclusive occupation of all Jews, disregarding the fact that those records do not tell whether the Christian debtors owed their Jewish creditors money for extended loans or for goods given on credit, or possibly for services rendered.[10] On the other hand, the entire tenor of the Kalisz Charter and the character of its credit provisions clearly demonstrate that the document was introduced and, in a sense, superimposed on all Jews in Poland, regardless of their occupation and origin, by a smaller group of Jewish financiers among the Ashkenazi element who migrated to Poland together with the German colonizers and in whose financial capacities the Polish rulers were particularly interested.[11] Aware of the rather propitious charter promulgated in 1244 by Frederick II of Austria, these Jews presented that document, with further ameliorations, to Boleslas the Pious of Kalisz and later to the architect of the unified Polish state, Casimir the Great, who, characteristically, granted the document *ad petitiones Judaeorum* (at the request of the Jews) fully cognizant of the benefits *Judeus nostri* would bring to the royal treasury and the country as a whole. Schipper puts it in these words:

> The organization of credit in medieval Poland was in the main based on western patterns and this is related to the fact that attempts were made in Poland to meet the growing [economic]

> needs as fast as possible and in the easiest way. This tendency led to the practice of drawing from foreign sources, instituting western legislative patterns (the entire municipal law, for instance) and relying on foreign labor (German colonists) before an indigenous Polish class of merchants and craftsmen could develop. . . . The same policy applied to Jews who from the thirteenth century on began streaming to Poland together with the German colonists as well as to those Jews who had been living on Polish lands much earlier. The point of view from which the establishment of relationships with Jews were seen as well as the frame in which the economic functions of the Jews were to be put were adopted from the West. The paragraph of the 1364 *Privilegium* which states "*utilitates camere nostre anquere cupientes*" clearly shows that Casimir the Great looked at the Jews mainly through the prism of fiscal interests. . . . The policy of safeguarding Jewish loans was dictated by those interests. Hence, the preponderance of security clauses in the charters.[12]

The true picture of Jewish economic relationships, however, cannot be determined by historians from an examination of the charters or the unsuccessful resolutions adopted by the Church at its synods in Kalisz (1264), Breslau (1266), Łęczyca (1285) and Buda (1279) to counteract Jewish economic activities, or the statutes adopted by the landed *szlachta* designed to protect their own interests as debtors. Far from reflecting actual economic practices, these documents were more often than not disregarded, to a greater or lesser degree, and superseded by the growing needs of the young Polish state. The demands of the country, which was behind in its development and therefore different in its socioeconomic structure from Germany, created economic functions and activities, means and devices, unforeseen and not reflected in the royal charters or other statutes.[13] In the process of meeting these demands, the Jews played a significant role not only as moneylenders but in other occupations as well. To determine that role, the historian must examine those sources that would tend to reflect the actual economic life situations that existed in medieval Poland: the municipal and country documents, the revenue books, and, above all, the court records. And it is in this respect that Schipper performed, indeed, a pioneering task, having been among the first to investigate and study such untapped source materials in order to present a fuller picture of the Jewish economic functions in Poland under the last Piasts and the Jagiellons.[14] Schipper emphasizes the importance of these sources several times in his *Studies*, and besides monuments of ancient Polish laws as well as municipal, provincial, and court records published by Helcel, Ulanowski, Lekszycki, Krzyżanowski, Czołowski, Hube, and others, he utilizes a number of unpublished primary sources that he himself searched out in the archives. He was also one of the first Polish-Jewish historians to make full use of Bershadski's *Russko-Yevreyskiy Arkhiv.* Thus he wrote in the introductory paragraphs to the *Studies*:

> The harvest has proved to be rich. . . . It has brought a full reservoir of heretofore unelaborated material, the added significance of which lies in the fact that it provides us with pictures from life instead of arid charter articles. To what extent the latter were implemented in life has been unknown to us until now.[15]

The examination and analysis of these materials provided Schipper not only with a body of new, informative facts and data which he brought to light in his *Studies*, but also enabled him to formulate his own general conclusions concerning the economic position and role of Jews in medieval Poland. Among these conclusions, two seem to stand out in particular:

1. That the power of the Polish rulers, the sponsors of Jewish *Privilegia*, was for a long time strong enough to withstand and disregard anti-Jewish pressures emanating from the ecclesiastical authorities or other centrifugally oriented classes in the Polish society when the interest of the kings and the country dictated favorable economic policies towards their Jewish protegés. While in the western countries the Jewish royalties were divided among many lords, land potentates, and city rulers, the royalties of the Polish Jews, as the *servi camerae* of the chief suzerain of the Polish state, belonged only to the latter until the very end of the Middle Ages. Attempts by nobles and cities to gain part of the revenues produced no results because the king wanted the Jews to have

ready money for his needs, and his power was strong enough to prevent consequential interference and infringement on the part of other powerful factors.[16]

2. That unlike the West where, with few exceptions, the policy of deriving revenues from Jews deteriorated to a shortsighted course of exploitation and sheer robbery accompanied by acts of violence, especially in the area of credit relationships, in medieval Poland no attempt was made by the state to exploit or seize Jewish material resources. Although it cannot be said that the Polish kings conducted a planned, long-range economic policy, it is a fact that they were, by and large, tolerantly disposed to their Jewish *servi camerae*, giving the Jews the necessary freedom and opportunities to develop their own economic potentialities.[17]

Credit Terms and Practices

Schipper's exposition of Jewish credit activities points to the fact that pertinent legislative regulations and court decisions in particular can be characterized as aiming to protect the moneylender and to provide him with quite favorable conditions for the profitable operation of his business. This fact is more than adequately demonstrated by Schipper in his detailed description of loan forms and contracts, interest rates, security provisions, creditor rights, etc. Thus, in discussing interest rates, he points out that the Kalisz Charter of 1264, unlike the document of Frederick II of 1244 after which it was patterned, does not set a maximum rate. It was deliberately omitted in order to give Jewish creditors a free hand in consonance with the king's wish, clearly stated in BIII that "Jews should have ready money for all our needs." Moreover, while the Little Poland Statute of 1347 (Code of Wiślica) set the allowed interest rate at about 54 percent, there is enough documentary evidence showing that this rate was charged only when creditors obtained adequate guarantees; in practice the prevailing rate was 108 percent.[18]

Similarly, the Code of Wiślica limited interest arrears to a period not exceeding two years, providing that if the creditor did not claim the loan through the courts during the two-year period he could later demand only the principal and two years' interest thereon, even in cases where the written conditions of the loan stated otherwise. In practice, however, this limitation was neither observed nor enforced. The debtors themselves, in whose interest the two-year limitation was legislated, did not demand its implementation, preferring to adhere to the terms of the contract. This placed them in a position to maintain their credit, and in case of litigation the courts often granted the creditor interest for as many as five, six, eight, ten, and even sixteen to seventeen years.[19] Schipper shows that in Greater Poland as well as in Little Poland the courts usually took into consideration the terms stated in the promissory notes and that Jewish creditors collected not only the regular interest for the entire period of the unrestored principal but the accrued usury from unpaid interest as well. Another important aspect of the credit transaction was that the interest was often remitted in agricultural goods (cattle, fowl, fish, fruit, corn, honey, etc.) because debtors were short of cash.[20]

Indeed, the research of court records produced three types of loan contracts:

1. Terminal loans with interest charged only if principal is not returned at the specified time;
2. Contracts providing for terminal payment of principal and interest with additional payment of compounded interest after the expiration of the agreed terminal point;
3. Terminal loans providing for an automatic increase of the principal sum and payment of interest on the latter following the expiration of the terminal point.

Noting the particular burdensome provisions of the last two types of loan contracts, Schipper points out that they were obviously designed to make sure that loans were paid up on time.

That the courts protected the creditors rather than the debtors is also evidenced by court decisions in favor of moneylenders who extended loans to underage borrowers, although the royal charter deemed such loans to be invalid.[21] The same general policy of safeguarding the interest of the moneylender is reflected in the analysis of the various forms of pledges against which credit was extended. Pointing to the fact that the royal charters (BI and BII) fail to prescribe the specific ways of credit transaction, although they recognize the fact that loans can be made against movable and immovable pledges, Schipper demonstrated that the country's growing need for credit dictated a number of significant developments that provided both the lender and the borrower respectively with the necessary protection and incentive. Thus, in practice, two methods of pledging real property were instituted:

1. The so-called *littera sigilatta*, a letter signed and sealed by the debtor in which he pledged his property and which the Jewish creditor could present to the king's functionaries (the voivode or *starosta*) and demand of them proper action if the conditions of the loan were not carried out by the debtor, and

2. The registration of property mortgages in public books, *i.e.*, the municipal or country books, depending on whether the debtor was a nobleman or burgher.[22]

Furthermore, since the royal charters did not expressly forbid Jews to lend money without any tangible security, so-called *listy dłużne* (letters of debt or promissory notes) were introduced in which the debtor's liability related not only to his possessions but also to his person. Here again Schipper emphasizes the fact that although the Statute of Little Poland of 1347 forbade this practice and made it obligatory for Jews to lend only against pledges, in view of the abuses, conflicts, and accusations that Jews forge the letters of debt, the practice not only continued but was almost always recognized by the courts. To protect themselves against the accusations of false notes, Jewish creditors requested their Christian debtors to sign separate documents[23] that not only would the payment of the loan be carried out according to the stated terms of the agreement but that the debtor would take no steps that might cause the creditor any loss or accuse the latter of having forged or altered the terms of the original letter of debt.[24] Eventually, as the money economy grew, underwriting by guarantors became a common method of securing loans, and court records reveal that the method introduced, which was one of collective obligation (*con-*

jucta manu) on the part of the borrower as well as his guarantor, also worked in favor of the Jewish moneylender.[25]

In his treatment of Jewish credit on mortgaged land, Schipper is of the opinion that the wording of article 25 of the Boleslas Charter of 1264 (BI) has been preserved in a corrupted form and therefore lacks explicit reference to this kind of security. His conclusion is based on a critical comparison of this article with its corresponding clauses in the prototypic charters of Austria, Hungary, and Bohemia (the *Fredericianum* of 1244, *Bellanum* of 1251, and *Ottocarianum* of 1254-1255) as well as on the fact that

> the aphoristically expressed article 25 in BI is complemented by article 26 of the charter granted by Casimir the Great in 1364 and 1367 in which the Jewish creditor is assured of protection in case he is attacked in his peaceful possession of land held as security for a loan.[26]

Furthermore, while the Hungarian charter of Bela IV provides that the Jewish lender is entitled only to the yielded produce (*fructus provenientes*) of the mortgaged land, articles 32 and 34 of BIII allow the Jewish creditor to hold such land in lease until the loan is paid up. Indeed, court records reveal many instances in which Jewish creditors took over temporarily mortgaged land or let it be administered by a Christian nobleman responsible to the creditor for the latter's proceeds from that land.

Courts in Greater Poland as well as in Little Poland also granted Jewish creditors ownership rights to mortgaged lands in instances in which loans were never paid up. In such cases the Jewish owner had the right to demand that the Christian population settled on the land carry out various public obligations. In this connection Schipper points out that professional moneylenders knew how to proceed in order to secure for themselves priority in claiming ownership rights to a mortgaged property when it had more than one lien.[27]

Regarding movable pledges, Schipper notes that Jewish moneylenders were allowed to accept all kinds of objects, with the exception of church articles and things showing blood stains, but the accepted pawns consisted mostly of furred clothing, especially embellished fur-lined topcoats used by the nobles, silk, woolens, rings and chains, expensive belts and sabres, etc. What is important is that the law (BI, articles 6, 33) protected the Jewish moneylender against any loss if he unwittingly accepted stolen objects. While the ecclesiastical authorities demanded at the Synod of Łęczyca (1285) that such pawns be returned to their rightful owners and that the Jewish moneylender suffer the loss, in practice the latter could claim his loan as well as the interest as long as he could prove that the stolen pawn was accepted openly during the daytime and declared his unawareness and innocence under oath. By making a deposit in gold, a Christian could obtain a warrant to search a Jewish home for stolen goods. But if the search did not produce the anticipated results, the gold was forfeited to the State, and this law persisted in spite of the numerous complaints by the burghers whose stolen goods were sold to Jews by thieves.[28]

Legislation and policies designed to safeguard the transactions of Jewish moneylenders are also reflected in the manner in which claim executions could be carried out. As indicated above, the creditor's claim on the debtor bore upon the latter's possessions as well as person. The voivode or *starosta* could put the delinquent debtor to work in the castle, where he remained until the creditor received his entire claim, and if the debtor did not report to work he could temporarily lose his personal freedom and become himself an object that could be pawned. At times the burden of work fell also on the debtor's relatives. In cities the municipal authorities carried out the same function of executing claims against burghers. Schipper points out, however, that one cannot find a single case in the court records of Cracow showing that a Jew deprived a Christian debtor of his freedom. But there is evidence showing that Christian debtors were expelled from the city as a result of unremitted Jewish claims.[29]

In actions taken against the debtor's possessions, the latter's right to regain pawned objects expired after one year and six weeks at the end of which the Jewish creditor could do with them as he pleased after showing the pledge to the voivode. In the case of mortgaged land or real estate, the debtor's right to regain it was valid for three years and three months after which the Jewish creditor could either sell it or claim title to it.[30]

The Evolution of Jewish Moneylending

In tracing the scope, dimensions, and evolution of Jewish participation in the credit business, Schipper discerns two main periods: (1) the early period prior to 1384 and (2) the later period from 1384 until the end of the fifteenth century.[31]

The Period of Unrestricted Credit Activities

Compared with the West, professional credit operations began in Poland rather late because cities and a merchant class did not exist in the country prior to the thirteenth century, that is, before the German colonization, and it was not until the turn of the fourteenth century that the growing cities needed credit. But even before the growth of cities and for a long time thereafter, the shortage of capital had already constituted an acute problem among the rulers and nobles as a result of frequent wars, the need to redeem land and estates from foreign occupants, limited amount of precious metals, poor currency policies, etc. Jewish arrivals from Germany seem to have been in a position to satisfy, to an extent, the need for credit because they either brought with them some capital from the West or accumulated money from commercial activities conducted in Poland. Many were fit to act as bankers and mint masters by virtue of their knowledge and experience. In addition, there were other circumstances which put the Jews, as providers of credit, in a preferred position. Chief among them was the hatred and distrust which developed between the German burghers and the indigenous landed population. The antagonism, stemming initially from ethnocultural differences, continued long after the Germans began to Polonize because it took on the form of an economic struggle between the countrymen and the city dwellers. The Polish *szlachta* saw its position threatened by the burghers, especially the city patriciate which was mostly of German extraction, when the latter's position and wealth began to show unmistakable signs of strength. In the view of the nobility, the growing wealth of the city patriciate stemmed from the organized pressures of the municipalities to keep the prices of agricultural products at the lowest possible level. This antagonism prompted the nobility to turn for credit to the Jews who also disliked the burghers for their Germanic descent, the anti-Jewish sentiments which they brought with them to Poland, and, above all, their continuous attempts to prescribe and limit Jewish economic activities in the cities. Schipper demonstrates that the court records of that period show indeed that Jewish credit transactions were made mainly with the nobility and that their financial relationships with the burghers were, as a rule, limited.[32]

The last decades of the fourteenth century and the first decades of the fifteenth century (the first phase of the later period, 1384-1423) are characterized by Schipper as the time during which Jewish credit transactions flourished. Its main centers of operation were Poznań (and Kalisz), Cracow, Warsaw, and to a lesser extent Lwów and Łuck. Besides doing business individually with the landed gentry as well as with petty landowners and burghers in the vicinity, Jewish bankers in these centers often organized partnerships and consortia to reach more distant territories all over Poland as well as abroad and to meet the demands of royalty, high nobility, and upper clergy.

The largest number of professional Jewish moneylenders, about fifty, is accounted for in Poznań. But only three of them can be considered to have been truly important bankers: Muszko the Rich (of Pyzdry), Aaron, and Jordan. Based on evidence gleaned from various sources, especially from the documents published by Lekszycki, Wuttke, and Piekosiński, Schipper describes the scope and details of their considerable activities. He is in a position to point out that of the three the most active banker was Aaron, who worked with his two sons. Besides the local gentry, their clients included King Ladislas Jagiello, the voivode of Kalisz, a number of castellans, and other high Polish dignitaries. The amounts of their single claims varied from 100 to 700 marks, and they became owners of foreclosed lands and demesnes since most of their loans were guaranteed by mortgages of rural properties. Jordan, who conducted his business together with his wife and son Abraham, pursued a similar policy. They lent their money to nobles only on mortgages or good guarantees. Among the bigger loans Schipper notes one, given by Muszko the Rich together with his son and another Jewish creditor, which amounted to 1,000 marks ($5,000). Muszko's debtors included rich landowners and ecclesiastical dignitaries in Great Poland as well as in Pomerania and Silesia. Other Jewish bankers in Poznań, David of Kalisz and Jacob of Kalisz, lent sums from 116 to 780 marks to the city of Breslau and other municipalities in Silesia.[33]

Although the number of Jewish professional bankers in Cracow was much smaller than that in Poznań, only about twenty, the credit operations conducted in this city, in which the Polish kings and the highest dignitaries resided, were quantitatively much greater and qualitatively more variegated. The greatest Jewish bankers—Lewko, Josman, Smerlin, Chaskel, and others—lived in Cracow, and among their debtors one can find the most prominent Polish personalities: kings, dukes, princes, archbishops, voivodes, castellans, and other high officials, even some important city patricians. That the Jewish bankers in Cracow were the richest in Poland can be seen from the sums of money which they lent to Polish kings, according to the sources. A consortium of Jewish bankers provided Casimir the Great with a loan of 15,000 marks ($75,000). Lewko, son of Jordan, gave Casimir's successor, the Hungarian King Louis of Anjou, a loan in the amount of 30,000 gulden, about $120,000! The same Lewko lent varying sums to King Ladislas Jagiello (1386-1434) and Queen Jadwiga (1374-1399). By the end of the fourteenth century all ducal real estate and movable possessions of Ziemowit II, Prince of Mazovia, which included also the province of Kujavia, were mortgaged to a group of Cracow bankers which besides Lewko included Smerlin, Josman, and Andreas. Ziemowit's debts were underwritten by Queen Jadwiga and eventually paid up in 1398 by her husband, Ladislas Jagiello.[34]

Noting that the great credit transactions were usually made by consortia rather than individual bankers and that Cracow bankers had the financial support of the experienced and competent Jewish bankers from Silesia, Schipper points out that the great majority of claims amounted here, as in Poznań, to no more than fifty *grzywny*, although apart from royal debts Jewish claims on the nobles were often quite sizable, from 450 to 1400 *grzywny* (*grossi*).[35]

Schipper devotes considerable space in his *Studies* to Lewko, the Jewish financial potentate of Cracow. Based on information in the oldest records of Cracow,[36] he constructs a genealogical table of the House of Lewko and describes in detail its financial activities, stressing the fact that Lewko's career and success were due, mainly, to his close relationship with Casimir the Great to whom he made available considerable sums of money. In return, Casimir protected and rewarded his *vir discretus*, as Lewko is referred to in some of the documents, in more than one way. Not only was Lewko assisted by the kings (Casimir and his successors) in collecting his claims from high nobles and burghers, but he became the lessee of royal mints and the salt mines in Bochnia and Wieliczka as well as collector of municipal fees (together with Jan Borek, the king's pantrymaster). Casimir the Great granted him, as a token of recognition for services rendered, two houses on the Jewish street in Cracow. Besides these and other houses, Lewko owned considerable real estate holdings in the city, a number of lots, and a brewery, since he was also a realtor in city lands and a creditor of the city fathers and prominent Cracow burghers, such as Wierzynek, with whom he entered in various commercial transactions. Legends developed around his riches and influence, but the complaints against him, submitted to the king and even to Pope Boniface IX by burghers as well as certain nobles, were useless. Even King Louis of Anjou, whose attitude can hardly be described as friendly, depended on Lewko's wealth. Although the credit of this Hungarian ruler of the Polish state was seriously questioned, Lewko granted him the requested loans when powerful magnates agreed to guarantee them. Lewko continued to be the chief creditor of Queen Jadwiga and Ladislas Jagiello, who at times guaranteed the loans made by certain dignitaries of their court while the huge sums they themselves borrowed were guaranteed by many powerful magnates. Some of these debts were indeed paid up by the guarantors to Lewko's wife and sons, who took over the extensive credit transactions of their father after his death. By 1409 when most outstanding claims were collected by the common effort of the family, Lewko's heirs began conducting their financial affairs, instances of which are cited by Schipper, individually. By 1422 they were conducted by his grandchildren, particularly Kanaan who, Schipper carefully notes, owned two villages.[37]

Schipper brings out also a number of interesting details concerning the credit transactions of the two other leading Jewish bankers in Cracow: Smoyl, with his son Smerlin, and Josman. While Smoyl dealt mostly with Cracow burghers, his son Smerlin, who began with a modest inheritance, became the creditor of nobles and the clergy and grew to be wealthy enough to be able to lend, in 1404, the sum of 700 marks on a mortgage of three villages. Smerlin's wealth became part of the Christian community because his wife and children converted to Christianity when he died. Although Josman's clients came mostly from among the petty nobles and burghers and his individual loans did not, as a rule, exceed eighty *grzywny*, except for a documentary entry showing one loan in the amount of 1,000 marks, he must have had at his disposal great capital resources. This can be seen by the number of his debtors, including the municipality itself and some city fathers, and by the fact that he was among the partners who financed the loan granted to Prince Ziemowit of Mazovia. Schipper notes also that Josman owned three houses in Cracow, a sizable lot, the Jewish bathhouse, and some other properties which he took over from his landed debtors elsewhere.[38]

The dimensions of Jewish credit transactions in Cracow are indicated by a court litigation in 1428 in which King Ladislas Jagiello, represented by the nobleman Mikołaj Dunda, accused a Cracow alderman of having appropriated to himself money advanced by the Jews to the royal treasury in the fantastic amount of 500,000 florins![39]

In contrast to Cracow, the hub of Jewish financial operations, credit transactions in the principal cities of other Polish regions were considerably smaller. Warsaw, for instance, had only a few second-rank bankers whose loans seldom exceeded twenty to thirty marks. In Volhynia the only known and important Jewish banker was Jacob Słomkowicz of Łuck who acted here as the creditor of the high nobility but whose major transactions were carried out in partnership with Lewko.

As for Red Ruthenia, Schipper infers from the pertinent sources that in comparison to the western parts of the country this region, as a whole, was lagging in its economic development. Financial operations were generally limited, with the exception of Lwów where the bulk of credit transactions betray a typically commercial character in view of the trade activities conducted there with the East. The loans of the only three professional moneylenders known in this region (Shlomo, Jacob, and Shana) were indeed small, short-term advances of money given as a rule at frequent intervals to local merchants. At the same time Schipper emphasizes that Wolczko and Detko, who acted in Red Ruthenia as the financial representatives of the king, performing a variety of economic functions, should not be put in the category of professional bankers, although their credit transactions were both sizable and extensive. They were actually drawn into moneylending by virtue of their positions and close relationships with state dignitaries who became their debtors, but it was not their main occupation.[40]

The Statute of Warta and the Credit Decline

The initial basic tendency of the royal charters to safeguard the interests of the Jewish creditors, echoed by the courts, began to give way when the opposition of the indebted nobility to the king's favorable policy towards his Jewish *servi camerae* became a serious political problem. The growing cries of debtors among the nobles that "the insatiable appetite of the Jews for usurious money is aiming to deprive the Christians of their wealth and possessions even more than of their religion" could be alleged by reason of the general rise of Jewish assets in the country and the fact that Jews began more often to occupy foreclosed properties mortgaged by their debtors. The accusations of the nobility were eagerly reiterated by the clergy at its synod in Wieluń-Kalisz held in 1420, which reinstated the old Church resolutions designed to separate the Jews culturally as well as economically. The synod demanded of the king that he limit usury in order to lighten the burden on the Christians. The pressures exerted by the *szlachta* and the clergy, and the anti-Jewish excesses in Poznań (1399) as well as in Cracow (1407 and 1423) where city dwellers attempted to get rid of their debts by acts of violence (characterized in the sources as signs of "God's wrath" on the Jews for their "usurious perversity"), led the king to confirm the statute, adopted by the noble estate which assembled in 1423 in Warta, forbidding Jews to lend money on mortgages and promissory notes.[41]

The Statute of Warta, Schipper demonstrates, had a decisive effect on Jewish credit operations. It marked the end of the prime period of that economic activity and the beginning of a new phase in which both the scope and character of Jewish moneylending underwent a strong decline. Since the new legislation prohibited the lending of money on mortgages and promissory notes, credit became a riskier business and therefore the size and duration of loans as well as the frequency of credit transactions decreased considerably. The interest rate dropped (36 percent to 86 percent compared with the previous 54 percent to 108 percent) and city dwellers (mostly petty merchants, shopkeepers, and artisans), rather than the landed gentry, became the clients of Jewish moneylenders. In view of the fact that the Warta Statute permitted the lending of money on the security of movable valuables only, the Jewish banks now assumed the character of pawnshops.[42]

All these changes, Schipper points out, are especially reflected in the sources from Great Poland and Little Poland, where the Jewish credit operations had flourished most and where the money economy attained a degree of development higher than in other parts. Thus, documents pertaining to Jewish credit in Greater Poland after 1423 are found mostly in the municipal records of Poznań, and these documents disclose loans to merchants, craftsmen, and peasants, but none to members of the *szlachta*. In addition to movable pledges, credit agreements with burghers were declared and registered in the city council which provided the Jewish creditor assurances that it would help him collect his claim. But there were also cases of loans given to burghers on mortgages of city real estate, and borrowers from among the peasants often pledged their land as security. Thus the prohibition of the Statute of Warta, Schipper points out, was not fully and strictly carried out even in Greater Poland when the credit transactions involved burghers or peasants. Nonetheless, credit operations diminished here to such an extent that only four Jewish moneylenders can be adduced from the Poznań records for the years 1423-1453. Most of their loans amounted to two or three marks and none exceeded fifty marks.[43]

A similar situation prevailed in Little Poland. In contrast to the preceding period, the Cracow records for 1425-1454 are almost silent. The Jewish moneylenders who continued to function in Cracow, only four in number, hardly resembled their predecessors: the Lewkos, Josmans, and Smerlins. While the place of the latter was taken by powerful bankers who arose among the Christians, the few Jewish moneylenders could now find their clients only among the artisans, and lending in exchange for pawned objects became the dominant form of Jewish credit. Noting that for a period of thirty years following the proclamation of the Warta Statute the records do not contain a single credit transaction based on a *littera obligatoria* or against mortgaged real estate, Schipper points to the fact that pawning became the source of all kinds of accusations on the part of the Christian borrowers. The lower city classes, the artisans and the laborers, accused Jews of knowingly accepting stolen goods as pawns, including items stolen from churches, and used these accusations in order to incite riots against their Jewish creditors, such as took place in Bochnia in 1445 and 1448.[44]

But the effect of the Warta Statute was not uniform in all of Poland. Its implementation depended to a great extent on the conditions and needs prevailing in the various regions of the country which differed in their economic development. Thus, in Mazovia, economically less advanced and politically particularistic for a very long time, local legislation regulating the relationship between landowners and their Jewish creditors continued to favor the latter. The law here remained strict with debtors who did not remit their debts on time. It provided creditors with special prerogatives in collecting their claims, including the right to dispossess. Hence, a certain increase in Jewish moneylenders (five in Warsaw) and credit transactions during the second quarter of the fifteenth century.[45]

The Warta Statute was even less meaningful and less effective in Red Ruthenia, as in the eastern regions of Poland generally, where the German colonization or urbanization under German law started comparatively late and proceeded at a much slower pace. Here the main sources, the *Akta grodzkie i ziemskie* (Town and Country Documents), besides disclosing an active participation of Jews in economic endeavors other than sheer moneylending, reveal a number of Jewish bankers whose credit transactions with high Polish dignitaries, magnates, and lords were as considerable as those of Lewko or Wolczko a generation earlier. The leading figure among those bankers was Szachna of Lwów who advanced money to the king (500 marks in 1444 on a mortgaged palace at Lwów), the voivode of Podolia (against mortgaged villages), Prince Świdrigełło (King Jagiello's youngest brother), the castellan of Chełm, the *starosta* of Trembowla, the Archbishop of Lwów, and others. But being involved in extensive commercial activities, Szachna also borrowed money from Christians and used the money of Jews who were encouraged to deposit their savings with him.

The nobility of Red Ruthenia borrowed also from other Jewish businessmen active in this region: Izaczko Sokołowicz of Halicz, David of Przemyśl, Izaczko of Lwów, all of whom extended their loans on land mortgages or promissory notes, both practices fully recognized by the courts as if the Warta Statute did not exist. Schipper also notes that the records of the city of Lwów for 1440-1448 provide a considerable amount of data pertaining to smaller credit transactions with the city dwellers, Armenians and Ruthenians, based on pledges of valuables and disclosing that many Jewish women acted here as moneylenders.[46]

The incongruity of the limitations imposed on credit operations by the Warta Statute with the prevailing economic needs of the country and their inapplicability in various regions is evidenced also in the attempts of the central power to eliminate the restrictions. In 1453, King Casimir IV (1447-1492) indeed succeeded in annulling the limitations, but he was soon forced to restore them. He reinstated the restrictions in the new Nieszawa Statute of 1454 in response to loud protests of the *szlachta* and the growing political power of the Church led by the energetic and influential Cardinal Zbigniew Oleśnicki. The latter's enmity towards the Jews was spread both by the local clergy and by the notorious Father John Capistrano who, having aroused Christians in Germany and Silesia to acts of violence against Jews, came in 1454 to Cracow to do the same in Poland.[47]

The Relative Reactivation

Although the intensive anti-Jewish propaganda had its repercussions in the form of tensions and strained relationships between Christians and Jews, Jewish credit operations experienced only a temporary recession which, in the case of Cracow, was equally due to a major conflagration in 1455 in which Jews suffered very great losses. In Cracow Jewish credit activities began to grow again in the 1460's. In Poznań signs of revived moneylending activities can be traced to a new immigration of Jews from Silesia after 1453 when a wave of persecutions swept Germanic lands. With new capital, financial experience, and the necessary spirit of enterprise, these Jews brought Jewish credit operations in Poland back to life.[48]

Thus, two Silesian Jews, Daniel and his brother, established a big bank in Poznań in 1457. Soon thereafter another Silesian Jew, Shlomo of Glogau, founded an even larger bank. A number of lesser moneylenders and pawnbrokers provided loans to local merchants and artisans.

In Cracow a similar development took place. A Jew from Frankfurt-am-Main, Moses Fischel, married to a rich widow who owned a bank in Prague, appeared on the scene and assumed the role played a century earlier by Lewko. The Fischels became the creditors of King Casimir IV and his successors, Jan Olbracht (1492-1501) and Alexander (1501-1506), as well as Cardinal Frederick, the son of Casimir IV. Citing various sources, Schipper brings out a considerable number of details concerning the extensive money transactions of the Fischels and the many court litigations in which they were involved. Among other things, he notes that in 1499 the king remitted his debts to Fischel by turning over to him the collection of the Jewish poll tax in Greater Poland. And in 1505 the debts of the royal family, in the amount of 2,000 marks, were made good by granting Fischel the right to collect that tax in the whole country.

Fischel's wife was a royal creditor in her own right. The fact that Casimir IV allowed her to live inside his Cracow palace bespeaks his considerable obligations to her. Both he and Jan Olbracht owed her money which King Alexander paid up in 1504 by granting her the right to mint coins of her own silver to the value of the principal loan (1,000 florins) and the accrued interest (600 florins). Among her clients there were also higher ecclesiastical dignitaries, as evidenced by the fact that one of her litigants in court was Jan Rzeszowski, the Bishop of Cracow, as well as mortgagors from among the rich burghers.[49]

None of the other Jewish moneylenders who were active in Cracow at that time and subsequently could compare with the Fischels, although there were among them substantial bankers like Abraham Bohemus and Ozer of Opoczno who became the leading court bankers in the beginning of the sixteenth century under the rule of Sigismund I (1506-1548). The other known creditors were David Głownia (Lapides) with his wife and sons, and Moses Lewko, the grandson of the famous Lewko of earlier times, but they dealt chiefly with the burghers of Cracow and their credit was based in the main on pledges of valuables. The pawnshop of the Głownia family was indeed a great storehouse of expensive objects and articles: jewelry, silver, textiles, clothing, etc. Generally, Schipper notes, the credit activities in Cracow by the end of the Middle Ages were burgher directed since the records of that city as well as the records of Kazimierz contain a great number of entries pertaining to small-size loans, seldom more than 200 florins, made by the city dwellers against movable securities.[50]

Significantly, the new Jewish immigration from the West in the second half of the fifteenth century had little or no effect in Mazovia and the eastern provinces of Poland. In contradistinction to the western regions and its main centers, Poznań and Cracow, where this immigration brought about a considerable reactivation of credit operations, the situation in Mazovia and Red Ruthenia remained unchanged almost till the end of the Middle Ages. The place of Szachna was taken by his son, Joseph, and men like Samson of Żydaczów, Joseph of Hrubieszów, and Szania of Bełz. Like their predecessors, these bankers were more involved in other economic activities than credit, the latter representing a concomitant to the former rather than a main occupation. Moreover, the credit was mainly extended to the nobility against land mortgages in spite of the existing legal prohibitions. The sources, for instance, do not show a single case of a loan given by Samson of Żydaczów on a pledge or even a promissory note, and Samson was the temporary owner of two villages mortgaged to him by Lady Anne and her son John in 1461 on a loan of forty *grossi.* While the royal treasury records show credit transactions with Casimir IV involving notes, one cannot say whether these transactions related to outright loans extended by the Jewish court bankers (Szania of Bełz and Joseph of Hrubieszów) or advances against collected royal duties. Generally, the court records of Lwów, Schipper notes, include only a limited number of cases relating to moneylending, and it appears that the Jews, rather than Christians, were in debt because they often bought goods from the Christian merchants on credit. The situation changed radically, however, in the last decade of the fifteenth century when, as a result of an intensive campaign initiated by the burghers of Lwów to undermine Jewish commercial activities, many Jews began to engage feverishly in moneylending.[51]

The natural reluctance and disinclination of Jews to enter into moneylending and make it their occupational source of income is even more perceptible and unmistakably evident in Lithuania.

United with the Polish monarchy through the marriage of Queen Jadwiga with Jagiello in 1386, the vast Lithuanian territory of pagans, who converted to Christianity five centuries later than the Poles, was still in its early stages of economic development. Great stretches of land were hardly touched by colonizing hands, and the few existing cities were as much agricultural in character as urban. The Jews who settled there in Grodno, Brest, Łuck, and Troki obtained their first *Privilegia* from Grand Duke Vitold, Jagiello's brother and the virtual authority in Lithuania, in 1388-1389 but, characteristically, these charters, although patterned after the Polish *Privilegium* of Boleslas, contain none of the provisions and regulations concerning moneylending transactions, so conspicuous in the Polish document. In fact, the Vitold charters make no mention of moneylending although they refer to a number of other economic activities (commerce, agriculture, leasing of industries and revenues, crafts) in which Jews were occupied. For a period of over a century (1389-1494) in which there were no conflicts with the Lithuanian gentry, the so-called boyars, or the city dwellers, who constituted still a relatively small and weak class, the Jews in Lithuania had neither reason nor need to engage in credit activities and to live from usury. Schipper notes that the Lithuanian sources mention only a single case of a loan, given to a nobleman in 1454 by Jaczko of Brest who was not a banker but the lessee of Prince Świdrigełło's customs. Even Silesian (or Polish) Jews who were moneylenders and who came to Lithuania in considerable numbers after the persecutions and expulsions of 1453-1455 chose to engage here in endeavors other than moneylending. Those with capital preferred to become the lessees of ducal enterprises and public revenues rather than bankers.[52]

In summarizing this Lithuanian period in which Jewish credit operations are so conspicuously absent, Schipper says:

> It is no accident that the historical sources, containing so many interesting details about Jewish land estates, commercial transactions and leasing, bring no information whatever about Jewish banking. Obviously, there were no professional Jewish moneylenders in Lithuania and the need for money on the part of the

Grand Duke and the magnates must have been adequately satisfied by public fees and rents which were paid on their behalf by the Jewish colonizers, leaseholders and merchants. Only by the very end of the fifteenth century did the Grand Duke and the boyars begin to borrow sizeable sums from Jews in order to pay for war disbursements and the expenses of sumptuous court life. When the Jewish resources became low, methods of exploiting the "treasury serfs", so often practiced in the West, were implemented; Jews were expelled from the [Lithuanian] duchy in 1495 and their remaining possessions were confiscated. A few years later, in 1503, the Duke again invited the Jews to Lithuania which was not worse a "transaction" than the expulsion because high fees were collected from the returnees for the privilege to return.[53]

Conclusions

In examining the evolution of Jewish participation in the business of moneylending, taking under consideration its scope, dimensions, geographic distribution, participants, and fluctuations, Schipper makes a number of important generalizations indicative of his approach and his interpretation of the pertinent historical material which he assembled. In the first place he concludes that, compared with the total number of Jews in medieval Poland, the number of professional moneylenders among them was indeed small. To demonstrate this conclusion, Schipper, besides attempting to determine on the basis of the sources the number of Jews primarily engaged in the credit business, assigned himself also the task of calculating the size of the Jewish population in the whole country, a task that he tackles several times in order to arrive at the nearest possible estimation as additional evidence was brought to light. Despite the obvious difficulties stemming from the limited and incomplete historical data, Schipper proceeds to trace the growth and size of the Jewish population on the basis of the number of Jewish communities mentioned in the primary sources and the extant tax records, the so-called *census annuns* lists, according to which Jews living in stone or mason-built houses paid four gulden to the king's treasury while those living in small wooden houses paid two gulden. Schipper's estimate of 12,000 Jews in his *Studies* was based on forty-five documented Jewish communities.[54] However, three years later in his special article devoted to the subject, the estimate rose to 16,000 Jews because an additional nine Jewish communities could be accounted for in the fifteenth century.[55]

The interesting table showing the historical growth as well as the geographic expansion of the Jewish communities in the *Virtshaftsgeshikhte* represents a reiteration of the data and method of calculation presented already by Schipper in his *Kultur-geshikhte fun di Yidn in Poyln beysn mitlalter* published in 1926. The number of communities listed here is still bigger as a result of new investigations (especially those conducted by Ringelblum in the province of Mazovia) which produced additional Jewish settlements, bringing the total number up to sixty-one (ten until the end of the fourteenth century, an additional eighteen during the first half of the fifteenth century, and still another thirty-three communities in the second half of the fifteenth century). Noting that the concentration of the older communities (established before the fifteenth century) in the western and southwestern regions was superseded by a growing number of new Jewish settlements in the northern and eastern regions during the fifteenth century, Schipper's estimate of the Jewish population in the sixty-one communities (ten in Greater Poland, ten in Little Poland, ten in Mazovia, five in Kujavia, two in Pomerania, seventeen in Red Ruthenia, three in Volhynia, three in Podolia) was increased to about 18,000. Based on the amount of Jewish taxes paid in certain cities and utilizing other data culled from various sources to determine the number of Jewish homes in various locations and the average number of Jewish dwellers in these homes, Schipper calculates that the three "big cities" in Poland (Poznań, Cracow, and Lwów) had about 1,400 Jewish inhabitants each and that the other fifty-eight communities comprised approximately 10,500 Jews, based on an average of twelve Jewish homes with fifteen dwellers in each of those communities. Thus, altogether he assumes that about 14,700 Jews lived in the sixty-one communities. In addition, there is documentary indication that some Jews settled in villages among Christians.

Assuming that their ratio to the latter was 1:5, based on the fact that documents from the seventeenth and eighteenth centuries disclose a proportion of 1:4, Schipper calculates the Jewish village population to have amounted at the time to 3,000 Jews. Therefore, the total Jewish population in Poland in the second half of the fifteenth century is estimated by him to have been around 18,000.

Finally, in his contribution on the subject to the encyclopedic volumes of *Żydzi w Polsce Odrodzonej* (Jews in Reborn Poland) published in the early thirties, Schipper further corrects his estimate of 18,000 Jews in the Polish "Crown" with an additional 6,000 Jews in Lithuanian communities, omitted in his previous calculations, thus bringing the total to 24,000.[56]

Compared with this relatively sizable number of Jews in the Polish-Lithuanian monarchy, the number of professional Jewish moneylenders was quite small. Even at the height of Jewish credit operations (1384-1423) when the number of Jewish communities was still limited (between ten and twenty-eight), not too many Jews engaged in moneylending, and those who did generally dealt in more substantial credit transactions with the Polish royalty and high nobility rather than with the people. In Cracow, the political and economic center of Poland, there were only twenty Jewish bankers in the first half of the fifteenth century among two hundred Jewish families settled there. In Warsaw, out of forty-five families, four to five families were engaged in professional moneylending.[57] In the subsequent phases of Jewish credit operations (after 1423 and after 1455) the number of professional Jewish moneylenders decreased as the Jewish population grew to more than twice as many communities as had existed before the Statute of Warta. Most importantly, in the newer communities established in the eastern regions, in Red Ruthenia and Volhynia, "we do not meet a single professional Jewish banker until after the rule of Ladislas Jagiello,"[58] and subsequently the extension of credit was here, as in Lithuania, seldom a professional occupation in itself. It was rather an "annex to commerce" while most of the accumulated capital in Jewish hands was invested in leasing public revenues and industries.

This was also true to an extent in Cracow where the great Jewish bankers like Lewko engaged in both commercial and leasing activities. But if the generalized stigma of the Jew as a "usurer" could be putatively expected in Greater Poland, it had hardly any justification in relationship to Jews who settled in Podolia, Red Ruthenia, Volhynia, and Lithuania.[59]

Secondly, Jews were not the only moneylenders in Poland. The theory that Jews could monopolize the money market and satisfy their "insatiable usurious lust" because Christians were forbidden by the Church to practice usury is false. In spite of repetitious and continuous threats of punishment in heaven and on earth and the officially reiterated prohibition at the Church Synods in 1320, 1402, and 1420, Christians engaged in moneylending at interest directly and openly or under various forms and disguises: loans for the use of land, purchase of rents, sales on credit, etc. In fact, the clergy itself must have engaged in outright usury if it was necessary for the Synod of 1402, at which the Breslau Bishop Kurowski admonished the clergy, to adopt the *ne clerici usuras exerceant* resolution. Citing documentary evidence, Schipper proves that during the fifteenth century, and especially by the end of it, all Polish classes, even the gentry, practiced usury. Credit agreements of Christian creditors often provided for an augmentation of the principal as a method of circumventing the canonical prohibition of charging interest. The Christian creditor also often utilized the so-called *damnum in Iudea perceptum* according to which he had the right to borrow money at interest from a Jew on the account of his Christian debtor if the latter did not remit his loan on time. Besides Gniezno, Poznań, and Cracow, Christian moneylenders were particularly active in Mazovia where the Statute of Warsaw was adopted in 1401 in order to prevent them from further ruining the Polish landowners in that province. All this evidence points unmistakably to the fact that credit operations in medieval Poland were not as exclusively Jewish as pictured in the popular opinion of Poles, historically nurtured by anti-Jewish propaganda.[60]

Thirdly, while some Jewish bankers, especially the court bankers, were in a position to extend huge loans to the Polish rulers and people in high positions, the sums of money often represented common efforts on the part of more than one Jewish creditor, in Poland and abroad, to raise the capital. The Jewish bankers from the West who migrated to Poland brought with them certain financial assets that were as important as capital, if not more so, namely: experience, connections, know-how, and competence in financial matters. They not only instituted the proper credit procedures but organized and coordinated their efforts by forming consortia and partnerships and by cooperating with one another. It is in this respect that the rather limited number of Jewish bankers in underdeveloped Poland played an important economic role. A "*hominus novi*"— as Schipper calls him—the Jewish banker represented at the time the indispensable, fermenting factor in the financial sphere of Poland. By introducing more complicated forms of financial transactions, the Jewish creditor was the trailblazer of Poland's progress towards a higher economic stage.[61]

Most importantly, the Jews—especially the Ashkenazi element which initially may have settled in Poland primarily as moneylenders—turned to various other economic activities. In contradistinction to the West where in a long occupational evolution, going back to the early Middle Ages, the Jews were reduced to one economic activity only, that of lending money to the poor, a reversed process took place in medieval Poland due to the specific political and economic conditions which the Jewish moneylenders from the West found in their new country. The Jews, characterized by Gumplowicz as a group with a specific economic function, became in Poland occupationally diversified. Schipper's *Studies* deals at length with the participation of Jews in leasing public revenues, in commerce, in agricultural colonization, handicrafts, and free professions, besides providing a thorough analysis of the forms and extent of Jewish credit operations. It is this occupational diversity that Schipper painstakingly uncovered and brought to light in order to fill an important gap in the history of Jews in Poland, as it was known until his time, and in order to dispel and dismiss the stereotyped views of assimilationists, apologists, and anti-Semites.[62]

Notes

1. *Supra,* Chapter I, pp. 27-29 and pertinent notes; *Studies, op. cit.*, pp. 49, 70.

2. *Studies, op. cit.*, p. 67; *Virtshaftsgeshikhte, op. cit.*, II, p. 103; *Dzieje handlu żydowskiego, op. cit.*, p. 10.

3. *Studies, op. cit.*, p. 42. Schipper cites here the findings and studies of Polish numismatists: I. Połkowski, *Wykopaliska głębockie średniowiecznych monet polskich* (Gniezno: 1876); K. Stronczyński, *Dawne monety polskie* (Piotrków: 1883); Z. Zakrzewski, "O brakteatach z napisami hebrajskimi," *Wiadomości numizmatyczno-archeologiczne*, I-IV (1911-1913). See also *Virtshaftsgeshikhte, op. cit.*, II, p. 101. Cf. Mahler and Ringelblum, *op. cit.*, pp. 23-26; Baron, *op. cit.*, vol. III, pp. 218, 338 n. 58; also, Baron and Kahan, *Economic History, op. cit.*, pp. 252-253.

4. See *Virtshaftsgeshikhte, op. cit.*, II, p. 103; "Dzieje gospodarcze Żydów," *op. cit.*, p. 118; *Dzieje handlu żydowskiego, op. cit.*, p. 10; *Studies, op. cit.*, p. 66. Cf. Baron, *op. cit.*, vol. X, p. 32.

5. *Studies, op. cit.*, p. 53. Schipper relies here mostly on Bondy-Dvorsky, *Regesten zur Geschichte der Juden in Böhmen, Mähren und Schlesien* (Prague: 1905); L. Oelsner, "Schlesische Urkunden zur Geschichte der Juden im Mittelalter," *Archiv für Kunde österreichischen Geschichte Quellen*, XXXI; M. Brann, *Geschichte der Juden in Schlesien* (Breslau: 1896). Cf. R. Rosenthal, "The Oldest Jewish Communities in Silesia," (in Polish translation), *Biuletyn, Żydowski Instytut Historyczny*, No. 34 (1960), pp. 3-27.

6. *Virtshaftsgeshikhte, op. cit.*, II, pp. 104-105.

7. Cf. Mahler and Ringelblum, *op. cit.*, p. 33.

8. *Loc. cit.; Studies, op. cit.*, pp. 67-68; "Dzieje gospodarcze Żydów," *op. cit.*, pp. 118-119; *Dzieje handlu żydowskiego, op. cit.*, pp. 12-13.

9. *Studies, op. cit.*, p. 50; *Dzieje handlu żydowskiego, op. cit.*, p. 13.

10. *Studies, op. cit.*, pp. 70-71. Cf. A. Eisenstein, "Prawda a lichwie żydowskiej w Polsce w XIV wieku," *Miesięcznik żydowski*, II (1932), pp. 161-164. See also Weinryb, *The Jews of Poland, op. cit.*, p. 58.

11. Schipper illustrates the interest of the Polish kings in settling Jews, as a profit-bringing element, on royal rather than private territories with the document cited by F. Piekosiński (*Kodeks Dyplomatyczny Małopolski*, I, No. 60) according to which Boleslas Wstydliwy (the Chaste, 1243-1279) allowed the Cisterians of Koprzywnica to admit any free colonizers on their land "except Jews." Schipper points out that far from being an anti-Jewish interdiction, this was the ruler's way of getting Jewish settlers for himself since immunity clauses

allowing colonists to settle on private lands took them out from under the jurisdiction of the princes and kings. See *Studies, op. cit.*, pp. 42-43. Cf. Baron, *op. cit.*, vol. X, pp. 31 and 313, n. 36. Cf. also B. Mark, "Rzemieślnicy żydowscy w Polsce feudalnej," *Biuletyn, Żydowski Instytut Historyczny*, Nos. 9-10 (1954), p. 8.

12. *Studies, op. cit.*, pp. 71-73. See also *Virtshaftsgeshikhte, op. cit.*, pp. 105-106. Cf. A. N. Frenk, *Ha-'Ironim veha-Yehudim be-Polin* (Warsaw: 1921), pp. 9-11; Halpern, "Jews in Eastern Europe," *op. cit.*, p. 300; Dubnow, *History of Jews in Russia and Poland, op. cit.*, pp. 45-47; B. Mark, "Rzemieślnicy żydowscy w Polsce feudalnej," *op. cit.*, p. 58. Speaking of the German influence in Poland and the charter of Frederick II as the model for charters in Eastern Europe, Parkes notes that the Frederician charter not only nullified the imperial grant of 1238 but abandoned forever the Carolingian model since it recognized that the primary occupation of the Jews in the West was no longer commerce but moneylending, and while charters in Germany were not revised along the lines of the Frederician model, the latter formed the basis of the Hungarian, Bohemian, Silesian, Polish, and Lithuanian charters. Parkes, *The Jew in the Medieval Community, op. cit.*, p. 178.

13. *Studies, op. cit.*, p. 75; "Początki," *op. cit.*, p. 58; "Dzieje gospodarcze Żydów," *op. cit.*, p. 119.

14. See M. Wischnitzer, "On the Occasion of Schipper's Book about the Economic Life of Jews in Poland in the Middle Ages," (in Russian), *Yevreyskaya Starina*, V (1913), p. 133.

15. *Studies, op. cit.*, p. 4; see also pp. 69-70 and the Addenda on pp. 328-351.

16. *Virtshaftsgeshikhte, op. cit.*, II, p. 107 and IV, p. 193. Cf. Halpern, *op. cit.*, p. 300.

17. *Virtshaftsgeshikhte, op. cit.*, IV, pp. 194 f. Quoting here in part the letter of protection issued by Ladislas Jagiello (1387-1434), a new convert to Christianity, and from the decree issued about a century later (in 1504) by Alexander, Schipper indicates to what extent the kings appreciated the Jews as an economic factor for the development of the country. A similar attitude was displayed by Casimir Jagiello (1447-1492) in spite of the opposition and pressures exerted by Cardinal Oleśnicki and the chronicler Jan Długosz. See also *Studies, op. cit.*, p. 73. Cf. Dubnow, *History of Jews in Russia and Poland, op. cit.*, pp. 47 f.; also Baron, *op. cit.*, vol. X, pp. 45 ff. as well as Weinryb, *The Jews of Poland, op. cit.*, pp. 36-37.

18. *Studies, op. cit.*, pp. 73, 80-81; "Początki," *op. cit.*, p. 58; *Virtshaftsgeshikhte, op. cit.*, II, pp. 106-107.

19. *Studies, op. cit.*, p. 82. In view of new evidence that apparently came to Schipper's attention after the publication of his *Studies*, the number of years of interest granted by courts, at least in certain instances, is raised to twenty and twenty-six in the *Virtshaftsgeshikhte, op. cit.*, IV, p. 239.

20. *Studies, loc. cit.*

21. *Studies, op. cit.*, pp. 82-83, 85.

22. *Studies, op. cit.*, p. 76. The *starosta* was the king's officer in charge of the administration of a territorial unit, usually a voivode. In certain parts of the country the *starosta* was in charge of greater territorial units, even of a whole province in which case he was called general *starosta.* Such matters as municipal autonomy in royal cities were under his jurisdiction. He also presided over the criminal courts in the royal cities. See Mahler and Ringelblum, *op. cit.*, p. 51, n. 2.

23. The separate documents, known as *littera fideiussoriae*, constituted a word of honor (*sub fide et honore*). Worded initially in Latin, they were later written in Hebrew also.

24. *Studies, op. cit.*, p. 78.

25. Schipper cites a galaxy of Polish celebrities who acted as guarantors in various loan transactions, especially in loans taken from Jewish bankers by the high nobility and the Polish kings, noting thereby that loans given to burghers were, as a rule, based on collateral security rather than guarantees. *Ibid.*, p. 92.

26. *Ibid.*, pp. 88-89.

27. *Ibid.*, pp. 90, 96.

28. *Ibid.*, pp. 86-87.

29. *Ibid.*, pp. 93-94.

30. *Ibid.*, pp. 91, 94. For sources substantiating the stated general position of the courts in litigations relating to credit transactions, see Mahler and Ringelblum, *op. cit.*, pp. 44-47.

31. See "Dzieje gospodarcze Żydów," *op. cit.*, p. 125. The division of periods varies somewhat in Schipper's earlier works. The *Studies* include in the early period the phase in which credit operations reached thriving proportions, 1384-1425, while the later period from 1425 to 1500 is divided into two phases, 1425-1454 and 1454-1500. The division in the *Virtshaftsgeshikhte* is more in tune with the general vertical division followed by Schipper in this work, that is, from 1241 to 1350 and from 1350 to 1500, distinguishing in the latter three phases: 1350-1423, 1423-1455, and 1455 to 1500.

32. *Studies, op. cit.*, pp. 99-101; *Virtshaftsgeshikhte, op. cit.*, II, pp. 229-231.

33. *Studies, op. cit.*, pp. 106-112; *Virtshaftesgeshikhte, op. cit.*, IV, pp. 233-234; "Dzieje gospodarcze Żydów," *op. cit.*, p. 125.

34. *Studies, op. cit.*, pp. 113-114, 121; *Virtshaftsgeshikhte, op. cit.*, IV, pp. 234-235. On the political relationship between the principality of Mazovia and the Polish kingdom and, in particular, the political considerations underlying the relationship of Prince Ziemowit II to Queen Jadwiga see *The Cambridge History of Poland, op. cit.*, pp. 190, 196.

35. *Studies, op. cit.*, pp. 113-114: *Virtshaftsgeshikhte, op. cit.*, IV, p. 237. The *grzywna* (*grossus*) was the basic silver unit of Polish currency in medieval times. Regarding its fluctuating value see *The Cambridge History of Poland, op. cit.*, p. 448.

36. *Acta scabinalia Cracoviensia; Consalaria Cracoviensia; Codex diplomaticus Universitatis Cracoviensia;* F. Piekosiński, *Kodeks dyplomatyczny miasta Krakowa*; B. Ulanowski, *Najstarsze księgi sądowe ziemi krakowskiej;* the *Kodeks dyplomatyczny Małopolski*, ed. by F. Piekosiński, the Sanguszko Archives, and others.

37. *Studies, op. cit.*, pp. 115-126; *Virtshaftsgeshikhte, op. cit.*, IV, p. 236. Cf. Bałaban, *Historja Żydów w Krakowie i na Kazimierzu*, vol. I, 1304-1655 (Cracow: 1928), pp. 16-23 and his *Historja i literatura żydowska*, vol. I, in the Hebrew translation in *Bet Yisrael be-Polin, op. cit.*, pp. 8-9; also, Weinryb, *The Jews of Poland, op. cit.*, pp. 48, 50, 63, 90-91, 97.

38. *Studies, op. cit.*, pp. 127-129; *Virtshaftsgeshikhte, op. cit.*, IV, pp. 235-237.

39. *Studies, op. cit.*, p. 137. In 1496 one Polish florin amounted to thirty *grossi.* See *The Cambridge History of Poland, op. cit.*, p. 448.

40. *Studies, op. cit.*, pp. 133, 136; *Virtshaftsgeshikhte, op. cit.*, pp. 237-239. Cf. Weinryb, *The Jews of Poland, op. cit.*, pp. 48, 58, 61.

41. *Studies, op. cit.*, pp. 74, 137-138; *Virtshaftsgeshikhte, op. cit.*, IV, p. 240; "Dzieje gospodarcze Żydów, *op. cit.*, p. 125. See Weinryb, *op. cit.*, pp. 43, 49, 60.

42. *Studies, op. cit.*, p. 258; *Virtshaftsgeshikhte, op. cit.*, IV, p. 241.

43. *Studies, op. cit.*, pp. 259-260; *Virtshaftsgeshikhte, op. cit.*, IV, p. 241.

44. *Studies, op. cit.*, pp. 261-263; *Virtshaftsgeshikhte, op. cit.*, IV, p. 242. See Weinryb, *op. cit.*, p. 60.

45. *Studies, op. cit.*, p. 264; *Virtshaftsgeshikhte, op. cit.*, IV, p. 242. Regarding the traditional separatist tendencies of Mazovia see *The Cambridge History of Poland, op. cit.*, pp. 104, 123, 135, 190, 242.

46. *Studies, op. cit.*, pp. 265-267; *Virtshaftsgeshikhte, op. cit.*, IV, pp. 242-243.

47. *Studies, op. cit.*, pp. 268 f. It should be noted that apart from the economic restrictions in relation to Jews, both the Warta and Nieszawa Statutes were the expressions of a political struggle. They aimed at weakening the power of the king, on the one hand, and strengthening the hand of the *szlachta*, on the other. See Mahler, "Di Yidn in amolikn Poyln," *op. cit.*, pp. 27-28. On the political power wielded by Cardinal Oleśnicki and the relationship between him and the liberal Casimir IV, see *The Cambridge History of Poland, op. cit.*, pp. 224-226, especially 233 ff. Regarding Capistrano's activities in Bohemia, Silesia, and Poland, see *Virtshaftsgeshikhte, op. cit.*, III, pp. 184-185; Dubnow,

History of the Jews in Russia and Poland, op. cit., pp. 62 ff.; Baron, *op. cit.*, vol. IX, p. 202 and vol. X, pp. 37, 47; Weinryb, *op. cit.*, pp. 49-50.

48. According to *Studies*, the stagnation of Jewish credit operations lasted until about 1480. In the *Virtshaftsgeshikhte*, however, Schipper amends his previous conclusion in the light of new evidence, especially the documents published by K. Kaczmarczyk, *Akta radzieckie poznańskie, 1434-1470* (Poznań: 1925). See *Virtshaftsgeshikhte, op. cit.*, IV, pp. 243-244 and *Studies, op. cit.*, pp. 268 f.

49. *Studies, op. cit.*, pp. 270-276; *Virtshaftsgeshikhte, op. cit.*, IV, pp. 244-245.

50. *Studies, op. cit.*, pp. 270, 277-278; *Virtshaftsgeshikhte, op. cit.*, IV, pp. 245-246.

51. *Studies, op. cit.*, pp. 278-280; *Virtshaftsgeshikhte, op. cit.*, IV, p. 247.

52. "Dzieje gospodarcze Żydów," *op. cit.*, p. 129; *Virtshaftsgeshikhte, op. cit.*, IV, pp. 266-267, 273. Cf. Mahler, "Di Yidn in amolikn Poyln," *op. cit.*, p. 37. It should be noted that the economic activities of Jews in Lithuania are not treated by Schipper in his *Studies.* Apparently he was not at the time in a position to discuss the subject adequately because he did not have at his disposal the necessary historical evidence. This deficiency, however, is well rectified in the *Virtshaftsgeshikhte*, and subsequent studies.

53. "Dzieje gospodarcze Żydów," *op. cit.*, p. 130. See also *Virtshaftsgeshikhte, op. cit.*, IV, p. 274. Cf. Mahler, "Di Yidn in amolikn Poyln," *op. cit.*, pp. 41-42; Friedman, "Geshikhte fun Yidn in Ukraine," *op. cit.*, pp. 27-28; Weinryb, *The Jews of Poland, op. cit.*, pp. 56-57.

54. *Studies, op. cit.*, Chap. X, pp. 148-156 and Chap. XVIII, pp. 306-324, *passim.*

55. "Razsyeleniye Yevreyev v Polshe i Litvye ot XV do XVIII vyeka," *Istoriya yevreyskogo naroda*, Vol. XI (1914), pp. 105-131.

56. See *Kultur-geshikhte, op. cit.*, pp. 146-150; *Virtshaftsgeshikhte, op. cit.*, III, pp. 189-192; and "Rozwój ludności żydowskiej na ziemiach Rzeczypospolitej," *Żydzi w Polsce Odrodzonej, op. cit.*, I, pp. 21-36. Relying on Schipper's calculations, Mahler suggests that it may be safely assumed that there lived, in fact, in the Polish-Lithuanian monarchy at least 30,000 Jews since besides the communities explicitly mentioned in the historical sources there must have also been other localities in which Jews established communities. Mahler, *Toledot ha-Yehudim be-Polin* (Merḥavia: 1946), pp. 28 f., 93 ff.; *idem.*, "Di Yidn in amolikn Poyln," *op. cit.*, pp. 10-11 and footnote. Cf. Baron, *op. cit.*, vol. X, pp. 36, 317 n. 44; also, the critical judgment of Schipper's calculations by Weinryb in *The Jews of Poland, op. cit.*, pp. 309-311.

57. *Virtshaftsgeshikhte, op. cit.*, IV, p. 233; "Dzieje gospodarcze Żydów," *op. cit.*, p. 121.

58. *Dzieje handlu żydowskiego, op. cit.*, p.14.

59. *Ibid.*, p. 22; *Virtshaftsgeshikhte, op. cit.*, IV, p. 235; *Studies, op. cit.*, p. 264. Cf. B. Mark, "Rzemieślnicy żydowscy w Polsce feudalnej," *op. cit.*, p. 6.

60. *Studies, op. cit.*, pp. 84, 102-103, 105, 261; *Virtshaftsgeshikhte, op. cit.*, IV, p. 232; "Dzieje gospodarcze Żydów," *op. cit.*, p. 125. Cf. Mahler and Ringelblum, *op. cit.*, pp. 49-51. The latter make the following remark: "Who knows whether the hidden usury [of the Christian moneylenders] which was neither controlled nor regulated by the government was not greater than that of the Jews." *Ibid.*, p. 50, n. 3.

61. *Studies, op. cit.*, pp. 99, 114, 131, 140; *Virtshaftsgeshikhte, op. cit.*, IV, p. 237.

62. See Foreword to *Studies, op. cit.*, pp. 1-3; also M. Wischnitzer, "On the Occasion of Schipper's Book . . .," *op. cit.*, pp. 133-137. Parkes also notes that although the new arrivals in Poland from the West "were already accustomed to the specialized life of moneylending . . . the backwardness of Eastern Europe gave them more opportunities for following other trades than they possessed in the West." Parkes, *The Jew in the Medieval Community, op. cit.*, p. 179.

5

Occupational Diversity

In the Polish society of Schipper's time, the stereotype of the Jew as a usurer had not only persisted as part of a historical anti-Jewish legacy but was actually fostered by nationalist anti-Semitic elements and parties. They portrayed the Jews as an unproductive and undesirable race, as an element which traditionally refused to be occupied in strenuous, constructive labor, preferring instead to engage in devious financial speculations and pecuniary trades through which they exploited the hardworking Christians and lived off the fat of the land like parasites.[1]

Thus, while it was important to set the historical record straight with regard to Jewish moneylending activities in medieval Poland, it was equally imperative to bring to light a factual picture of Jews engaged in occupations other than moneylending. And here again Schipper's indefatigable research of the sources, the court records and the aforementioned *Town and Country Documents* in particular, and his critical examination of the available published materials[2] enable him to present an interesting and revealing picture of active Jewish participation in a relatively wide gamut of economic activities: in leasing or managing state enterprises and revenues, in foreign and domestic trade, in agricultural colonization, in the free professions, and in the crafts. Moreover, the information and data were substantial enough to go beyond the mere description of the extent of Jewish involvement in these activities. They provided Schipper with ample evidence for a number of inferences regarding the role of the Jews, even the extent of their indispensibility, in various occupations and in different spheres of economic endeavors. Thus he could decisively prove unfounded the assertions of certain contemporary politicians, churchmen, and professional anti-Semites who sought to discredit the Jews in every possible way and by every possible means, as well as those historians who wittingly or unwittingly served the aims of the former by misreading or distorting the historical record of Polish Jewry.

Management and Lease of Industries and Revenues

Adverting to the fact, already discussed in the *Anfänge des Kapitalismus bei den abendländischen Juden*, that during the early Middle Ages, especially before the rise of urban centers, Jews in the West were often the only currency experts and money changers, and that in the early stages of the Polish state certain Jews from the West were either the masters and managers of the Polish mints (in Gniezno, Poznań, and Cracow) or the lessees of these mints in their capacity as court bankers,[3] Schipper proceeds to show that in enterprises which required financial resourcefulness and administrative experience, the young Polish state could hardly do without Jews.

Even though the documentary evidence for the thirteenth and fourteenth centuries is rather scanty and limited, the mere fact of the repeated Church interdictions at the synods (Breslau in 1267, Buda in 1279, and Łęczyca in 1285) against involving Jews in financial and administrative functions of a public character clearly demonstrates that the Polish kings and nobles indeed entrusted Jews with such functions. Obviously, the disregard for the vigorous opposition of the ecclesiastical leadership was dictated by sheer necessity, not by any Judeophilia.

The importance of the Jews in the area of financial management, on one hand, and the total impractibility and ineffectiveness of the Church interdictions in this respect, on the other, are made more evident by the fact that even the Polish clergy turned to Jews to administer financial matters. Apparently there was no other choice.[4]

The dependence on Jews in managing or leasing the collection of such public revenues as customs, tolls, and rents or the administration of such industries as the royal mints and salt mines are already clearly indicated in the documentation relating to Lewko during the reign of Casimir the Great. It comes even more to the fore in the sources of the fifteenth century. Lewko of Cracow was not only the banker of three Polish kings but also, together with some partners, the lessee of the famous Wieliczka and Bochnia salt mines during the sixties of the fourteenth century.[5] He also managed the Cracow mint and acted as the agent of Bodzianty, the king's administrator (vice regent) of Cracow, in collecting the city taxes from the burghers.[6]

On the basis of the multiple charges by burghers that Jews were counterfeiting money,[7] it is reasonable to assume that there must have been Jews other than Lewko who leased royal or princely mints during the reign of Casimir the Great as well as that of Ladislas Jagiello. However, the documentation from the fifteenth century, which is far more extensive than that of the preceding century, indicates that, rather than managing or leasing mints and taxes, Jews with the necessary funds preferred to lease the collection of royal as well as private customs and tolls. This was an enterprise profitable in many ways because of its direct link to commerce and the fact that duty on the transit of goods was obligatory regardless of the direction in which the wares were shipped. A table, put together by Schipper on the basis of the sources at his disposal, enumerates thirty-one different names of Jewish customs lessees who operated in thirty different localities, some of whom appear several times, during the period extending from 1414 to 1510.[8] Characteristically, most of the localities shown on the table were situated in the less urbanized and Germanized eastern provinces of Poland (Podolia, Red Ruthenia, Volhynia, the regions of Chełm and Lublin) where,

Schipper notes, there was hardly a customs house that was not leased or administered by Jews from 1423 to 1485. A similar situation prevailed in Lithuania during the second half of the fifteenth century. However, this should not lead one to the conclusion that in Greater Poland or Little Poland Jews were not involved to some extent, at least, in the same type of activity, as can be seen from the fact that King Alexander leased the Cracow and Rawa duties to Ozer of Opoczno in 1503. It may seem that way only because documents for that period relating to the western provinces are limited, but what Justus Decius, the liberal-minded private secretary of King Sigismund I and admirer of the Reformation, had to say about the dominant and indispensable role of Jews seems to Schipper to represent a statement closely reflecting the actual situation, rather than an exaggeration, inasmuch as his own investigations provided enough evidence to warrant its acceptance.[9]

At the same time, the wealthier Jewish financiers also leased industrial mines. These enterprises, also mostly in the eastern regions and Lithuania, required more administrative and technical know-how and still larger investments of money which, judging by the evidence, only Jews were in a position to provide. Natko, for example, paid an annual rent of 1,000 *grossi* for the lease of the Lwów customs and another 3,050 *grossi* for leasing the salt works in Drohobycz for a period of two years. The latter sum, according to Schipper, equaled 39,650 Austrian kronen.[10]

Samson of Żydaczów, too, must have had at his disposal considerable capital resources to be in a position, in the years 1466-1473, to lease the mines of Kolomyja, Drohobycz, Dolina, and Żydaczów and at the same time be the leaseholder of transit duties in Kolomyja, Gródek, and Lwów. In 1471 he paid 2,363 *grossi* and delivered a bale of red textile, called *koftyr*, to the royal court for the annual rent of the Lwów and Gródek duties as well as the Drohobycz mine.[11] Entries in the records of the royal treasury for the years 1484-1488 indicate, among other things, that Josko of Hrubieszów paid the sum of 1,146 *grossi* and 319 florins (about 17,609 Austrian kronen) to Casimir IV on account of his three-year lease.[12] The Fischels of Cracow, the greatest lessees of royal revenues in various localities and the leaseholders of the Jewish taxes in Greater Poland, paid 2,500 gulden (about $8,500) in 1504, two Polish stones (64 pounds) of saffron, and ten stones (320 pounds) of pepper for the customs of Łuck. Other big leaseholders in the eastern provinces included, besides the aforementioned Wolczko of Lwów and those indicated above, Jacob Słomkowicz of Łuck, Izaczko Sokołowicz of Hrubieszów, and, in Josko's family, his brother Szania and son Jacob.[13]

The capital resources and experience of the Jews were utilized even more in Lithuania. The so-called "Lithuanian *Metrica*," containing the documents of the Grand Duke's chancery for 1463-1494, abounds with information revealing that the Grand Duke let the Jews manage almost all his ducal revenues and enterprises: duties, estates, mines, breweries, inns, etc. Among the richest and most active Jewish lessees, Schipper includes Enko Ickowicz of Grodno, Sadko Danilowicz and his brother Shamak of Troki, Sason Krawczyk and Doktorowicz of Kiev, Hirsh and Abraham of Brest, Enig (Enoch) Motolivi, Szachna Pesachowicz, Elkon Danilowicz, Israel, Judko, and Jaskal (Ezekiel) of Łuck, and many others. All of these are mentioned in the documents as the Duke's lessees of one enterprise or another, including such industries as the manufacture of wax and pitch, the brewing of beer, the distilling and selling of alcohol in the Duke's inns and taverns. But Schipper notes that here, too, Jews formed partnerships and consortia in order to be able to lease the Duke's great salt and wax industries.[14]

The prevailing system of leasing to Jews, Schipper shows, was both beneficial and responsive to the need of the country and its rulers. The Jews provided the kings and lords with vast sums of ready cash and relieved them of the difficult responsibilities of managing financial and industrial affairs, for which they could hardly find competent people among the native population. Jews also paved the way for further economic development by setting an example of how to run important economic activities efficiently and profitably. This lasted until the petty nobility concluded that it should push the Jews out of these activities in order to take them over themselves.

But until the first signs of this inevitable transposition began to appear in the beginning of the sixteenth century, the Jewish lessees derived considerable profits and other advantages from their investments and hard work. While their returns, obviously, depended on the size of the leased enterprise and their operational efficiency, the documented number of Jewish leaseholders, the growing sums of money put into leasing, and the turnover of invested capital led Schipper to conclude that the business was lucrative enough to justify the efforts of the Jews to be in it, as Decius indicated. The profits, Schipper points out, were often augmented by fifty percent of the confiscated goods to which the lessee was usually entitled, according to the terms of the lease, and the numerous opportunities for engaging in commercial transactions which the leasing of transit duties afforded. As for possible risks on the part of the leaseholders, these were considerably reduced by the fact that the agreements usually included a clause guaranteeing the lessee a reduced rent in case of war or other unforeseen major calamities (*vis major*). Furthermore, in view of their direct contact with the royal court, the big magnates and dignitaries, the Jewish leaseholders often gained individual privileges and special letters of safe conduct which facilitated and protected their economic activities. The royal lessee, in particular, could not be interfered with by any local authority. They were directly responsible to no one but the king or the voivode, and they could not be brought before any other court.[15] This not only gave them special status but also afforded a measure of independence and influence in the general society, a state of affairs which was irksome to the ecclesiastical authorities.

By the beginning of the sixteenth century the fundamental and historically implanted opposition of the Church to the toleration of Jews in public positions of control and influence found increasingly more adherents among the socially and politically discontented lesser gentry which, for purely economic reasons, began to demand the profitable positions of the Jewish leaseholders for themselves. This demand found its first expression in one of the resolutions adopted at the Diet of Radom in 1505. But neither this resolution nor the interdiction included in the Edict of Toruń (Thorn) in 1520 was of much avail, judging by the fact that the complaints and demands of the petty nobility continued for over a century, having been voiced repeatedly at various Diets (in 1532, 1538, 1562, 1565). Indeed, the leasing of public and industrial enterprises by Jews did not disappear for a long time, particularly in the eastern provinces and in Lithuania.[16]

Foreign and Domestic Trade

In depicting the participation of Jews in commerce, the occupation in which, in Schipper's view, most Jews were engaged in medieval Poland, Schipper adverts to the particularly favorable circumstances which enabled the Jews to play an important role and to make a significant contribution in that area of the Polish economy in the Middle Ages.

In the first place, the German-Polish commercial class in the cities did not have in Poland the degree of political power which burghers attained in the West where they were able to thwart Jewish competition almost completely. The explanation for this lies in the attitude of the Polish kings, the Piasts as well as the Jagiellons, to the Christian middle class, on one hand, and to the Jews, on the other. With the single exception of Casimir the Great, the Polish rulers did not conduct a purposeful trade policy. Their decisions and regulations, usually made in response to petitions submitted, individually or collectively, by the burghers or the Jews, were determined by the king's personal concerns rather than the economic interest of the Polish middle class. The Jagiellons, whose financial credibility was questionable due to their perpetual financial difficulties stemming—in no small measure—from frivolity and extravagance, found it even more necessary to give special considerations and concessions to the Jews, the "supporters of the royal treasury," in order to assure themselves of the latter's credit. The position of the Jagiellon kings that easy personal credit from their Jewish *servi camerae* was the proper means of solving their financial problems was decisive in granting the Jews special rights, which the kings—as a rule—were not inclined to grant Christian merchants, and in preventing the latter from undermining the economic positions of the Jews or interfering with their ability to provide credit and revenues. Hence, the provisions of the royal charters giving Jews unlimited freedom of movement, a free hand in all spheres of trade activities, including the trade in victuals, and protection against possible abuses.

Schipper emphasizes the fact that both Queen Jadwiga and Ladislas Jagiello confirmed in 1387 and 1424 the measures of the Boleslas-Casimir *Privilegium* against uncalled-for intrusions into Jewish commercial activities. (In 1432 these regulations were extended to include the Jews of Volhynia as well.) Reaffirming the right of Jews to internal autonomy, Jagiello and the subsequent kings expressly exempted Polish Jews from being responsible to the municipal councils or municipal courts which were controlled by the burghers. Even state mint officials were forbidden to hold Jews on false currency charges unless in the presence of the voivode or a royal representative. Thus Schipper concludes that:

> Such important commercial concessions as autonomy in Jewish internal matters, complete exemption from the German laws (*i.e.*, the Magdeburg Law granted to the early German city settlers) and from the juridical dependence on municipal authorities, which were entirely composed of contentious city merchants, complete freedom to travel and equality in the payment of duties on goods, were important, if not the most important, factors in the growth of Jewish commerce in Polish territories.[17]

And it was mainly commerce, Schipper stresses, that yielded the profits and the capital that enabled Jews to provide the loans or to lay out the considerable sums needed for leasing various enterprises.[18]

But there were other propitious factors. The Polish *szlachta*, like the kings, saw in the Jews not only their creditors, whose economic position must be protected, but also convenient partners in their attempts to hold the middle class in check. Besides ethnic and cultural factors, the Christian merchants being mostly Germans, there existed conflicts of interest. Politically, the *szlachta* could not stand the fact that many Christian merchant families (the Melsztyns, Kmits, Herburts, Wierzyneks, Firleys, Boners, Morsztyns, and others) grew extremely rich and wielded much power and influence in the cities. Economically, the *szlachta* was fearful of organized merchants aiming to dictate low prices for agricultural products. And so, in order to counteract the growing wealth and power of the city patricians, and the middle class in general, the *szlachta*, guided by the *similia similibus* maxim, found it most expedient to patronize Jewish merchants. Cognizant of the fact that Jewish wealth was less dangerous than that of the burghers, the Polish gentry expected to benefit from it in two ways: (1) to impede the economic growth and capacities of the burghers and (2) to receive more revenues for themselves for the protection and privileges they extended to the Jews who, indeed, paid quite handsomely for them.[19]

Because the nobility looked askance at the middle class and because the Jagiellons, too, were not, as a rule, wholeheartedly interested in the cities and their dwellers, the Polish burgher class was weak politically and otherwise. It lacked the tightly organized system and the coordination of action that was characteristic of the medieval burghers in the West. Citing the research done by Professor Kutrzeba, Schipper points out that in Polish sources of the Middle Ages there is no trace of strong Christian merchants' guilds except for the guild in Cracow. And here, in the foremost urban center, it was established as late as 1410 and might have existed only a few years in view of the fact that its activities remained unknown. Although the Christian merchants were well represented in and protected by their municipal councils, they could not limit or control Jewish commercial activities, at least until 1485, because the Jews were independent of these councils and had recourse to the king or the lords whenever necessary.[20]

In contradistinction to the municipal councils, which for a long time constituted separate governing bodies lacking intercity relationships and common policies, the Jewish communities displayed a high degree of solidarity. One can find a great deal of evidence in the court records showing that individual Jews guaranteed for one another and that Jewish communal leaders, the *kahal* elders, acted on behalf of the merchants who, as a rule, constituted the controlling majority in every *kahal.* Moreover, well aware of their status as "strangers" within the general Christian society, the Jews in their individual autonomous *kahals* strove to regulate not only their internal affairs but also their relationships with other *kahals* in all important matters, including economic policies and common economic actions, in order to safeguard their commercial interests. In addition, the Jewish communities, widely spread over all Polish provinces, maintained contact with Jewish communities abroad, reaching in the West to Flanders and in the East to Constantinople and the Black Sea. Obviously, the contiguity with Jewish centers in Germany, Silesia, Bohemia, Hungary, Italy, Byzantium, etc. gave the Jewish merchants in Poland, whose own legacy of experience and knowledge was by no means limited or inconsequential, the indispensably important advantages of commercial anchorage, protection, information, and advice. Most important of all—and this Schipper states with added emphasis—was the communal solidarity and national unity. It determined their contributions and success in commercial endeavors domestically and even more so internationally. All this the Christian merchants were lacking. They could not undertake as readily and as effectively the kind of foreign ventures and transactions in which the Jews pioneered and in which they became most proficient.[21]

The importance of the Jews in commerce, Schipper notes, is reflected in the fact that until 1485 the historian cannot find, in the sources, any indications of official steps taken to limit or restrict the commercial activities of the Jews. The first successful attempt to do so, which was carried out in that year by the municipal council of Cracow in a written agreement with the Jews who allegedly accepted it "voluntarily," should not be taken, in Schipper's view, as an act formally legalizing the restrictive conditions which had already existed for some time, as Kutrzeba would have it. The agreement expressed rather the pious wish of the Polish merchants which they undoubtedly harbored, with the encouragement of the clergy, before 1485 but which even later remained, in the main, on paper. Citing a number of inconsistencies in Kutrzeba's work, *The Trade of Poland with the East* (Polish), Schipper politely but firmly points out that the esteemed Polish professor was too bent upon demonstrating that Jews were engaged exclusively in usury to be able to treat of Jewish commercial activities impartially. Since, however, the 1485 agreement is indicative of the oncoming and progressively growing economic struggle between the Christian townspeople and the Jews, Schipper takes the 1485 date to demarcate this period of Jewish commercial activities in medieval Poland as a period of undisturbed expansion.[22]

Schipper's description of the scope and content of Jewish trade in the 1384-1485 period is devoted more to foreign trade than to domestic commerce. That the former type should be more probative and significant is explained by the fact that since the annexation of the vast Ruthenanian territories in the second half of the fourteenth century (Red Ruthenia and part of Volhynia in 1349, Moldavia in 1387, Wallachia in 1389, Bessarabia in 1396) Poland became again a transit land and an international artery of trade with the Orient. In fact, the Polish push to the southeastern territories was in no small measure motivated by the ambition of the Jagiellons to control the river ways leading to the Italian Black Sea colonies, more of which were founded and developed by the Republic of Genoa during the fourteenth century. When the Jagiellons, with the cooperation of the Lithuanian Grand Duke Vitold, extended their possessions as far as the coast of the Black Sea, between the Dniester and the Dnieper rivers, the Oriental wares from Basra, Baghdad, and Constantinople which reached the Genoese colony of Kaffa or the Moldavian ports of Bialgorod (Akerman) had to travel through the eastern cities of the Jagiellonian monarchy in order to get to the West (Breslau, Augsburg, Nuremberg, even Bruges) or to the North (Danzig, Königsberg, Riga). Hence, there came about a renaissance of such commercial centers as Lwów, Kiev, Łuck, and Vladimir, which were also the receiving points of goods coming through the "Tartar Route," and a concentration of substantial Jewish commercial activities in Podolia, Red Ruthenia, Volhynia,and Lithuania. On the other hand, in Little and Greater Poland, where the cities were more advanced and the nobility was in greater need of credit capital, the participation of Jews in large scale foreign trade was comparatively smaller.[23]

Initially, Schipper took the position that even in the fourteenth century the Oriental trade was almost entirely in the hands of Jews and Armenians with insignificant participation by Christian merchants, limited only to forwarding some of the merchandise from Lwów and Cracow further to the West. Admitting that pertinent sources for that period are rather limited, he nevertheless assumed this position on the basis of the documentary evidence relating to the last decades of the fourteenth century and the beginning of the fifteenth which indicates that Jews of Volhynia and Red Ruthenia, in particular, were active in the trade with Kiev and Breslau and had a hand in the transit of wares from Kaffa to Podolia and Poland via the "Tartar Tract." In time, however, Schipper modifies this viewpoint somewhat, stating that although Jews were, no doubt, engaged in the traffic of Oriental wares, it is hard to determine whether their role in the fourteenth century was as dominant as it had been before 1241 since it has been shown that, besides the Armenians and some Italians, the aforementioned famous German-Polish burgher families, who gained their fortunes during the fourteenth century, were also actively engaged in this trade.[24] That Volhynian and Red Ruthenian Jews played at least as significant a role as the Italians becomes more evident in the beginning of the fifteenth century since a number of indicative facts can be ascertained regarding some leading Jewish merchants. For instance, that Jacob Słomokowicz of Łuck, who became the royal purveyor of Ladislas Jagiello and who often dealt in partnership with Lewko of Cracow, provided the Polish magnates and patricians of Lwów with Oriental wares. It is also known that Jacob's sons, Isaac of Vladimir and Simcha of Łuck, were delivering Oriental goods to Cracow. Jews from Lwów, who apparently were suppliers to the royal court, were the king's guests and their names appear in the fiscal records (bills) of the court. Finally, the known *officiales nostri*, Wolczko Czolner (Zollner) of Lwów and Dziatko of Drohobycz, who acted as royal creditors and leaseholders, conducted a very active and extensive East-West trade in spices, silk, furs, Lwów wax, and English cloth. Judging by the municipal records of Lwów, which contain a considerable number of notations regarding these two court-Jews, they must have been leading merchants in the eastern trade, and this, in turn, accounts for their ability to lay out large sums of money for lending or leasing purposes.[25]

The portrayal of a fuller and more definitive picture becomes possible after 1435, when the Ruthenian *Town and Country Documents* were instituted. These records provided Schipper with more information and details about the commercial contacts of Polish and Lithuanian Jews with the Black Sea colonies and Constantinople. Among the pertinent data cited,[26] Schipper emphasizes the evidence relating to the presence of Byzantine and Italian Jews in Poland. One of those was Caleb Judeus de Kaffa who used to visit Lwów to transact his trade affairs with Szachna. The latter, being the leaseholder of royal duties, exempted Caleb from paying customs on Oriental wares which he brought to Poland in great quantities. In 1442 Caleb settled in Poland and he established business connections with Tarnów and Cracow. He enjoyed the special protection of the Voivode Peter Odrowąż of Lwów, who tendered a considerable surety sum on behalf of Caleb when the latter became involved in one of his court litigations with Szachna and others.[27]

Following the fall of the Byzantine Empire in 1453, the routes from the East leading through Poland gained in importance. In view of the unfriendly relations with the Turks, the Italian merchants who had been traveling from their Black Sea colonies to Italy via Constantinople began to make greater use of the Polish transit ways, and wares from the East began coming to Lwów and Cracow in greater volume. But, Schipper notes, the competition of the Italians did not affect the Jewish merchants adversely, since there were only six to eight Italian merchants staying in Poland for a longer period of time, although one can find in the documents at least one case of contention, brought to the attention of King Casimir IV by the doge of Venice, in which Jews traveling from Kaffa to Poland in 1464 allegedly took away goods worth 600 ducats from the Italian of Tana, Nembrot Valenti.[28] When the relationship between the Turks and the Italian colonies grew worse and the two parties began to engage in hostilities, the richer Italian Jewish merchants from Kaffa began to settle in Poland because of the commercial relationship which they maintained with that country. One such Jew was Jacob Anselmi, originally of Venice, who obtained a special letter of safe conduct from Casimir IV and who in 1474, a year prior to the fall of Kaffa, settled in Poland together with his family, relatives, and friends.[29]

The commercial contacts of Polish Jews with the East were not entirely interrupted by the fall of the Italian settlements. When they could not be maintained any longer via the routes leading to the northern shores of the Black Sea, Jews shifted the trade in eastern goods to the only route left open, the one leading through Podolia, Moldavia, Wallachia, to Constantinople. This route, Schipper notes, must have been popular for a long time before, even though the sources about its utilization became explicit only from the times of the fall of Byzantium, or else it would be difficult to explain the fact that "from 1453 Jews were almost the only agents of commerce between Poland and Turkey for a number of decades."[30] Thus, at a critical and difficult time when the Turkish expansion interrupted the lines to the Near East and adversely affected the trade of Poland with that part of the world as well as with Hungary, [31] and when it seemed that Lwów would lose its importance as a commercial center, Jews from Constantinople appeared on the scene and saved the situation. Thanks to them, Lwów could still for a time maintain its position as an international market. Judging by the evidence of the municipal records, Jews of Constantinople virtually monopolized all Polish-Turkish trade shipped to Lwów in 1467-1479. One of them, David, had in Lwów his own representative whom he supplied with such goods as alum from Asia Minor, lemons, spices, and wine in return for woolens and satin from England and Flanders. David's goods were also delivered by his representative to other Polish cities: Kamieniec Podolski, Trembowla, and Chocim. Another Jew from Constantinople named Abraham brought to Lwów great amounts of pepper and other spices, judging by the fact that in 1479 Lwów merchants, particularly Armenians, owed him 2300 florins. Besides David and Abraham, the records continue to mention until 1481 the names of two other Jews of Constantinople, Moses and Zechariah, whose transactions with other cities, going as far to the north as Lublin, and their municipal councils were quite sizable.[32]

While the Jews of Lwów may have been most active in the distribution of the eastern products throughout Poland and beyond, numerous notes in the *Town and Country Documents* indicate that Jews from different cities and towns along the main routes to the West and North came to the Lwów fairs to purchase considerable amounts of these products in order to resell them in various parts of the country, including Silesia. The biggest among the buyers, however, were the court purveyors, men like Michael of Hrubieszów, Szachna of Lwów, Szania and Joseph of Bełz, Samson of Żydaczów, etc., who either received special letters from the king exempting them from the payment of royal duties or were themselves the lessees of such duties. And having direct connections with Jewish merchants abroad, some of these court-Jews were in a position to import such articles as textiles, furs, and wine.[33]

Finally, in connection with the eastern trade, Schipper points out that contact with the Near East brought about a reactivation of the slave trade, a fact clearly evidenced in the court records of 1440-1450, some of which indicate that slaves were placed with Jews as security for extended loans.[34] He is, however, careful to stress two important mitigating circumstances. First, that "slavery was recognized as a legal institution in Poland throughout the Middle Ages." As late as the sixteenth and the beginning of the seventeenth centuries, Nicolas Buciella, the court physician of the Kings Stephen Batory (1572-1586) and Sigismund III (1587-1632), owned a few slaves, men and women who, in accordance with his will, were transferred to his relatives and friends.[35] Secondly, that the export of slaves, which at times used Lwów as a station, was continuously directed to the commercial centers of the Italian republics, and while Jews as well as Armenians participated in it to some extent, it was mostly in the hands of the Christian Italian merchants who were its chief traffickers. To substantiate the latter point, Schipper again makes use of Kutrzeba's work as well as that of Heyd.[36]

For the Jewish foreign-trade dealers of Ruthenia and Little Poland, at least until the bloody events of 1453, the market of Breslau constituted the main center of interest. This can be discerned from the Cracow records which mention Jews traveling to the Breslau fairs or from the information about Polish Jews maintaining their representatives there. However, the Volhynian, Mazovian, and especially Lithuanian Jews directed much of the eastern and local products to the north, particularly to the port of Danzig. The lively trade in this direction was undoubtedly determined by two facts: (1) that in 1423 the Lithuanian Grand Duke Vitold granted the Jews the right of free trade in the territories of the Teutonic Order and (2) that the relationships between the latter and the Polish rulers, which had been strained for a long time, improved during the 1430s. Thus, according to the records of Danzig and Königsberg, which Schipper found in the works of Hirsch and Jolowicz, substantial Jewish merchants from Troki, Grodno, Brest, and Łuck shipped to, or exported through, Danzig, individually and in partnerships, Oriental wares as well as wood, wax, furs, hides, silver belts, etc. In the local trade with Danzig and other Prussian cities, the most enterprising Jews were those living along the Bug and Narew who used these waterways for rafting agricultural products, mostly grain, pitch, and charcoal to Prussian markets. All this was accomplished in spite of the forceful and acrimonious attempts on the part of the Prussian cities to keep away all foreign competitors. That the Jewish merchants did not yield easily to pressures and intimidations is evidenced by the fact that King Casimir IV intervened on behalf of Słonia (Solomon) of Grodno to the Grand Master of the Teutonic Order, the message being delivered by none other than Mazovian Jews. But Jewish trade with Danzig and Prussia became even livelier when Danzig was given the status of a free city under Polish authority in 1454 and when all of Pomerania and other districts held by the Order became part of Poland in accordance with the Thorn Peace Treaty of 1466. Following this event Polish Jews began to settle here in increasing numbers and their commercial activities with the northern countries on the Baltic Sea expanded considerably.[37]

Speaking of the Lithuanian Jews, Schipper emphasizes that besides being active in the northern trade they also traveled to Italy. This can be seen from the fact that in 1483 a Jew from Brest sued a Jew of Warsaw for unpaid travel expenses to Venice, a matter which, according to a Hebrew document submitted to the court by the defendant, had been settled before the Jewish "doctors" (rabbis). The fact is significant for it shows that Jews initiated contact with Italy even before 1497, which is considered in the Polish literature of economic history to be the date marking the beginning of the period when eastern goods began coming to Poland from the West since the fall of the Italian Black Sea colonies made the import of these goods very difficult.[38]

To complete the picture of Jewish participation in the foreign trade of Poland, Schipper cites the evidence found in the *Town and Country Documents* indicating that in the vicinity of Jarosław and Rzeszów, cities located on the borderline of Red Ruthenia and Little Poland, Jews were active for a long time in marketing horned cattle, especially oxen, delivered from Podolia and Moldavia by Ruthenian Jews from Lwów, Ostróg, Żydaczów, and Halicz, and shipped to Silesia and Germany. In the western parts of Little Poland, on the other hand, Jews imported horses from Hungary.[39]

In the area of domestic trade, Schipper points out that Jewish participation can be determined in almost all important branches of that trade, but there were certain branches that were specifically Jewish in the sense that they were either in Jewish hands or introduced by Jews. In the western provinces, especially in cities like Cracow, Poznań, and Warsaw, many Jewish merchants dealt in a variety of objects and secondhand wares retained by Jewish moneylenders as unredeemed pledges. A great deal of commerce in alcoholic beverages was also in Jewish hands in various parts of the country, because Jews either owned or leased breweries. Similarly, the trade in salt was almost completely monopolized by Jews, especially in the Russian territories where they were more often than not the sole leaseholders or managers of the salt mines. In Central Poland, particularly in Mazovia, Jews were known for their dominant participation in the marketing of agricultural products and by-products.

As for new branches of trade introduced by Jews, the example offered by Schipper is that of fish. Initially, Jews used to bring fish in salted or dried form from the Black Sea colonies or from deep Russia to Poland in order to ship it further to other European countries. But, realizing the great possibilities of home-grown fish, they soon became fish farmers, breeding new species of fish from the Black, Azov, and Caspian Seas as well as from the Don in Polish waters leased or bought from the *szlachta.* With the development of the fish industry, Jews expanded the domestic trade in fish to considerable proportions.[40]

Agriculture

As has been pointed out in dealing with the origins of Jews in Poland, documentary evidence which explicitly or implicitly indicated that Jews in medieval Poland owned arable land and were engaged in the cultivation of land, was of particular interest to Schipper.[41] The reason for this interest is stated by Schipper himself in his *Studies* when, speaking of the economically multifarious Wolczko as a colonizer of villages in Ruthenia, he said:

> The example of Wolczko Czolner (Zollner) eloquently proves that the rooted opinion in the historical literature, up to this time, that Polish Jews did not participate in the agricultural economy because of legal prohibitions (which we could not discover in the sources until the end of the fifteenth century) or because they were not eager to engage in it, is by far one-sided. Generally, it is given to infer that the participation of Jews in Polish agriculture, although not as distinct as in commerce or credit, was quite substantial. . . . It was not until the Diet of Piotrków in 1496 that Jews were forbidden to buy fields. But the implementation of this

> decision seems to us to be highly questionable if only for the information provided by the chronicler Miechowita who lived at the end of the fifteenth century. Writing about the Jews, Miechowita stressed the fact that he found among them a "third kind", not only usurers and merchants but farmers settled on the lands of Ruthenia. . . . And, indeed, court records of the fifteenth century quite often mention Jewish grounds and settlements located in farming terrains.[42]

Although Schipper wrote a special monograph on the agrarian colonization of Jews [43] and devoted an entire chapter to their participation in the rural colonization of Ruthenia in which he stresses that the involvement of Jews in this economic process was consonant with and determined by the consistent policy of the Polish rulers to populate Ruthenia through outright grants of virgin lands or through putting such lands on the free market,[44] a more comprehensive treatment of the extent of Jewish involvement in agriculture is presented in the *Virtshaftsgeshikhte.* This treatment is also more noteworthy because it came many years after the critique and the polemics on the subject (reference to which will be made later) had been aired and there had been time for a reexamination of the material.

From the source materials attesting the ownership of land by Jews, Schipper finds the situation in Poland to have been, in this respect, quite similar to that which existed in the Middle Ages only in Spain and such islands as Sicily. As in Castile and Aragon, to which Schipper devotes a considerable amount of space in his *Virtshaftsgeshikhte*,[45] Jews in Poland acquired land and became, directly or indirectly, involved in agriculture in three ways: (1) by retaining mortgaged land which debtors failed to redeem; (2) by colonizing uncultivated lands received from the king; and (3) by becoming either tenants in villages established by Jewish colonizers or small farmers living from their own fields and gardens. The first method, prevalent in the western and central provinces (Greater and Little Poland) and substantiated by Schipper with court records showing that in litigations Jews were granted not only the right to use the foreclosed land but also the actual title to it,[46] was curtailed by the Statute of Warta (1423) which, however, had no effect in Ruthenia, as has been already pointed out.[47] The second and third methods were significantly operative in the eastern regions, especially in Red Ruthenia when, in spite of the frequent Tartar attacks, this province underwent a period of intensive colonization, and in Lithuania where the stretches of uncultivated land were even vaster and the agricultural character of the existing cities was still quite distinct.

As far as the Lithuanian portion of the country is concerned, the very fact that its economic level of development was lower than that of other parts of the Polish kingdom actually compelled Jews to be more actively engaged in agricultural pursuits. This is reflected in the Grodno Charter of 1389, granting Jews the right to own land, as well as in the "Lithuanian *Metrica*" which furnishes specific information about the considerable participation and leading role of Jews in the agricultural colonization of the country. There were Jews like Lewon Szalomicz, known to have owned the villages of Niewiarów and Kornicza, and there were others like Bogdanowicz, Chaczkowicz, and Kunczyc who owned granges, meadows, fisheries, and mills. Also, a fairly large percentage of Jews in the cities engaged in the cultivation of orchards and grew produce on their city plots or suburban parcels of land.[48]

In Red Ruthenia, where Jews were drawn into the colonization process, along with the Polish knights and burghers, by the kings and the nobility who wished to bring this territory under their control, the role of the Jews in the agricultural aspects of this colonization is illustrated by Schipper with the documentation concerning Wolczko Czolner. This notable and versatile entrepreneur, already mentioned in connection with his banking, leasing, and commercial activities, acted also as the king's authorized bailiff in a number of villages which were founded by him with the help of Jews whom he brought to the new settlements as tenants. According to the sources, Wolczko was appointed by Jagiello in 1423 as the bailiff of the village Werbiż. In 1425 he was authorized to establish the village of Werbeza, of which he became the bailiff in 1427 and in which the king granted him land, meadows, a house, a mill, a pond, one-third of the royal revenues, and one-sixth of all other revenues in return for one-third of the flour produced in the mill and the delivery of a horse in the event of war in Ruthenia. In 1427 he also founded the village of Karcz, and there, too, the office of bailiff belonged to him. It is quite reasonable to assume, in Schipper's view, that the energetic Wolczko established many other agricultural sites in view of the numerous villages which existed at that time in Ruthenia bearing such names as Wolczków, Wolczkowce, Wołkowa, and Wołków, although there is no other direct evidence to substantiate this.

That other Jews must have entered, like Wolczko, into special agreements with the king or the magnates to colonize land, and that Jews were often among the colonists in the newly founded settlements, can also be inferred from the names by which some of the villages were known, such as Żydatycze, Żydowska Wola, Żydów, etc.[49] All these indications become relevant and meaningful when taken in conjunction with the direct evidence from the Ruthenian *Town and Country Documents*, the "Lithuanian *Metrica*," and the testimony of the aforementioned Miechowita. They all point to the conclusion that Jews played a part, by no means small, in the agricultural colonization of the eastern provinces at least until the Diet of Piotrków in 1496 made the first attempt to put a stop to it.

This conclusion could hardly become a matter of dispute since temporary or permanent Jewish ownership of land and agricultural cultivation is irrefutably demonstrated in the sources. However, certain explicit or implicit inferences which Schipper derives from this fact were not readily accepted. Immediately following the publication of the aforementioned monograph on Jewish agrarian colonization, a reviewer questioned the validity of Schipper's inference that the Jewish colonizers were actively engaged in the tilling of the soil. Jewish landowners might very well have been the collectors of rents rather than the actual land workers or peasants, as the case of the rich Wolczko would indicate.[50]

Wischnitzer took a similar position in his review of Schipper's *Studies*, stating that in treating the subject of agricultural colonization Schipper made a sweeping generalization in which the differentiation between landowner and actual tiller is disregarded and that, in fact, the weakest point of the *Studies* is the author's attempt to place Jews among the people who lived and worked on the land.[51]

In an article referred to previously,[52] Bałaban took issue with Schipper on the same point, although in a somewhat different vein. He questioned Schipper's contention that because Wolczko was a Jew, a favorite and confidant of the king who was given a free hand in the operation of his enterprises, he must have colonized his newly founded villages with Jewish farmer-settlers. Whether he did, indeed, is nowhere stated. Therefore, one may only assume on the basis of the circumstances the possibility that Jews settled in these villages as farmers, but it cannot and should not be asserted with any degree of certainty that it must have been so, especially if one considers the attested facts that there were quarrels with the Christian settlers, that Wolczko was forced to transfer the village of Werbiż to the capitulary of the Lwów Cathedral, and that Wolczko was forced to sell his office as bailiff of Karcz to a Christian burgher. These facts, in Bałaban's view, render Schipper's thesis that Jewish farmers were among the colonizers quite untenable.[53]

Schipper's reply to Bałaban's critique appeared two years later in *Yevreyskaya Starina*. Like a skillful polemicist he points out in the first place a contradiction in Bałaban's own argumentation which, on one hand, uses the opposition of Christian settlers to Wolczko and the eventual loss of his rights to Karcz in favor of the clergy and, on the other, admits the possibility of the existence of Jewish settlers. The quarrels that took place at times and that were eventually settled by a special royal commission in favor of Wolczko certainly do not prove the absence of Jewish settlers, and the transfer of Karcz to the clergy points only to the latter's agitation and intrigues against Wolczko who, in spite of the king's magnanimity and expressed anticipation, did not convert to Christianity. But the possibility of Jewish farmers in Wolczko's villages becomes not only a probability but even a certainty when one considers the evidence that Bałaban chose to ignore, namely: the explicit references in the court records to Jews in Red Ruthenia who lived in villages, the testimony of Miechowita, and the analogous situation that existed in Lithuania where the evidence concerning Jewish participation in agricultural occupations is even more pronounced. These are, in Schipper's view, the *facta concludentia* in the case of the Wolczko villages, notwithstanding the lack of direct evidence to substantiate the conclusion that Jewish farmers must have lived in those villages.[54]

As has been noted above, Schipper saw no reason for amending his position in the matter in the *Virtshaftsgeshikhte* which was published seventeen years later. And to conclude, it might be worthwhile to quote Halpern's concise statement on the question of the extent of Jewish participation in actual agricultural activities:

> In several districts of Poland and more in Lithuania, there were Jewish burghers and villagers engaged in various branches of agriculture. The town was still semiagricultural, and among the burghers there were also Jews who owned gardens, fields, and pastures. In the eastern districts, especially, the Jews sometimes acquired rural properties as collateral for temporary cultivation, and sometimes, by authority of the prince or king, they even acquired full ownership of the properties. We know some of these property holders by name as wealthy merchants and tax farmers who certainly did not work their properties themselves. We do, however, find occasional references to Jewish tillers of land.[55]

Free Professions and Crafts

Besides credit, leasing, commerce, and agriculture—which were often interrelated and complementary—the gamut of occupations in which Polish Jews were engaged also included certain free professions and the crafts. Of the former Schipper singles out in particular the Jewish physicians and surgeons, although many religious functionaries and administrative clerks or bookkeepers already existed in the evolving organizational structure of the *kahal*[56] as well as in the bigger banking and leasing enterprises of the known "court-Jews."

Jewish physicians were known in the Middle Ages in the Mediterranean countries as well as in Western Europe, and their professional services were sought by all segments of the Christian population—the rulers, the secular and religious dignitaries, the nobility, and the common people—in spite of repeated admonitions by the Church, going back to the Trullan Council in 692, which threatened excommunication for accepting medical treatment from Jewish physicians.[57] In Poland the Jewish medical practitioners enjoyed the same popularity. It is reflected in the sources that come from the second half of the fifteenth century, presumably because of the increased immigration from the West, although it may be reasonably assumed, in Schipper's view, that Jewish physicians had already practiced in Poland before that time. While in the *Studies* the list of physicians gathered by Schipper from the sources of 1465-1519 includes thirteen names, the list presented in the *Virtshaftsgeshikhte*, culled from sources corresponding to the more extended period of 1435-1547, contains twenty-one names. In examining the latter one will find that of the twenty-one Jewish physicians and surgeons, five served at various times at the royal court. Besides these court doctors, eight lived and practiced in Cracow while four functioned in Warsaw, among them the wife of the known Jewish banker Alexander; two in Lwów; one in Gniezno, attached to the Primate and Archbishop of Poland; and one in Novy Sącz. At least four came to Poland from Spain, Jerusalem, and Silesia and two served as ophthalmologists.[58] Among the other interesting and indicative facts Schipper notes that Jacob Isaac of Spain, the personal doctor of King Jan Olbracht, was granted in 1501 such special privileges as exemption from all royal taxes and duties and direct royal jurisdiction; that the correspondence between King Sigismund I and his Jewish doctor, Moses of Brest, discloses a very intimate personal relationship between them; that Israel Medicus of Warsaw, who apparently escaped from Silesia during the Capistrano days, was requested by Princess Barbara to appear before the Warsaw court because the Bishop of Breslau claimed of him 300 gulden; and that Izaczko, the Jewish physician in Lwów, engaged in moneylending and various commercial transactions besides practicing medicine. Altogether, Schipper infers, the practice of medicine by Jews and the close relationships which Jewish physicians usually maintained with the royal court and people of the upper classes contributed, to a certain extent, in the accumulation of capital among Jews. On the other hand, they contributed in no small measure to the dissemination of Jewish and secular knowledge among Jews and Christians since there were among them men of great learning and ability.[59]

In attempting to depict the actual participation of Polish Jews in various industries and crafts, Schipper is moved, as in the case of agriculture, to expose the fallacy of the stereotyped notion that there were no craftsmen or laborers among the Jews because they shunned hard work, as the Jew-baiter would have it, or because they were barred from membership in the Christian guilds, as apologists among the Jewish historians explain it. But in addition, Schipper is interested in depicting not only the activities of the bigwigs, the Jews noted for their large-scale enterprises and transactions in banking or commerce or agricultural colonization, but also—and perhaps even more so—the daily activities of the common and simple folk, who, he thinks, constituted the majority in the Jewish society of medieval Poland.[60] Proof for the latter contention Schipper finds in the brochure bearing the self-explanatory Latin title *Ad querelam mercatorum Cracoviensium responsum Judaeorum de mercatura* (An Answer of Jews Concerning Commerce to an Accusation of Cracow Merchants), which appeared in 1539 and in which the assertion is made that at the time (beginning of the sixteenth century) the Jewish craftsmen outnumbered Jewish merchants three to one. It would therefore appear that the Jewish working class (craftsmen, artisans, and laborers in the cities and in the countryside) was, in fact, greater than all the other socioeconomic classes of the Jewish community put together, especially if one bears in mind that the majority of small shopkeepers were actually craftsmen selling their self-made products.[61]

But the task of presenting a definitive picture of the participation of Jews in craftwork was not easy for, as can be expected, the court records or the other sources would usually yield sparse knowledge about craftsmen whose business seldom brought them to court or the municipal offices.[62] Moreover, whatever direct and specific information Schipper was able to gather was of rather late origin, that is, from the second half of the fifteenth century. And yet, Schipper not only pioneered in laying solid foundations for further investigations and studies, but he also assembled enough evidence and indications to show that Jews, far from considering the crafts as a drudgery, actually contributed to the development of certain handicrafts in spite of or because of the discriminatory policies of the Christian craft guilds.

In the first place, even if one is to assume that the Christian guilds, which began to appear in the greater Polish cities in the second half of the thirteenth century, succeeded immediately in implementing industrial monopolies, Jews must have practiced some crafts which could not be interfered with by the Christian guilds. Guaranteed the freedom of religious observance in the royal charters, the Jews certainly had their own butchers and bakers, to assure themselves of kosher meat and bread prepared in accordance with religious demands, as well as their own weavers and tailors to produce their prayer shawls and to observe the biblical prohibition of *sha'atnez* in their clothing, as was the case in all countries in which Jewish communities existed in the Middle Ages.[63] But from a 1460 document noting that in Lwów some Jews were tanners "since old times," it may be deduced that besides the religiously determined crafts they were also engaged in other crafts. This is supported by the evidence from the Lwów court records of the fifteenth century in which some of the Jewish litigants are called *laboriosi*, a term used in addressing artisans and peasants, and the fact that the municipal records in the last decade of the fifteenth century mention Jewish glaziers.[64]

Even more indicative are certain evidences from Cracow. Of these, the fact that in 1465 the Council of Twelve of the Cracow *kahal* listed among its members a representative of the Jewish craftsmen (*Lazar Israhel, faber*) is undoubtedly most telling, for it goes to show that the Jewish artisans in Cracow were numerous and strong enough to warrant the participation of one of their ranks in one of the *kahal* organs that were dominated and controlled by an oligarchy of wealthy bankers and merchants in association with the acknowledged spiritual leaders.[65] Furthermore, while it may be justifiably assumed that Jewish breweries and distilleries in Cracow employed Jewish workers, although this is not explicitly stated in the extant sources, it appears certain that Jews in Cracow manufactured great quantities of fur collars and garments if in the 1485 agreement between the *kahal* elders and the Cracow municipality the Jewish craftsmen producing these items were allowed to sell them freely even on nonmarket days. It is also apparent that these Jewish furriers and tailors produced not only for individual orders but for general consumption, indicating the existence of a putting-out system and a higher form of production among the Jewish craftsmen in Cracow.[66]

Other agreements between Jews and Christian guilds in Cracow and Kazimierz in the last decades of the fifteenth century indicate that Jewish craftsmen sought a certain *modus vivendi*, a framework within which they could function in spite of increasing resentment shown by the Christian guilds against their growing productivity. However, the opposition of the Christian guilds and their attempts to eliminate the ever growing Jewish competition intensified by the beginning of the sixteenth century. This is reflected in the 1527 decree prohibiting Jewish craftsmen in Warsaw (who were apparently successful in plying their trades) from living in that city or even within a two-mile radius of it. That Jewish craftsmen were being pushed out of the city proper is evidenced by the *Country Documents* of the Błonie district (adjacent to the city of Warsaw) as well as the *Town and Country Documents* of Warsaw proper.[67]

The only indication that Jewish weavers may have resided in Poznań is provided by the fact that the "Jewish street" in that city was also known as the *Wullenwebirgasse*, the street of wool weavers. In general, however, the evidence of Jewish participation in crafts, though meager, is sufficient to corroborate Schipper's thesis that the ensuing struggle between the Christian guilds and the Jewish artisans in the sixteenth century had its roots in the preceding medieval period during which the latter had already constituted a well-established economic reality.

Taxes and Fiscal Obligations

To cast more light on the scope of the economic relationships of the Jews in Poland, especially on their economic contributions to the feudal state, Schipper undertakes the task of ascertaining the various taxes and levies that Jews were obliged to pay. Although the research did not produce as much source material as one could wish for, Schipper pioneers here, too, in presenting a comprehensive picture of the Jewish fiscal duties and, to an extent, of their actual payments. He deals with the problem several times and presents his findings, with slight variations in form rather than substance, in the *Studies*, the *Virtshaftsgeshikhte*, the *Kultur-geshikhte*, and finally, in a special essay on the subject written for the aforementioned encyclopedic volumes of *Jews in Reborn Poland.*[68]

In tracing the documentary evidence germane to Jews as taxpayers, Schipper notes a characteristic evolution indicating that the revenues derived from Jews grew progressively in importance to the Polish state until they became a matter of contention. Initially, the Kalisz Charter of 1264 made no mention at all of special Jewish tax obligations on behalf of the king's treasury, tantamount to the state treasury, except for the customary duties and tolls payable on the transport of goods by all merchants, Jews and Christians alike. However, the later Boleslas-Casimir Charter not only refers to the Jews as belonging to the royal treasury but expressly forbids the voivodes and *starostas* to collect from them the so-called *opłatki* (payments) or *dany* (tributes) because "we maintain them for our own treasury." Still later, in the fifteenth century, when the character of the economy became increasingly sumptuary and dependent on capital, the financial obligations of the Jews increased while assuming new forms. Based on fiscal documents from the chancery of Ladislas Jagiello, providing the oldest information on the subject, direct and ordinary revenues which Jews contributed to the state entailed at least five different categories:

1. The annual census (*exaccio Judaica*), a quota determined by the king for each Jewish community according to its size and means and collected by the *kahal* seniors who were responsible for its payment. By the end of the fifteenth century the criterion for taxing communities was two or four florins per Jewish house, depending on whether it was a wooden or stone building;
2. Tariff duties on goods;
3. Payments for individual or collective charters and special royal letters (*privilegia*) which constituted an important source of income to the Crown;
4. Appropriations of Jewish estates with no heirs;
5. Payments remitted to royal officials which included fines for trespassing royal laws as well as various gift contributions.

In addition, the sources reveal extraordinary imposts levied at various times in special circumstances. These included: (1) war imposts such as that levied by King Jan Olbracht in 1496; (2) coronation tributes; (3) state duties in kind and labor which, according to 1475 and 1523 documents relating to Jews in Lwów and Lublin respectively, entailed deliveries of wagons, horses, spices, and the like at such special occasions as the king's visit in the city, work impositions in the royal castle and industrial enterprises, transportation obligations, etc.; and (4) penalties for various transgressions.[69]

The growing importance of revenues derived from Jews and the consequent increased interest of the Crown in these revenues is also reflected in the changes that were instituted in the method of collecting the Jewish annual tax, although judging by the fragmentary and somewhat heterogeneous data culled by Schipper from various sources, the taxes remitted by the individual Jewish communities were by no means excessive.[70] In analyzing the tax-collection procedures, Schipper points to the fact that until the latter part of the fifteenth century the system of collection was rather decentralized. Between the Crown and the Jewish taxpayers stood the seniors of the individual *kahals.* They were addressed by the Crown, and they were responsible to the Crown for the tax assessment. However, as the number of Jewish communities increased and efficient control over the assessment as well as the collection began to miss the mark, either because of too high assessments or because royal exemptions obtained by rich and influential Jews affected negatively the solvency of their respective communities, the Crown became interested in centralizing the system. Hence, Sigismund I (1506-1548) decided to appoint Jewish tax prefects in the main provinces of the country to represent the Crown treasury *vis à vis* the *kahals* and to carry out the task of assessing and collecting. The *kahals'* elders lost thereby some control in their own communities as well as the benefits derived from being in direct contact with the royal court, and they saw in the new procedures an infringement of their autonomy. When the resentment and opposition to the new system on the part of the local *kahals* became unmistakably apparent, the king did not hesitate to engage the leading rabbis in Poland to act as the Crown's approved "spiritual judges" (*doctores legis*) who should use religious sanctions, if necessary, to compel the *kahals* to cooperate with the provincial prefects and to discharge their tax obligations in a manner satisfactory to the state. Thus, Schipper points out, the matter of taxes became the *causa proxima* of: (1) the first serious encroachment by the state into such an important internal matter of the Jewish communities as the appointment of rabbis, since the state began to exert pressure on the *kahals* not to engage rabbis without the Crown's approval; (2) a prolonged inner struggle within the Jewish community reflected in the banishment of Rabbi Jacob Polak, the famous Talmudist and the first Jewish Primate (Chief Rabbi of Polish Jewry) appointed by the king; and (3) the first serious aggravation in the relationship between the Crown and the Jews, although Sigismund I was not personally ill-disposed to them.[71]

Furthermore, Jewish revenues were substantial enough to become a bone of contention towards the end of the Middle Ages. According to the principle laid down in the General *Privilegia*, Jews were not subject to any other jurisdiction but that of the Crown, and as such they were exempt from any and all payments in behalf of the municipalities or the local secular and ecclesiastical lords. Although the kings carefully watched that the Jews should not become a source of obligatory income to the nobles, the clergy, and the cities, in practice Jews found themselves paying increasingly more to these centers of power as their demands became stronger and the central power of the Crown weakened. The Church succeeded in implementing the decision of the Wieluń-Kalisz Synod (1420) according to which Jews were obligated to pay to the Church the contributions or fees of those Christians whose homes were either mortgaged or sold to and occupied by Jews. The cities soon adopted the same principle. First in Cracow and soon thereafter in Poznań Jews were asked to pay, to begin with, a property tax for homes acquired from Christians. Eventually, in 1506 the king had to enter into an agreement with the *kahal* of Lwów whereby he relinquished fifty percent of its annual state tax in favor of the city. A few years later the same happened in Chełm. The lords, too, began collecting all kinds of payments from Jews in their private, patrimonial cities and estates. In Tarnów, for instance, John Amor, the lord of this private city, collected an annual fee from Jews trading in cloth called *Krajówka.*

Eventually, a radical change in the relationship between the nobility and the Jews came about in 1539 when, by virtue of the Statute of Sigismund I, Jews settled in private lands became subject to the jurisdiction of the lords who, at the same time, obtained the right to collect annual rents from their Jews. Even the royal officials who were not supposed to collect any payments or contributions from the Jews, unless the latter offered such of their volition, must have received considerable amounts in Jewish "gifts" for the obvious reason that in practice the Crown Jews depended very much on the direct intervention of the royal officials rather than the indirect protection of the kings.[72]

Based on these developments and the various forms of direct and indirect taxation to which Jews were gradually subjected, Schipper concludes that, besides the contribution which Jews made towards the development and expansion of the economy of medieval Poland through their capital, initiative, work, and productivity in various areas of economic endeavor, they also supplied the state treasury and other coffers with considerable and ever-growing sums of money in the form of various taxes, levies, and imposts.[73]

In concluding the discussion on Schipper's exposition of the occupational diversity of the Jews in medieval Poland, it should be noted that besides pioneering in an area that was hardly touched upon in the histories of Polish Jews before his time, Schipper laid solid foundations that were fully utilized and further built upon by subsequent Jewish historians. If, for instance, "the story of the medieval Jewish craftsmen (in the European countries) has not yet been told in full detail," according to Baron, and if "because of the paucity of readily available sources and monographic studies, references to them are relatively scarce even in the two Jewish economic histories of G. Caro and I. Schipper,"[74] it is nonetheless true that Schipper made not only a significant initial step but also turned the attention of historians to this particular area of investigation. It can undoubtedly be said that Wischnitzer, the author of *A History of Jewish Crafts and Guilds*, with whom Schipper wrote a monograph in Russian in 1914, was indebted to the latter for some of the spadework and data provided in the *Studies* as well as in the *Virtshaftsgeshikhte*.[75] A cursory examination of the historical works by Mahler and Mark, published after World War II, will suffice to convince that Schipper's work and contribution in unfolding the diverse and ramified activities of Polish Jews, as well as his inferences and conclusions, were duly appreciated and fully accepted. This is true not only of Mahler and Mark, Marxist-oriented historians to whom Schipper's economic findings were of particular interest, but also of a historian like Halpern who does not look at Jewish history from an economically determined point of view and who generally has not been uncritical of Schipper's work and views. With regard to the matter of occupational diversity, however, Halpern's succinct description of the subject quite faithfully follows Schipper's findings, now part and parcel of the historiography of Jews in Poland in the Middle Ages.[76]

Notes

1. See *supra*, Chap. I, pp. 6-7.

2. See *supra*, Chap. IV, p. 122.

3. *Onhoyb, op. cit.*, p. 43; *Studies, op. cit.*, p. 235. See also *supra*, Chap. II, p. 63 and Chap. III, p. 97. Cf. Baron, op. cit., vol. IV, p. 210. Cf. Weinryb, *The Jews of Poland, op. cit.*, pp. 57-58.

4. *Studies, op. cit.*, p. 236; *Virtshaftsgeshikhte, op. cit.*, IV, p. 224. See also Mahler and Ringelblum, *op. cit.*, p. 58, n. 1 and Weinryb, *ibid.*, p. 43, 63.

5. Salt was the main product of Poland, and the mines of Wieliczka and Bochnia constituted Poland's largest industrial enterprise in the Middle Ages. It should also be noted that Casimir the Great, who was very much interested in increasing production in the salt mines, issued a special legislative statement designed to promote this aim. In the light of this, the fact that he entrusted the salt mines into the hands of Lewko and other Jews is most noteworthy. See *The Cambridge History of Poland, op. cit.*, pp. 446, 179.

6. *Studies, op. cit.*, p. 237; *Virtshaftsgeshikhte, op. cit.*, IV, p. 224. Cf. Mahler and Ringelblum, *op. cit.*, pp. 56-57.

7. Schipper cites in his *Studies* five cases based on different sources. See p. 237.

8. For instance, the transit duties in such an important trade center as Lwów were leased by Wolczko Czolner (Zollner) in 1424-1434, by Szachna in 1440-1448, Natko (Nathan) in 1452-1459, Samson of Żydaczów in 1466-1474, the latter's widow in 1476, Elias in 1481, Moses Jordan in 1494, Josko (Joseph) in 1502-1508.

9. *Studies, op. cit.*, pp. 238-241, 277; *Virtschaftsgeshikhte, op. cit.*, IV, pp. 225-228; "Dzieje gospodarcze Żydów," *op. cit.*, pp. 126, 129; *Kultur-geshikhte, op. cit.*, pp. 200-206. Cf. Friedman, "Geshikhte fun Yidn in Ukraine," *op. cit.*, p. 26. The statement quoted by Schipper from Decius' work, *De Sigismundi regio temporobis* published in 1516, is as follows: "At this time, and this had already begun much earlier, the value and rights of the Jews are increasing. There is almost no tax or duty which they do not manage or which they would not wish to be in charge of. Christians are generally dependent on Jews and there is hardly one among the magnates and the foremost gentlemen in the Republic who would not appoint a Jew over his estate and give him power over Christians." The last point, Schipper notes, was the main reason why the Church vehemently, but unsuccessfully, opposed the placing of Jews in positions of public trust. *Studies, op. cit.*, p. 241. Cf. Weinryb, *The Jews of Poland, op. cit.*, p. 51.

10. *Studies, op. cit.*, p. 273. In the *Virtshaftsgeshikhte* Schipper computes Natko's annual rent for leasing the Lwów customs and the Drohobycz salt works to have been about $13,000. See *Virtshaftsgeshikhte, op. cit.*, IV, p. 225.

11. *Studies, loc. cit.*, and p. 278.

12. *Ibid.*, p. 244.

13. *Ibid.*, p. 275. *Virtshaftsgeshikhte*, IV, *loc. cit.*; "Dzieje gospodarcze Żydów," *op. cit.*, p. 127. According to Rybarski the weight of the Polish stone varied but it generally amounted to thirty-two pounds. See R. Rybarski, *Handel i polityka handlowa Polski w XVI stuleciu* (Warsaw: 1958), vol. II, pp. 332-340.

14. *Virtshaftsgeshikhte, op. cit.*, IV, pp. 267-268; "Dzieje gospodarcze Żydów," *op. cit.*, p. 129.

15. *Studies, op. cit.*, pp. 245-246; *Virtshaftsgeshikhte, op. cit.*, pp. 226 ff.

16. *Studies, op. cit.*, pp. 247-248; *Virtshaftsgeshikhte, op. cit.*, IV, p. 229. Cf. Mahler, "Di Yidn in amolikn Poyln," *op. cit.*, pp. 60 f. and Weinryb, *The Jews of Poland, op. cit.*, p. 121; also, Baron and Kahan, *Economic History, op. cit.*, pp. 125 ff.

17. *Studies, op. cit.*, p. 166. See also *Der Anteil der Juden am Grosshandel, op. cit.*, p. 18; *Virtshaftsgeshikhte, op. cit.*, IV, p. 208; *Dzieje handlu żydowskiego, op. cit.*, pp. 16, 17. It should be noted that in asserting the lack of a consistent and purposeful economic policy on the part of the Jagiellons, Schipper relies completely on the conclusions of Prof. S. Kutrzeba (*Handel Krakowa w wiekach średnich*, Cracow: 1903) to whom he refers several times but with whom he eclectically agrees and disagrees.

18. *Dzieje handlu żydowskiego, loc. cit.*

19. *Studies, op. cit.*, p. 167; *Der Anteil . . . am Grosshandel, op. cit.*, p. 20; *Virtshaftsgeshikhte, op. cit.*, IV, p. 209; *Dzieje handlu żydowskiego, op. cit.*, p. 16. Cf. Weinryb, *The Jews of Poland, op. cit.*, p.8.

20. *Studies, op. cit.*, pp. 167-168; *Der Anteil . . . am Grosshandel, op. cit.*, p. 19; *Virtshaftsgeshikhte, op. cit.*, IV, p. 210; *Dzieje handlu żydowskiego, loc. cit.* The reference to Kutrzeba relates to his *Handel Polski ze Wschodem* (The Trade of Poland with the East), (Cracow: 1903), p. 97. Regarding the weak political position of the Polish burgesses, see also *The Cambridge History of Poland, op. cit.*, pp. 424-425.

21. *Dzieje handlu żydowskiego, op. cit.*, pp. 16, 17; *Studies, op. cit.*, pp. 169, 170; *Der Anteil . . . am Grosshandel, op. cit.*, p. 19; *Virtshaftsgeshikhte*, IV, *loc. cit.*

22. *Studies, op. cit.*, p. 171; *Dzieje handlu żydowskiego, op. cit.*, p. 15; *Virtshaftsgeshikhte*, IV, *loc. cit.* Regarding the Cracow agreement of 1485 see also M. Bałaban, *Historja Żydów w Krakowie i na Kazimierzu* (Cracow: 1928), vol. I,

p. 48. According to Weinryb, Jewish retail trade was limited and circumscribed even before 1485; see his *The Jews of Poland, op. cit.*, pp. 64-65.

23. *Der Anteil . . . am Grosshandel, op. cit.*, pp. 20-21; *Studies, op. cit.*, p. 172; *Virtshaftsgeshikhte, op. cit.*, IV, p. 210; *Dzieje handlu żydowskiego, op. cit.*, p. 18; "Dzieje gospodarcze Żydów," *op. cit.*, pp. 122, 124. On the Polish expansion towards the Black Sea see *The Cambridge History of Poland, op. cit.*, pp. 177, 201, 206, 225, 253.

24. Cf. *Der Anteil . . . am Grosshandel, loc. cit.*; "Dzieje gospodarcze Żydów," *op. cit.*, p. 123; and *Dzieje handlu żydowskiego, loc. cit.*

25. *Studies, op. cit.*, pp. 173-175; *Virtshaftsgeshikhte, op. cit.*, IV, pp. 211-212; "Dzieje gospodarcze Żydów," *op. cit.*, p. 123; *Dzieje handlu żydowskiego, loc. cit.*

26. See *Virtshaftsgeshikhte, op. cit.*, IV, p. 213 and *Dzieje handlu żydowskiego, op. cit.*, p. 19.

27. *Studies, op. cit.*, p. 177; *Virtshaftsgeshikhte*, IV, *loc. cit.; Der Anteil . . . am Grosshandel, op. cit.*, p. 23. *Dzieje handlu żydowskiego, loc. cit.* The entry in the *Akta grodzkie i ziemskie* of Lwów regarding Caleb's presence in Lwów in 1440 is cited by Mahler and Ringelblum, *op. cit.*, p. 42.

28. *Studies, op. cit.*, pp. 178-179; *Virtshaftsgeshikhte*, IV, p. 214; *Dzieje handlu żydowskiego, loc. cit.; Der Anteil . . . am Grosshandel, op. cit.*, p. 24. Regarding the number of Italian merchants staying in Poland, Schipper cites Kutrzeba, *Handel Polski ze Wschodem, op. cit.*, p. 60.

29. *Studies, op. cit.*, p. 180; *Virtshaftsgeshikhte, loc. cit.; Dzieje handlu żydowskiego, loc. cit.; Der Anteil . . . am Grosshandel, loc. cit. See also Mahler and Ringelblum, op. cit.*, p. 42.

30. *Studies, op. cit.*, p. 180; *Dzieje handlu żydowskiego, op. cit.*, p. 20.

31. Cf. *The Cambridge History of Poland, op. cit.*, pp. 446-447.

32. *Studies, op. cit.*, p. 181; *Der Anteil . . . am Grosshandel, op. cit.*, pp. 25-26; *Virtshaftsgeshikhte, op. cit.*, IV, pp. 215-216; *Dzieje handlu żydowskiego, loc. cit.* See also Mahler and Ringelblum, *op. cit.*, p. 43.

33. *Studies, op. cit.*, pp. 183-184; *Der Anteil . . . am Grosshandel, op. cit.*, p. 28; *Virtshaftsgeshikhte, op. cit.*, IV, p. 217; *Dzieje handlu żydowskiego, loc. cit.*

34. Cf. Mahler and Ringelblum, *op. cit.*, pp. 43-44.

35. *Kultur-geshikhte, op. cit.*, p. 233. Cf. J. Ptaśnik, *Kultura włoska wieków średnich w Polsce* (Warsaw: 1922), p. 78. See also Friedman, "Geshikhte fun Yidn in Ukraine," *op. cit.*, p. 28.

36. *Studies, op. cit.*, p. 182; *Der Anteil . . . am Grosshandel, op. cit.*, pp. 26-27; *Kultur-geshikhte, op. cit.*, p. 234; *Virtshaftsgeshikhte*, IV, *loc cit.; Dzieje handlu żydowskiego, loc. cit.* Cf. Kutrzeba, *op. cit.*, p. 72 and Heyd, *op. cit.*, pp. 180, 542.

37. *Virtshaftsgeshikhte, op. cit.*, IV, pp. 218-219, 269-270; *Studies, op. cit.; Der Anteil . . . am Grosshandel, op. cit.*, p. 28; "Dzieje gospodarcze Żydów," *op. cit.*, p. 21. Cf. T. Hirsch, *Danzigs Handels-und Gewerbegeschichte*, (Leipzig: 1858), pp. 165, 176-177; H. Jolowicz, *Geschichte der Juden in Königsberg* (Posen: 1867), pp. 3 f. On the complicated relationships with the Teutonic Order and their final resolution, see A. B. Boswell, "Jagiello's Successors: the Thirteen Years War with the Knights," *The Cambridge History of Poland, op. cit.*, vol. I, pp. 232-249. The letter of King Casimir IV to the Grand Master of the Teutonic Order regarding Słonia of Grodno is reproduced by Mahler and Ringelblum, *op. cit.*, pp. 39 f. Concerning the participation of the Volhynian Jews in the northern trade see also Friedman, "Geshikhte fun Yidn in Ukraine," *op. cit.*, pp. 27, 29. On the subject of foreign trade, see also Weinryb, *The Jews of Poland, op. cit.*, pp. 65-67.

38. *Virtshaftsgeshikhte, op. cit.*IV, pp. 271 f.; *Dzieje handlu żydowskiego, op. cit.*, p. 22; "Dzieje gospodarcze Żydów," *op. cit.*, p. 130. Regarding the litigation between Zusman of Brest and Ruben of Warsaw revealing trade relations with Venice, see also Mahler and Ringelblum, *op. cit.*, p. 41.

39. *Studies, op. cit.*, pp. 188-189; *Virtshaftsgeshikhte, op. cit.*, IV, p. 219; "Dzieje gospodarcze Żydów," *op. cit.*, p. 124; *Dzieje handlu żydowskiego, op. cit.*, p. 21. Cf. Mahler and Ringelblum, op. cit., pp. 35-36.

40. *Studies, op. cit.*, pp. 190-192; *Virtshaftsgeshikhte, op. cit.*, IV, pp. 219-220; "Dzieje gospodarcze Żydów," *loc. cit.; Dzieje handlu żydowskiego, op. cit.*, pp. 21-22.

41. *Supra*, Chap. III, pp. 96-97, 106-107.

42. *Studies, op. cit.*, pp. 161-162.

43. "Agrarkolonisation der Juden in Polen," *Jüdische Fragen* (Vienna: 1909), pp. 64-78.

44. *Studies, op. cit.*, pp. 157-163.

45. With regard to land ownership and farming, see in particular vol. I, pp. 126-128; 150-152. Cf. I. F. Baer, *Toledot ha-Yehudim bi-Sefarad ha-Notsrit* (Tel Aviv: 1959), pp. 27 f., 84, 124 f., 502 n. 20.

46. Schipper cites cases ranging from 1386 to 1432. *Virtshaftsgeshikhte, op. cit.*, IV, pp. 201-203.

47. *Ibid.*, p. 204. See also *supra*, Chap. IV, pp. 136 f.

48. *Virtshaftsgeshikhte, op. cit.*, IV, pp. 266, 269; "Dzieje gospodarcze Żydów," *op. cit.*, p. 129. Cf. Mahler, "Di Yidn in amolikn Poyln," *op. cit.*, pp. 37-38.

49. "Agrarkolonisation der Juden in Polen," *op. cit., passim. Studies, op. cit.*, pp. 159, 161; *Virtshaftsgeshikhte, op. cit.*, IV, pp. 205-207; "Dzieje gospodarcze Żydów," *op. cit.*, p. 128. See also Mahler and Ringelblum, *op. cit.*, p. 55.

50. D. Pasmanik, "Review of Schipper's 'Agrar-Kolonisation der Juden in Polen'," *Yevreyskaya Starina*, I (1909), pp. 144-146.

51. M. Wischnitzer, "On the Occasion of Schipper's Book about the Economic Life of Jews in Poland in the Middle Ages," *Yevreyskaya Starina*, V (1913), pp. 133-137.

52. *Supra,* Chap. I, p. 26.

53. M. Bałaban, "Dwa pryczynki do stosunków Jagiełły z Żydami lwowskimi," *op. cit.*, pp. 231-232. See also *idem., Z historji Żydów w Polsce: Szkice i studja* (Warsaw: 1920), pp. 3-17.

54. "Sporniye voprosi epokhi Vladislava Yagiello," *op. cit.*, pp. 106-107.

55. Halpern, *op. cit.*, p. 303. Cf. Weinryb, *The Jews of Poland, op. cit.*, pp. 61-62; also, Baron and Kahan, *Economic History, op. cit.*, p. 110.

56. See Schipper, "Wewnętrzna organizacja Żydów w dawnej Polsce," Żydzi w Polsce Odrodzonej, *op. cit.*, pp. 97-98.

57. *Studies, op. cit.*, pp. 249 f. Cf. Baron, *op. cit.*, vol. XII, pp. 80 ff. and vol. III, pp. 175, 194.

58. Cf. *Studies, op. cit.*, p. 251 and *Virtshaftsgeshikhte, op. cit.*, IV, pp. 249 f. The list of Jewish physicians in the latter is given again in the *Kultur-geshichte, op. cit.*, pp. 195 f.

59. *Studies, op. cit.*, pp. 249, 252; *Kultur-geshikhte, op. cit.*, pp. 196-197, 206-207.

60. Regarding Schipper's sentiment on the subject of the common folk, see *infra*, pp. 251 ff.

61. *Virtshaftsgeshikhte, op. cit.*, IV, pp. 250-251.

62. See Mahler and Ringelblum, op. cit., p. 53, n. 1.

63. *Studies, op. cit.*, p. 254; *Virtshaftsgeshikhte, op. cit.*, IV, pp. 251-252. While the matter of kosher (ritually acceptable) meat and other foods is part of the complex dietary laws expounded in the Talmud and the vast halakhic literature, the prohibition of *sha'atnez* (mixing wool with linen) is unequivocally stated twice in the Bible, *Lev.* 19:19 and *Deut.* 22:11. Both the dietary laws and the *sha'atnez* prohibition were strictly adhered to by all Jews up to recent times. Cf. Baron, *op. cit.*, vol. XII, p. 45.

64. On the basis of Schipper's evidence and later investigations, Mahler concluded that the theory relating Jewish crafts to religious factors is completely false, since Jews engaged in a whole series of crafts which had nothing in common with religious rituals and needs. There were among them furriers, tanners, glaziers, rope makers, etc. See Mahler, "Di Yidn in amolikn Poyln," *op. cit.*, pp. 79-80. Adhering to the same conclusion, Mark goes a step further in arguing that the existence of Jewish craftsmen in Poland goes back to the very begin-

ning of Jewish presence in that country, well before the Tartar invasion, and that from the very beginning they served not only their own coreligionists but also the Christian population in the cities and villages. See Mark, "Rzemieślnicy żydowscy w Polsce feudalnej," *op. cit.*, pp. 11, 15-17. Regarding Jewish craftsmen in Lwów, see L. Charewiczowa, "Ograniczenia gospodarcze nacyj schizmatyckich i Żydów we Lwowie XV, XVI wieku," *Kwartalnik Historyczny* (1925), p. 216. Cf. Weinryb, *The Jews of Poland, op. cit.*, pp. 67-68; also, Baron and Kahan, *Economic History, op. cit.*, pp. 151-153.

65. *Virtshaftsgeshikhte, op. cit.*, IV, p. 254; *Kultur-geshikhte, op. cit.*, pp. 133, 207; "Wewnętrzna organizacja Żydów w dawnej Polsce," *op. cit.*, pp. 87-88, 96; cf. Mahler, "Di Yidn in amolikn Poyln," *op. cit.*, pp. 33-34.

66. *Studies, op. cit.*, p. 257; *Virtshaftsgeshikhte, op. cit.*, IV, p. 253. Cf. M. Wischnitzer, *A History of Jewish Crafts and Guilds* (New York: 1965), p. 211. See also Mark, *op. cit.*, p. 88.

67. *Virtshaftsgeshkihte, op. cit.*, IV, p. 253. See also Mahler and Ringelblum, *op. cit.*, pp. 52-53; J. Shatzky, *Geshikhte fun Yidn in Varshe* (New York: 1947-1953) vol. I, p. 37; Wischnitzer, *loc. cit.*

68. "Świadczenia Żydów na rzecz państwa i patronów," *Żydzi w Polsce Odrodzonej, op. cit.*, vol. I, pp. 200-210 (cited in the following as "Świadczenia").

69. *Studies, op. cit.*, pp. 307, 317-321; *Virtshaftsgeshikhte, op. cit.*, IV, pp. 196-198; "Świadczenia," *op. cit.*, pp. 201-203.

70. The table compiled by Schipper on the basis of these sources shows, for instance, that in the last decades of the fifteenth century the Jewish community of Cracow paid only 100 florins in 1479 and 1504; the community of Poznań 160 florins in 1487 and 200 florins before 1493; Lwów, 200 florins in 1466 and in years thereafter. Other communities (Gniezno, Sandomierz, Łęczyca, etc.) paid considerably less. Besides the individual Jews who were by special royal letter exempted from the annual tax, certain communities were also, at times, either completely exempted or granted assessment reductions mainly because of major misfortunes (*vis major*). See *Studies*, pp. 307-309.

71. *Studies, op. cit.*, pp. 311-316; *Kultur-geshikhte, op. cit.*, pp. 135-143. The first provincial tax prefects for Greater Poland were Shlomo and Samuel, superseded in 1512 by Abraham Bohemus whose territory included also the province of Mazovia, Ephraim Franczek for Little Poland and Red Ruthenia, and Michael Ezofowicz for Lithuania. Although the biography of Rabbi Jacob Polak, the father of the Polish school of *pilpul* (a specific analytical method of Talmudic study), is not without unclarified and controversial points, it has been established that he was appointed the State-Primate of Polish Jewry in 1503 and forced to leave the city of Cracow soon thereafter. But he returned to Cracow in 1509 and founded, with the help of his rich mother-in-law, Rachel

Fischel, who was one of the king's financiers, the academy that became known as a great center of Talmudic studies. Cf. M. Balaban, "Yakov Polyak, otyets polskogo rabinisma," *Yevreyskaya Starina*, VI (1912), pp. 225-245; *idem., Dzieje Żydów w Krakowie i na Kazimierzu* (Cracow: 1913), vol. I, pp. 403 f.; I. Zinberg, *op. cit.*, vol. III, pp. 169 ff. For some additional details about Rabbi Jacob Polak see Weinryb, *The Jews of Poland, op. cit.*, pp. 91-92.

72. *Studies, op. cit.*, pp. 321-324; *Virtshaftsgeshikhte, op. cit.*, IV, p. 199; "Swiadczenia," *op. cit.*, p. 202.

73. *Studies, op. cit.*, p. 306. Regarding the subject of Jewish taxes, see also Mahler, "Di Yidn in amolikn Poyln," *op. cit.*, pp. 29-30, where Schipper's findings and contentions are closely followed in a comprehensive manner. Cf. Weinryb, *The Jews of Poland, op. cit.*, pp. 52-55.

74. Baron, *op. cit.*, vol. XIII, p. 267, n. 43.

75. The monograph that Schipper wrote together with Wischnitzer at the invitation of Dubnow, the editor of the encyclopedic *Istoriya yevreyskogo naroda*, the eleventh volume of which was devoted to the history of Jews in Poland, is entitled: "Ekonomicheskiy bit Yevreyev v Polshe: Torgoviye promisli otkupa i arenda." Two other monographs that Schipper wrote himself for the same publication are entitled: "Podatnoye oblozheniye Yevreyev" and "Razsyeleniye Yevreyev v Polshe i Litvye of XV do XVIII vyeka."

76. See *supra*, Chap. III, pp. 103-104 and I. Halpern, *The Jews in Eastern Europe, op. cit.*, pp. 302-303. Also, R. Mahler, *Toledot ha-Yehudim be-Polin* (Merḥavia: 1946), pp. 36-45; B. Mark, *Di geshikhte fun Yidn in Poyln* (Warsaw: 1957), pp. 255-283.

6

Economic Antagonism and Rancor

In analyzing and evaluating the financial obligations of the Jews towards the Polish state, Schipper carefully emphasizes that, although these obligations became increasingly burdensome, the Jews in Poland fared comparatively well because of the Crown's prudently tolerant policies towards them. Schipper writes:

> The liberal attitude of the Polish kings to Jews is best illustrated when one compares the Jewish burdens in Poland with the ravaging exploitation of the Jewish *regale* by the Western rulers. Beginning approximately with the twelfth century, the "patrons" of the Jews in the West implemented a shrewd system of plundering the possessions of their "treasury serfs." More than once had the patron himself had a hand in the pogroms in order to collect for himself, through his officials, the remaining ownerless Jewish belongings. The system included numerous expulsions of Jews calculated to obtain high ransom for extending them the right to return. A special method of robbing Jews consisted of liquidating Jewish claims for a proper recompense paid by the debtors to the

"patron" of the Jewish creditors. None of these methods of exploiting the Jewish *regale* can be determined in the Polish Crown.[1]

The Motives and Nature of Anti-Jewish Excesses

Nonetheless, there were numerous pogroms and anti-Jewish excesses in medieval Poland. Jews suffered from humiliations, terror, and outright attacks which erupted in various cities at one time or another and which made Jewish life quite insecure, notwithstanding the royal charters and their explicitly stated guarantees of protection.

In denouncing the blindness and naiveté of the assimilationist Jewish historians who, on the basis of these charters, painted a rather idyllic picture of Polish-Jewish relationships at the time, Schipper notes:

> If one wishes to form an opinion about the situation of the Jews in medieval Poland only on the basis of the General *Privilegia* which the Jews received from the Polish kings, the impression one will get is that the highest authority in Poland cared and used the strictest penalty sanctions to insure peace and security in the Jewish quarter. However, should one peruse the pages of the hundreds and thousands of court records preserved from the Middle Ages one will perceive that the royal sanctions were often no more than letters on paper.

In support of this contention Schipper offers a long list of documented facts relating the story of the typical medieval accusations leveled against Jews in Poland—well poisoning, host desecrations, ritual child murder, arson, and the like—and the criminal assaults perpetrated on their possessions and lives.[2]

Since a proper understanding of the anti-Jewish actions involves the position taken by the Polish clergy towards the Jews, Schipper discusses at length the policies and attitude of the Church regarding the presence and status of the Jews in the country. Pertinent sources being rather scanty, he presents the official thinking of the Church on the basis of canonical resolutions adopted at the Synods in Breslau (1266), Buda (1275), Łęczyca

(1285), and Wieluń-Kalisz (1420). These resolutions included: (1) the demand that Jews should be removed and excluded from all public activities (collection of tolls and customs, administrative functions, etc.); (2) the demand that Jews should live in separate areas; (3) the prohibition of social relationships with Jews (eating and celebrating together, attending the public baths together, etc.); (4) the prohibition on buying meat and other victuals from Jews; (5) the demand that Jews wear identification badges; (6) the demand that pawns and pledges deposited with Jewish creditors be returned to their Christian owners if stolen; and (7) the demand that Jews living in houses originally occupied by Christians pay the same contributions which had been paid to the local parish by the Christian occupant. The underlying objective of the Church reflected in the resolutions, which became crucial in the evolving relationships, was to keep the Christians and Jews separate. In Poland, where Christianity was still a relatively young plant, this objective was even more important than in the West.[3]

However, unlike the West, it was many years before the ecclesiastical authorities in Poland were in any position to press the secular rulers into adopting the economic resolutions or taking repressive action against Jews. In the first place, the decisions adopted at the synods utterly contradicted the royal *Privilegia.* Specific articles of the *Privilegia* not only expressly permitted Jews to use public facilities and places together with Christians but went as far as to impose upon the latter the obligation to assist Jews whenever mistreated or attacked. Secondly, the wishes of the Church were in diametrical opposition to the interest of the State, and the Church was not strong enough, especially under the Piasts, to interfere with the legitimate economic interests and aspirations of the growing Polish kingdom. Thirdly, the Polish clergy, which for political reasons obtained from the Polish kings great latifundia, soon discovered in the Jew the same indispensable commercial agent for the sale of their agricultural products and the purchase of foreign goods as the Polish nobility did. Moreover, capital began to accumulate in their coffers, and they had to put it in Jewish hands to be used for credit at interest. Thus, keeping in mind the very practical considerations and benefits, the official position of the Church was often disregarded by the Polish clergy itself. In fact, unofficially, it was interested in the Jews no less than the king and the nobility. "The Church, therefore, had to close its eyes to the fact that all its synod decisions regarding the Jews had no practical meaning."[4]

But the Church did not hide its official attitude to Jews. On the contrary, its attitude was manifested by means of propaganda conducted at the grassroots, especially in the cities where the German influence was strong. As the position and power of the Church grew stronger under the Jagiellons, the synod resolutions were echoed more often and in ever-wider circles. Nevertheless, Schipper goes on to prove, even the anti-Jewish excesses and pogroms in the second half of the fourteenth century, and surely those in the fifteenth century, although ostensibly justified by the need to protect Christianity and the Christians from the perfidious Jews who poison wells, murder children, desecrate Hosts, etc., were in actuality the product of economic frictions and antagonisms rather than religious animosity. The Jews were attacked not so much by the Christians as by the burghers and artisans, most of whom were Germans.

The distinctive feature of the earliest persecutions and actual killings of Jews in the years of the Black Death, attested by Jan Długosz and, more specifically, by the Italian chronicler Matteo Villani, is not that the Jews were accused of poisoning the wells but the fact that the assaults took place at a time when cities like Breslau and Cracow attained a high point in their development and that even a tutelary ruler like Casimir the Great could not prevent it. True, the testimonies of the chroniclers do not reveal to what extent socioeconomic factors determined or influenced the tragic events of 1348-1349, but in 1367 when a bloody pogrom took place in Poznań, again under the rule of Casimir the Great and in spite of a direct appeal by the Pope, the court documents of that city clearly indicate that the economic relations between the Jews and the Christians were extremely strained. Similarly, the ruthless punishment of Jews that was carried out in Poznań in 1399 because they allegedly desecrated the Host had its roots in the growing hostility between the Jewish money-lenders and their Christian debtors, as can be deduced from court records of 1397, showing that a nobleman organized an attack on a Jewish banker in order to remove the latter from his mortgaged property, and from other sources of 1398 revealing credit frictions with burghers.

Influenced, apparently, by the news about Jew killings in Silesia and Bohemia, the burghers of Cracow, especially the artisans among them, attacked the Jews and pillaged their homes in 1407 under the pretext of avenging a ritual murder. But this, too, was preceded by charges of Jewish counterfeiting and the burning of an alleged Jewish counterfeiter. Moreover, the Cracow artisans fought at the time with the leading city patricians for political leverage in the municipal autonomy. In this struggle, the patricians, accused by the artisans of siding with the Jews, arrested the rioters en masse fearing that the latter would attack them as well. However, not too many years later, in 1423, when Cracow was again the scene of anti-Jewish excesses, a royal investigation found the city patricians guilty of instigating these excesses and the Cracow voivode took punitive steps against them.[5]

Schipper demonstrates further that the religious pretexts to justify anti-Jewish acts of violence were utilized only until the beginning of the fifteenth century. From that time on, the accusation of arson, which the burghers found more convenient to hurl at the Jews, became the generally accepted excuse for burning and looting Jewish homes. The only exception to that seems to have been the 1463 massacre in Cracow which, organized by crusaders in connection with the expedition against the Turks, was still justified *ad maiorem Dei gloriam.* Citing the fact that the city chroniclers of Poznań often note that "part of the city was burned down and for this reason Jews were killed," Schipper lists pogrom participants in that city in 1464 to show that its leaders included only artisans and craftsmen. Even the anti-Jewish riots in Cracow in 1455, imputable to Capistrano's visit and campaign in Poland, were sparked by a fire set to the house of a Christian alderman in which Jews kept their own wares and the pledges of their debtors. In spite of this, the Jews were blamed, as in all cases of fire, including those that erupted in Cracow in 1464, 1477, and 1494.

In Cracow the city council was at best neutral and inactive while Jews were being killed and their possessions plundered. In fact, it quietly supported the sacking of Jews by the crusaders in 1463. As a result, Casimir IV initiated court proceedings against the city, and Cracow was fined to the extent of 3,000 florins and forced to post a high bond of 10,000 *grossi* as a guarantee that all disputes with Jews would be settled without resorting to violence and that the city would protect the Jews in the future. But a year later, when the city gave its consent to the expulsion of Jews, the king found it again necessary to sue, and the city was penalized with a fine of 2,000 ducats. In spite of court litigations (there was another one initiated by the king in connection with the fire that broke out in 1477) and arrests of individual city councilmen, the terrible conflagration that took place in Cracow in 1494 caused the king to ask the Jews to leave the city and settle in the suburb of Kazimierz. Thus, by means of intimidation and terrorization, the burghers of Cracow achieved, for a time at least, their objective of getting rid of their Jewish competitors.[6]

What is most significant, however, is that the growing anti-Jewish sentiment in Poland in the last century of the Middle Ages was not evenly distributed throughout the country. There were no anti-Jewish excesses at all in the Ruthenian lands until the very end of the fifteenth century. Even if one is to limit oneself to the land of the Crown alone, Schipper points out, one can easily perceive the fact that anti-Jewish actions spread from the economically more-developed provinces to the less-developed ones where such actions inevitably came to pass, but not until the economic interests and competitive tensions reached a certain degree of acuteness. This is manifestly borne out by the fact that the crusaders who, instead of following the orders of Pope Pius II calling for a military campaign against the Turks, turned against the Jews in the cities, found in Cracow overt and covert accomplices. But in Lwów, located in the eastern province of Red Ruthenia, they met with little success. The city council of Lwów not only rejected the demand of the crusaders that the Jews be delivered into their hands but also declared that it would defend the Jews and the city in case of attack. Clearly, unlike Cracow, the Jews in Lwów were still needed in the sixties of the fifteenth century; hence, the willingness and readiness of this city to protect them. But four decades later, in 1498, the attitude of the burghers and council of Lwów was no longer the same. The reversal in their attitude is evidenced in the fact that they did not oppose the attacks of the crusaders that took place in the last years of the fifteenth century. On the contrary, this time the city dwellers of Lwów openly participated in the plunder of Jewish homes and the court records reveal many charges of murder brought against individual adventurers.[7]

In summarizing the state of anti-Jewish violence and persecutions in medieval Poland, Schipper notes:

> We are far from the view that differences of descent and creed did not play an important role in instigating pogroms against Jews. We believe, however, that the economic motives were more decisive and significant in the matter. Otherwise, how can one explain the phenomenon that in spite of all the bills issued by the Popes to deny and dispel the accusations of ritual murder as groundless rumors and in spite of the charters forbidding the populace to accuse Jews of using Christian blood, the medieval society clung to the opposite view. Obviously, under the mantle of religion this society fought not for religious but for quite material objectives. . . .[8]

In Poland the hostility toward Jews prevailed almost exclusively among the city dwellers, particularly among the Christian artisans, and it persisted even though the Polish rulers watched over Jewish life and property and punished, indeed, those responsible for attacking Jews.

True, "at times the city dwellers were supported by the clergy, but the role of the Church in the persecutions was of secondary importance. At best it acted as a spark falling into a barrel of powder."[9]

Furthermore, the correctness of the view that the outbursts of anti-Jewish violence are explicable mainly in terms of the process of economic development can be seen from the pattern of these outbursts. They began at first in Greater and Little Poland and came to pass in the central region (Mazovia) much later and in Ruthenia still later, not before the very end of the Middle Ages. In other words, "wherever city life developed earlier, collisions with Jews also occurred earlier, and wherever Jewish facilitation, their credit and commerce, were needed longer, there the pogroms and Jew-pillage took place later."[10]

Again, assentingly referring to Roscher's thesis that the pogroms represented a medieval form of social revolution, Schipper expresses the same idea somewhere else in a more aphoristic form by saying that "the degree of the Jews' personal and material security in the Middle Ages stood in converse proportional relationship to the level of economic culture."[11]

The Struggle for Residence Rights

The opposition to Jews for economic reasons is also reflected in nonviolent areas, especially in attempts of the Christian city dwellers to implement legislation designed to limit Jewish rights and to curb their economic activities. The two main targets of these attempts were (1) to prescribe the residential rights of the Jewish population and (2) to regulate and control their commercial affairs in compliance with the best interests of the Christian burghers.

The freedom of movement guaranteed to Jews in the royal charters was complemented in the same charters by articles granting Jews the right to live in the Polish realm wherever they wanted. The oldest information concerning the Jewish quarter in Cracow, found in the municipal records of 1304, relates that Christian burghers also had their homes, shops, lots, and breweries in that quarter. On the other hand, other sources reveal that a number of Jews owned homes and property outside the Jewish section. It would appear therefore that a Jewish quarter existed as a matter of choice rather than imposition. There was no segregation as such, nor was there initially any opposition on the part of the Christian burghers to that state of affairs. The only institution that opposed it and attempted from the very beginning to undermine the indiscriminative residence rights of the Jews was the Church which deemed it necessary to keep Jews in a *vicus Judaicus*, apart and away from Christians, in order to protect the "young Polish seedling of Christianity" from harmful Jewish influences. But even though the demand of the ecclesiastical authorities to restrict the residence of Jews to ghettos was reiterated at all Church synods of the thirteenth century, it had little effect and produced no visible change because until the end of the fourteenth century the economic role and position of the Jews in the cities could not be and was not yet challenged by any segment of the population. However, when the same demand was voiced again at the Wieluń-Kalisz Synod in 1420 (presided by Nicolas Trąba, the militantly anti-Jewish archbishop of Gniezno and Primate of Poland), it got an unmistakable echo in the cities because it now coincided with the economic interest of the burghers among whom the German colonizers, assimilated by now with the local Polish population, constituted the leading and most influential element. Thus, noting that "the economic laws of daily life were more powerful and decisive than the royal charters and the Church resolutions in the question of Jewish residence rights," Schipper emphasizes that the Church became in time the natural ally of the Christian city dwellers in opposing the Jews, not for religious reasons but for the very practical reason of eliminating the Jewish competitor.[12]

The evolving struggle for residence rights is well illustrated by the story of Cracow which Schipper reproduces in considerable detail. On the basis of available sources, principally the municipal records, it appears that until the second half of the fourteenth century and beyond, the Jews in Cracow did not experience any restrictions in the purchase of lots for the purpose of building and that, in general, they were buyers rather than sellers of properties. By the end of the fourteenth century, however, clauses designed to thwart the purchase of properties by Jews began to appear in the contracts. Citing a number of characteristic cases, Schipper goes on to show that these clauses reflect the growing insistence of the burghers that Jews be required to carry the same responsibilities towards the municipality as all its other citizens, even though they were formally not subject to city jurisdiction and exempted, on the basis of the principle implied in their legal status, from city obligations. Obviously, it was not a question of jurisdiction as much as a question of additional income for the city. Indeed, from 1435 the Cracow records include a number of contracts in which the Jewish purchasers assumed the obligation of paying an annual property fee, unknown heretofore, which was collected by certain distinguished burghers, or directly by the city, or by ecclesiastical institutions. This property fee, Schipper notes, was a well-established fact in Cracow in the fourth decade of the fifteenth century.[13]

The persistent effort of the Cracow burghers to undermine the position of the Jews intensified in the second half of the fifteenth century and took on the form of a campaign to limit the residence rights of Jews to the *vicus Judaicus* by impeding their right to buy homes outside the *vicus.* Although the Jews did not occupy properties in the marketplace proper and their section of residence, mainly St. Anne Street, was only adjacent to it, the burghers, in their desire to retain for themselves the entire retail trade, made every possible attempt to move the boundaries of the Jewish section further away from the marketplace. Eventually, in 1469, the center of Jewish residence shifted because Jagiello decided to build the Jagiellonian Collegium (*Studium*) on the St. Anne Street, and the Jewish *kahal* agreed to surrender two synagogues, a hospital, a bath house, a cemetery, and other Jewish buildings located there. But this did not satisfy the burghers who wanted to get rid of the Jews altogether by removing them to the suburb of Kazimierz. Being in no position to do so, they began to frustrate the ability of Jews to buy homes.[14] Although the Jews knew how to circumvent obstacles, the situation grew worse until it erupted in the 1494 conflagration during which the Christians plundered all Jewish homes located outside the Jewish quarter. The homeless Jews apparently had no choice but to transfer to Kazimierz where Jan Olbracht offered them some land and homes. Having accomplished their aim once by the sheer force of violence, the burghers continued to use it. In the year 1500 bloody riots took place again in Cracow as well as Kazimierz which led to the arrest of some city councilmen, who acted in collusion with the pogrom leaders, and the imposition of a bond in the amount of 10,000 *grossi* on the city to guarantee future peace. But the king, realizing that the burghers would continue with their attacks until the Jews were prevented from making their way into Christian areas, issued a decree forbidding the Jews to buy, build, or rent outside their *vicus* under threat of confiscation or the nullification of contracts. In his desire to avoid further riots, he even justified his decree by stating that the dominant and ruling Christians should strive to limit the growth of the Jewish race. Thus the burghers triumphed and the Middle Ages in Poland ended with the establishment of a Jewish ghetto.[15]

In Poznań the pattern of the struggle for space and the right to reside outside limited areas was, in the main, similar to that of Cracow. The burghers here were no less relentless in their efforts to impose upon Jews all city burdens while, at the same time, impeding their right to buy properties outside the area of Jewish concentration which, in effect, consisted of two streets, although many Jewish families lived among non-Jews. In spite of this, in the fifteenth century, Jews of Poznań, apparently supported in their efforts by the gentry, were somehow able to build around their streets and to penetrate even in the center of the marketplace where they either bought or rented stores and shops. In the face of mounting opposition, they even obtained an official statement from the king sanctioning their right to property in the marketplace. By the beginning of the sixteenth century, however, the burghers were strong enough to bring about a reversal in the king's position. In 1523 Jews were forbidden, by an order of Sigismund I, to live or maintain commercial enterprises in the marketplace of Poznań, and in 1532, as a result of an influx of Jewish war refugees which prompted the city fathers to clamor in protest, the king issued a decree limiting the residence right of the Jews to the old Jewish quarter only and interdicting their right to purchase homes from Christians. Thus, here too, a Jewish ghetto was created by the beginning of the second quarter of the sixteenth century.[16]

Around the same time a number of Polish cities began to secure for themselves the special right of excluding Jews altogether in order to ward off Jewish competition in commerce and in other economic activities. According to Schipper, in the 1520-1597 period alone, at least nineteen cities secured for themselves the privilege *de non tolerandis Judaeis* which became a source of prolonged and bitterly obstinate struggles best illustrated by the story of Warsaw.[17]

But, as in the story of anti-Jewish violence, the question of residence rights and space was hardly a matter of strife in the eastern regions. In Lwów the Jews, organized at the time in three communities (*kahals*), lived in the center of the city as well as in its suburbs and experienced no restrictions whatever in the purchase of land for building homes. Even high Church dignitaries were not opposed to the acquisition of city properties by Jews, as can be seen from the fact that in 1468 Archbishop Gregor himself sold real estate to Jews, and nobles did likewise whenever they were offered a proper price for their houses in the city. As late as the end of the fifteenth century Jewish transactions in city real estate were still of quite considerable proportions. The conditions were not yet ripe at the time for the economic struggle to enter into the phase in which the restriction of residence rights for Jews became a major demand of the Lwów burghers.[18]

The Struggle for Commercial Rights

The persistent attempts of the cities to restrict Jewish living space and the consequent struggle for residence rights on the part of the Jews constituted only one aspect of the wider economic conflict between the growing Polish middle class and the Jews, the first signs of which became distinct in the second half of the fifteenth century when, following the anti-Jewish campaign of Capistrano in 1454, the agitation of the clergy met with growing approbation among the city commonalty and the Christian merchants. The former—ignorant, poor, and in debt—saw in the Jewish moneylender the source of all its misfortunes and the latter wished to get rid of the Jews because they saw in them an element endangering the established, noncompetitive monopoly of their trade in the cities.[19]

It was not until 1485, however, that the first restrictions on

Jewish commercial activities became a matter of fact, although it is highly improbable that the *kahal* seniors of Cracow would have "voluntarily" (*obsque omni coactione*, according to the Latin wording) entered into a covenant with the city agreeing to relinquish virtually all trade without having been under unbearable duress for a long time before. According to this "voluntary" agreement, the Jews "agreed" to limit their trade to forfeited pledges and self-manufactured caps and collars which could be sold only on two specific days of the week and at fairs. Furthermore, the city was given the right to arrest Jews engaged in trade other than forfeited pledges and to confiscate their wares. In any event, Schipper considers this date to represent a turning point and a historical boundary between the preceding period of unrestricted Jewish commercial activities and the following centuries of unending struggle for commercial rights. That the 1485 Cracow agreement represented the first signal and the beginning of a new period in Jewish commercial relationships in Poland is evidenced by the fact that it served as a precedent for other cities and continued to be invoked later at every possible occasion.[20]

Several types of anti-Jewish measures were employed. An attempt was made to check the growth of the Jewish population in the cities by limiting the number of houses available to Jews and by forcing the *kahals* to expel newcomers. The burghers demanded that Jewish shops and warehouses be banned from the city marketplaces and main streets to special inferior sections or outside the city altogether. The program of the Polish middle class consisted of those specific postulates designed to undermine Jewish trade which had been already carried out in the West and around which the struggle for commercial rights began to evolve in Poland during the 1485-1572 period with increasing intensity. These postulates, Schipper shows, included:

1. The premise that the Jews were not part of the national commercial class but foreign merchants. In practice this implied two crucial limitations on the ability of Jews to sell. First, as "foreigners," they would be expected to comply with the municipal law of compulsory unloading and storage which provided the city with an income as well as control over the imported

goods and which also gave the local Christian merchants the first option to buy them. Secondly, it meant that Jews could sell directly to the consumers only on market days and fairs;

2. The prohibition of engaging in retail trade which the Christian merchant considered to be his exclusive prerogative not to be interfered with by outside merchants;

3. The need to limit the wholesale trade of the Jews to certain commodities only, depending on local conditions and the interest of the burghers; and

4. The need to control and limit the competition of the Jews by forbidding them (a) to keep their stores open at times other than market and fair days, (b) to keep goods and merchandise in their own homes, and (c) to peddle and practice any type of undercutting.[21]

In addition, the clergy demanded at its synod in 1542 and again in 1589 that Jews be forbidden to keep their stores open, or to do business otherwise, on Sundays and on Christian holidays. Even the *szlachta*, the most privileged class of the Polish society which frowned upon the growing power of the Polish middle class, resenting particularly the latter's ability to dictate through its organized guilds low prices for grain and other agricultural products, began, officially at least, to interfere with the right of Jews to free trade. In the fifteenth century the *szlachta* readily used the Jews to sell its grain, pitch, and charcoal abroad, thus keeping the burghers in check economically; but by the beginning of the sixteenth century, realizing that its agricultural products were in great demand abroad, the *szlachta* began acting on its own in disposing of its goods. The fact that the Jew ceased to be so economically useful to the nobility is reflected in the position taken by the *szlachta* at its Diet of Piotrków in 1538 where it resolved that Jews be forbidden to carry on trade in the villages. "If the laws of the land," the resolution states, "forbid Christians to trade in the countryside and to have market days there, we have even less reason to let the Jews do so." Moreover, "the Jews are not entitled to unlimited freedom of trade. They must conform to the regulations established in the kingdom and abide by the agreements which exist in certain big cities."[22]

Thus it would seem that by the middle of the sixteenth century Jewish merchants found themselves under a cross fire from both the city and the countryside. The course of the struggle for commercial rights, characterized by repetitious ups and downs and by a tenacious effort on the part of the embattled Jews to hold on to their positions wherever possible, is described by Schipper in considerable detail in his *Studies.* The best case in point is provided by Lwów for which Schipper had more pertinent sources at his disposal.

Immediately following the 1485 Cracow agreement, the king unexpectedly granted the petition of the Christian merchants of Lwów to bar Jews from retail trade in all goods and wholesale trade in textiles and cattle. Since the king's decree left the Jews nothing but trade in forfeited pledges, Jewish commercial activities in Lwów immediately experienced a severe crisis as evidenced by the fact that the court records which, up to that time, contained many commercial entries, disclose mostly credit transactions and some real-estate investments and speculations in 1488-1493. It took some years before the Jews of Lwów initiated action to regain their positions in commerce. At first they obtained from the king an interim period during which they were permitted to trade 1800 oxen annually for a specified quantity of textiles to be sold wholesale in the cities of Jarosław and Przemyśl. Although the burghers could not by themselves revitalize the commercial activities of the city, which declined sharply when trade relations with the East were interrupted following the fall of Bialgorod in 1482, they insisted that the movements of Jews and other "foreigners" (Armenians, Russians) in the city proper be restricted. Jews, therefore, began to conduct limited trade outside the city limits, and by the end of the fifteenth century they even reestablished contact with Constantinople in spite of the obstacles put in their way by the burghers who now attempted to stem Jewish trade outside the city as well.

While the limitations on retail trade in yard goods and clothing fixed by the so-called *laudum* of 1499 remained in force, Jewish merchants found it to their advantage to conduct their retail trade in outlying towns and hamlets by avoiding whenever possible the need to unload in the city, although this could result in the confiscation of their goods when intercepted. In circumventing city regulations they often found tacit support among the nobles. But they relied mostly on their own ingenuity and, especially, on the influence they had with the king and the court. Thus, Josko of Hrubieszów, the lessee of royal duties and the king's purveyor of textiles and furs, was instrumental in helping the Jews of Lwów transport goods from Wallachia. He was also helpful in obtaining the 1503 royal decree which lessened considerably the erstwhile restrictions by allowing the Jews to engage in every type of retail trade on market days and fairs. This decree was confirmed again in 1506, the opposition of the burghers notwithstanding, with the added extenuating provision that the Jewish merchants be exempted from certain city tolls, the same as other city dwellers. When Sigismund I confirmed these commercial rights, the burghers initiated a vicious anti-Jewish campaign including false accusations, abuse, and illegal confiscations. This caused the king to issue a stern order to the city of Lwów in 1514 to stop the unfair methods of oppressing Jews and return to the latter illegally confiscated goods. But the struggle continued, and in 1515 Sigismund issued a temporary order according to which the Jews of Lwów were permitted to trade in all commodities except textiles and cattle without restrictions. Retail trade in textiles was limited to fairs only, and the annual quota of oxen to be bought and sold by Jews could not exceed 2,000. The constant appeals of the burghers to annul this order resulted in a temporary *salvum conductum* which led the burghers to intensify their political pressures because it did not meet with their demands.

Although the king promised to take up the matter at the Diet in Piotrków, the burghers decided to act for the first time in cooperation with other cities. A letter sent to all major cities called upon burghers to organize in order to limit the commercial rights of the Jews by a common effort.[23] Judging by the fact that in 1521 increased and intensified anti-Jewish actions were carried out in Lublin, Cracow, Poznań, and Lwów, it appears that the letter brought about a united front of burghers which had indeed a political effect. The Diet in Piotrków, held the same year, produced a royal decree designed to put an end to Jewish commerce in accordance with the wishes of the Polish merchants. It allowed the Jews to trade in four articles only: textiles, oxen, wax, and hides, with certain qualifications. The first could be bought and sold wholesale and retailed only at fairs. The second was limited to 2,000 head; the third and fourth could be sold but not purchased and could be disposed of only on market days and fairs. In addition, Jewish girls were forbidden to carry in their baskets and peddle pepper, spices, linen, silk, saffron, etc., and all Jews were forbidden to keep wares in their homes. The decree applied to Jews residing in the city proper and to those residing in its suburbs as well as to alien Jews visiting in Lwów.[24] Schipper emphasizes, however, the fact that this decree, too, could not and did not bring the Jews to surrender their rights and to capitulate. Although the king authorized local officials to enforce the restrictions of the 1521 decree, the Jews found ways and means to circumvent them while lobbying energetically for their repeal. Their actions produced in 1527 a short-lived victory in the form of a new royal decree granting again unlimited commercial freedom. They lost no time in taking advantage of it, and a number of big commercial enterprises sprang up in the suburbs of Lwów. But the ensuing reaction of the burghers was so vehement that the king was again compelled to retract.

A period of bitter contentions and negotiations followed. The burghers claimed that their economic position was dangerously jeopardized by Jewish merchants and that the latter were not deserving of equal rights because they could not claim bona fide citizenship either by virtue of their status in the city or by virtue of their obligations on behalf of the city. The Jews contended that restrictions would not only damage their own economic position but would ultimately mean a loss to the king's treasury. Indeed, when following the burghers' rejection of compromises proposed by the king, the Jews declared that the restrictions would force them to go bankrupt or to leave the city altogether, the king, realizing the financial losses which these alternatives might entail, summoned the burghers of Lwów and warned them to come to an agreement with the Jews or suffer the consequences, as a result of which the city finally agreed to grant the suburban Jews full municipal rights in return for certain fees.[25]

Except for variations determined by local circumstances, the struggle for commercial rights followed basically the same pattern in other urban centers of Poland during the period under discussion. In Cracow, in spite of the 1485 agreement and the anti-Jewish riots in 1494 and 1500, Jewish merchants not only continued to operate but actually intensified their activities to counteract the designs of the burghers. What made it possible was the influx of Jews from Bohemia who brought with them considerable amounts of capital. The burghers could not withstand the vigor, competence, and resourcefulness of the Jewish financial figures, the aforementioned Fischel family, Ozer of Opoczno, Franczek, Abraham Bohemus, and others who were not only court bankers and collectors of leased state duties and Jewish taxes, but also purveyors of great quantities of goods. They were engaged in a very extensive net of commercial transactions all over Poland. Citing a number of illustrations, Schipper shows that even the leading Christian merchants depended on them if they wished to share in the distribution of goods or even gain at times the king's favor. In fact, the 1485 agreement was never invoked by the city patricians who were transacting a great deal of business with their Jewish counterparts. To the lesser burghers, however, this agreement constituted an important precedent which Sigismund I could not overlook in his decree of 1521. While the Jews of Cracow considered the king's confirmation of the 1485 agreement to be a temporary device of policy, the burghers continued to press their demands to eliminante Jews completely from all trade with increased vigor, using the old arguments that Jews could not claim equal commercial rights since their legal status in the city was not that of citizens and their obligations to the city were not the same as those of legitimate burghers. The king finally responded with a decree in 1535 in which he confirmed again the validity of the 1485 agreement for the city of Cracow proper but left the commercial rights of the Jews outside the city unimpaired.[26]

The friction in Poznań also revolved, in the main, around the right of Jews to engage in retailing and the fact that here they still maintained shops and booths in the very center of the marketplace. For a long time the burghers' appeals to the king remained apparently unanswered. In fact, in 1517 Sigismund I warned the municipal council members of Poznań not to harass their Jewish competitors. But in 1520, as the political strength and pressures of the burghers, cloaked in religious terms, mounted, the king found it advisable to disallow Jews the right to sell their wares in the marketplace. In 1523 he issued one of the broadest and most specific decrees known for that period of time. It excluded Jews from the retail market altogether while prescribing particular limitations and rates on the wholesale trade of certain textiles, jewelry, spices, hides and leather, victuals, etc. It enjoined Jewish merchants against buying any merchandise brought to the city before local burghers had a chance to see it on the open market. It did not permit Jews to maintain stores and booths in the marketplace. Only during the annual fair were all restrictions lifted. Although this decree was obviously one-sided and discriminatory, the Jews nevertheless accepted its terms, not without misgivings but also not without hope that in spite of the trammels they would somehow manage.[27]

A more decisive victory over Jews was won by the burghers in Warsaw in 1525 when Janusz, the last Mazovian prince of the house of Piast, issued a decree rendering illegal the practice of commerce and crafts by Jews as well as their presence in the city of Warsaw and the localities adjacent to it within a two-mile radius. In 1527, within a year after Warsaw and the entire principality of Mazovia were incorporated in the Crown, Sigismund I confirmed the city's privilege of not tolerating Jews. The king's move, in Schipper's view, was dictated by the strong Teutonic influences which had existed here for a long time, reflected in the fact that since the Cracow peace treaty of 1525, which brought

East Prussia under fealty to the Polish Crown, there was not a single Diet without the Prussian cities demanding the expulsion of Jews and their elimination from local trade activities.[28]

Propitious Factors

The numerous decrees and agreements which appeared in the latter part of the fifteenth century and the first decades of the sixteenth century received their official formulation at the 1538 Diet in Piotrków, referred to above.[29] At this Diet the nobility officially took an anti-Jewish position for the first time. But, Schipper points out again, Jewish commerce, restricted in various degrees in the main Polish cities, continued to operate quite successfully and with the support of the king and the nobility in the eastern provinces of the kingdom: in Podolia, Volhynia, and Lithuania. The same Sigismund I who issued restrictive decrees in response to the demands of the burghers in Cracow, Poznań, and Warsaw did not hesitate in 1518 to grant complete commercial freedoms to the Jews of Kowel, the same as those enjoyed by the Jews of Brest Litovsk, or to provide a clause in the Magdeburg Charter, bestowed upon the city of Krzemieniec in 1536, granting the Jews of that city full commercial rights. It was both possible and desirable as long as there was not yet a substantial Christian middle class to object. Indeed, Jews of Volhynia continued to trade undisturbed in grain and other land products and shipped great quantities of charcoal, produced in the forests of Sanguszko, to Danzig. A similar favorable situation prevailed in Lithuania where the most active Jewish merchants concentrated in Brest Litovsk. The leading merchant here was the powerful Michael Ezofowicz, a banker and agent of the court who was even given the title of a noble. In Podolia, too, Jewish commerce experienced no limitations.[30]

But generally, even in the western provinces and the bigger urban centers, "reality was not as hard as would appear from the [royal] edicts and pacts. The restrictions on Jewish commerce prescribed by agreements or court decisions were only temporary or were not implemented at all. . . ." This was so because there existed at the time certain "factors [which] had a much greater effect on the practical course of life than the royal pronouncements and decrees . . . or the paper pacts which the municipalities, taking advantage of certain propitious circumstances, were able to impose upon the Jews."[31]

Schipper discusses several factors which not only mitigated but actually helped the Jews overcome the inimical designs of the burghers. In the first place, the Polish *szlachta* played an important role in keeping the burghers in check. Aware of the political power and role of the urban financial aristocracy in Western Europe, the Polish nobility quite deliberately utilized the Jews in its selfish pursuit of economic and political hegemony. In relation to the central power of the state, the *szlachta* had been trying relentlessly for a long time to arrogate to itself ever more rights and privileges. This resulted in a gradual weakening of the king's power and a growing amplification of the political position of the *szlachta* which went as far as to demand exclusive jurisdiction over Jews living on its lands and in its private towns. It was advantageous for the nobles to have their "own Jews," rather than Christians, function as the commercial agents of their estates. They knew that (1) Jews would safeguard their exclusive monopoly in exporting land products; (2) the Jews would bring them higher prices for their products; and (3) the Jews would sell them foreign goods at lower prices. To assure themselves of the latter, the *szlachta* put through tariff regulations at the diets which discriminated against the Jews, forcing them to sell at lower prices and receive narrower margins of profit, but which also compelled the Jews to seek ways and means of competing successfully. To fulfill the expectations of the *szlachta* and to assure themselves of the latter's protection as well as the benefits it might bring, the Jews, for their part, were anxious to cooperate and work harder. Their efforts produced a considerable increase in the volume of trade. They also concentrated their efforts on marketing articles of mass consumption. This, Schipper notes, was too much for the Christian merchants who simply could not keep up with the Jews in volume, variety, and prices.

Citing a number of typical illustrations, Schipper points also to the fact that leading burghers, once they attained wealth and land, often left the ranks of the Polish middle class to become part of the nobility. Because of this, the burghers as a class lacked the power to regenerate themselves steadily which, in turn, weakened their ability to compete with the Jews.[32] Moreover, Polish Jewry continued to receive Jewish immigrants from Spain, Italy, Germany, Bohemia, and Turkey. Besides additional capital, these new arrivals continuously reinforced and enriched the accumulated experience of the Jewish merchants in Poland with new knowledge of trade techniques as well as with up-to-date information about foreign markets. These factors, emanating from the Jews themselves, were even more important in their struggle with the burghers.

However, most decisive—and this Schipper makes a point of, directly or indirectly, in this as in other contexts—was the "agility" or "commercial aptitude" of the Jews, implying thereby their ability to adjust and to seize on opportunities as well as such psychological assets as tenacity, indefatigability, and perseverence. The fact that the Jews were undaunted and intrepid in their fight for commercial rights and that under the adverse conditions of duress and disadvantage they put their enterprising spirit and experience to good use, helped them, indeed, to emerge victorious from this fight.[33] Decrees, restrictions, and injunctions had little or no effect. They remained on paper while Jewish commercial activities, of one type or another, grew in intensity and importance. This is substantiated by the aforementioned anonymous brochure of 1539 which, even if inaccurate and exaggerated by reason of its polemical character, is very significant when it contends that 3,200 Jewish wholesalers were active in Poland at the time as against 500 Christian wholesalers, that Jewish merchants were selling at lower prices and were satisfied with smaller profits while practicing prudence and frugality in their calculations and expenditures, and that they were not at all cowed by the burgher, being well aware of the king's interest and protection.[34]

The General Effect

The best evidence, however, of Jewish economic advances despite the obstacles is provided by the numerous and repetitious protests and complaints about the monopolization of Polish commerce by Jews submitted to the king during the major part of the sixteenth century. "That these complaints were not exaggerated is demonstrated by the considerable amount of information, preserved from that period (*i.e.*, 1485-1572) about the growing dimensions of Jewish trade illustrating the participation of Jews in the foreign trade of Poland as well as in its domestic trade."[35]

The considerable amount of information which Schipper refers to resulted from his extended delving into Jewish source materials as their increased quantity and availability made it more possible. Thus, with reference to the period under discussion, Schipper is in a better position to supplement his evidence from the archival materials, the *Town and Country Documents*, the published official records, and the germane studies by Polish and Jewish historians with pertinent passages from the Responsa literature of the leading contemporary rabbis: Solomon Luria, Joseph ben Mordecai Gershon, Me'ir ben Gedaliah of Lublin, Joel Sirkes, and others, all of whom were well acquainted with the economic situation and activities of the Jewish communities in which they served.[36]

Based on this information, Schipper draws the wide panorama of Jewish economic activities, especially in the area of commerce, under the rules of Sigismund I (1506-1548) and Sigismund Augustus (1548-1572), depicting their unmistakably significant contributions to the economy of the Polish kingdom which, compared with countries in the West, was still in the Middle Ages.

In Foreign Trade

Thwarted to a greater or lesser degree in the field of domestic trade, Polish Jews became increasingly more active in Poland's commercial relations with other states, assuming an important role in such European markets as Constantinople, Adrianople, Venice, Florence, Hamburg, Frankfort-am-main, Leipzig, Breslau, Danzig, and Riga. In fact, they reached even more distant places such as Moscow, Rhodes, Alexandria, the Crimea, and as far as India.[37]

The fact that Jews were in a position to reactivate a lively trade with the East, especially with Turkey, was due mainly to the migration of the expelled Jews from Spain and Portugal, two-thirds of whom (about 90,000) settled in the European and Asian parts of the Ottoman Empire and some of them came from there to Poland.[38] Having established contact with their brethren in the southeastern provinces of Poland, the Turkish Jews, known in Poland as "Frenks," provided the former with new trade opportunities which were fully taken advantage of, especially when the Polish rulers entered into a series of commercial agreements with the Turkish sultans (Sigismund I with Selim I and Soliman II in 1519 and 1525, and Sigismund Augustus with Soliman II in 1553 and 1560). Because these agreements put Turkey and Poland in the position of leading commercial intermediaries between the Orient and the West, the contact between Constantinople and Lwów became a vital link of exchange, and the Jews, according to Schipper, became the mainspring in that link. The Jews acted as the leading middlemen who maintained and directed the organization of the movement of Oriental goods, outstripping in that respect the Armenians who, although very active, were fewer in number.

Besides citing the report of Commendone, the papal legate to Poland, to the ambassador of Venice in 1564, Schipper offers a series of pertinent examples to illustrate his point. According to the records, many Jews of Lwów traveled to Moldavia and further south. Moses and Solomon of Lwów received a special royal letter to conduct unlimited trade with Turkey. Even Jews of Poznań were engaged in the trade with the East. Jacob Tłusty, possibly the biggest Jewish merchant, and Ḥayim Somulowicz, the court purveyor, as well as others, exported a Polish red dye called *czerwiec* to Turkey and Kaffa. Following the expulsion from Lithuania in 1495, a number of Lithuanian Jews settled in Turkey and set up an active trade with Poland.[39] The most important role, however, was played by the so-called "Frenks," that is, the Jews who immigrated to Poland from Turkey. They were so active and effective in their trade operations that the Christian merchants in Lwów found it necessary to resort to the underhanded spread of malicious rumors accusing the Turkish Jews of being spies, as a result of which one of them was jailed and executed.[40] Nevertheless, the commercial operations of the "Frenks" continued, although rendered somewhat difficult for a while, thanks to the support of the interested leading nobles such as Jan Zamojski whose favorable attitude and extended protection are described by Moses de Mosse, one of the leading merchants among the "Frenks," in a letter to his brother in Constantinople. The commercial activities of the Turkish Jews were to a great extent facilitated by Don Joseph Nasi, the wealthy Portugese Marrano who became the sultan's minister and Duke of Naxos in Turkey, where he returned to Judaism, and who conducted a friendly correspondence with Sigismund Augustus. Citing from this extant correspondence, Schipper points out that, thanks to Don Joseph Nasi, storehouses and outlets for Turkish malmsey and muscatel were established in Lwów. These enterprises were managed by Don Joseph's agents, Ḥayim Cohen and Abraham de Mosso, who received in 1567 exclusive royal rights for unlimited trade in these wines in all of Poland for a period of five years. Their transactions in 1567-1569 amounted to tens of thousands of florins, and although they were bitterly opposed and fought against by Lwów burghers, the king stood at their side mindful of Poland's reputation abroad, in general, and of its friendly relations with Turkey, in particular.[41]

The activities of Abraham de Mosso were carried on in Poland by his sons, Moshe and Mordecai, who also brought to the business Don David Passis. The latter operated from Constantinople, providing the company in Lwów with a variety of goods and gold. Eventually, a certain Rabbi Jacob Sydis joined the muscatel and malmsey monopoly of the de Mossos whose business transactions became very extensive and reached as far as Salonika, Safed, Venice, Samos, etc. Based on the municipal records of Lwów, Schipper describes the volume of their transactions, which ran into hundreds of barrels of wine and thousands of florins or thalers, pointing out that this expansion and success of the de Mossos and other "Frenks" (Jacob Rafajlowicz, Jacob Sadisa, etc.) caused not only the Christian merchants but also the local Jews of Lwów to see in them an uninvited and undesirable element.

Even though the sojourn of the "Frenks" in Poland did not last too long,[42] their activities had a profound effect on the future commercial operations of the Jews in Poland. Schipper puts it in these words:

> Their short stay in Poland did not occur without effect on Polish Jewry, despite ill-will and animosity. On one hand, the "Frenks" broke completely the competition of the Armenians in the area of Oriental trade. . . . On the other hand, they indirectly influenced the Jewish merchants in Poland in the sense that they lifted their levels of operation lending them broader directions of development and method which in an astonishing way were realized in the West European markets—in Danzig and Leipzig, Nuremberg and Frankfort—in the seventeenth and the first half of the eighteenth centuries.[43]

Besides the "Frenks" from Turkey, Lwów attracted Jewish merchants from other countries as well: the "Portugese" Chaskel, Abraham Gambai, Solomon Marcus and Abraham Mizraḥi of Venice, Joseph Kohen of Candia, and others. On the other hand, Jews from Poland and Ruthenia traveled in pursuit of business transactions to such places as Adrianople, Kaffa, and Rhodes. This is attested by information which Schipper cites from the Responsa of Rabbi Joel Sirkes and the rabbinical volume *Sh'erit Yosef* by the rector of the Cracow yeshiva, Joseph ben Mordecai Gershon.[44]

With the successful expansion of the Polish Crown to the north, Jews of Greater Poland and Lithuania began playing an increasingly important role in the trade to Toruń (Thorn), Elbląg (Elbing), and Danzig which—based on documentary evidence from 1526, 1532, 1551—enjoyed the special attention and support of the king and the great nobles. Barred from settling in Danzig proper, many Jews overcame this obstacle by settling in the nearby estates of nobles, even in the bishopric of Kujavia, from which they descended on the city on market days and fairs. In this way, the Jewish settlement of Szotland came about. Persistent in getting over difficulties, the Jews eventually developed large-scale operations attested in the documents of the Crown Register which indicate that Jewish merchants shipped huge amounts of grain and charcoal to Danzig from the estates of the great Polish magnates, Sanguszko and Ostrogski. In Danzig proper a number of them functioned in the capacity of *Judaei regii* (Jewish royal servants) who enjoyed the special and direct protection of the king and who, according to the records of 1552-1572, were the biggest merchants in the trade with Danzig.[45]

Following the inclusion of Livonia (Livland) in 1561, Jewish merchants from Lithuania and White Russia began to appear more often in Riga. In fact, the very Act of Incorporation speaks of Jews as the commercial liaison between Poland and Livonia. This is quite understandable in light of the fact that even prior to that date Lithuanian Jews maintained lively commercial relationships with Königsberg and Kowno, especially in the export of grain and import of salt. Lithuanian Jews even ventured to penetrate to Muscovy, via Novgorod and Smolensk, during the first half of the sixteenth century, the frequent attacks on merchants in that country notwithstanding and in spite of the fact that the intercessions of the Polish kings with the rulers of Muscovy were of no avail.[46]

Important trade relationships with the West were maintained by Jews of Poznań and Cracow who reached such centers in Germany as Hamburg, Frankfort-am-Main, Leipzig, Nuremberg, Breslau, etc. The participation of Polish Jews in the fairs of Frankfort, for instance, is mentioned in documents from 1540. Other documents and the data cited by Koczy, which Schipper utilizes, show that Jews of Poznań had connections with the Augsburg kings of copper, the Herwarts and the Relungs, and that at least seven Jewish exporters and importers in Poznań, among them the noted Jacob Tłusty, conducted large-scale operations with various cities in Germany in furs, horned cattle, horses, wax, *czerwiec*, and especially hides. Poznań Jews played a great part in Breslau and Brzeg (Brieg), the main markets for cattle driven by Jews from Wallachia, Podolia, and Red Ruthenia. In fact, in 1517 Breslau burghers owed great sums of money to Polish Jews which necessitated the intervention of Sigismund I on their behalf.

Eventually, Lithuanian Jews, following in the footsteps of their brethren from Great Poland, also began to travel to German cities, noticeably to Leipzig which was known already at the time for its great fairs.[47]

Some documented and interesting facts, although limited in number, indicate direct commercial contacts and transactions of Polish Jews with Venice and Florence. Among these facts Schipper points to the visit of Regina di Jacob of Poznań in Florence in 1460, the assignment given by Sigismund I to Lazar of Cracow to buy precious stones in Venice in 1525, and a similar mission carried out in Venice by Isaac Schwartz of Cracow in 1553.[48]

Finally, in the field of foreign trade Schipper provides the evidence, especially the statements found in the Responsa of Rabbi Me'ir of Lublin and other rabbis, which indicate that Jews of Red Ruthenia and Little Poland who resided near the southern border of Poland conducted intensive trade in Hungarian wine and horses as well as other articles.[49]

In Domestic Trade

Turning to the field of domestic trade, Schipper proceeds to show that by the end of the fifteenth century there was no fair in Poland or Lithuania without Jewish participation. In fact, judging by the scope of their trade activities at the great annual fairs held in Lublin, Jarosław, Przemyśl, Kamieniec, and other cities, Jews must have played an outstanding role in the exchange of domestic goods. These goods, according to the sources, included a wide variety of items: oxen, horses, hides, furs, wax, saltpeter, tallow, ashes, grain, wine, herring, soap (self-made), iron articles, expensive fabrics, foreign and domestic linens and textiles, ready-made clothing, and groceries.

Based on data culled from various sources and the works of other historians, especially the two volumes by Professor Rybarski published in 1928, Schipper provides in *Dzieje handlu żydowskiego na ziemiach polskich*, his very extensive and comprehensive *magnum opus* on the entire history of Jewish commerce in Poland, a detailed description of the Jewish domestic trade activities in the various geographic areas of the country, showing their leading participants, main items of exchange, and—what is most important—the scope and volume of exchange.[50]

But, indebted as he is to Rybarski for certain facts, Schipper disagrees with the latter's general conclusion that "by the middle of the sixteenth century, at the time when Polish commerce was in full bloom, the participation of Jews in it was generally very weak," and he sets out to disprove this contention by demonstrating its inaccuracy and fallaciousness.

Already in discussing the trade in horned cattle conducted by Jews, Schipper points out the falsity of Rybarski's inference that cattle shipments by Jews diminished while overall shipments increased as a result of the aforementioned 1515 and 1527 royal decrees issued in Lwów.[51] In the first place, the Jews of Lwów did not adhere to the imposed limitations of 2,500 oxen a year. This can be seen from the records of Lwów customs in 1533-1534, 1548, and 1549 which show the respective figures of 2,904, 3,023, and 3,482 oxen brought in by Jews. Secondly, Rybarski arrives at his false generalization as if only Jews of Lwów participated in the transport of oxen, forgetting that Volhynian, Lithuanian, and other Ruthenian Jews participated in it also, even to a greater extent, as attested in the relevant documents of the *Russko-Yevreyskiy Arkhiv* and the Responsa of Rabbi Me'ir of Lublin.[52]

But the evidence which is of decisive validity and cogency in his refutation of Rybarski's view about the minor role of Jews, Schipper adduces from the 1530-1531 record of the Lublin customhouse. This document is most revealing and conclusive because Lublin became an important commercial center in Poland in the sixteenth century. Strategically located, it became a meeting place for merchants from all provinces of the country and, according to Rybarski himself, the turnover of goods was probably greater here than in Lwów. Because of its growing importance as a commercial center and because of its annual fair, which became known all over Poland, Lublin became in 1540 the seat of the highest Jewish court and four decades later the highest governing body of Jewish autonomy in Poland known as the *Va'ad Arba Aratsot* (the General Diet of Polish Jewry which drew its delegates from four major parts of the country) began to convene here regularly.[53] Thus, not only local Jews but mostly Jewish merchants from various parts of the country converged here for business, and their trade activities are well reflected in the 1530-1531 customs table. Another advantage of this document is the fact that it distinguishes between Jewish and non-Jewish merchants, making it possible to determine with sufficient accuracy the comparative role of Jews in the Lublin exchange of goods.

The table clearly demonstrates that Jews had a definite edge over non-Jews in such items of trade as cattle, hides, furs, honey, cotton, wax, tallow, groceries, red dye, eastern fabrics, linen, ready-made clothing, caps, and soap. They took second place in the trade of such articles as fish and herring, iron, copper, lead, scythes, sickles, shoes, medicaments, and flax. In the exchange of eastern wares, for instance, Jews brought to Lublin, according to the table, 51.5 stones and thirty-seven pounds while non-Jewish, native merchants brought twenty-one stones and a nameless "Turkish merchant," thirty stones and thirty-six pounds. Characteristically, the Jewish deliverers of these wares were all from the southeastern regions and Lithuania. Another interesting fact is that the entire shipment of *czerwiec*, the Polish red dye, was brought by Jews only. Although Jewish merchants were not as active in the trade in eastern fabrics compared with other articles, they could still account for three times as much of this commodity as the amount of it credited to non-Jewish native merchants if the amount brought by the anonymous Turkish merchant is to be disregarded. Even in horned cattle, the item which Rybarski used as an indicator for his thesis, the ratio, according to the Lublin table, was 503 to 310 in favor of the Jewish merchants.[54]

In addition to the data of the 1530-1531 Lublin table of customs, Schipper points out that there were at least seventeen known Jewish merchants, whose names he lists, acting as the main suppliers of Sigismund I and Sigismund Augustus. That these Polish rulers found it desirable to engage the services of so many Jewish *servi regii* in a period known as the "golden age" of Polish commerce is obviously a characteristic phenomenon which, like the Lublin customs table, speaks for itself. These facts and many other details about the commercial activities of the Polish Jews in the period of struggle for commercial rights lead Schipper to sum up the situation in the following words:

> 1. In the foreign trade of Poland Jews had a definite advantage over non-Jews due to their extensive relationships with Jewish communities abroad.
>
> 2. In the domestic trade the advantage of Jews can be ascertained in a whole series of very important commercial branches.
>
> 3. The dominant role of Jews in the development of the famous Lublin fairs is visible already in 1530-1531, and in the development of the fair in Lithuania in 1539.
>
> 4. The number of *servi regii* recruited from among Jewish merchants goes to prove that there must have been among the Jews of Poland individuals of outstanding mercantile qualifications.

And all this goes to show that Professor Rybarski's evaluation of the Jewish role in Poland's commerce during its "golden age" is hardly in agreement with the actual historical facts.[55]

Notes

1. "Świadczenia," *op. cit.*, p. 202; cf. *Studies, op. cit.*, p. 147. Regarding the term *regale*, see *supra*, Chap. II, p. 79 n. 60.

2. *Kultur-geshikhte, op. cit.*, pp. 244, 246-249; *Studies, op. cit.*, pp. 110-112, 118, 133, 141, 142-146, 185, 282-285, 295-296, 310-311. Cf. Weinryb, *The Jews of Poland, op. cit.*, pp. 46-47.

3. *Kultur-geshikhte, op. cit.*, pp. 57-58; *Studies, op. cit.*, p. 289.

4. *Kultur-geshikhte, op. cit.*, p. 59; *Studies, op. cit.*, pp. 133, 139, 142, 290. Cf. Frenk, *op. cit.*, p. 12 and Weinryb, *The Jews of Poland, op. cit.*, pp. 42-43.

5. *Kultur-geshikhte, op. cit.*, p. 60; *Studies, op. cit.*, pp. 141-142, 145-146; *Virtshaftsgeshikhte, op. cit.*, IV, pp. 258-259. Cf. Dubnow, *History of the Jews in Poland and Russia, op. cit.*, pp. 55-57; Baron, *op. cit.*, vol. X, pp. 33-36, especially p. 316, n. 43.

6. *Studies, op. cit.*, pp. 282-285; *Virtshaftsgeshikhte, op. cit.*, IV, pp. 260-263. Regarding Schipper's explanation of the king's decision to have the Cracow Jews transferred to Kazimierz, see *infra*, pp. 201-203, and especially n. 15 below.

7. *Studies, op. cit.*, pp. 281-282, 286; *Virtshaftsgeshikhte*, IV, *op. cit.*, p. 263.

8. *Studies, op. cit.*, p. 140.

9. *Virtshaftsgeshikhte, op. cit.*, IV, p. 255. Cf. Weinryb, *The Jews of Poland, op. cit.*, pp. 139-141.

10. *Virtshaftsgeshikhte, op. cit.*, IV, p. 256.

11. *Studies, op. cit.*, p. 141. Cf. Roscher, *op. cit.*, pp. 14, 24.

12. *Kultur-geshikhte, op. cit.*, pp. 151-153; *Studies, op. cit.*, pp. 288 ff.

13. *Studies, op. cit.*, pp. 291-295.

14. Schipper illustrates this with his finding that from 1408 to 1470, out of twenty-two recorded real-estate transactions involving Jews, eighteen represented sales of Jewish homes to Christians, three purchases from Christians, and one rental of a municipal house near the synagogue. See *Studies, op. cit.*, p. 300.

15. *Studies, op. cit.*, pp. 296-297, 299-301; *Virtshaftsgeshikhte, op. cit.*, IV, pp. 261-262. It should be noted that in the matter of the transfer of Cracow Jews to Kazimierz in 1495, Schipper differs from the position taken by Bałaban that it represented a total expulsion carried out by the order of the king, maintaining that it was rather an unavoidable solution under the circumstances, especially for those Jews in Cracow whose homes were destroyed, to move to Kazimierz where Jews had been residing for over a century, since 1386 according to historical evidence cited by Schipper. Another pertinent factor in the king's position which, in Schipper's view, Bałaban did not fully appreciate, was the role that the Italian humanist, Philip Callimachus, who was the king's teacher and very influential counsellor, played in averting an official expulsion. In support of his view, Schipper cites Callimachus' three letters, published by J. Szujski in his *Odrodzenie i reformacya w Polsce* (Cracow: 1881), pp. 145-146, in which he appealed to the king on behalf of the Jews and which undoubtedly affected the thinking and ultimate decision of the king in spite of the anti-Jewish pressures exerted by the burghers and the king's own brother, Cardinal Frederick. See Schipper's article "Humanizm a sprawa żydowska w XV wieku," *Moriah*, XI, No. 8, pp. 231-237, and *Studies, op. cit.*, pp. 297-298. Cf. M. Bałaban, *Dzieje Żydów w Krakowie i na Kazimierzu* (1913), pp. 50 ff; *idem.*, "Ha-Kehilot ha-Gedolot bi-Ymey ha-Beynayim," *op. cit.*, p. 20; *Bet Yisrael be-Polin, op. cit.*, p. 20.

16. *Studies, op. cit.*, pp. 302-304.

17. *Dzieje handlu żydowskiego, op. cit.*, pp. 27, 198-199; "Razsyeleniye Yevreyev v Polshe i Litvye," *op. cit.*, pp. 150 ff.; "Rozwój ludności żydowskiej," *op. cit.*, p. 27. Regarding the precarious history of Jewish rights to reside in Warsaw, see E. Ringelblum, *Żydzi w Warszawie od czasów najdawniejszych do ostatniego wygnania w r. 1527* (Warsaw: 1932), pp. 15 ff.

18. *Studies, op. cit.*, pp. 304-305. Regarding the attempts to limit the right of Jews to reside, see also the summary presented by Frenk, *op. cit.*, p. 34 and Weinryb, *The Jews of Poland, op. cit.*, pp. 135-136.

19. *Studies, op. cit.*, p. 193. "Dzieje gospodarcze Żydów," *op. cit.*, p. 122; *Dzieje handlu żydowskiego, op. cit.*, p. 15.

20. *Studies, op. cit.*, pp. 194 f.; *Virtshaftsgeshikhte, op. cit.*, IV, pp. 220-221; "Dzieje gospodarcze Żydów," *op. cit.*, p. 131; *Dzieje handlu żydowskiego, op. cit.*, pp. 23, 25. Cf. Bałaban, *Dzieje Żydów w Krakowie i na Kazimierzu, op. cit.*, pp. 47 ff., and in *Bet Yisrael be-Polin, op. cit.*, pp. 19, 23. See also Baron, *op. cit.*, vol. X, p. 38 and Weinryb, *The Jews of Poland, op. cit.*, p. 138.

21. "Dzieje gospodarcze Żydów," *loc. cit.; Dzieje handlu żydowskiego, op. cit.*, pp. 27-28. On the struggle and methods used by the Christian merchants in the cities of medieval Europe to maintain a monoply in the urban centers, see Weber, *op. cit.*, pp. 166-168.

22. *Dzieje handlu żydowskiego, op. cit.*, p. 29; *Studies, op. cit.*, pp. 229-230. The excerpt from the Piotrków resolution is quoted by Schipper on the basis of *Volumina legum* I B, p. 524, *Studies, loc. cit.* Cf. Dubnow, *History of the Jews in Russia and Poland, op. cit.*, pp. 77-79 and Weinryb, *The Jews of Poland, op. cit.*, p. 121.

23. Schipper cites the full text of the letter sent by the burghers of Lwów to Poznań according to J. Łukaszewicz, *Obraz statystyczno-historyczny Poznania* (Poznań: 1838). See *Studies, op. cit.*, pp. 350-351.

24. *Studies, op. cit.*, pp. 197-219. *Dzieje handlu żydowskiego, op. cit.*, pp. 25-26; *Virtshaftsgeshikhte, op. cit.*, IV, pp. 221-222.

25. *Studies, op. cit.*, pp. 220-222.

26. *Ibid.*, pp. 209-212, 224-226.

27. *Ibid.*, pp. 214-215, 226-228.

28. *Ibid.*, pp. 228-229.

29. *Supra*, Chap. VI, p. 206.

30. *Studies, op. cit.*, pp. 205-208, 223 f.

31. *Dzieje handlu żydowskiego, op. cit.*, p. 24.

32. "Dzieje gospodarcze Żydów," *op. cit.*, pp. 130-131; *Dzieje handlu żydowskiego, loc. cit.* See also J. Ptaśnik, *Miasta i mieszczaństwo w dawnej Polsce*

(Cracow: 1934), pp. 358-387. Cf. Frenk, *op. cit.*, pp. 36 f.; I. Halpern, *op. cit.*, pp. 305-306.

33. "Dzieje gospodarcze Żydów," *loc. cit.*, and *Dzieje handlu żydowskiego, loc. cit.*

34. *Supra*, Chap. V, p. 177. Regarding the date of the brochure, Schipper differs from the position taken by Bershadski, *op. cit.*, and H. Nussbaum, *op. cit.*, vol. V, pp. 136-139, that it is of much later provenance. Referring again to Decius and germane statements made by Peter Kmita, he contends that Polish Jews were economically strong and wealthy enough to oppose the burghers openly and actively by means of polemical literature such as the brochure in question. See *Studies, op. cit.*, pp. 231-233; "Dzieje gospodarcze Żydów," *op. cit.*, p. 132.

35. *Dzieje handlu żydowskiego, op. cit.*, p. 30.

36. Since the days of Rabbi Jacob Polak who came to Poland from Bohemia by the end of the fifteenth century and established in Cracow his yeshiva which became famous for the so-called *pilpul* method in the study of the Talmud (*supra*, Chap. V, p. 190, n. 71), Talmudic learning and Jewish literary productivity in general began to flourish in Poland. The four rabbis named above were among the distinguished Talmudists and teachers who served as spiritual leaders or heads of academies in the major Jewish communities of Poland (Cracow, Lublin, Lwów, Brest Litovsk, and others) during the sixteenth century, and their views on religious matters and on questions of religio-civic jurisprudence, in particular, were widely sought and respected. The volumes of their Responsa reflect their erudition, their independence in judgment, and some of the basic issues and problems of their times. For their written legacies (responsa, commentaries, *novellae*, etc.) and methods of interpretation, see Zinberg, *op. cit.*, vol. III, pp. 177-179, 190-191. Also, *The Jewish Encyclopedia*, VII, p. 268; VIII, p. 201; VIII, p. 212; XI, p. 397.

37. Regarding connection with India, Schipper maintains that although the fall of Constantinople in 1453 and the discovery of America forty years later reduced the importance of the old established routes to the Orient, Jews settled in India earlier and assisted significantly in the colonization attempts undertaken by Europeans, especially the Portugese who established the new route to India via the Indian Ocean. In support of his contention that Polish Jews, too, were involved in this, Schipper refers to M. Kayserling (*Christoph Columbus und the Juden*, 1894, p. 105) who points out that Don Isaac Abrabanel (1437-1508), the Jewish philosopher, statesman, and financier in Spain, received definite information about great merchants among the Jews in India who originally lived in Poland, and the report cited by Baros (*Asia*, I, IV, p. 360) according to which Vasco da Gama met a Jew in the territory where he founded the Portugese colony of Goa. This Jew was the son of a refugee from Poland, who had escaped to Alexandria. These references Schipper substantiates further

with the information provided by Rabbi Moses ben Joseph di Trani (1505-1585) in his collection of Responsa (HaMaBIT, II, No. 78) according to which a certain Polish Jew named Me'ir Ashkenazi who came to Goa from Egypt appeared in Cracow in 1567 as the ambassador of a Tartar prince. See *Anteil der Juden am Grosshandel, op. cit.*, pp. 29-30; "Dzieje gospodarcze Żydów," *op. cit.*, p. 133; *Dzieje handlu żydowskiego, op. cit.*, p. 34.

38. Schipper points out also that, following the discovery of America, the Atlantic did not become at once the *nervus movens* of all European commerce and that the center of commercial gravity moved gradually, for a period of about two hundred years, from Southern Europe to the Northwest. This is why a lively trade with the Orient was still possible in Poland in the sixteenth century. See *Anteil der Juden am Grosshandel, op. cit.*, p. 30.

39. *Dzieje handlu żydowskiego, op. cit.*, pp. 31-32; "Dzieje gospodarcze Żydów," *op. cit.*, pp. 132-133. Nuncio Commendone's report is cited by Schipper on the basis of I. Albertrandi, *Pamiętniki o dawnej Polsce*, I, pp. 99-102. See *Anteil der Juden am Grosshandel, op. cit.*, p. 32. Regarding the special role of this nuncio in the process of the "Counter-Reformation" in Poland see *The Cambridge History of Poland, op. cit.*, p. 402. As for Lithuanian Jews settled in Turkey, Schipper refers his reader to S. Rosanes, *Toledot ha-Yehudim be-Turkiya* (1930), pp. 36, 264.

40. Noting that Bershadski and Nussbaum failed to interpret correctly the causes of the espionage affair, Schipper refers the reader to a manuscript from 1543 which he found in the Ossolineum Archives (Ms. 172, pp. 109-110) to show that the accusations were propagated by jealous Christian burghers for strictly economic reasons. See *Anteil der Juden am Grosshandel, op. cit.*, p. 33.

41. *Ibid.*, p. 34; "Dzieje gospodarcze Żydów," *loc. cit.*; *Dzieje handlu żydowskiego, op. cit.*, pp. 32-33.

42. By the beginning of the seventeenth century there were hardly any "Frenks" left in Poland. In explaining their disappearance, Schipper follows the assumption of Bałaban, whose research on the subject he respectfully acknowledges, that the death of the great Chancellor Jan Zamojski, who fully appreciated the contributions of the "Frenks" and staunchly protected them from the hostility generated among Jews and non-Jews, caused them to withdraw from Poland. Schipper also refers his readers to M. Schoor and W. Łoziński who also brought to light many relevant details about the "Frenks," the former in "Zur Geschichte des Don Joseph Nassi," *Monatschrift für Geschichte und Wissenschaft des Judentums* (1897) and the latter in *Patrycjat i mieszczaństwo lwowskie w XVI i XVII wieku* (Lwów: 1902). *Der Anteil der Juden am Grosshandel, op. cit.*, p. 36. Cf. Bałaban, *Żydzi lwowscy na przełomie XVI i XVII wieku* (Lwów): 1906), pp. 39 ff.

43. *Der Anteil der Juden am Grosshandel, op. cit.*, pp. 36-37.

44. *Dzieje handlu żydowskiego, op. cit.*, p. 25.

45. *"Dzieje gospodarcze Żydów," op. cit.*, pp. 134-135; *Dzieje handlu żydowskiego, op. cit.*, pp. 38-40. Besides the Crown Register, Schipper cites also the testimony of Rabbi Solomon Luria, found in his Responsa, regarding two Jews from Brest on the Bug who floated wares to Danzig using Jewish help. And to substantiate further the point that Jews played a dominant role in the development of Poland's trade through Danzig, Schipper cites the conclusion of L. Koczy, *Handel Poznania do polowy XVI wieku* (Poznań: 1930), that thanks to Jews, Polish trade with Danzig experienced an unusual degree of stimulation. Among the *Judaei regii* in Danzig, Schipper names Ḥayim Samuelowicz of Poznań, Isaac Brodawka of Brest on the Bug, Dr. Marek-Me'ir Reimbach of Poznań and his son-in-law, Abraham.

46. "Dzieje gospodarcze Żydów," *loc. cit.; Dzieje handlu żydowskiego, op. cit.*, pp. 41, 45. Schipper cites the letter of Sigismund Augustus to Ivan IV in 1550 which is also mentioned in the Responsa of Solomon Luria.

47. *Dzieje handlu żydowskiego, op. cit.*, pp. 42-44; "Dzieje gospodarcze Żydów," *loc. cit.*

48. *Ibid.*, p. 136; *Dzieje handlu żydowskiego, op. cit.*, pp. 43-44.

49. *Ibid., loc. cit.*; "Dzieje gospodarcze Żydów," *op. cit.*, p. 133.

50. *Dzieje handlu żydowskiego, op. cit.*, pp. 46-57. The work by Professor R. Rybarski, *Handel i polityka handlowa Polski w XVI-tym wieku* (The Trade and Commercial Policy of Poland in the Sixteenth Century), 2 vols. (Poznań: 1928), represented at the time the most authoritative treatment of the subject. It was republished again in Warsaw in 1958. The second volume is devoted to an annotated reproduction of documentary materials and contains a wealth of data based mostly on the records of customs chambers in various localities.

51. See Rybarski, *op. cit.*, I, p. 227 and II, pp. 218, 253-254.

52. *Dzieje handlu żydowskiego, op. cit.*, p. 36.

53. The need for coordinating the activities of the individual Jewish *kahals* and the emergence of the *Va'ad Arba Aratsot*, Schipper discusses in his extensive monograph "Wewnętzna organizacja Żydów w dawnej Rzeczypospolitej" in *Żydzi w Polsce Odrodzonej, op. cit.*, pp. 81-110, which deals with the entire history of the Jewish autonomy in Poland. Regarding the permanent Jewish tribunal of arbitration established in Lublin and the periodic convocations of the Central *Va'ad* in that city, see pp. 90 and 94 of this monograph. Schipper also deals with various aspects of the Jewish autonomous organs in special studies: "Beiträge zur Geschichte der partiellen Judentage in Polen um die Wende des XVII und XVIII Jahrhunderts" in *Monatschrift für Geschichte und Wissenschaft des Judentums*, LVI (1913); "Der tsuzamenshtel funem Vaad Arba Arotses," *Historishe Shriftn of YIVO*, I (1929); "Poylishe regestn tsu der geshikhte funem Vaad Arba Arotses," in *ibid.*

54. *Dzieje handlu żydowskiego, op. cit.*, pp. 37-38, 54-57; "Dzieje gospodarcze Żydów," *op. cit.*, pp. 136-137.

55. *Dzieje handlu żydowskiego, op. cit.*, pp. 57-58. Cf. Mahler, *Toledot ha-Yehudim be-Polin, op. cit.*, pp. 98 ff. as well as Baron and Kahan, *Economic History, op. cit.*, pp. 245-246.

7

The People's Historian

Post-Rankean historical thought utilizes the concepts of relativism and sociology, pointing out that history as well as the historian who writes it are subject to conflicting interests, to rational or irrational motives and purposes, and to specific sociological and psychological factors. Consequently, "written . . . history is to be best understood not only by an analysis of its structure and documentation, but also by a study of the possible attitudes arising from the life and circumstances of the author."[1] If one accepts this point of view then one should attempt to identify the factors underlying Schipper's exposition of the economic history of Jews in medieval Poland—his approach, method, and views on the subject—in the light of his own times, his own situation and predilections.

Schipper himself, as a historian, subscribed by and large to the ideas promulgated by post-Rankean historicism. He was convinced that the contention of the historiographical empiricists or positivists that history is nothing less than a scientific discipline and that the historian can and must write history *wie es eigentlich gewesen ist* (as it really happened) is both impossible and invalid.

History and the Historian's Role

Although Schipper's writings do not include a treatise expressly devoted to a presentation of his views on the study of history and the role of the historian, the basic propositions of modern historicism are implied in all his works and certain pertinent statements on the subject are found in some of his essays, especially in the evaluations of books written by others. It is these statements that should be cited before anything else.

Back in 1917, when the fate of European states was about to be decided and the demands of Poles for an independent Poland became more realistic, Schipper wrote the following critically poignant remarks in a review of Bałaban's newly published book, *The History of Jews in Galicia and in the Republic of Cracow, 1772-1868*:[2]

> In a time like the present, when the problem of a new orientation in the Polish-Jewish question makes it obligatory to engross our minds retrospectively in the history of the mutual Polish-Jewish relationship, Bałaban's book . . . portends to serve not only as a scientific work, of interest to experts only, but in equal measure as a work of thought which, by its timeliness, is of vital concern to the general public. Alas, after reading it, the expert as well as the pretentious laymen will of necessity experience a disappointment. . . .
>
> The basic fault of the book lies in Bałaban's method, or lack of method. The knowledge of additional thousands of historical details—and Bałaban's book undoubtedly brings a great deal of details—is by no means a substitute for knowledge which is organic and deep. If we submerge ourselves in the waves of our history, it is not in order to emerge to the surface with a handful of news, good or bad, interesting or of little consequence. Our aim is always the present. It is the understanding of the present that we seek in our history. One must want something from the past. One must ask of her bold questions and then the locks with which she is sealed will open. . . .
>
> Bałaban does not want or is unable (perhaps he does not know how) to pose such questions! And for that reason his books are lacking a spinal column. You read them, and they interest you like . . . the pictures shown in the cinema where the eye is satisfied but the mind is at rest. . . . They are sort of better chronicles,

> *silvae rerum!* The defendant would say in accordance with Tacitus' recipe, "untendentiousness is praiseworthy!" But our answer to this is: Let them call it "objectivity" or "untendentiousness"; to our mind it is nothing but the absence of an orientation in the Jewish present. Hence, the tendency to a romantic interest in the currents of worlds gone by.
>
> About the book proper there is little else we can say since it is not the author who speaks in it but the material which, we should add, is raw and still in need of an author. . . . All [other] animadversions are reducible to the basic one, to the author's method which reflects, in turn, his particular mentality eminently suitable for a *researcher*, a publisher of materials, but not for a creative *scholar* whose analytical abilities are coupled with the gift of constructing.[3]

More than twenty years later, in 1938, when both Schipper and Bałaban had to their credit a prodigious body of historical studies and writings, Schipper had occasion to speak at the celebration of Bałaban's sixtieth birthday. What he said in his characteristically candid way amounted to a synoptic repetition of the observation cited above.

The implications of his remarks are obvious. Schipper has no use for piling up historical data and details as an end in itself, nor does he consider the historian who has no point of view, who has no "serious outlook," and who does not write history for the sake of the present and its problems as having fulfilled his task and duty. Such a man is at best only a chronicler, while the role of the historian is to "forge a sword for battle out of knowledge."[4]

In an essay devoted to the subject of Jewish motifs in the historical novels of Lion Feuchtwanger, Schipper wrote in 1931:

> We can confidently categorize the historical novels by Feuchtwanger as documents reflecting the thought of the contemporary Jew who is trying to find himself in the world. . . . And this is why they interest us. They would not have been of interest to us had they been—as so often happens with historical novels—only an escape from oneself, from the struggles and problems of the present. They have nothing in common with "history," with the "past," as if the author has been fully cognizant of the fact that "history"—"past" is a corpse which can be of interest only to the

> chronicler standing on the margin of events. Chronicles of obscure times? Of what concern can they be to a writer of Feuchtwanger's calibre? An artist-thinker for whom only the rhythm of the *living* spirit exists! For him the "annals" the "past" are only a means, as paints are for the painter. Only when the creative vision of an artist, his living thought—his cognition and the love or hate that ties in with it—blends the paints into a picture do they become alive.[5]

Schipper's philosophy reflects to a great extent the critical position taken by Benedetto Croce vis à vis the scientific, or positivistic, trends of nineteenth century historicism which, influenced by Ranke and his contemporaries as well as successors of the Prussian Historical School, proclaimed that historiography is nothing else but the strictest presentation of facts tested by a systematized, scientific method.[6] Schipper's reference to history as being contemporary, to the historian as a man whose springboard into history must be the present, and to the past as a "corpse" unless related to the present, reminds one very much of Croce's famous proposition that "every true history is contemporary history," that the past is indeed dead except insofar as it is "unified with an interest of the present life," and that "only an interest in the life of the present can move one to investigate past facts."

The distinction that Schipper makes between the historian and the chronicler is also based on Croce's views. To Croce, "history is a living chronicle" while "chronicle is dead history; history is contemporary history, chronicle is past history; history is principally an act of thought, chronicle an act of will." Furthermore, "the real distinction between chronicle and history," Croce points out, "enables us to reject a very common presupposition —namely, that of the *priority* of chronicle in respect to history. . . . Precisely the opposite of this is [true]. . . . *First comes history, then chronicle.* First comes the living being, then the corpse; and to make history the child of chronicle is the same thing as to make the living be born from the corpse, which is the residue of life, as chronicle is the residue of history." And one more sagacious point made by Croce which is equally crucial to the understanding of Schipper's attitude toward history: "Sources, in the extrinsic sense of the empiricists, like things, are equal with chronicle, which is a class of those things, not anterior but posterior to history."[7]

Obviously, Schipper considered himself to be a historian, not a chronicler. By the very definition of his role as a historian, he had to be involved in the immediate problems of his own world —his society, nationality, religion, political and socioeconomic conditions. He had to seek in history those phenomena that have something to say, something to contribute to the questions of the present. Like Ranke, he may not have intended, necessarily, to judge the past (although in the process of selecting, interpreting, and explaining past events the historian can hardly avoid it), but —unlike Ranke—he certainly "assigned to history the office of instructing the present." Hence, the historian's task, for Schipper, does not lie primarily in relating what happened in the past but in explaining why it happened and in giving a pragmatic sense to that explanation. It follows that just the accumulation of facts, data, and details, in or of itself, is not the main prerequisite for the writing of history if it contributes little to the explanation of the historical processes, to the understanding of underlying motives and relationships, and to the needs of the present, especially the needs of those for whom the historian writes.[8]

Facts and Phenomena, Interpretation and Synthesis

Indeed for Schipper, a single piece of evidence or even a clue may be more important to the historian dealing with a specific historical problem than many "facts" which yield him nothing. Those who knew Schipper personally relate that he used to call historians enthused about every old document as a "find," "collectors of old galoshes," especially when the "find" revealed little and served no specific purpose. Altogether, he maintains, it is the historian who should be the master over his materials rather than the other way around, for it is up to the historian to pose his own problems and to seek those materials which might provide him with a full, partial, or even a possible answer to his questions.[9]

That is not to say that he minimizes the value of source materials, of documentary evidence, statistical data, numismatics, epigraphy and archeology, of all these things commonly categorized as "historical facts." Nor does he minimize the critical or "scientific" examination of these facts. But still, they are subordinate to history (or, as Croce expressed it, "posterior to history"); they are means in the hands of the historian who, because of his specific, contemporary problem and demand, imbues these facts with new life and meaning. While Schipper knows this to be a subjective treatment of historical facts, he feels it cannot be avoided since the historian must select, explain, interpret, and arrange his facts.

The extrinsic existence of historical facts cannot be empirically repeated and tested under the same or different conditions, as a physicist or chemist would experiment and test his facts in the laboratory. As Becker put it:

> The actual past is gone; and the world of history is an intangible world, recreated imaginatively, and present in our minds. . . . By no possibility can the historian present in its entirety any actual event, even the simplest. . . . The event itself, the facts, do not say anything, do not impose any meaning. It is the historian who speaks, who imposes a meaning. . . . The only external world he [the historian] has to deal with is the records. He can indeed look at the records as often as he likes, and he can get dozens of others to look at them; and some things, some "facts," can in this way be established and agreed upon. . . . But the meaning and significance of these facts cannot be thus agreed upon, because the series of events in which it has a place cannot be enacted again and again, under varying conditions, in order to see what effect the variations would have. The historian has to judge the significance of the series of events from one single performance, never to be repeated, and never, since the records are incomplete and imperfect, capable of being fully known or affirmed.[10]

This is why Schipper always insisted that, unlike the chronicler, the historian must have a "serious world outlook," a *Weltanschaung*, a theory, or—to use a term styled by Collingwood—an "a priori imagination,"[11] which will enable him to accept or reject, to modify, interpret, or reinterpret his source materials in a way that makes sense to him, that leads him to a coherent historical narration. Such a narration cannot be produced without an interpretation of the historical facts and the relationships between them, and an interpretation cannot be given without a theory.

Of course, the more pertinent the source materials, the fuller the narration. And whenever Schipper has at his disposal sufficient evidence, he goes about analyzing it in a way that ultimately produces a synthesis revealing the dynamics of the historical process, the significant and cogent interconnections of historical episodes and the characteristic phenomena of social development. In this regard he was the guiding spirit of a synthetic trend that developed among certain Jewish historians in Poland following the end of World War I.[12]

A typical synthesis which runs like a refrain throughout his economic story of the Jews is the general observation made by Roscher that "the medieval policy toward the Jews is almost the reverse of the general economic trend." Schipper illustrates this contention by often pointing to the basic difference between the economic situation of Polish Jews living in the economically more advanced western provinces and those of the economically retarded eastern regions.

Related to this general proposition are its concomitant socioeconomic phenomena, which Schipper, guided by Roscher's contention,[13] brings to the fore in all his works in one connection or another, namely:

1. The role of the Jew as economic pioneer and trailblazer, whether in commerce (domestic and foreign), or credit, or even in agriculture;
2. The conflict between Jews and the growing classes of indigenous economic agents;
3. The position of the Jew as a pawn or instrumentality in the hands of rulers and classes, or in the socioeconomic and sociopolitical antagonisms between them;
4. The hostility of the Christian masses to Jews when the latter became reduced to lenders of consumptive credit;
5. The distinction in the general status and situation of Polish

Jews as compared with Jews in the West, reflecting the difference in the level of economic development as well as the particular conditions of place and time;

6. The general observation that the difference between Jewish occupations and those of the local population was basically quantitative rather than qualitative.

In all these salient developments Schipper points to the strong and inseparable interdependence of the economic and the political factors.

But the existence and position of the Jews depended not only on external factors. The Jews themselves determined to a great extent their fate and history, a phenomenon that Schipper brings to the fore, directly or indirectly, at every possible opportunity with varying degrees of emphasis, but never in the form of an understatement. Rejecting metaphysical, theological, or idealistic explanations of Jewish existence and survival,[14] Schipper emphasizes the continuous struggle for existence, the will to persist, the *élan vital* of the Jews. He misses no occasion to show that even under the worst circumstances the Jews had the vitality and the will to counteract, to persevere, to adapt to new circumstances, to draw on their unity, connections, and experience, to overcome inimical interests by inventing new avenues of survival, by seizing on new opportunities, by actuating and stimulating new areas of economic activities.

Schipper exposes, one might say, a Darwinian view of the ability of the Jews, as a people, to overcome the forces threatening their existence. The Jews have survived because they have accumulated a collective resourcefulness and developed a fitness to survive. Schipper considers this to be a fundamental lesson of paramount importance for the contemporary problems facing his own generation of Jews in Poland, and elsewhere.

In his critical evaluation of the contribution which Schipper made with his *Virtshaftsgeshikhte*, Friedman underscored this very point when he said that:

> Schipper's description of the economic and fiscal oppressions in Germany after 1340 points to the vitality and indestructible vigor of the Jew in the face of economic catastrophes as well as to the

> question whether Jews will continue to be strong enough to withstand the pressures of modern times, whether they will find it within themselves to persevere as a people. . . .[15]

Conjecture and Historical Theory

When faced with problems and periods lacking in historical data and direct evidence, Schipper considers it his duty to probe and to investigate, to look for clues, to discover new leads, hidden threads, and relationships between seemingly unrelated facts and pieces of information, in order to wrest possible answers to posed questions. He cannot quite agree with the maxim, "*quod non est in actis, non est in mundo.*" He is much more in accord with the sentiments expressed by Pirenne that "a considerable portion of historical data has no other foundation than conjecture and is certified by no source," that "it would be an error to conclude that it is necessary to postpone writing history until all the materials are assembled," and that the "historian cannot abstain from making a synthesis on the pretext that he does not possess all the elements of his synthesis."[16] For, in the last analysis, all necessary sources and facts will never be known and the scientific apparatus, indispensable as it is, cannot always be successfully employed in the writing of history. Unless the historian has within himself the necessary "creative imagination," an intelligent synthesis and comprehensive historical narrative would be hardly possible.

When confronted with only indirect pieces of evidence, Schipper tends to present his narrative in hypothetical rather than affirmative terms. To be sure, his hypotheses are based on a synthesis. This is true of the Khazar theory of the Jewish origins in Poland, the theory of Jewish participation in agriculture, of Jewish capitalism in the Middle Ages, and so on. Schipper's natural enthusiasm for penetrating unexplored grounds, his intellectual insight and creative ability combine seemingly unrelated and indirect facts into a comprehensive account. And this is why the reader may get the impression that the narrative of the hypothesis relates what actually, rather than what probably, happened. Schipper's critics seized on this to accuse him of sheer fantasy since there is no direct evidence or too few substantiating documents.

Of course, Schipper would have liked to have more source materials and more facts directly bearing on his theories. Even in the times of the Nazi terror, when the destiny of Polish Jews rather than their origin was at stake, he continued to defend his theory, stating that he found additional, new evidence.[17] But regardless of whether or not he had at his disposal new supporting data or facts, his basic position in this and other theories is that the historian must not be limited only to direct historical documentation and he must not strike out possible episodes or segments of history only because of lack of direct evidence. On the contrary, the historian has not only the right but the duty to postulate and to fill in as long as his synthesis of indirect evidence demonstrates a reasonable degree of probability, a reasonable approximation of the "objective" historical truth.[18] For, after all, "all historical narrative [that is, including also the narrative based on 'solid' and 'direct' facts] is at once a synthesis and a hypothesis. It is a synthesis inasmuch as it combines the mass of known facts in an account of the whole; it is a hypothesis inasmuch as the relations that it establishes between these facts are neither evident nor verifiable by themselves."[19] As far as Schipper is concerned, it is the degree of common sense, of the perception and insight, that ultimately determines the validity and viability of a historical theory, its synthetical as well as hypothetical aspects.

In view of the indirect facts and of what we generally know from experience and from the nature of human behavior—Schipper would ask—isn't it reasonable to assume that with Khazar Jews being in Hungary and in Kievan Russia they were also in the regions of Poland situated between these two countries, especially after the fall of Itil and in the wake of the Mongolian invasion?[20] Or, isn't it more logically credible that Jewish capital in the early Middle Ages derived initially from the rent and sale of land rather than from the times prior to the destruction of the Roman Empire? Or, would it be reasonable to conclude that a Jew like Wolczko, given a mandate by the Polish king to colonize virgin lands in Ruthenia and appointed bailiff of a number of newly established villages, carried out his assignments without engaging his coreligionists and without giving other Jews the opportunity to settle in those villages and work on their own land?

The critics detected in this approach and in the enunciated theories a tendentiousness and bias typical of their author. Bałaban stated without reservations that the theory of the Khazar origins of Jews in Poland betrays the signs of "being rather a political tendency and not a desire to find the historical truth,"[21] intimating thereby that Schipper tends to manipulate his materials for his own purposes. If that implied deliberate misrepresentation, distortion, or falsification of data to advance some political propaganda, Schipper would vehemently, and quite rightfully, deny it. But if it meant an intellectually honest interpretation of the materials reflecting a definite point of view and bearing upon contemporary conditions, Schipper would not only accept it but, indeed, be flattered by it.

In fact, "his study of history was not meant to politicize [historical] knowledge but to actualize it."[22] In this process, a subjective outlook, a value-charged position, on the part of the historian is not only unavoidable but imperative. Does that preclude the possibility of getting to the truth? Not at all, Schipper would answer. The explanation or conclusions of a historian considered biased because of preconceived ideas may be indeed closer to the truth than those arrived at by historians who claim "objectivity." The insight and the historical narrative of the "biased" historian may be not only warranted and credible but may reflect the past events "as they really happened." Sidney Hook said:

> The possession of bias or passion on the part of the historian does not preclude the possibility of his achieving objectivity in testing his hypothesis any more than a physician's passion to relieve men from the possibility of a discovery of a medical . . . truth.[23]

Method and Purpose

The only change—more correctly, modification of no essential consequence—that can be detected in Schipper's works, taken in their chronological order, relates to his method of presentation. In the earlier books and monographs (*Anfänge des Kapitalismus*, the *Studies*, etc.) Schipper utilizes in the main the deductive method. First, he poses the problem and in doing so alludes to the general assumptions, revealing, as it were, his own point of view or, as others would term it, preconceived ideas. He then proceeds to provide the evidence. But in his later books (the *Virtshaftsgeshikhte* and, especially, *The History of Jewish Commerce in Poland*) the method is inductive, creating at times the impression that the author has no special axe to grind.[24] He lets the facts speak for themselves, so to say. It is because of that method of presentation that Friedman wrote about the *Virtshaftsgeshikhte*:

> With all its objectivity as well as calm, factual, and strictly scientific analysis of facts and problems, this work by Schipper represents a powerful "J'accuse" against those who ruled over Jews in the Middle Ages. Not rhetorical accusations, but cold figures, data and facts show irrefutably that the persecutions of Jews in England, France, Germany, Spain, etc., were not so much the result of religious fanaticism, the influence of clergy and momentary suggestions, as of coldly planned financial operations contrived with Satanic precision, although camouflaged with a pious mantle of religious hypocrisy.[25]

In *The History of Jewish Commerce in Polish Territories*, his latest and most extensive work, Schipper presents an even greater quantity of details—demographic data, economic facts, statistical tables, etc.—which he organizes and utilizes with remarkable facility and which represents a storehouse of invaluable information. Mahler quite accurately stated that "today no study on the history of the economy of the Jews in Poland is possible without reference to Schipper's *History of Jewish Commerce in Polish Territories*."[26] But the immense amount of collected materials and the inestimable magnitude of the research that must have gone into it were not merely an exercise in scholarship for its own sake. As has been shown above, Schipper gladly engaged in digging and searching for details and used every free moment of his time to do so[27] but only for the purpose of fortifying his conclusions and driving his point home.

Schipper wanted, above all, to bring Jewish history to the attention of the embattled Jewish masses of his own time, to those who for centuries of discrimination and degradation were reared in Jewish religious lore but remained ignorant of their own story. To Schipper's mind the knowledge and understanding of the past was an essential tool in the hands of the Jewish masses in their struggle for emancipation, for the attainment of political rights and equal economic opportunities as well as for the enhancement of their national awareness and self-respect. Ringelblum said:

> The leader of the *Poale Zion* movement in Galicia [*i.e.*, Schipper] who made out of the anomaly of the contemporary structure of Jewish economic life the cornerstone of his party platform searched in the past for the roots of the problems of the present.[28]

Indeed, Schipper believed that by knowing and understanding his history, especially its socioeconomic phenomena and developments, the Jew of his generation could free himself from the forces that had been victimizing him. This was part and parcel of Schipper's Crocean philosophy that "every true history is contemporary history" and of his contention that it is the task of the historian to "forge out of knowledge a sword for battle."

The writing of history in response to the needs of the time is not an unknown phenomenon in Jewish historiography. It is generally agreed, for instance, that the idea of the historical mission of Jews to mankind as the carriers of a "higher" morality, the leitmotif of the historians of the *Wissenschaft des Judentums* school in Germany in the nineteenth century,[29] grew out of the specific conditions and interests of German Jewry in the period of disillusionment following the promise and hopes of Enlightenment in Central Europe. It was meant to justify the existence of Judaism, to show the greatness of its noble teachings to the Gentile world, which was hopefully expected to practice these teachings (neighborly love, fraternity, etc.) towards Jews, as well as to the Jews themselves, many of whom were leaving the religion of their fathers. No doubt, it reflected the desire of the Jewish middle class in Germany to attain the rights of equal and full-fledged citizens.[30]

But half a century later, in Galicia and Poland, the apologia of the *Wissenschaft* school ceased being the theme of Jewish historiography. It was no longer considered an adequate answer to the three main problems facing the Jewish communities:

1. Externally, Polish anti-Semitism which concentrated its main assault on Jews in the sphere of economic activities;[31]

2. Internally, the trend toward assimilation which undermined the unity of the Jewish communities culturally and politically and was misleading the Jewish masses into believing that their salvation lay in an identification with the majority population;[32] and again

3. Internally, the task of strengthening the new nationalist orientation of the Jews with measures of self-defense as well as a broad and far-reaching program of cultural, economic, and political aspirations.[33]

The Economic and Sociocomparative Approach

Schipper knew that an answer to these problems couched in theological or idealistic terms would not do for an age familiar with the Marxist and socialist schools of thought, the materialistic approach to the understanding of social conditions and the history of societies. This approach required of the historian a new sociocomparative method of studying the past, a method that takes as its point of departure the economic facts of life and analyzes the economic and social relationships of specific developments and periods in the history of groups. It must be noted, however, that Schipper did not turn his attention to the socioeconomic factors in Jewish history because he was a convinced Marxist, in a doctrinal sense, or because he accepted a materialistic view of history as a matter of dogma. He stated himself that:

> . . . on account of the book [*i.e., Virtshaftsgeshikhte*] it seems safe to say that I will be described as an adherent of the "materialistic

> view of history." This has already occurred in connection with my previous historical economic monographs. If under the "school of materialistic history" one understands a philosophy that denies the influence of ideological motives on history, then I must state that I have nothing in common with such a primitive and raw understanding of history. . . . The materialistic interpretation of history as one of the best methods of historical investigation is something I do believe in. But I do not think that a method should be elevated to the level of a *Weltanschaung.*[34]

This is indeed reflected in Schipper's general tenor and in a number of specific statements.[35] He could not see how the history of the human experience can be relegated to materialistic motives only. Surely, there are other factors which determine, to a greater or lesser degree, the actions of man, and no one factor is the sole, exclusive determinant. In accord with this view, Schipper points out in his critique of Weber's theory that:

> . . . by ascribing to religion the predominant influence in the development of [Jewish] economic ethics, Weber introduced a doubtful hypothesis. It is true that both religion and economic ethics show a very significant parallelism in the life of a nation, but it does not follow that economic ethics is solely the consequence of religion. Equally hazardous seems to us the assumption that religion has the predominant influence not only on economic ethics but also on economic activity.[36]

Pointing out further that the difference between the Jewish and non-Jewish economy in the Middle Ages as well as in modern times is quantitative rather than qualitative, Schipper states that the quantitative differences were indeed influenced by religious factors, "but these were not the sole or even the predominant ones, because political, social and economic elements were also at work." And he provides a number of examples to illustrate this point.[37]

It might be added that in the same essay Schipper is also critical of Weber's "typological methodology" because it is one-sided and fails to take under consideration individual, specific features and particulars which are often of basic significance to historical dynamics. "We believe," he writes, "that historical dynamics is the result of a compromise between typical ('regular') phenomena and specific, individual factors, rather than the result of a supremacy of the first over the second."[38]

Thus, theoretically and in practice, Schipper is far from being doctrinaire and unidimensional in his view and approach to history. He recognizes the old Biblical adage that "man does not live by bread alone," and a great deal of his research and studies are also devoted to specific aspects of the cultural history of Polish Jewry.[39] But what is new and of pioneering significance in Schipper's approach is that economic factors and relationships constitute a basic key for the understanding of many, but not all, phenomena in the life of a people, and that the history of the Jews must therefore be reexamined in the light of these factors and relationships.[40] Moreover, the contemporary problems and needs of the Jewish people, especially those of its broad, pauperized masses in Eastern Europe, could not be answered with the old Jewish histories. Those were histories of Jewish suffering or of Jewish spiritual achievements (religious disputes and movements, great men, philosophers, literature), or both. A history of the struggles of the people for their daily sustenance and the lessons to be derived from those struggles was missing. A down-to-earth history understandable to the broad masses in terms of their own economic and political contentions as well as in terms of their national aspirations was waiting to be written.

In 1917, in an article dedicated to the hundredth anniversary of Graetz's birth, Schipper wrote:

> Urged by our sense of national duty we reach into the past not only to justify our existence . . . but to find in it the arsenal which contains the means of our defense and the means of our reconstruction. . . . We are not interested so much in defining the position of the Jews in the universe (as is still the case with Graetz) as in a place of existence . . . where we can productively utilize for ourselves . . . our entire historical experience. Graetz was the first modern historian, on a large scale, who reached into the depths of the Jewish awareness of kinship. But we are still waiting for a

> historian of similar dimensions who will give us the national history of the Jewish people's toil.[41]

Such a history, Schipper admitted, was the dream of his youth, a dream that he realized only in part through his *Virtshaftsgeshikhte*.[42] In the Preface to the *Studies* he formulated his position in words which became classic:

> They [the great men of Jewish historiography to date] have given us a splendid picture of the spiritual leaders of Diaspora Jewry. We are, however, left completely in the dark about the history of the hundreds of thousands whose claim to recognition does not rest on the riches of the spirit but on their toil and labor. We know the Sabbath Jew with his holiday spirit, but it is now high time to become acquainted with the history of the weekday Jew and the weekday ideas, and cast a beacon of light on Jewish labor.[43]

With this in mind, Schipper entered an area of Jewish historiography that was hardly touched before. With the exception of Herzfeld's and Caro's first and fundamental works in Jewish economic historiography as well as a limited number of monographs,[44] an economic history of Jews was badly lacking. The *Virtshaftsgeshikhte* and the many monographic studies that preceded it complemented Caro's work and put Schipper in the forefront of the Jewish economic historiography of his time. Certainly, with regard to Polish Jewry, he not only pioneered in telling its economic past in a comprehensive and didactic manner but erected a lasting monument to its centuries of economic efforts, activities, enterprises, and contributions. In this respect his place in modern Jewish historiography has been fully recognized, although all kinds of reservations have been expressed with regard to one or another detail or question in his works.[45]

Schipper always keeps in mind the fact that in the case of Jewish history an analysis of the economic factors and relationships must take under consideration not only the Jews but also the people among whom they lived. Jewish historiography suffered from a tendency to disregard the general historical setting, and it is Schipper who rectified this to a great extent. Aware that Jewish economic activities did not function in a vacuum, that those activities related and depended to a great extent on general economic factors, he always looks for the key to the understanding of Jewish economic phenomena and specific problems in the general setting.[46] This led him quite naturally to search more intensively and more often in the non-Jewish, external sources rather than in the internal, Hebrew sources, while not in any way minimizing the intrinsic value of the latter.[47]

The same comparative approach dictated also a broader treatment of the economic history of the Jews in medieval Poland, a treatment which would take into consideration the medieval history of Jews in other countries as well. For the history of Polish Jewry was part of a long medieval history of Jews in various countries, and the proper understanding of the former depends on a knowledge of the latter. It is with this in mind that Schipper moved, so to say, from the one to the other. Having made his first steps in the early history of Polish Jews, he turned to a study of the Jewish economic relationships in all of early medieval Europe prior to the publication of his *Studies* as well as following that publication. With this broad, comparative background, he returned again to the economic history of Polish Jewry and produced the monumental *History of Jewish Commerce in Polish Territories.*[48]

As Schipper sees it, the general background of his subject includes not only Poland but Western as well as Eastern Europe. That background contains certain key factors or elements against which Polish Jewry is seen in much better light, such as:

1. The character of Jewish commerce in the early Middle Ages, and its connections with the Near East, Southeastern Europe, and Western Europe;

2. The general economic and political causes of the change from commerce to moneylending activities which took place in medieval Western Europe;

3. Jewish credit as a phenomenon determined by the economic development of those social classes of the general society which needed it, either for productive or consumptive purposes;

4. The economically determined changes in the attitudes to the Jews on the part of the secular and ecclesiastical authorities

and on the part of the different social classes of the medieval society;

5. The aforementioned general observation by Roscher that "medieval policy towards the Jews is almost an inverse function of general economic development."

Against these features the similarities or dissimilarities in the economic and sociolegal position of the Jews in Poland are perceived in their proper perspective; for instance:

1. The early commercial connections with the East and the West, and the role of Jews in the development of Poland's foreign as well as domestic trades;

2. The dissimilarities between the Kalisz Charter of 1264 and its Austrian model;

3. The functions and operations of Jewish credit in Poland and the specific character of the Jewish bankers in Poland;

4. The refutation of Kutrzeba's theory that until the fifteenth century Jews in Poland were engaged only in usury;

5. The presentation of fiscal policies towards the Jews in distinction to those practiced in the West;

6. The relationship between pogroms and the economic development of the country;

7. The evidence of Jewish participation in the colonization of Ruthenian and Lithuanian territories;

8. Jewish participation in certain crafts, etc.

All these new and distinct contributions to the understanding of the economic role of Jews in medieval Poland are presented by Schipper in a realistic, rather than an idealized, vein. He dislikes the empty pathos of the descriptive history employed by Bałaban and the other Jewish historians who preceded him. Conscious that a generation of Jews fighting for social and national emancipation does not require an idealization of a sad past but a realistic assessment of those socioeconomic and political factors that played a decisive role in shaping the position of the Jews, Schipper presents his narrative of history in a way that appeals to common sense rather than sentiment. Facts, episodes, and trends become interesting and revealing because in speaking to reason and the critical faculty of the mind and in pointing to the underlying reasons and relationships, his narrative becomes both dialectical and didactic. It reflects Schipper's personality, his broad vision, intellectual curiosity and insight, his search for basic conceptions and implications, connections and relevances. He proceeds like a pedagogue who is bent upon challenging his students to gain a deeper understanding of the past and to derive the proper conclusions from it.

In setting forth his theories and in posing questions for which conclusive answers could not be given due to the paucity of source materials, Schipper challenges also his contemporaries—historians and students alike—not to rely on past histories, on the accepted clichés, routines, and methods, but to look for new ways and approaches, to search for new answers or to come up, at least, with tenable hypotheses. Schipper introduces in his works methods of historical inquiry scarcely employed before: considerable statistics, demographic data, numismatics, and such an unknown quantity in Jewish historiography as toponymy.[49] And in presenting his own theories (on Jewish origins in Poland or on early Jewish agricultural activities) he surely meant to put new problems on the agenda of the historian's desk, to arouse discussions and polemics, and to create thereby a greater interest in Jewish history on the part of the general Jewish public, especially Jewish youth and the Jewish masses with whom he identified and to whom he felt a deep sense of responsibility.

It is that sense of intimate, organic identification and genuine dedication to the people, stemming from coexperiencing its history, that Schipper admires in Graetz, although he certainly disagrees with the latter's philosophy of Jewish history. In writing about Graetz and his monumental work Schipper says:

> The permanence of Graetz lies in the folk-character of his work and in his sense of responsibility for the continued existence of the Jewish people. . . . He proved and deepened the awareness and faith that we are and will be! Thus he created a broad base for Jewish activism.[50]

But he also notes that this is as far as Graetz went. Guidelines for the future are missing in Graetz's history, and it is up to the nationalist historians to show the way to the disenthrallment of the Jewish people, to their self-reliance and self-respect, to their future of productivity, dignity, and self-determination.

For the Sake of the People and National Emancipation

For Schipper, the continuation of Jewish existence depended on an intelligent identification expressed in terms of modern Jewish nationalism in its Zionist formulation. That nationalist consciousness among Jews in Poland depended, in turn, on an inner emancipation of the Jewish masses in every respect—socio-economically, politically, culturally, and psychologically. His work as a historian was meant to foster the national awareness of the Polish Jews and to aid in the process of their nationalist emancipation. Hence, Schipper's pronounced interest not only in the history of the "everyday Jew" and his means of sustaining himself but also in the daily aspects of his culture, his language, and his creative efforts.

Believing that Jewish historiography should not be concerned with literature, scholars, and spiritual leaders only, Schipper made the unique attempt to recreate a picture of everyday life of the common folk in medieval Poland: their customs, habits, and other aspects of daily culture. In spite of the admittedly meager source materials,[51] he succeeded in presenting seven chapters, of necessity short and sketchy but with interesting illustrations of the medieval Jewish home, its furniture, utensils, and other objects, Jewish attire and adornments, jewelry and art, festive occasions and games, and such sociologically revealing aspects of daily life as misdemeanors, criminal transgressions, imputations, superstitions, etc.[52] Some of the details Schipper extracted from various archival documents, others from illuminated manuscripts, still others from antiques and historical monuments such as paintings in synagogues and churches. In scrutinizing the details of all these historical vestiges, he finds, in his characteristic way, a great deal more than meets the eye about the habits in Jewish life as well as about Jewish art and artists.[53] All this is set forth in his *Kultur-geshikhte fun Yidn in Poyln beysn mitlalter (Cultural*

History of the Jews in Poland During the Middle Ages) published in 1926.

In delving into the history of the common people, their day-to-day efforts at making a living as well as their social and cultural patterns, Schipper is not unmindful of the fact that the life of the Jews, like that of any other group, had its lighter side, its moments of entertainment and joy. It is both natural and typical of Schipper to be interested in the joys of the simple and downtrodden people and to show that life in the Jewish quarter or ghetto was not as dark and impregnably isolated as might be assumed. In the latter respect his interest centers especially on expressions of Jewish dramatic art because of his distinct propensity and love for the Jewish theater.[54] He saw in the theater, in the dramatic literature of known and anonymous authors as well as in the dramatic folklore, substantial and significant aspects of Jewish history organically related to the ways and modes of life of the people in the past as well as the present. Stimulated by this conviction, Schipper devoted several years to the extremely difficult task of researching the past of the Jewish theater and published three volumes in Yiddish on the *History of Jewish Theatrical Art and Drama.*[55] He viewed the Jewish theater as a folk theater and expected it to serve not only as a rostrum for high artistic and aesthetic expressions but also as an instrumentality projecting the style and ideas of the Jewish people, the idiom and traits, the spirit and aspirations of Jewish nationalism.[56]

Schipper's deep affection and regard for the people, his empathy with the masses, is best reflected in his appreciation of their folklore of which he was an avid collector and, especially, in his profound interest in Yiddish, the people's vernacular. In 1908 the Jewish intelligentsia in Galicia was still oriented either to German or, more so, to Polish. The Zionists for their part also belittled Yiddish as a poor and unworthy "jargon" which must ultimately yield to Hebrew. Schipper, however, being most sensitive to the cultural needs of the Jewish multitudes, had no doubts about the vitality and importance of Yiddish as an intrinsic vehicle of cultural emancipation and the most natural asset towards the realization of the national aspirations of the people.[57] Schipper's positive attitude to Yiddish as the national language of the Jewish people is remarkable for two reasons. The first is that Schipper was an intellectual who was educated within the framework of the Polish and German cultures rather than within the Jewish fold. As a lawyer, a historian, an author, a deputy to the Polish Sejm, he certainly had more in common with the refined and the sophisticated, with the educated intelligentsia and the professional upper crust than with the so-called "*amkho*."[58] Secondly, while a convinced Zionist, he seemed to take the position of the Yiddishists who, by and large, contraposed the Zionist idea of rebuilding Palestine with the idea of a Jewish cultural autonomy in the Diaspora in which Yiddish would play the dominant role.[59] But these very facts go to show that Schipper's foremost consideration was the people, the broad masses of his fellow Jews. His European, non-Jewish acquisitions were at best secondary to his true and overriding inner identificationn with "*amkho*," and surely there was no better means of identifying with "*amkho*" than Yiddish. Chided by his fellow Zionists for his associations and concurrence with the Yiddishists, Schipper used to retort astutely that "Yiddish is not a monopoly of the Yiddishists but the property of the entire Jewish people,"[60] and it was the cultural emancipation of the entire people that Schipper believed to be of paramount importance. Without negating the role of Hebrew as the historical language of the Jews and certainly as the language of Jews in Palestine, Schipper enthusiastically saluted every new achievement in the field of Yiddish linguistics and Yiddish literature. As early as 1913 he foretold that Yiddish would become a major field of research for Jewish scholars and scientists, and he even projected a study of the old and new Yiddish literatures. He expressed these sentiments in an indicatively sympathetic and pragmatic essay written in connection with the publication of the Festschrift, *Der pinkos*, edited by Niger (Wilno: 1913), which contained pioneering studies in Yiddish philology and which Schipper considered to symbolize the beginning of a new period in the development of Yiddish literature and Yiddish scholarship. His essay, entitled "A New Era in Our Struggle for

Yiddish," appeared in a jubilee issue of *Der Yidisher Arbeter*.[61]

Schipper, the economic historian, also devoted a great deal of his time to the history of Yiddish and its literature. Although initially by no means an authority on the subject in view of the lack of formal preparation, he eventually became one. His deep interest and research resulted in numerous studies and essays published in various journals and periodicals which put together would constitute a very sizable and significant volume. He deals mostly with the origins and oldest traces of Yiddish, the character of Old Yiddish literature, the oldest Yiddish publications, the first translations into Yiddish, etc.[62] Major works on the history of Yiddish literature provided him with opportunities to write extensive critical essays in which he discussed some of the fundamental problems relating to the history of the old as well as the character of the new Yiddish literature.[63]

As in the case of Jewish economic history, Schipper believes that the historian of Yiddish literature must aim at detecting the threads that bind the literary records and expressions with the sociological aspects of the people's life. He must perceive the synthesis inherent in the literary heritage of the people, rather than limit himself to an analysis and critical evaluation of literary documents and works, and he must focus on Yiddish literary creativity in a sociocomparative way.[64] That Schipper became an authority on the subject of the Yiddish language and Yiddish literature can be seen from the fact that he was invited to co-author the entries relating to these two subjects in the *Encyclopaedia Judaica* published in Berlin in 1927-1933.[65]

But to Schipper, Yiddish was much more than a matter of scholarly investigations and academic discussions. It was essentially and mainly a means of communicating with the people, of educating the masses, and of sharing with the Yiddish reading public his historical studies as well as his views and opinion concerning the problems facing the Jewish people. In the Foreword to the Yiddish translation of his *Studies*, Schipper explains apologetically to the Yiddish reader why this book, which had been written for the Yiddish reader in the first place, remained "in exile" for twenty years. In the same Foreword he stresses the fact that the Jewish working masses helped him materially and morally in the publication of the Yiddish translation of *Anfänge des Kapitalismus* in 1920 and that "the intensified interest of the Jewish reader in scientific studies in Yiddish makes it clear that the time has come to put an end to the wandering of Jewish books among non-Jews."[66]

Experienced in the work of journalism since his youth both as a contributor and editor, [67] Schipper was very conscious of the educative value of the periodicals and press in Yiddish, and he utilized these to write in a popular vein on historical curiosities and cultural topics whenever possible. His work as a publicist was indeed very prolific and the dozens of articles which he contributed to various Yiddish journals and such dailies as the *Haynt* and *Moment* in Warsaw and *Der Morgn* in Lwów,[68] all written in a light, anecdotal manner, reflect better than anything else Schipper's national plebeian thesis, his dedication to the cause of the people's edification and their national renaissance.[69]

Schipper himself exemplified to a great extent his own ideals of national regeneration and renewal. Those who were often in his presence, either as associates or students, and who knew him personally described him as one of the most attractive representatives of the modern Jewish renaissance, a man who personified a harmonious synthesis of different influences and ideas, of the old and the modern, the conservative and the radical, the European and the specifically Jewish, and a man who by virtue of his erudition, personality, and dedication to his people, served as a perfect example of the modern, nationalist Jew.[70]

Notes

1. See *Theory and Practice of Historical Study: A Report of the Committee on Historiography*, Social Science Research Council, Bulletin No. 54 (New York: 1946), p. 135. For a concise and comprehensive treatment of modern historicism and its evolution, see the Introduction in H. Meyerhoff's *The Philosophy of History in Our Time, An Anthology* (Garden City, N.Y.: 1959), pp. 1-25. See also D. E. Lee and R. N. Beck, "The Meaning of Historicism," *The American Historical Review*, LIX, No. 3, pp. 568-577.

2. M. Bałaban, *Dzieje Żydów w Galicyi i w Rzeczypospolitej krakowskiej, 1772-1868* (Lwów: 1916).

3. *Moriah*, XII (1917), No. 9-10, pp. 434-435.

4. See *Księga jubileuszowa dla uczczenia sieśćdziesięciolecia Profesora Majera Bałabana* (Warsaw: 1938), pp. 28-29.

5. "Motywy żydowskie w powieściach historycznych Liona Feuchtwangera," *Miesięcznik Żydowski*, I (1931), p. 417.

6. See Meyerhoff, *op. cit.*, pp. 12-14. An interesting comparative study of Leopold von Ranke and the great Jewish historian of the nineteenth century, Heinrich Graetz (1817-1891), is provided in the volume entitled *History and Jewish Historians* which is composed of essays and addresses by S. W. Baron, compiled by A. Hertzberg and L. A. Feldman (Philadelphia: 1964), pp. 269-275.

7. This quote of B. Croce as well as the preceding ones are from his *History: Its Theory and Practice* (New York: 1921), pp. 12, 19, 20, 23 f. That Schipper was well acquainted with Croce's philosophy of history can be seen from the fact that he refers to him in his critical essay on Max Weber's thesis regarding the sociological basis of the Jewish religion. In it he notes that Croce is a "great historian and philosopher who maintains that all historical writings are but mirrors of the living present." See "Socjologiczne podłoże religji żydowskiej. Sprawozdanie krytyczne z dzieła Maksa Webera," *Nowe Życie*, I (1924), pp. 39-47, 204-210. The English translation thereof by P. Glickson can be found in *The Jewish Journal of Sociology*, I (Dec. 1959), pp. 250-260.

8. In connection with the last statement, it might be noted that in the brief introductory remarks to Croce's selection included in his anthology, Meyerhoff says that the pragmatic approach to history "seems to correspond to the sentiments of the 'general reader' who tends to feel that history is an archaic, dead discipline unless it has something to say to him which is pertinent to his own life and times." See Meyerhoff, *op. cit.*, p. 44.

9. See Mahler, "I. Schipper," *YIVO Bleter*, XXV (1945, pp. 19-32), p. 19.

10. C. L. Becker, "What Are Historical Facts?," *The Western Political Quarterly*, VIII, 3 (Sept. 1955), pp. 333-336, or in Meyerhoff's anthology, *op. cit.*, pp. 128-129, 131-132.

11. R. G. Collingwood, *The Idea of History* (New York: 1956), pp. 241 ff. or Meyerhoff, *op. cit.*, pp. 76 ff.

12. See Ph. Friedman, "Pokłosie historiografji żydowskiej lat ostatnich w Polsce," *Miesięcznik Żydowski*, V, (1935), pp. 182 ff. Also, *idem*., "Polish Jewish Historiography between the Two Wars (1918-1939)," in *Jewish Social Studies*, XI (1949), p. 374.

13. See, for example, the places where Schipper refers to Roscher directly:

Onhoyb, op. cit., p. 32; *Studies, op. cit.*, p. 140. Cf. J. Shatzky, "Shney Historyonim Kedoshim," *Metsuda* (London: 1945), p. 418. Roscher's famous essay on the Jews' function in the economy of the Middle Ages entitled "Die Stellung der Juden in Mittelalter, betrachtet vom Standpunkt der allgemeinen Handelspolitik" has been mentioned already in this study in its English translation by S. Grayzel. See *supra*, Chap. II, p. 57 and Chap. VI, p. 200. An excellent critical evaluation of Roscher's essay and his theory was written by G. Kisch under the title, "The Jews' Function in the Medieval Evolution of Economic Life," *Historia Judaica*, IV (1944), pp. 1-12.

14. See *infra*, p. 244 f.

15. Friedman, "Dzieło na czasie," *Miesięcznik Żydowski*, I (1931), p. 557.

16. H. Pirenne, "What Are Historians Trying to Do?," in *Methods in Social Science*, ed. by S. A. Rice (Chicago: 1931), p. 441.

17. See H. Seidman, *Yoman Geto Varsha* (Tel Aviv: 1946), p. 301; or *idem., Togbukh fun varshever geto* (Buenos Aires: 1947), pp. 99-100. Ringelblum wrote in his last notes (*Fun di letste notitsn*) that during the war Schipper actually completed a sizable and conclusive work on the Khazars based on the research and studies that were brought to light since 1918, the year in which his espousal of the Khazar theory was again presented in "Początki." See E. Ringelblum, "Der boyer fun der moderner historiografye," *Bleter far Geshikhte*, XI (1958), p. 9. Schipper would, no doubt, have welcomed and utilized the scholarly contribution made by Golb and Pritsak with respect to the discovery of the Kiev Document and their reexamination of the Cambridge Document. As a result of their study, Golb has concluded that the Khazar Jews became a part of Eastern European Jewry in the Ukraine after the Khazar kingdom fell. To that extent, at least, he seems to support Schipper's thinking, inasmuch as not long thereafter major parts of Western Ukraine came under Polish rule. See Golb and Pritsak, *Khazarian Documents, op. cit.*, p. xv.

18. Cf. Seidman, "Ḥayyav shel Dr. I. Shiper Zal," *I. Shiper*, ed. by Eidelberg, *op. cit.*, p. 61.

19. Pirenne, "What Are Historians Trying to Do?," in *Methods in Social Science, loc. cit.*

20. Cf. D. M. Dunlop, *The History of the Jewish Khazars* (New York: 1967), pp. 261-263.

21. Bałaban, "Kiedy i skąd przybyli Żydzi do Polski?," *Miesięcznik Żydowski, op. cit.*, p. 113.

22. Mahler, "I. Shiper," *YIVO Bleter, loc. cit.*

23. C. A. Beard and S. Hook, "Problems of Terminology in Historical Writing," in *The Theory and Practice of Historical Study, op. cit.*, p. 126.

24. Cf. A. Tartakover, "Darko shel I. Shiper be-Ḥeker ha-Kalkala ha-Yehudit," in *I. Shiper, op. cit.*, pp. 25-26.

25. Friedman, "Dzieło na czasie," *Miesięcznik Żydowski*, I (1931), *loc. cit.*

26. Mahler, "I. Shiper u-Meḥkarav ha-Historiyim," in *I. Shiper, op. cit.*, p. 44.

27. In the Foreword to the *Virtshaftsgeshikhte* Schipper notes that in the ten years following World War I, a period during which he served as a representative in the Polish Sejm and was preoccupied with important political issues and problems of the General Zionist Party, his research and studies were not completely neglected. He continued to spend as much time as possible in the libraries and archives of Warsaw and collect source materials during his oft-taken trips abroad. See *Virtshaftsgeshikhte, op. cit.*, p. 111. Cf. Ringelblum, "Der boyer fun der moderner yidisher historiografye," *op. cit.*, p. 8.

28. *Ibid.*, p. 6.

29. Krochmal, Zunz, Jost, Geiger, Graetz, and others.

30. See Mahler, "Teorje żydowskiej historjografji o rozwoju dziejowym kultury żydowskiej," *Miesięcznik Żydowski*, III (1933), p. 7 and *passim.*

31. *Supra*, Chap. I, pp. 6-7. Also, *Dzieje handlu żydowskiego, op. cit.*, pp. 602. 607-609, 633-641.

32. *Supra*, Chap. I, p. 6. How utterly disgusted Schipper was with Jewish assimilationists can be seen in a critical review which he wrote on Z. Mayer's book *Die Wiener Juden* (Vienna: 1917) in which he derisively describes the author as "a man who suppresses himself in the face of his time. He passed the route from the ghetto of Pressburg to the mid-town of Vienna and on the way lost the Jew within himself. He is the known type of the 'progressive Jew' (*Zivilisationjude*) with his tragicomical spiritual situation branded by Aḥad Ha-Am as inner bondage." *Moriah*, XIV (1918), p. 196.

33. *Supra*, Chap. I, pp. 7 f.

34. *Virtshaftsgeshikhte, op. cit.*, in the Foreword, p. vi.

35. See, for instance, *supra*, Chap. VI, p. 199 or Chap. V, pp. 178 f.

36. Quoted from P. Glikson's translation of Schipper's "Socjologiczne podłoże religji żydowskiej. Sprawozdanie krytyczne dziela Maksa Webera," *op. cit.*, p. 259.

37. *Ibid.*, p. 260.

38. *Ibid.*, p. 259.

39. See *infra*, pp. 251 f., 253 f.

40. Cf. Mahler, "I. Shiper," *op. cit.*, p. 20; Seidman, "Ḥayyav shel Dr. I. Shiper Zal," *op. cit.*, p. 62.

41. "Graetz: W setną rocznicę urodzin historyka żydowskiego," *Moriah*, XIII (Nov. 1917), pp. 55-56.

42. Initially the *Virtshaftsgeshikhte* was proposed to Schipper by the "Central" publications company in Warsaw, as an economic supplement to the eleven volumes of the *Geschichte der Juden* by Graetz. When it was realized, however, that such a project would not be feasible, Schipper proceeded to plan an independent work to extend to the middle of the seventeenth century. The four volumes of the *Virtshaftsgeshikhte* did not go beyond the year 1500, but Schipper hoped that he would find it possible to bring it up to the present time. See *Virtshaftsgeshikhte, op. cit.*, pp. iii-iv of the Foreword.

43. *Studies, op. cit.*, p. 11.

44. L. Herzfeld, *Handelsgeschichte der Juden des Altertums, op. cit.*, which in Baron's words "has not yet been superseded by any other comprehensive work of this type," (Baron, *History and Jewish Historians, op. cit.*, p. 322) and G. Caro, *Sozial- und Wirtschaftsgeschichte der Juden im Mittelalter*, 2 vols. (Leipzig: 1908 and 1920) which only went up to 1350. The special monographs by M. Hoffman, L. Davidsohn, F. Baer, J. Krakauer, U. Cassuto, and others are mentioned by Schipper in the Foreword of the *Virtshaftsgeshikhte* and are listed in its extensive bibliography.

45. See Friedman's opening remarks in his review of Schipper's *Dzieje handlu żydowskiego* in *Jewish Social Studies*, II (1940), p. 102 f. *Idem*, "Pionier nowej historigrafii żydowskiej," *Opinia* (Lwów: 1934), No. 46; *idem*, "Polish Jewish Historiography between the Two Wars (1918-1939)," *op. cit.*, pp. 380-381; *idem*, "Dzieło na czasie," *op. cit.*, p. 555; A. Tartakover, *op. cit.*, p. 32; Mahler, "I. Shiper," *op. cit.*, pp. 29, 31-32; M. Wischnitzer, "Dr. I. Schipper," *Historia Judaica*, VI (1944), pp. 98-100; Shatzky, "Dr. I. Shiper (1884-1943)," *Zamlbikher* (New York: 1946), No. 4.

46. Cf. Mahler, "I. Shiper u-Meḥkarav ha-Historiyim," *op. cit.*, p. 35.

47. In this connection it should be added that some reviewers noted that Schipper's works are lacking because he neglected to utilize adequately the primary Hebrew sources in support of his narrative and views. Without indicating any particular Hebrew sources which might have been used by him and which would have had a direct bearing on his comparative method and conclusions, insofar as the medieval economic history of Polish Jews is concerned, these critics ascribed the alleged shortcoming to Schipper's inadequate knowledge of Hebrew due to the fact that he had received, as a young man, a European and secular, rather than traditional, type of education. Schipper's educational background is, of course, a matter of record, and it may be quite true that he was no Hebraist in the accepted sense of the word. But it seems that the extent of his utilization or neglect of Hebrew sources had little to do with his Hebraic pro-

ficiency or lack of it. With regard to Schipper's specific problems, there was simply a paucity of primary Hebrew sources. On more than one occasion he complained about this paucity and, as has been shown elsewhere in this study, Schipper was anxious to lay his hands on pertinent Hebrew source materials and indeed he utilized them whenever he succeeded in his search. (*Supra*, Chap. III, pp. 92 ff; Chap.VI, p. 215.) See Y. M. Biderman, "I. Shiper ke-Ḥoker Toldoteha shel Yahadut Polin," *Hadoar*, XLVII (June, 1967), p. 550, column 1; I. Halpern, "On Schipper's *History of Jewish Commerce in Polish Territories*", *op. cit.*, pp. 209-210.

48. Cf. Mahler, "I. Shiper u-Meḥkarav ha-Historiyim," *op. cit.*, pp. 34-35.

49. Cf. Altbauer, "Meḥkaro shel I. Shiper al ha-Yesod ha-Kuzari-Yehudi be-Mizraḥ Eyropa," *op. cit.*, p. 53.

50. "Graetz un zayn monumental verk," an essay in the Yiddish edition of Graetz's *Yidishe geshikhte*, 7 vols. (Warsaw: 1927), pp. xxxiv-xlvi. Schipper wrote also a similar essay in the Polish edition of Graetz's history published in Warsaw in 1939. Cf. Baron, *Jewish History and Jewish Historians, op. cit.*, pp. 274-275.

51. See Preface to Part VI of the *Kultur-geshikhte, op. cit.*, p. 211.

52. It is of interest to note that with regard to criminal transgressions, Schipper states that the crimes of which Jews were accused were both true and fictitious. On the basis of cited documented cases involving theft and robbery, trading in stolen goods or accepting such goods as pledges, falsification of currency, assaults, libel, smuggling of goods, disobedience of market regulations (*Kultur-geshikhte, op. cit.*, pp. 235-240), he points out that while "the Jewish crimes at that time were mainly of the so-called 'occupational' category, that is, crimes induced by the type of business practiced in the locale or class to which the offender belonged, we must note as very characteristic the fact that among the numerous disclosures about Jewish offenses preserved in the medieval sources we could not find a single court case nor a single memorandum in church documents or municipal councils . . . which would mention a Jewish murderer or a Jewish spy!" *Ibid.*, pp. 240-241.

53. To present more details about the attire and adornments of the Jews in medieval Poland, Schipper goes into a thorough dissection of a miniature illumination on a manuscript from the twelfth or thirteenth century which belonged to a church in Kruszwice, two stained glass windows from the fourteenth century in the Cathedral of Włocławek, and two paintings from the fifteenth century in the Church of St. Catherine in Cracow, all of which portray Jewish figures. And to provide some information about Jewish art, he describes the "Old Synagogue" of Cracow and the medieval synagogue of Sandomierz, both of which attest to Jewish architecture and wall painting as well as gold and silver smithery. He also describes in great detail two illuminated manuscripts which had not been noted by any bibliographer, a siddur on parchment going back to

the Middle Ages found in the synagogue of Sandomierz, and fragments of the *Sefer ha-Mitsvot* found in the Main Archives of Warsaw, both done by anonymous scribes and both attesting not only to the existence of Jewish artists but also to the high quality of their art. *Ibid.*, pp. 212-230.

54. Sigmund Turkow, the famous actor of the Yiddish theater in Poland, relates in his memoirs many interesting facts about Schipper's active involvement in the affairs of the Yiddish theater in Warsaw in the twenties. He describes him as an insider in the theatrical circles. Not only did Schipper attend the premiere of every play and the parties following the premieres in the cafés of Warsaw where the Jewish actors used to gather, but he actually participated in the professional and technical discussions of various theatrical projects. Turkow notes that Schipper had theatrical conceptions for staging and directing which were original and impressive and that he often came up with proposals and remedies worthy of true professionals. At the rehearsals of certain plays his opinions and instructions were not only accepted by actors but actually sought after. He was considered an expert on the subject of the *Purimshpil*, the traditional folk plays performed on the day of Purim, having devoted many years to the study of its historical development. See Z. Turkow, *Fragmentn fun mayn lebn* (Buenos Aires: 1951), pp. 20-22.

55. Written in Yiddish, the title of this work is *Geshikhte fun der yidisher teater-kunst un drame* (Warsaw: vols. I-II, 1927; vol. III, 1928). A fourth volume of the work remained in manuscript. See especially Schipper's Foreword to the first volume as well as p. 151 in vol. I, p. 75 in vol. II, and p. 100 in vol. III. A critical assessment of this work was written by Shatzky, "Di ershte geshikhte fun yidishn teater, tsu Dr. Shiper's verk," *Filologishe Shriftn fun YIVO*, II (1928), Wilno. See also *idem.*, "Dr. I. Shiper (1884-1943)," *Zamlbikher, op. cit.*, pp. 475 f.

56. See "Tsukunft-fragn funem yidishn teater," *Yidish Teater* (Warsaw: 1921), No. 1.

57. See *supra*, Chap. I, pp. 19-20.

58. A Hebrew expression meaning "your people" which in popular Yiddish or Hebrew usage denotes the common people, the Jewish masses.

59. The foremost proponent of a Jewish cultural autonomy in the Diaspora, based on the proposition that the Jews represent a spiritual (cultural-historical) nationality in the midst of political nations, was the great historian Simon Dubnow. With regard to the place of Yiddish as a means of strengthening Jewish cultural self-determination and as a bastion against cultural assimilation, Schipper's position was analogous to that of Dubnow. See Dubnow, *Nationalism and History, Essays on Old and New Judaism*, ed. by K. S. Pinson, *op. cit.*, Part I, *passim*, especially p. 190 and 50-53 of the editor's introductory essay.

60. See J. Hirschaut, *op. cit.*, p. 229.

61. See *supra*, Chap. I, p. 19. As indicated there, the essay by Schipper was considered at the time to represent the official position of the *Poale Zion* party

in Galicia on the issue of Yiddish, but Schipper's position was not dictated by his party affiliation, for his attitude to Yiddish remained the same after he parted with the *Poale Zion* in 1920 and became a leading figure in the party of the General Zionists of Poland. See also Hirschhaut, *op. cit.*, p. 201; Shatzky, "Dr. I. Shiper (1884-1943)," *Zamlbikher, op. cit.*, p. 474.

62. On Schipper's contributions in the area of the oldest Yiddish literature, one should mention two essays which he wrote in 1934 and 1935 because they contain a comprehensive summary of his investigations and findings. The first is entitled "Problemen fun der alt-yidisher literatur-geshikhte" published in the *YIVO Bleter* (Wilno: 1934), VII, Nos. 1-2, pp. 36-46; the second, "Kultur-geshikhtlekher fon fun der eltster yidisher literatur," *YIVO Bleter* (Wilno: 1935), VIII, pp. 44-60. For his other contributions, published mostly in the journal *Di Yidishe Velt*, see the Bibliography in this study, pp. 277 ff.

63. Notable among these are two series of articles published in the *Literarishe Bleter*: "Oyfn rand fun Maks Eriks bukh vegn alt-yidishn roman un novele," *Literarishe Bleter* (Warsaw: 1926), Nos. 112, 113, 114, 116, 118; "Vegn Eriks geshikhte fun der yidisher literatur," *Literarishe Bleter* (Warsaw: 1928), Nos. 11, 12, 17, 19, 22.

64. See "Kultur-geshikhtlekher fon fun der elster yidisher literatur," *Di Yidishe Velt* (Warsaw: 1928), Book II, pp. 232-247.

65. See "Jiddisch" and "Jiddische Literatur," *Encyclopedia Judaica*, vol. IX (Berlin: 1932), pp. 112-127 and 127-180 written together with S. Birnbaum and N. Meisel respectively.

66. See *Di virtshafts-geshikhte fun di Yidn in Poyln beysn mitlalter, op. cit.*, "Foreword."

67. See *supra*, Chap. I, p. 20. In 1919-1920 Schipper served again as the editor of the *Poale Zion* organ, *Di Yidishe Arbeter-Tsaytung.* He was also the editor of the Polish dailies which the General Zionists published in the twenties and early thirties but which existed only for limited periods of time. See H. Seidman, "Ḥayyav shel Dr. I. Shiper Zal," *op. cit.*, pp. 60-61.

68. See the Bibliography in this study, pp. 277 ff.

69. In connection with Schipper's dedication to the cause of educating the masses, it may be appropriate to note here that in dealing with the subject of Jewish physicians and surgeons in medieval Poland, Schipper emphasizes the fact that besides benefiting the common Jewish folk through their relationships with the royal court and the great lords, the Jewish physicians were the disseminators of general knowledge in the Jewish quarters and this is why he takes such a great interest in them. See *Kultur-geshikhte, op. cit.*, p. 194.

70. Cf. Mahler, "I. Shiper u-Meḥkarav ha-Historiyim," *op. cit.*, p. 37; J. Cyneman, "Dr. I. Shiper," *Kiyum* (Paris: 1950), Nos. 6-7, p. 1602; J. Shatzky, "Shney Historyonim Kedoshim," *op. cit.*, p. 419.

Postscript

In dealing with outstanding figures it often becomes apparent that their contributions and lives are intertwined. That this is particularly true in the case of Schipper has already been demonstrated to an extent. Schipper's constant preoccupation with Jewish history and his active involvement in the sociopolitical and cultural affairs directly affecting the Jewish community in Poland went hand in hand. Both were rooted in deep nationalist convictions; both complemented one another in thought and action; and both are typical of the thinking and character of the man who occupied an eminent place and played a distinctive role not only as a historian but also as a leader and statesman, a teacher and tribune of his people. Accordingly, a brief sketch of Schipper's life and activities following World War I seems to be in order.

In the Hub of Political Activities

Schipper did not escape the havoc brought upon Galician Jews by the shifting Russo-Austrian front in the initial phase of World War I. He became, like many Jews of Eastern Galicia, a refugee in Vienna. Even though the conditions were wretched, Schipper utilized his stay there for intensive research in the famous library of the Viennese Jewish kehilla and in other archives. The accumulated materials were meant for the general economic history of the Jews which Schipper was already planning.[1] But in

1916, when he was called into the army, this work had to be interrupted and postponed for many years.[2] In fact, in the years following the war, Schipper's pursuits as a historian became secondary to his life as a political activist. He wrote:

> I considered other tasks to be more important. At a time when "history is being made," when the foundations for a new life, under changed conditions, are being laid—and such indeed were the difficult but elated days which I lived through together with my brethren in Poland—it is hard to write history. . . . Only at "breathing spells" from my political and social preoccupations could I return to my scientific workshop and seek there some rest from the contemporary history which kept spinning before my eyes. . . .[3]

Although at first a regular soldier, Schipper was eventually transferred to Cracow to serve as a military judge. Notwithstanding his position of trust and the risk involved, he engaged in the political activities of the *Poale Zion*, which became increasingly anti-Austrian in the last two years of the war. Schipper, in fact, presided over the secret meeting of his party at which its official pro-Polish resolution was adopted.

In the autumn of 1918, the nationalities of the Austro-Hungarian Empire, realizing that the rule of the Hapsburg dynasty was coming to an end, readied themselves for the impending great changes in the geopolitical structure of Europe. Schipper represented the *Poale Zion* at the Party Council of Zionist Organizations in Galicia organized in August of 1918 to formulate the political postulates of the Jewish national minority. At the mass demonstration in October which was called by the Party Council to declare to the world its demands for Jewish national rights, Schipper delivered a fiery speech on behalf of *Poale Zion.* He called for the formation of a Jewish National Council which would include also the Jewish non-Zionist parties in order to protect, by common effort, the Jewish interests during the transition period from Austrian to Polish sovereignty, to ensure the national minority rights of the Jews in Poland, and to bring about a democratization of Jewish life internally and a broad people's representation for external purposes.[4]

When the Jewish National Council of Western Galicia was indeed formed in the wake of spreading anti-Jewish excesses and riots throughout Galicia designed to intimidate the Jews, Schipper became a member of its three-man Presidium, representing the *Poale Zion*, and served on the Council's Executive Committee. He was among the leading initiators in organizing, in cooperation with the Polish Liquidation Commission, voluntary reserve units of Jewish officers and soldiers to protect the lives and possessions of the Jewish population in Galicia against the Polish rabble.[5]

Following the end of the war and the proclamation of an independent Poland, Schipper returned to Tarnów where he became a candidate of the *Poale Zion* for the first Constituent Assembly of the resurrected Polish state, known as the Constitutional Sejm. Although he did not obtain the necessary number of votes in the election, Schipper soon became a full-fledged deputy when the only elected *Poale Zion* representative, Dr. Max Rosenfeld, died. Schipper, who was recognized as one of the foremost leaders in his party and next in line on its list of candidates, took Rosenfeld's place.[6] In 1919, Schipper already lived in Warsaw, working at the headquarters of his party and in the office of its chief national organ, *Di Arbeter Tsaytung*, which became a popular daily among the Jewish masses thanks to its high level of sociopolitical and literary journalism.[7]

As intraparty strife increased between the radical Marxists and the moderate socialists,[8] Schipper realized that the Polish *Poale Zion* was becoming a party of narrow political dogmatism, a party swayed by Marxian fanatics. He left the *Poale Zion* altogether, although his personal outlook had a lot in common with its general ideology, for to him the interests of the people, of *klal Yisrael* (the entire Jewish community), came before the narrow interest of his, or any other, party. He had expected the *Poale Zion* to be a broad and general Jewish folk movement motivated and governed by a liberal and open program of national and social progress.[9] When it turned out otherwise, Schipper joined the General Zionist Party in which he remained active for the rest of his life.[10] He at once became one of its leading figures and held its national chairmanship for a number of years. A candidate of his new party to the Parliament, he was reelected on the list of national minorities and continued to serve as deputy in the Polish Sejm from 1922 to 1929. True to his convictions, he considered himself a representative of Polish Jewry, vigorously fighting against laws designed to discriminate against Jews and steadfastly defending their rights. These rights were often threatened by the Polish centers of power which were, by and large, ill-disposed to the Jews.

In the Sejm, Schipper distinguished himself with his eloquent speeches in various committees. While serving on the Constitution Committee of the First Sejm, he vigilantly contributed to the liberal formulation of the Polish constitution, seeing to it that the rights of Jews were adequately protected. He would not let the special investigating committee of the First Sejm cover up the despicable pogrom on Jews in Pińsk. In the Second Sejm, he continued to fight courageously against any compromises with the Polish government in matters concerning the legitimate rights of the Jews. He fought for their right to rest on the Sabbath and work on Sundays, their right to attend the universities and to pay taxes in a way that did not discriminate between Jew and non-Jew, or their right to maintain their own recognized schools and institutions of cultural and social self-government. In the intra-Jewish political discussions and in the strifes between various factions, Schipper always attempted, often at the risk of his own political career which he enjoyed and considered important, to abate the differences and wranglings for the sake of unity and the common objectives.[11]

With Students and Young Historians

Although preoccupied politically in the twenties in the Sejm, in the Zionist Party, and in other organizations or institutions, which included innumerable conferences and meetings, Schipper did not neglect his other interests and avocations. He found the time and energy to be involved in the activities of the Jewish theater, to collect Jewish folklore, to do a considerable amount of journalistic writing on sociopolitical and literary topics in periodicals as well as the daily Yiddish and Polish press, to serve as the chairman of the Union of Jewish Writers and Journalists, to do additional research for his historical studies, to publish two major books and monographs,[12] and—above all—to be in touch with the people, especially with its youth, through his many speaking engagements and lectures. The latter activity was a labor of love as he always considered the task of educating the working people to be of utmost importance. He notes in the Foreword of the *Virtshaftsgeshikhte* that his contact with the working people and youth dispelled his doubts about the timeliness of his book: "During the lectures which I gave them [the youth and workers' circles], I noticed how little the old approach to Jewish historical questions satisfied them."[13] And his audiences respected him for his knowledge, for his fresh interpretations and broad historical perspective. They also liked his friendliness, his direct, affable, and intimate approach to people.[14]

He was even more popular with students whom he greatly influenced through his lectures as well as personal contacts.[15] Many of these young men became his admirers and disciples. They were impressed by his pioneering efforts in the field of historical inquiry, by his insights and vision, and they were overwhelmed by his sincerity, open-mindedness, nationalist-progressive outlook, and youthful enthusiasm sprinkled with considerable doses of wit and humor. Mahler, one of the younger Jewish historians and admirers of Schipper, writes that Schipper never seemed to get old in spirit or personal appearance, that he looked young, thought young, and always acted young by virtue of his impulsive temperament, his contagious enthusiasm as well as his natural, unaffected disposition.[16] "The [proverbial] *kin'at sofrim* (scholars' jealousy)," Mahler writes, "was alien to Schipper in relation to any new, young face appearing in the field of Jewish historical inquiry." On the contrary, he encouraged young historians who came to his attention, he was genuinely happy with their progress and achievements, and he respectfully appreciated their contributions.[17]

It was, therefore, quite natural for Schipper, when his political career as a deputy to the Polish Sejm ended, to become the Lecturer of Jewish Economic History at the Institute of Jewish Studies in Warsaw, a modern institution for higher Jewish learning established in 1927, and to assume the directorship of the Jewish Academic Home which housed the finest element of Jewish university students. Thus Schipper continued to be in close touch with the Jewish academic youth. As he became increasingly more active in YIVO,[18] especially in its history department in Warsaw, he was also in close contact with the group called *Yunge Historiker* (Young Historians) which gravitated around YIVO.[19] At the same time he continued to be in the hub of Zionist action, occupying a place in the Presidium of the Zionist Organization, serving all the time on its Central Committee, participating in the Congresses of the World Zionist Organization, and playing an active role in important deliberations and decisions.[20] In fact, there was hardly any important Zionist activity in Poland in the twenties or thirties with which Schipper was not directly associated.[21]

In the Ghetto of Warsaw

In 1935 Schipper became the director of the *Keren ha-Yesod* (Palestine Development Fund) in Poland and by that time, or soon thereafter, he apparently began thinking about the possibilities of settling in Palestine. On his visit to Palestine in 1937, from which he returned very much captivated by and enthused with the Jewish achievements in reclaiming the land and restoring the country, Schipper conferred about his prospects for a *cathedra* in Yiddish at the Hebrew University in Jerusalem.[22] For some reason, his plans were not realized in the years immediately preceding World War II, and then it was too late.

It is very possible that Schipper was prevented from settling in Palestine by the onset of symptoms of a serious heart ailment in the last years before the war. By 1939, he was in fact so exhausted and ill that people could hardly recognize him. He looked incurable and many thought that he was fast approaching the end of his life. But when the war broke out, and following the prolonged and merciless bombardment of Warsaw (witnessed by the writer of this book) when Jews in the city began experiencing the ruthlessness of the Nazi rule, Schipper, to everybody's amazement, began to regain his strength.[23] As if to verify the truthfulness of the Yiddish folksaying that "*tsores shtarkn*" (sufferings strengthen), he became active again. It is reasonable to assume that the psychological awareness of the calamity facing his people put him back on his feet. His sole objective became to help, to succor, and to comfort. He did so within the framework of the exigently organized Jewish Relief Service, serving as a member of its board of directors and attending especially to the needs of the Jewish intellectuals, who were the first to lose all sources of income, and to the needs of the young men who were driven off to forced labor camps outside the city.[24] He was also very active in the special watchdog committee appointed to scrutinize the activities of the Warsaw *Judenrat* (Jewish Council).

In the closed-off ghetto of Warsaw, Schipper participated in various public and secret meetings. He regularly attended the so-called *Oneg Shabbat* (Sabbath evening) gatherings. His speeches at some of the cultural public events organized in the ghetto became a source of comfort and solace to the abased, mortified, and despairing inhabitants.[25] He became generally known as a chronically undaunted optimist, turning every piece of information about the war into glad tidings for the immured community eager to detect a ray of hope. Even the obviously bad reports were interpreted by Schipper as signs of Hitler's inevitable defeat, and the clearly incredible rumors that spread from time to time in the ghetto he accepted as possible truths.[26]

People who had known him as man who had always dealt with the realistic aspects of Jewish history and with the down-to-earth sociopolitical actualities of Jewish life were amazed at his credulity and total lack of realism. Some, especially the so-called "realists," were annoyed and angry with him. They believed that Schipper was using his prestige to mislead and delude the people at a time when it was necessary for them to know the grim truth.[27] But Schipper persisted in his optimism, guided by a deep conviction that Nazism would be defeated. He was equally confident about the Jewish *élan vital.* He had no doubt that the Jewish people would survive and continue to exist and that a remnant of Polish Jewry would not only see the day of victory but also witness the establishment of a Jewish state in Palestine which would attract the best elements of Jewry from all over the world.[28]

True to these beliefs and to his lifelong dedication and commitment to the people, Schipper could not help but be the messenger of good tidings, however unrealistic. This was his way of helping the despairing ghetto inhabitants to withstand, to persevere, and possibly to survive.

Even when the SS men began deportation actions in the summer of 1942, Hillel Seidman writes, Schipper seemed to ignore completely the daily grim realities.[29] He busied himself with the study of the old documents, seriously preparing a book on the history of the Warsaw rabbinate. Or else, he was speaking about the inevitable bright future, even about his professorship at the Hebrew University in Jerusalem.[30] Obviously, to be able to withstand the grimness of the situation, he let the past and future overshadow the present and with this kind of sublimation he remained as optimistic as ever, encouraging others also to hope and to have faith.

Confronted, as he often was, with the question of mounting terror and torment, the ever-increasing number of Jewish deaths and victims, Schipper replied: "We are combatants in this war and we must, therefore, suffer losses," implying that in the wider context of the struggle against evil, the Jews were involved in the war as much as soldiers in the battlefields. However, when the underground Jewish National Committee began planning active Jewish resistance, Schipper, who participated in the meetings and deliberations,[31] opposed moves that would further endanger Jewish lives. Citing historical instances of active as well as passive resistance, he insisted that active fighting was doomed to defeat and would only result in additional countless deaths of Jews who might otherwise survive. Committed, as always, to the preservation of Jewish lives and the perpetuation of Jewish existence, he wanted the surviving remnant to include as many as possible. Hence, as far as he was concerned, no one had a moral right to endanger the lives of those still remaining in Warsaw and in other parts of Poland.[32]

A Martyr's Fate and Faith

When the planned uprising did erupt and the heroic fighting of the Jewish defenders spread throughout the ghetto, the Germans seized Schipper in his hiding place and sent him to the Maidanek concentration camp. There, separated from his family, cruelly beaten by an SS man, suffering from hunger and from terribly diseased, swollen feet which could no longer support him,[33] he was able to keep alive for some time through the aid and protection of his fellow inmates. Although it was by no means easy, they placed him in the kitchen peeling potatoes, a "soft" job reserved only for the privileged.[34] They also saw to it that he was carried to the morning roll calls and, when the danger of selecting the weak and the sick for elimination was imminent, they found ways to conceal him.[35]

According to Alexander Donat, a co-worker in the camp kitchen who knew him personally for many years, Schipper was so emaciated and weak that he often lost consciousness during the morning roll calls and even the potato peeling was too much for his debilitated body.[36] But, like the historical Jewish martyr, Schipper maintained his faith. Bent upon knowing what was going on in the outside world, he somehow managed to obtain information about current developments, even to get a Polish newspaper from Lublin every day,[37] and he continued to remain unshaken in his beliefs. In this respect, his conversations with Donat in the last days of his life are most interesting and revealing. He is quoted by Donat as having said:

> The money the Ż.O.B. had collected in the Ghetto should have been used to organize the escape of the most socially valuable elements to the Aryan side rather than spent for arms. . . . The destruction of Polish Jewry did not mean the destruction of the Jewish people; it was merely an episode from the historian's point of view, terrible to be sure, but comparable to other disasters in Jewish history. . . . The last word has not yet been said about the

> historical antithesis between the warrior and the martyr. The defenseless martyr attains heights of dignity which will forever remain beyond the scope of the warrior, however brave. And what should the historical testament of Polish Jewry be, the clanking of arms, like everyone else, or the power of the spirit? The testament of the heroic warrior or of the saintly martyr?[38]

But his view concerning the historical "truth" about Jewish martyrdom is even more characteristically Schipperian:

> "There is no such thing as historical truth," he [*i.e.*, Schipper] would say with his sad smile when we dreamed about how after the war the survivors of the camps would tell the world *the whole truth*. "There is just interpretation. It depends on who writes the history of our time. Should *they* write the story of this war, our destruction will be presented as one of the most glorious exploits in world history. But if *we* write the story we will have the thankless task of proving to a disbelieving world that we really are Abel, the murdered brother."[39]

Although mentally and spiritually alert, Schipper's physical constitution was too weak to withstand for long the rigors and the terror of Maidanek. Sick and exhausted, he succumbed in the beginning of July, 1943.[40]

It is characteristic that until the day of his death Schipper was carried to the morning roll calls by a young, illiterate *balegole* (coachman) who intuitively felt that the "learned doctor" was his kind of man, a man interested in and understanding of the poor, uneducated Jews like himself.[41]

We know today to what extent subsequent history has vindicated Schipper's staunch beliefs in the ultimate outcome of the war, the survival of a remnant of Polish Jewry, the continuation of the Jewish people and Jewish existence, the establishment of a Jewish state, and the historical "truth" about the tragic events.

In his martyr's death, as throughout his dynamic and creative life, Schipper reflected the milieu, sentiments, and aspirations of the Jewish community in Poland between the two World Wars. He was an illustrious and illustrative son of that community which came to an abrupt and tragic end after a long existence of almost ten centuries, an existence to which Schipper devoted a lifetime of research and study as if he knew that his testimony would constitute a unique monument for the burned homes, tortured people, and obliterated graves.

Notes

1. See the Foreword to the *Virtshaftsgeshikhte*, p. ii, where he writes: "My notes during that time were in the tens of thousands and the plan for a general Jewish economic history became so ripe that I began, a little later, to work on the development of Yiddish from the early Middle Ages until the eighteenth century. . . ."

2. Nonetheless, in 1917 and 1918, Schipper wrote a number of historical essays and polemical articles for *Moriah* which was transferred at the time from Lwów to Vienna: "Germanie a Żydzi," "Żydzi Polsko-Litewscy a Palestyna," "Autonomia Żydów w Polsce w średniowieczu," "Synagoga, Kościół i zbory różnowiercze." In 1918 the *Almanach Żydowski* published Schipper's monograph on the Jewish origins in Polish and Ruthenian lands ("Początki Żydów na ziemiach ruskich i polskich," *op. cit.*) which, together with the preceding two items, were later included in his *Kultur-geshikhte*. Still another monograph concerning Galician Jewry appeared in the *Neue jüdische Monatshefte* (Berlin: 1918), Nos. 9-10, entitled "Die galizische Judenschaft 1772-1848 in wirtschafts-statistischer Beleuchtung." Schipper's friend, Chomet, who was also stationed in Cracow, notes that during the years of the war Schipper even wrote a book on the history of Jewish poverty that was never published because the manuscript was stolen. See Chomet, "Yidishe visnshaftler, literatn un publitsistn fun Torne," *Torne, op. cit.*, p. 334.

3. *Virtshaftsgeshikhte, op. cit.*, Foreword, pp. ii-iii.

4. See Chomet, "Di tsiyonistishe bavegung in Torne," *op. cit.*, pp. 382-385.

5. *Ibid.*, pp. 386-388; also, Hirschhaut, *op. cit.*, pp. 204-205.

6. Kenner, *op. cit.*, p. 168.

7. Chomet, "Di tsiyonistishe bavegung in Torne," *op. cit.*, p. 476.

8. See *supra*, Chap. II, p. 74 n. 3.

9. Cf. Sokol, *op. cit.*, p. 11; Cyneman, *op. cit.*, pp. 1603-1604.

10. The General Zionists, the centrists in the ideological spectrum of Zionist groups, originated in Poland at the beginning of the twentieth century when socialist and religious parties emerged in the World Zionist Organization, and

Zionists who could not identify with either the socialists or the religious elements saw a need for a general group.

11. See Seidman, "Ḥayav shel Dr. I. Shiper Zal," *op. cit.*, pp. 57-60; Hirschhaut, *op. cit.*, pp. 206-207, 209.

12. The aforementioned *Kultur-geshikhte* and the three-volume *History of the Jewish Theatrical Art and Drama*, and such important monographs on the history of Yiddish as "Der onhoyb fun loshn Ashkenaz in der balaykhtung fun onomatishe kveln," *Yidishe Filologye*, I (Wilno: 1924), pp. 101-112, 272-287; "Maynungen un proyektn fun Polyakn vegn der shprakh-frage bay Yidn in meshekh fun 16-tn biz der helft fun 18-tn yorhundert," *Bikher-Velt*, No. 2 (May, 1928), pp. 22-26; and others.

13. *Virtshaftsgeshikhte, op. cit.*, p. iv.

14. See Sokol, *op. cit.*, p. 10.

15. *Loc. cit.* See also Sh. Z. Shazar, "I. Shiper," in *I. Shiper*, ed. by Eidelberg, *op. cit.*, p. 20.

16. See Mahler, "I. Shiper (1884-1943)," *op. cit.*, p. 23, or *idem.*, "I. Shiper u-Meḥkarav ha-Historiyim," *op. cit.*, p. 36. Mahler recalls that at a festive event held in honor of Schipper's fiftieth birthday at the YIVO branch of Warsaw, the chairman, Joseph Yashunski, said: "It would be completely fictitious to say that Schipper has reached the age of fifty. Schipper's appearance has only one identification, the identification of youth!" *Ibid.*, p. 36, n. 3.

17. *Loc. cit.* See also Shatzky, "Shney Historyonim Kedoshim," *op. cit.*, p. 419.

18. The Yiddish Scientific Institute known today as the Institute of Jewish Research.

19. The recognition and respect which Schipper enjoyed in YIVO is reflected in the fact that he was a member of its central administrative board as well as a member of its Presidium. The celebration of his fiftieth birthday was sponsored by YIVO in Wilno as well as in Warsaw in a most laudative and memorable manner. See Hirschhaut, *op. cit.*, pp. 238-239.

20. *Ibid.*, p. 240.

21. However, in the thirties Schipper devoted most of his time and energy to further investigations and studies in the history of Polish Jewry, going beyond the Middle Ages and up to his own times. In 1932, in connection with the centennial anniversary of the Polish November Uprising, Schipper published a volume in Polish entitled *The Jews of the Polish Realm in the Days of the November Uprising*, after a number of his articles and essays pertaining to this subject appeared in various Yiddish and Polish periodicals. He utilized this opportunity to prove the absurdity of those growing elements in the Polish society which, attuned to Hitler's propaganda coming ever louder from neighboring Germany, questioned the loyalty of the Jews in Poland. In 1932-1935, Schipper contrib-

uted nineteen essential and comprehensive monographs to the encyclopedic two volumes of *Żydzi w Polsce Odrodzonej* of which he was co-editor. Many of these monographs deal with the general history of the Jews and with their role in various economic fields of endeavor in post-medieval and modern Poland. In 1937 Schipper's voluminous and impressive *History of Jewish Commerce in Polish Territories* appeared. In between these major publications, there were numerous articles and essays of a popular as well as scientific nature. Most important in the latter category were his studies of the social and financial aspects of the Jewish autonomous bodies in the later stages of their existence. (See the Bibliography for specific items.) Judging from a note in his *Dzieje handlu żydowskiego* (p. 191, n. 71), he actually prepared a book on Jewish autonomy in Poland which, however, was never published. Another manuscript which remained unpublished, a monograph on the history of Jews in Drohobycz, was written by Schipper in 1936. Hirschhaut saw and read it in 1943 in the ghetto of Drohobycz. See Hirschhaut, *op. cit.*, pp. 248-249. Both of these manuscripts seem to have been lost during the Holocaust years.

22. *Ibid.*, p. 240. See also Shazar, *op. cit.*, p. 20. In spite of his extensive achievements as a historian and writter, Schipper was never given the opportunity to teach at a Polish university, mainly because of the anti-Semitic tendencies that prevailed in the government as well as in the administrations of the academic institutions. Schipper often sarcastically referred to the Polish professors, whose erudition and accomplishments could hardly compare with his, as "guild scholars" or "*Zunftgelehrte*." See Mahler, "I. Shiper (1884-1943)," *op. cit.*, p. 24.

23. See Seidman, "Ḥayyav shel Dr. I. Shiper Zal," *op. cit.*, p. 63; Hirschhaut, *op. cit.*, pp. 250-251.

24. The Jewish Relief Service, known by its Polish name as *Zydowska Samopomoc Społeczna*, operated with funds of the American Joint Distribution Committee. It became a rallying point for Jewish leaders of the various political parties which existed in the Jewish community before the war. See Seidman, *Togbukh fun varshever geto* (Buenos Aires: 1947), p. 138; Hirschhaut, *op. cit.*, pp. 251-252; J. Tenenbaum, *Underground* (New York: 1952), p. 77.

25. Seidman, *Yoman Geto Varsha* (Tel Aviv: 1946), pp. 303-304. Referring to the Purim celebration organized by the Zionists in the ghetto in 1941 under the most trying conditions, Chaim A. Kaplan noted in his diary—translated by Professor Abraham Katsh—that the "credit for this heroic achievement goes to Dr. I. Schiper. . . ." See *Scroll of Agony: The Warsaw Diary of Chaim A. Kaplan*, trans. and ed. by Abraham I. Katsh (New York: 1965), p. 256, also p. 236.

26. Seidman, *op. cit.*, p. 299; *idem., Togbukh fun varshever geto, op. cit.*, pp. 82-83.

27. See Hirschhaut, *op. cit.*, p. 253.

28. See Seidman, *Yoman Gheto Varsha, op. cit.*, pp. 301-302.

29. Hillel Seidman was at the time in charge of the kehilla archives where Schipper, Bałaban, and other important scholars, writers, and rabbis were placed in "special" jobs to protect them against the deportation selections.

30. Seidman, *Yoman Geto Varsha, op. cit.*, pp. 300, 302; *idem., Togbukh fun varshever geto, op. cit.*, pp. 68-69, 102, 108-109. Ringelblum stated in his *Last Notes* that Schipper actually wrote a history of Hasidism in the nineteenth century based on materials of the kehilla archives. See Ringelblum, "Der boyer fun der moderner yidisher historiografye," *op. cit.*, p. 9.

31. M. Neustadt, *Ḥurbn un oyfshtand fun di Yidn in Varshe* (Tel Aviv: 1948), p. 138; Hirschhaut, *op. cit.*, p. 255.

32. Cf. Friedman (ed.), *Martyrs and Fighters* (New York: 1954), p. 194 and L. S. Davidowicz, *The War Against the Jews 1933-1945* (New York: 1976), pp. 408-409.

33. See N. Blumenthal (ed.), *Dokumenty i materiały*, vol. I (Łódź: 1946), pp. 168-169.

34. See M. Schtrigler, *Maidanek* (Buenos Aires: 1947), pp. 146-147.

35. Blumenthal, *op. cit.*, pp. 169-170.

36. A. Donat, *The Holocaust Kingdom: A Memoir* (New York: 1965), p. 210.

37. *Loc. cit.*; also, M. Schtrigler, "Im Dr. I. Shiper be-Maydanek" in *I. Shiper*, edited by Eidelberg, *op. cit.*, pp. 66-67.

38. Donat, *op. cit.*, pp. 210-211. The Ż.O.B. mentioned in the quote relates to the *Żydowska Organizacja Bojowa* (Jewish Fighting Organization), one of the two militant organizations, headed by Mordecai Anilewicz, which prepared for and led in the Warsaw Ghetto Uprising. Organized in October of 1942, it was composed of anti-Fascist Zionist groups.

39. Donat, "Armageddon," reprint from *Dissent* (Spring, 1963), p. 3.

40. See Blumenthal, *op. cit.*, p. 170; see also Friedman, "Polish Jewish Historiography between the Two Wars," *op. cit.*, p. 404.

41. See Schtrigler, "Im Dr. I. Shiper be-Maydanek," *op. cit.*, pp. 65-68.

Bibliography

I.

The bibliography of Yitzhak Schipper's writings compiled by J. Hirschaut includes 144 items without counting three manuscripts no longer extant. It has been of great help to the present writer who has been able to locate another thirteen items, bringing the total to 157. They are in Yiddish, Polish, German, Russian, and Hebrew and are listed below in chronological order. Works discussed or mentioned in the present study are indicated by an asterisk at the left of each title.

*"Ustawodawstwo Kazimierza Wielkiego w stosunku do Żydów," *Moriah*, I. Lwów: 1902-1903.

*"Żydzi w Polsce za Piastów," *Moriah*, III. Lwów: 1904-1905.

*"Współczesny dramat żydowski," *Moriah*, III. Lwów: 1904-1905.

*"Żydzi za czasów Kazimierza Wielkiego," *Moriah*, IV. Lwów: 1905-1906; pp. 46-50, 74-79, 104-107.

*"Żydzi w Tarnowie do końca XVIII wieku," *Kwartalnik Historyczny*, XIX. 1905; pp. 228-237.

*"Geneza lichwy żydowskiej w średniowieczu," *Moriah*, V. Lwów: 1906; pp. 178-182, 226-230.

*"Anfänge des Kapitalismus bei den abendländischen Juden im früheren Mittelalter," *Zeitschrift für Volkswirtschaft, Sozialpolitik*

und Verwaltung. Vol. XV. Vienna: 1906. Also, Verlag W. Braumiller, 1907. 66 pp.

*"Przyczynek do dziejów żydowskich własności ziemskich w średniowieczu," *Moriah*, VII. Lwów: 1908-1909; pp. 42-46, 70-75.

*"Vegn dem yidish renesans," *Literarishe Monatshrift*. Wilno: March, 1908; pp. 105-112.

*"Tsum artikl fun H. F. Klayn, 'Di yidishe shprakhlere'," *Kunst un Lebn*. Ed. by A. Reisen. June, 1908; pp. 61-67.

*"Przegląd krytyczny literatury odnoszącej się do historji Żydów w Polsce średniowiecznej," *Wschód*, IX. Lwów: 1909; No. 5-6, 11-13.

*"Agrar-Kolinisation der Juden in Polen," *Jüdische Fragen*. Vienna: 1909; pp. 64-78.

*"Początki ekonomiki żydowskiej w Polsce. Najwcześniejszy handel żydowski w Polsce (VIII-XII w.)," *Almanach Dra Leona Reicha*. Lwów: 1910; pp. 165-173.

*"Yevreyskiy kredit v Polshe v XIV vyeke," *Yevreyskaya Starina*, III. 1910; pp. 542-568.

*"Ranniye stadyi yevreyskoy kolonizatsyi v Polshe," *Yevreyskaya Starina*, IV. 1911; pp. 161-179, 348-371.

* *Studya nad stosunkami gospodarczymi Żydów w Polsce podczas średniowiecza*. Published by the Wawelberg Fund. Lwów: 1911; 379 pp.

* *Der Anteil der Juden am europäischen Grosshandel mit dem Orient*. Czernovitz: 1912. Reprint from Sammelwerk Heimkehr, Berlin: 1910.

"Żydzi neofici i prozelici w Polsce do roku 1569," *Kwartalnik poświęcony badaniom historii Żydów w Polsce* No. 2. Warsaw: 1912.

"W walce z pamfleciarstwem polskim," *Moriah*, XII, Nos. 6-7. Lwów: 1912-1913.

* Sporniye voprosi epokhi Vladislava Yagello," *Yevreyskaya Starina*, VI. 1913; pp. 102-107.

*"Beiträge zur Geschichte der partiellen Judentage in Polen um die Wende des XVII und XVIII Jahrhunderts bis zur Auflösung des jüdischen Parlamentarismus (1764)," *Monatschrift für die Geschichte und Wissenschaft des Judentums*, LVI. 1913, pp. 458-477, 602-611, 736-744.

"Di poylish-litvishe Yidn in Palestine, 1531-1821," *Togblat*. Lwów: Apr. 21, 25, 27 and May 1, 2, 1913.

*"A naye tkufe in undzer kamf far yidish," *Der Yidischer Arbeter*, Jubilee Issue 49-50. Lwów: 1913; pp. 17-24.

*"Humanizm a sprawa żydowska w XV wieku," *Moriah*, XI. Lwów: 1914; pp. 231-237.

*"Razsyeleniye Yevreyev v Polshe i Litvye ot XV do XVIII vyeka," *Istoriya yevreyskogo naroda*, Vol. XI. Moscow: 1914; pp. 105-131.

*"Ekonomicheskiy bit Yevreyev v Polshe: Torgoviye promisli otkupa i arenda," *Istoriya yevreykogo naroda*, Vol. XI. Moscow: 1914; pp. 243-285. Written together with M. Wischnitzer.

*"Podatnoye oblozheniye Yevreyev," *Istoriya yevreyskogo naroda*, Vol. XI. Moscow: 1914; pp. 300-319.

*"Żydzi Polsko-Litewscy a Palestyna: Przyczynek historyczny do romantycznej epoki syjonizmu," *Moriah*, XII. Vienna: 1916-1917; pp. 20-28, 60-68, 157-165, 190-199.

"Matthias Mieses, *Die Entstehungsursache der jüdischen Dialekte*," (review), *Moriah*, XII.Vienna: 1916-1917; pp. 124-125.

"Jizchok Leib Perez: *Die goldene kette*," (review), *Moriah*, XII. Vienna: 1916-1917; p. 214.

*"M. Schorr, *Die Hauptprivilegien der polnischen Judenschaft*," (review), *Moriah*, XII. Vienna: 1916-1917; pp. 432-433.

"Dr. J. Zoller, *Die Seeversicherungen und die Juden in Triest*," (review), *Moriah*, XII. Vienna: 1916-1917; pp. 433-434.

*"Dr. Majer Bałaban, *Dzieje Żydów w Galicji i w Rzeczypospolitej krakowskiej, 1772-1868*," (review), *Moriah*, XII. Vienna: 1916-1917; pp. 434-435.

*"Germanie a Żydzi," *Moriah*, XIII. Vienna: 1916-1917; pp. 486-489.

*"Graetz: W setną rocznicę urodzin historyka żydowskiego," *Moriah*, XIII. Vienna: 1917-1918; pp. 52-56.

"Germanie a Żydzi: Uwag kilka w odpowiedzi," *Moriah*, XIII. Vienna: 1917-1918; pp. 70-72.

"Zejde (Shalom Jakób Abramowicz)," *Moriah*, XIII. Vienna: 1917-1918; pp. 127-129.

*"Synagoga, Kościół i zbory różnowiercze," *Moriah*, XIII. Vienna: 1917-1918; pp. 266-280, 402-416.

"Początki Żydów na ziemiach ruskich i polskich (od najdawniejszych czasów do r. 1350)," *Almanach Żydowski.* Vienna: 1918; pp. 236-265. Yiddish translation: *Bleter far Geshikhte*, XIII. 1960, pp. 25-59.

*"Die galizische Judenschaft 1772-1848 in wirtschaftsstatistischer Beleuchtung," *Neue jüdische Monatshefte*. Berlin: 1918; Nos. 9-10, pp. 223-233.

*"Zygmunt Mayer i jego dzieło: Uwagi na marginesie książki *Die Wiener Juden, 1700-1900*," *Moriah*, XIV. Vienna: 1918-1919; Nos. 5-6, pp. 196-205.

*"Autonomia Żydów w Polsce w średniowieczu," *Moriah*, XIV. Vienna: 1918-1919.

"Sprawa żydowska w przededniu reformacji na Zachodzie i w Polsce," *Moriah*, XIV. Jan. 1919, No. 1.

"Vegn Dr. Maks Rozenfeld," *Di Arbeter Tsaytung*, No. 23. Warsaw: 1919.

* *Onhoyb fun kapitalizm bay di Yidn in Mayrev-Eyrope*. Transl. from German by Hillel Maimon. Warsaw: Arbeter Heym Publ., 1920. 88 pp.

"Marcin Luter a Żydzi Polscy," *Chwila*. Lwów: 1921; Nos. 743-745.

"Polski projekt utworzenia państwa żydowskiego przed 80 laty," *Nowy Kurier*. Warsaw: May 24, June 4 and 7, 1921.

*"Tsukunft-fragn funem yidishn teater," *Yidish Teater.* Warsaw: 1921; No. 1, pp. 23-32.

"Molier," *Yidish Teater.* Warsaw: 1922; Nos. 2-3, pp. 3-11.

"Premyeres in Tsentral," *Yidish Teater.* Warsaw: 1922; Nos. 4-5, pp. 52-57.

"Retsenzye vegn M. Gideman: *Yidishe kultur-geshikhte in mitlalter,*" *Bikher-Velt.* Warsaw: 1922; No. 1, cols. 44-46.

"Problemen fun yidisher kultur bay Oswald Spengler," *Bikher-Velt*, II. Warsaw: 1923; p. 306, col. 306.

"Vegn Y. M. Nayman: *Shabes-oybst*," *Bikher-Velt*, II. Warsaw: 1923; col. 363.

"Vegn Sholem Ash un vegn *Kidush hashem*," *Bikher-Velt*, II. Warsaw: 1923; cols. 447-454.

*"Der onhoyb fun loshn Ashknaz in der balaykhtung fun onomatishe

kveln," *Yidishe Filologye*, I. YIVO, Wilno: 1924; pp. 101-112, 272-287.

*"Socjologiczne podłoże religii żydowskiej: Sprawozdanie krytyczne z dzieła Maksa Webera," *Nowe Życie*, I. Warsaw: 1924; pp. 39-47. English transl. by Glikson in *The Jewish Journal of Sociology*, I. Dec. 1959; pp. 250-260.

"Shtimen vegn dem universitet in Yerushalayim," *Literarishe Bleter*. Warsaw: 1925; No. 53, p. 6.

"Der oyftu fun A. Goldfaden," *Literarishe Bleter*. Warsaw: 1925; No. 74, p. 133.

*"Oyfn rand fun Maks Eriks bukh vegn alt-yidishn roman un novele," *Literarishe Bleter*. Warsaw: 1926; pp. 413-415, 430-431, 450-452, 479-481, 516-517.

* *Di virtshafts-geshikhte fun di Yidn in Poyln beysn mitlalter*. Transl. from Polish by Dr. Emanuel Ringelblum and Daniel Leibel. Warsaw: 1926. 324 pp.

"Di firshtin Radziwil un di Yidn fun altn Poyln," *Der Moment*. Warsaw: 1926; No. 277.

"Vegn Maks Brods roman Dovid Reuveni," *Tsiyonistishe Bleter*. Warsaw: 1926; No. 1.

"Vegn Lion Foykhtwangers historishn roman *Yude Zis*," *Tsiyonistishe Bleter*. Warsaw: 1926; No. 3.

* *Kultur-geshikhte fun Yidn in Poyln beysn mitlalter*. Warsaw: 1926. 312 pp.

"Dr. Meyer Balaban, tsu zayn 50-yorikn yoyvl," *Haynt*. Warsaw: 1927; No. 82.

"Di broder zinger," (a series of articles), *Der Morgn*. Lwów: from March 12 to April 30, 1927.

"An umbakanter kemfer far yidish mit 50 yor tsurik," *Literarishe Bleter*. Warsaw: 1927; No. 13, pp. 242-243.

"Dr. Moyshe Markozo, a kemfer far yidishn folksgezunt in XVIII yorhundert," *Toz-Zhurnal*. Warsaw: May 13, 1927.

"Di frage fun sheḥite-gelter in likht fun yidish-poylisher geshikhte," *Der Moment*. Warsaw: 1927; No. 12.

"Yidishe legionen in kamf far Erets Yisroel," *Der Moment*. Warsaw: 1927; Nos. 48, 54.

"Yisroel Kempinski, der yidish-poylisher kemfer in Napoleons armey," *Der Moment.* Warsaw: 1927; No. 156.

"Di nitsḥoynes iber di otseanen in sof fun mitlalter un der poylisher Yid Meyer Ashkenazi," *Der Moment.* Warsaw: 1927; No. 222.

"An umbakanter poylisher barikht vegn yidishe 'kantonistn' un zeyer rol beys dem poylishn oyfshtand fun di yorn 1830-1831," *Der Moment.* Warsaw: 1927; No. 231.

*"Grets un zayn monumental verk," in Grets *Yidishe geshikhte,* 7 vols. Warsaw: 1927; pp. xxxiv-xliii.

* *Geshikhte fun der yidisher teater-kunst un drame.* Warsaw: vols. I-II, 1927; vol. III, 1928.

"Der nomen 'Galitsyen' shtamt fun hebreishn vort 'ḥalutsim'," *Der Morgn.* Lwów: Jan. 13, 1928.

"Meshumodim in Khmelnitskis tsaytn," *Yidisher Togblat.* New York: Jan. 20, 1928.

"Di nayeste matoneh funem Yidish visenshaftlekhn institut," *Literarishe Bleter.* Warsaw: March, 1928; pp. 186-187.

"Di eltste shpurn fun der yidisher shprakh un literatur," *Di Yidishe Velt,* I. Warsaw: April, 1928; pp. 121-130.

*"Maynungen un proyektn fun Polyakn vegn der shprakh-frage bay Yidn in meshekh fun 16-tn biz der helft funem 18-tn yorhundert," *Bikher-Velt.* Warsaw: May, 1928; No. 2, pp. 22-26.

*"Kultur-geshikhtlekher fon fun der eltster yidisher literatur," *Di Yidishe Velt,* II. Warsaw: 1928; pp. 232-247.

*"Vegn Eriks geshikhte fun der yidisher literatur," *Literarishe Bleter.* Warsaw: 1928; pp. 213-214, 236-237, 328-330, 363-364, 421-423.

"Yidishe tanakh iberzetsungen," *Literarishe Bleter.* Warsaw: 1928; pp. 891-892.

"Di eltste yidishe druker-mishpoḥe un dos eltste yidish-daytshe bukh in Poyln," *Bikher-Velt.* Warsaw: 1928; No. 3, pp. 24-28; No. 4, pp. 16-23.

"Bilder fun der yidisher literatur-geshikhte—Dr. M. Vaynraykh," *Bikher-Velt.* Warsaw: 1928; No. 5, pp. 42-48.

"Żydowska pieśń ludowa w Powstaniu 1863 r.," *Nasz Przegląd.* Warsaw: Feb. 19, 1928.

"'Judaica' w Zakładzie Narodowym im. Ossolinskich we Lwowie," *Nasz Przegląd*. Warsaw: June 3, 1928.

"Yidn mit berd un Yidn on berd," *Der Moment*. Warsaw: 1928; No. 27.

"Napoleon un di poylishe Yidn," *Der Moment*. Warsaw: 1928; Nos. 86, 98.

"Di zikhnbirger geyrim," *Der Moment*. Warsaw: 1928; Nos. 109, 115.

"Der ershter kidush hashem in Poyln, 1529-1534," *Der Moment*. Warsaw: 1928; No. 126.

"Legendes vegn der aynvanderung fun di Yidn keyn Poyln un zeyer geshikhtlekhe opshtamung," *Der Moment*. Warsaw: 1928; No. 138.

"Di poylishe Ester hamalke," *Der Moment*. Warsaw: 1928; Nos. 198, 210.

"Di Yidishe legendes vegn Martin Luter," *Der Moment*. Warsaw: 1928; No. 248.

"Poylishe Yidn oyfn lebnsveg fun Moyshe Mendelson," *Der Moment*. Warsaw: 1929; No. 221.

*"Der tsuzamenshtel funem 'vaad arba arotses'," *Historishe Shriftn of YIVO*, I. Wilno: 1929; pp. 73-82.

*"Poylishe regestn tsu der geshikhte funem 'vaad arba arotses'," *Historishe Shriftn of YIVO*, I. Wilno: 1929; pp. 83-114.

"Tsu der eltster geshikhte fun yidishe doktoyrim in Poyln," *Toz-Yedies*. Warsaw: 1929; Nos. 1-2, 5, 6, 8-9, 10-11, 12.

"Tsu der elster geshikhte fun yidishe doktoyrim, 17-ter yorhundert," *Toz-Yedies*. Warsaw: 1930; Nos. 3-4, 5-6.

"Umbakante zikhroynes fun a poylishn Yid funem 18-tn yorhundert," *Poylisher Mantshester*. Feb. 1930; pp. 35-36.

"Profesor Haynrikh Grets," *Haynt*. Warsaw: 1930, No. 91.

"Ber Mayzels," *Der Moment*. Warsaw: 1930; No. 91.

"Yidishe geshtaltn fun der tsayt fun poylishn oyfshtand, 1830-1831," *Der Moment*. Warsaw: 1930; Nos. 247, 253, 254, 271, 277.

"Di stikhye: Sholem Ash," *Literarishe Bleter*. Warsaw: 1930; No. 51, p. 966.

* *Yidishe geshikhte (Virtshaftsgeshikhte)*. 4 vols. Warsaw: 1930.

"Żydzi w Powstaniu Listopadowym," *Nasz Przegląd.* Warsaw: Nov. 30, 1930.

*"Motywy żydowskie w powieściach Liona Feuchtwangera," *Miesięcznik Żydowski*, I. Warsaw: 1930-1931; pp. 416-430.

"Judaica na Wystawie Listopadowej w Muzeum Narodowym w Warszawie," *Miesięcznik Żydowski*, I. Warsaw: 1930-1931; pp. 470-472.

*"Samorząd żydowski w Polsce na przełomie wieku XVIII i XIX (1764-1831)," *Miesięcznik Żydowski*, I. Warsaw: 1930-1931.

"Początki haskali na ziemiach Centralnej Polski," *Miesięcznik Żydowski*, II. Warsaw: 1931; pp. 311-327.

"Udział Żydów w Powstaniu Listopadowym," *Sprawy Narodowe.* Warsaw: 1930; pp. 695-699.

"Żydzi Warszawy w czasie wypadków, 1831," *Trybuna Akademicka.* Warsaw: 1930; Nos. 11, 12.

*"Portretn fun dray barimte yidishe doktoyrim fun der tsayt funem poylishn november oyfshtand, 1830-1831," *Sotsyale Meditsin.* Warsaw: 1931; Nos. 1-2, 3-4.

"Der ershter yidisher 'mons pietatis' (Lombard) in Varshe," *Di Kooperative Bavegung.* (Warsaw: 1931.

"Komisja Warszawska: Przyczynek do dziejów autonomii Żydów w Polsce," *Księga jubileuszowa ku czci Dra Markusa Braudego.* Published by Institute of Judaic Studies; III-IV. Warsaw: 1931; pp. 147-157.

"Dr. Shloyme Etingers varshever kroyvim un fraynd," *YIVO Bleter*, III. Wilno: 1932; pp. 371-384.

"Finantsyeler ḥurbn fun der tsentraler un provintsyeler otonomye fun Yidn in Poyln, 1650-1764," *Ekonomishe Shriftn fun YIVO*, II. Wilno: 1932; pp. 1-19.

*"Jiddisch," *Encyclopedia Judaica*, vol. IX. Berlin: 1932; pp. 112-127. Written together with Dr. S. Birnbaum.

*"Jiddische Literatur," *Encyclopedia Judaica*, vol. IX. Berlin: 1932; pp; 127-180. Written together with Nachman Meisel.

"Bergsohnowie," *Nowe Słowo.* Warsaw: 1932.

* *Żydzi Królestwa Polskiego w dobie Powstania Listopadowego.* Warsaw: 1932.

Loshn Ashkenaz berekh 14-tn un 15-tn yorhundert," *Archiv far yidisher shprakhvisnshaft, literatur-forshung un etnologye*. Warsaw: 1926-1933.

"Y. Opatoshus naye historishe dertseylungen—a tog in Regensburg: Eliyohu Bohur," *Literarishe Bleter*. Warsaw: 1933; pp. 370-371, 389-391, 402-403.

"Araynfir-verter in der yidisher folks-kentenish," *Landkentnish*. Warsaw: 1933; No. 1.

"Alt-yidisher folklor in shpan fun 'Toz' arbet," *Sotsyale Meditsin*. Warsaw: 1933; No. 708.

"Di mishpohe Teplits," *Haynt*. Warsaw: 1934.

*"Problemen fun der alt-yidisher literatur-geshikhte," *YIVO Bleter*, VII. Wilno: 1934; pp. 36-46.

* *Żydzi w Polsce Odrodzonej: Działalność społeczna, gospodarcza, oświatowa i kulturalna*. Eds. Dr. Ignacy Schipper, Dr. A. Tartakover, and Alexander Haftka; 2 vols. Warsaw: 1932-1935.

*"Rozwój ludności żydowskiej na ziemiach dawnej Rzeczypospolitej," *Żydzi w Polsce Odrodzonej*, I. Warsaw: 1932-1935; pp. 21-36.

*"Wewnętrzna organizacja Żydów w dawnej Rzeczypospolitej," *Żydzi w Polsce Odrodzonej*, I. Warsaw: 1932-1935; pp. 81-110.

*"Dzieje gospodarcze Żydów Korony i Litwy w czasach przedrozbiorowych," *Żydzi w Polsce Odrodzonej*, I. Warsaw: 1932-1935; pp. 111-190.

*"Świadczenia Żydów na rzecz państwa i patronów," *Żydzi w Polsce Odrodzonej*, I. Warsaw: 1932-1935; pp. 200-210.

"Język potoczny Żydów polskich i ich ludowa literatura w dawnej Rzeczypospolitej," *Żydzi w Polsce Odrodzonej*, I. Warsaw: 1932-1935; pp. 225-235.

"Apologeci i polemiści żydowscy w dawnej Rzeczypospolitej," *Żydzi w Polsce Odrodzonej*, I. Warsaw: 1932-1935; pp. 236-244.

"Nauki świeckie wśród Żydów w dawnej Rzeczypospolitej," *Żydzi w Polsce Odrodzonej*, I. Warsaw: 1932-1935; pp. 245-254.

"Sztuka plastyczna u Żydów w dawnej Rzeczypospolitej," *Żydzi w Polsce Odrodzonej*, I. Warsaw: 1932-1935; pp. 308-336.

"Żydzi galicyjscy w dobie wojny światowej," *Żydzi w Polsce Odrodzonej*, I. Warsaw: 1932-1935; pp. 413-422.

"Dzieje Żydów na ziemiach Księstwa Warszawskiego i Królestwa Polskiego," *Żydzi w Polsce Odrodzonej*, I. Warsaw: 1932-1935; pp. 423-471.

"Dzieje syjonizmu na ziemiach polskich (do 1918 r.)," *Żydzi w Polsce Odrodzonej*, I. Warsaw: 1932-1935; pp. 518-530.

"Żydzi pod zaborem pruskim," *Żydzi w Polsce Odrodzonej*, I. Warsaw: 1932-1935; pp. 551-562.

"Żydzi na Kresach północnych i wschodnich w czasach porozbiorowych," *Żydzi w Polsce Odrodzonej*. Warsaw:' 1932-1935; vol. I, pp. 563-574; vol. II, pp. 5-23.

"Rozwój literatury żydowskiej w Polsce porozbiorowej," *Żydzi w Polsce Odrodzonej*, II. Warsaw: 1932-1935; pp. 91-102.

"Żydzi polscy a sztuki piękne (muzyka i śpiew—teatr malarstwo, grafika, rzeźba—przemysl artystyczny) do 1918 r.," *Żydzi w Polsce Odrodzonej*, II. Warsaw: 1932-1935; pp. 114-147.

"Żydzi w rolnictwie na terenie Malopolski," *Żydzi w Polsce Odrodzonej*, II. Warsaw: 1932-1935; pp. 424-431.

"Żydzi w bankowości i kredycie," *Żydzi w Polsce Odrodzonej*, II. Warsaw: 1932-1935; pp. 455-463.

"Żydzi w przemyśle polskim," *Żydzi w Polsce Odrodzonej*, II. Warsaw: 1932-1935; pp. 479-541. Written together with A. Haftka.

"Udział Żydów w komunikacji i transporcie," *Żydzi w Polsce Odrodzonej*, II. Warsaw: 1932-1935; pp. 542-549.

* *Toledot ha-Kalkala ha-Yehudit*. Vols. I-II. Translated from Yiddish by A. Kariv and D. Kal'ee. Tel Aviv: 1935.

*"Kultur-geshikhtlekher fon fun der eltster yidisher literatur: Der lebnshtayger fun daytshe Yidn in der tsayt fun di ershte kraytstsugn biz dem shvartsn toyt," *YIVO Bleter*, VIII. Wilno: 1935; pp. 44-60.

"Ludność żydowska w Warszawie a ciągu 19-go stulecia: Szkic demograficzno-gospodarczy," *Krajoznawstwo*. Nos. 2/20, June 1935; No. 1/21, January 1936.

* *Dzieje handlu żydowskiego na ziemiach polskich*. Warsaw: 1937. 791 pp.

"Vi ikh hob gezen dem Bal Shem Tov," *Haynt*. Warsaw: Jubilee Issue, 1908-1938.

"Heores tsu Purim-shpiln," *Philologishe Shriftn fun YIVO*, V. Wilno: 1938; pp. 312-318.

Siedemset lat gminy żydowskiej w Płocku. Lwów: 1938. Yiddish transl. by L. Zhitnitzky, Buenos Aires: 1946.

"Di geshikhte fun Yidn in Poyln: A sintetisher iberblik," *Yidisher Gezelshaftlikher Leksikon*, I. Ed. by Dr. R. Feldschuh. Warsaw: 1939; pp. 50-90.

"A yidisher libe-roman fun mitlalter," *YIVO Bleter*, XIII. Wilno: 1939; pp. 232-245.

*"H. Graetz i jego monumentalne dzieło," *Historja Żydów*, transl. by L. Szenhak. Warsaw: 1939.

II. Other Primary and Secondary Sources Utilized in the Study

Abrahams, I. *Jewish Life in the Middle Ages.* Cleveland: Meridian Books, 1961.

Adler, E. *Jewish Travellers*. London: 1930.

Altbauer, M. "Meḥkaro shel I. Shiper al ha-Yesod ha-Kuzari-Yehudi be-Mizraḥ Eyropa," *I. Shiper.* Sh. Eidelberg, ed. New York: 1968; pp. 47-53.

Arkin, M. *Aspects of Jewish Economic History.* Philadelphia: 1975.

Aronius, J. *Regesten zur Geschichte der Juden in fränkischen und deutschen Reiche bis 1273.* Berlin: 1903.

Ashtor, E. "Ibrahim ibn Ya'qub," *The World History of the Jewish People.* Vol. II. New Brunswick, N.J.: Rutgers University Press, 1966; pp. 305-308.

Baer, I. F. Toledot ha-Yehudim bi-Sefarad ha-Notsrit. Tel Aviv: 1959.

Bałaban, M. "Dwa przyczynki do stosunków Jagiełły z Żydami lwowskymi," *Kwartalnik Historyczny*, XXV, 1911; pp. 234-239.

__________. *Dzieje Żydów w Galicyi i w Rzeczypospolitej krakowskiej (1772-1868).* Lwów: 1916.

__________. *Dzieje Żydów w Krakowie i na Kazimierzu.* Vol. I (1304-1655). Cracow: 1913.

_________. "Ha-Kehilot ha-Gedolot bi-Ymey ha-Beynayim." in *Bet Yisrael be-Polin*, I. Halpern, ed. Vol. I. Jerusalem: 1948; pp. 16-25.

_________. *Historja i literatura żydowska ze szczególnym uwzględnieniem historji Żydów w Polsce.* Vol. I. Lwów. 1924.

_________. *Historja Żydów w Krakowie i na Kazimierzu.* Cracow: 1928.

_________. "Kiedy i skąd przybyli Żydzi do Polski?", *Miesięcznik Żydowski*, I. 1931; pp. 1-12, 112-121.

_________, "Korot ha-Yehudim bi-Ymey ha-Beynayim," in *Bet Yisrael be-Polin*, I. Halpern, ed., Vol. I. Jerusalem: 1948; pp. 1-16.

_________. "Yakov Polyak, otyets polskogo rabinisma," *Yevreyskaya Starina*, VI, 1912; pp. 225-245.

_________. *Z historii Żydów w Polsce: Szkice i studja.* Warsaw: 1920.

_________. *Żydzi lwowscy na przelomie XVI i XVII wieku.* Lwów: 1906.

Baron, S. W. *A Social and Religious History of the Jews.* Vols. III-XII, 2nd ed. Philadelphia: 1962-1967.

_________. *History and Jewish Historians: Essays and Addresses*, compiled by A. Hertzberg and L. Feldman. Philadelphia: 1964.

Baron, S. W. and Kahan, A. et al. *Economic History of the Jews.* New York: 1975.

Beard, C. A. and S. Hook. "Problems of Terminology in Historical Writing," *Theory and Practice of Historical Study.* Social Science Research Council, Bulletin No. 54. New York: 1946.

Beard, M. *A History of Business: From Babylon to the Monopolists.* Ann Arbor Paperbacks: 1962.

Becker, C. L. "What Are Historical Facts?", *The Western Political Quarterly.* VII, 3, Sept. 1955; pp. 327-340.

Bershadski, S. *Russko-Yevreyskiy Arkhiv.* Petersburg: 1903.

Bergl, J. *Geschichte der Ungarischen Juden.* Leipzig: 1879.

Biderman, I. *Mayer Balaban: The Historian of Polish Jewry.* New York: Dr. J. M. Biderman Book Committee, 1976.

_________. "I. Shiper ke-Ḥoker Toldoteha shel Yahadut Polin," *Hadoar*, XLVII, June 1967; pp. 549-551.

Blazer, Y. "A blik ibern religyezn yidntum in Torne," in *Torne*, A. Chomet, ed. Tel-Aviv: 1954; pp. 215-224.

Bloch, Ph. *Die Generalprivilegien der polnischen Judenschaft.* Posen: 1892.

Blumenkrantz, B. "Germany 843-1096," *The World History of the Jewish People.* Vol. II. New Brunswick: Rutgers University Press, 1966; pp. 162-174.

Blumenthal, N. (ed.) *Dokumenty i materiały.* Vol. I. Łódź: 1946.

Borokhov, B. *Di klasn-interesn un di natsyonale frage.* Wilno: 1906.

_________. "Undzer platform," in *Poale-Zion Shriftn*, Vol. I. New York: 1920; pp. 109-320.

Boswell, A. B. "Jagiello's Successors: the Thirteen Years' War with the Knights," *The Cambridge History of Poland.* W. F. Reddaway *et al.*, eds. Cambridge: 1950; pp. 232-249.

_________. "Territorial Division and the Mongol Invasion," *The Cambridge History of Poland.* W. F. Reddaway *et al.*, eds. Cambridge: 1950; pp. 85-107.

Brann, M. *Geschichte der Juden in Schlesien.* Breslau: 1896.

Bretano, L. *Die Anfänge des modernen Kapitalismus.* Munich: 1916.

Brutzkus, J. "Di ershte yedies vegn Yidn in Poyln," *Historishe Shriftn*, I. YIVO, Warsaw: 1929; pp. 55-72.

_________. "Di geshikhte fun di Berg-Yidn oyf Kavkaz," *Historishe Shriftn*, II. YIVO, Wilno: 1937; pp. 26-42.

_________. "Di handls-batsiungen fun di Mayrev-Yidn mitn altn Kiev," *Shriftn far Ekonomik un Statistik*, I. Berlin: 1928; pp. 69-75.

_________. "The Khazar Origin of Ancient Kiev," *Slavonic and East European Review*, XXII, pp. 108-124.

Cambridge History of Poland. W. F. Reddaway, J. H. Penson, O. Halecki, R. Dyboski, eds. Vol. I. Cambridge: 1950.

Caro, G. "Die Juden des Mittelalters in ihrer wirtschafts Betätigung," *Monatschrift für Geschichte und Wissenschaft des Judentums.* Breslau: 1904; pp. 423-439, 576-603.

_________. *Sozial-und Wirtschaftsgeshichte der Juden im Mittelalter und der Neuzeit.* 2 vols. Leipzig: 1908 and 1920.

Caro, Jacob. *Vorträge und Essays.* Gotha: 1906.

Cassel, P. *Magyarische Alterthümer.* Berlin: 1848.

Charewiczowa, L. "Ograniczenia gospodarcze nacyi schizmatyckich i Żydów we Lwowie XV i XVI wieku," *Kwartalnik Historyczny*, XXXIX, 1925; pp. 193-227.

Chomet, A. "Di tsiyonistishe bavegung in Torne," in *Torne*. A Chomet, ed. Tel Aviv: 1954; pp. 351-595.

__________. "Tsu der geshikhte fun Yidn in Torne," *Torne.* A. Chomet, ed. Tel Aviv: 1954; pp. 3-186.

__________. "Yidishe visnshaftler, literatn un publitzistn fun Torne," *Torne.* A. Chomet ed. Tel Aviv: 1954; pp. 320-343.

Chvolson, D. *Achtzehn hebräische Grabschriften aus der Krim.* St. Petersburg: 1865.

__________. *Corpus inscriptionum Hebraicum.* St. Petersburg: 1882.

__________. *Ibn Dosta izvyestiya o Khazarakh.* St. Petersburg: 1869.

Collingwood, R. G. *The Idea of History.* New York: 1956.

Croce, B. *History: Its Theory and Practice.* New York: 1921.

Cyneman, J. "Dr. I. Shiper," *Kiyum.* Paris: 1950; Nos. 6-7.

Czacki, T. *Rozprawa o Żydach i Karaitach.* Wilno: 1807. 2nd ed. Cracow: 1860.

Dawidowicz, L. S. *The War Against the Jews, 1933-1945.* New York: Bantam edition, 1976.

Depping, G. *Die Juden in Mittelalter.* Stuttgart: 1834.

Donat, A. "Armageddon," *Dissent.* Spring, 1963.

__________. *The Holocaust Kingdom: A Memoir.* New York: 1965.

Dubnow, S. H. *Nationalism and History: Essays on Old and New Judaism,* ed. by K. S. Pinson. Philadelphia: JPS, 1961.

__________. *History of the Jews in Russia and Poland.* Vol. I. Philadelphia: 1916.

Dunlop, D. M. "The Khazars," *The World History of the Jewish People.* Vol. II. New Brunswick: Rutgers University Press, 1966; pp. 325-356.

__________. *The History of the Jewish Khazars.* New York: Schocken Books, 1967.

Eisenstein, A. "Prawda a lichwie żydowskiej w Polsce w XIV wieku," *Miesięcznik Żydowski,* II. 1932; Nos. 7-8, pp. 161-164.

Ettinger, G. "Kievan Russia," *The World History of the Jewish People.* Vol. II. New Brunswick: Rutgers University Press, 1966; pp. 319-324.

Feldstein, H. *Przysłość Żydów: Z powodu rozprawki Wernera Sombarta.* Lwów: 1912.

Finkel, L. and S. Starzyński. *Historya uniwersytetu lwowskiego.* Lwów: 1894.

Finkelstein, L. *Jewish Self-Government in the Middle Ages.* 2nd. ed. New York: 1964.

Flannery, E. H. *The Anguish of the Jews.* New York-London: 1965.

Fraehn, Ch. M. J. *De Chazaris: Experta de Scriptoribus Arabicis.* St. Petersburg: 1821.

Frenk, A. N. *Ha-Ironim veha-Yehudim be-Polin.* Warsaw: 1921.

Friedman, Ph. "Dzieło na czasie," *Miesięcznik Żydowski*, I. 1931; pp. 556-559.

__________. "Dzieje Żydów w Galicji, 1772-1914," *Żydzi w Polsce Odrodzonej.* Warsaw: 1932-1935; pp. 377-412.

__________. "Geshikhte fun Yidn in Ukraine," *Yidn in Ukraine.* Vol. I. New York: 1961; pp. 1-68.

__________. *Martyrs and Fighters.* New York: 1954.

__________. "Pionier nowej historiografji żydowskiej," *Opinia.* Lwów: 1934; No. 46.

__________. "Pokłosie historiografji żydowskiej lat ostatnich w Polsce," *Miesięcznik Żydowski*, V. 1935; pp. 182-194.

__________. "Polish Jewish Historiography between the Two Wars (1918-1939)," *Jewish Social Studies*, XI. 1949; pp. 373-408.

__________. "Schipper, I. *The History of Jewish Commerce in the Polish Territories*" (review), *Jewish Social Studies*, II. 1940; pp. 102-105.

Geffen, Y. "Dos yidishe-religyeze Torne", in *Torne.* A. Chomet, ed. Tel Aviv: 1954; pp. 205-216.

Gelber, N. M. *Toledot ha-Tenu'a ha-Tsiyonit be-Galitsya.* Jerusalem: 1958.

Golb, N. and O. Pritsak. *Khazarian Documents of the Tenth Century.* Ithaca and London: 1982.

Goldschmidt, S. *Geschichte der Juden in England von den ältesten Zeiten bis zu ihrer Verbannung.* Berlin: 1886.

Gumowski, M. *Wykopaliska monet z X-go i XI-go wieku.* Cracow: 1906.

Gumplowicz, L. *Prawodawstwo polskie względem Żydów.* Cracow: 1867.

Gumplowicz, M. *Początki religii żydowskiej w Polsce.* Warsaw: 1903.

Halpern, I. "Jews in Eastern Europe," *The Jews, Their History, Culture, and Religion.* L. Finkelstein, ed. New York: 1960; pp. 287-320.

__________. "On Schipper's *History of Jewish Commerce in Polish Territories*," (in Hebrew), *Kiryat Sefer*, XV. 1938; pp. 206-210.

Harkavy, A. *Ha-Yehudim u-Sefat ha-Slavim.* Vilna: 1876.

_________. "So'obshcheniya o Khazarakh," *Yevreyskaya Biblioteka.* St. Petersburg: 1880; Vol. VII, pp. 143-165; Vol. VIII, pp. 135-159.

Herzfeld, L. *Handelsgeschichte der Juden des Alterthums.* Brunswick: 1879.

Heyd, W. *Geschichte des Levantehandels im Mittelalter.* Leipzig: 1865.

Hirsch, T. *Danzigs Handels-und Gewerbegeschichte.* Leipzig: 1858.

Hirschfeld, H. *Das Buch al-Chazari.* Breslau: 1865.

_________. "Mittelalterliche Berichte von Arabern über die Slaven," *Zeitschrit der historischen Geselschaft für Provinz Posen*, IV. 1889; pp. 432-437.

Hirschaut, I. "Dr. I. Shiper—zayn lebn un shafn," in *Fun Noentn Ovar.* Congress for Jewish Culture. New York: 1955; pp. 183-264.

Hirshler, E. E. "Medieval Economic Competition," *The Journal of Economic History*, XIV. 1954; pp. 52-58.

Hoffman, M. *Der Geldhandel der deutschen Juden während des Mittelalters bis zum Jahre 1350.* Altenburg: 1910.

Hube, R. "Przywilej żydowski Bołesława i jego potwierdzenia," Biblioteka Warszawska. Warsaw: 1880.

The Itinerary of Benjamin of Tudela. Ed. and trans. by M. N. Adler. London: 1907.

Isaac b. Moses of Vienna. *Or Zaru'a.* Zhitomir: 1862; Jerusalem: 1887, 1890.

Jacob, G. *Der nord-baltische Handel der Araber im Mittelalter.* Leipzig: 1887.

Jacobs, J. *The Jewish Contribution to Civilization.* Philadelphia: 1919.

Jolowicz, H. *Geschichte der Juden in Königsberg.* Posen: 1867.

Joseph b. Joshua ha-Kohen. *Emek ha-Bakha.* Ed. by M. Letteris. Cracow: 1895.

Kaczmarczyk, K. *Akta radzieckie poznańskie.* Poznań: 1925.

Katsh, A. I., trans. and ed. *Scroll of Agony: The Warsaw Diary of Chaim A. Kaplan.* New York: 1965.

Kayserling, M. *Christoph Columbus und der Anteil der Juden an den spanischen und portugiesischen Endeckungen.* Berlin: 1894.

Kenner, J. *Kvershnit.* New York: 1947.

Kisch, G. "The Jewish Law of Concealment," *Historia Judaica.* Vol. I. 1938; pp. 3-30.

__________. "The Jews' Function in the Medieval Evolution of Economic Life," *Historia Judaica.* Vol. VI. 1944; pp. 1-12.

Klausner, J. *Historya shel ha-Sifrut ha-Ivrit ha-Ḥadasha.* 6 vols. Jerusalem: 1960.

Koczy, L. *Handel Poznania do połowy XVI wieku.* Poznań: 1930.

Kowalski, T. *Relacja Ibrahima ibn Jakuba z podróży do krajów słowiańskich w przekazie al-Berkiego.* Cracow: 1946.

Kraus, S. *Studien zur bizantisch-jüdischen Geschichte.* Vienna: 1914.

Kraushar, A. *Historya Żydów w Polsce.* Warsaw: 1865.

Księga jubileuszowa dla uczczenia sześćdziesięciolecia Profesora Majera Bałabana. Warsaw: 1938.

Kulisher, M. "Review of Schipper's *Anfänge des Kapitalismus bei den abendländischen Juden,*" Yevreyskaya Starina, I. 1909; pp. 140-144.

Kunik, E. and K. Potkański. "Lechcica," *Kwartalnik Historczny,* XII. 1898; pp. 1-20, 291-300, 497-514.

Kupfer, F. and T. Lewicki. *Źródła hebrajskie do dziejów Słowian i niektórych innych ludów środkowej i wschodniej Europy.* Wrocław-Warsaw: 1956.

Kutrzeba, S. *Handel Polski ze Wshodem.* Cracow: 1903.

__________. *Handel Krakowa w wiekach średnich.* Cracow: 1903.

__________. "Stanowisko prawne Żydów w Polsce w XV stuleciu," *Przewodnik naukowy i literacki,* XXIX. Lwów: 1901; pp. 1007-1018, 1147-1156.

Kutschera, H. *Die Chazaren.* Vienna: 1909.

Landau, J. "Yidish-sotsyalistishe partay, Zh. P.S.," *Torne.* A. Chomet, ed. Tel Aviv: 1954; pp. 632-640.

Lee, D. E. and R. N. Beck. "The Meaning of Historicism," *The American Historical Review,* LIX, No. 3; pp. 568-577.

Leniek, J. "Tarnów za czasów Leliwitów," in *Dzieje miasta Tarnowa.* Tarnów: 1911.

Lewicki, T. "Hebreishe mekoyrim tsu der geshikhte fun di slavishe felkershaftn in der tsayt fun frier mitlalter," *Bleter far Geshikhte,* IX. 1956; pp. 16-35.

Lopez, R. S. and I. W. Raymond. *Medieval Trade in the Mediterranean World.* New York: 1955.

Lord, R. H. *The Second Partition of Poland: A Study in Diplomatic History.* Cambridge: 1915.

Łoziński, W. *Patrycjat i mieszczaństwo lwowskie w XVI i XVII wieku.* Lwów: 1902.

Łukaszewicz, J. *Obraz statystyczno-historyczny Poznania.* Poznań: 1838.

Mahler, R. "Di Yidn in amolikn Poyln," *Di Yidn in Poyln.* New York: 1946; pp. 1-402.

__________. and E. Ringelblum. *Geklibene mekoyrim tsu der geshikhte fun Yidn in Poyln un mizraḥ Eyrope.* Warsaw: 1930.

__________. "Teorje żydowskiej historjografji o rozwoju dziejowym kultury żydowskiej," *Miesięcznik Żydowski*, III. 1933; pp. 208-226.

__________. *Toledot ha-Yehudim be-Polin.* Merḥavia: 1946.

__________. "Tsi zenen Yidn alemol geven a handlsfolk," *YIVO Bleter,* VII; pp. 20-35.

__________. "I. Shiper," *YIVO Bleter*, XXV. 1945; pp. 19-32.

__________. "I. Shiper u-Meḥkarav ha-Historiyim," *I. Shiper.* Ed. by Sh. Eidelberg. New York: 1966; pp. 33-45.

Mark, B. "Rzemieślnicy żydowscy w Polsce feudalnej," *Biuletyn, Żydowski Instytut Historyczny*, Nos. 9-10. 1954; pp. 5-89.

__________. *Di geshikhte fun Yidn in Poyln.* Vol. I. Warsaw: 1957.

Marylski, A. *Dzieje sprawy żydowskiej w Polsce.* Warsaw: 1912.

Meyerhoff, H. *The Philosophy of History in Our Time: An Anthology.* Garden City, N.Y.: 1959.

Neufeld, S. *Die Halleschen Juden in Mittelalter.* Berlin: 1915.

Neustadt, M. *Ḥurbn un oyfshtand fun di Yidn in Varshe.* Tel Aviv: 1948.

Nussbaum, H. *Historya Żydów od Mojżesza do epoki obecnej,* Vol. V of *Żydzi w Polsce.* Warsaw: 1890.

Oelsner, L. "Schlesische Urkunden zur Geschichte der Juden in Mittelalter," *Archiv für Kunde österreichischen Geschichte Quellen*, XXXI. Vienna: 1864; pp. 57-144.

Oelsner, T. "Wilhelm Roscher's Theory of the Economic and Social Position of the Jews in the Middle Ages," *YIVO Annual of Jewish Social Studies*, XII. 1958-1959; pp. 176-195.

__________. "The Place of the Jews in Economic History as Viewed by German Scholars," *Yearbook of the Leo Baeck Institute*, VII. 1962; pp. 183-212.

Parkes, J. "Christian Influence on the Status of Jews in Europe," *Historia Judaica*, I. 1938; pp. 31-38.

__________. *A History of the Jewish People.* Baltimore, Maryland: Penguin Books, 1964.

__________. *The Jew in the Medieval Community.* London: 1938.

Pasmanik, D. "Review of Schipper's 'Agrar-Kolonisation der Juden in Polen'," *Yevreyskaya Starina*, I. 1909; pp. 144-146.

Petaḥia b. Jacob of Regensburg. "Sibbuv," in *Exercitatione* by J.C. Wagenseil. Noriberga: 1687; pp. 167-203; or *Travels of Rabbi Petachia of Ratisbon.* Ed. and trans. by A. Benisch. London: 1856.

Pirenne, H. *Economic and Social History of Medieval Europe.* New York: 1937.

__________. "What Are Historians Trying to Do?", *Methods in Social Science.* Ed. by S. A. Rice. Chicago: 1931; pp. 435-445.

Poliak, Ab. N. *Kazariya: Toledot Mamlakha Yehudit be-Eyropa.* Tel Aviv: 1943.

Połkowski, I. *Wykopaliska głębockie średniowiecznych monet polskich.* Gniezno: 1876.

Potkański, K. *Kraków przed Piastami.* Cracow: 1897.

Ptaśnik, J. *Kultura włoska wieków średnich w Polsce.* Warsaw: 1922.

__________. *Miasta i mieszczaństwo w dawnej Polsce.* Cracow: 1934.

Rabinowitz, L. *Jewish Merchant Adventurers: A Study of Jewish Radanites.* London: 1948.

__________. "The Route of the Radanites," *Jewish Quarterly Review*, XXXV. 1945; pp. 251-280.

Rakowski, K. *Wewnętrzne dzieje Polski.* (*Zarys rozwoju społecznego i ekonomicznego.*) Warsaw: 1908.

Reich, N. "Capitalism and the Jews: A Critical Examination of Sombart's Thesis," *The Menorah Journal*, XVIII. Jan. 1930; pp. 5-19.

Responsa of Rabbi Me'ir of Rothenburg. Prague. ed., ed. by M. Bloch. Budapest: 1895. Contains responsa from *Sefer ha-Dinim* by Judah b. Me'ir ha-Kohen, Nos. 451, 861, 873-913, 935.

Ringelblum, E. "Dzieje zewnętzne Żydów w dawnej Rzeczypospolitej," *Żydzi w Polsce Odrodzonej.* I.Schipper, A. Tartakower, A. Haftka, eds. Warsaw: 1932-1935, pp. 37-80.

__________. "Fun di letzte notitsn: Der boyer fun der moderner historiografye," *Bleter far Geshikhte*, XI. Warsaw: 1958; pp. 5-14.

__________. *Żydzi Warszawie od czasów najdawniejszych do ostatniego wygnania w r. 1527.* Warsaw: 1932.

Rosanes, S. *Divrey Yemey Yisrael be-Togarma.* 2nd ed. Tel Aviv: 1930.

Roscher, W. "The Status of the Jews in the Middle Ages Considered from the Standpoint of Commercial Policy," *Historia Judaica*, VI. New York: 1944; pp. 13-26.

Rosenthal, R. "The Oldest Jewish Communities in Silesia," (in Polish translation), *Biuletyn, Żydowski Instytut Historyczny*, No. 34. Warsaw: 1960; pp. 3-27.

Roth, C. "Economic Life and Population Movements," *The World History of the Jewish People*, second series, Vol. II. New Brunswick: Rutgers University Press, 1966; pp. 13-48.

__________. "The Early Jewish Settlements in Central and Eastern Europe," *The World History of the Jewish People.* Vol. II. New Brunswick: Rutgers University Press, 1966; pp. 302-304.

Rubach, L. *Tarnów i najbliższa okolica.* Warsaw: 1953.

Rudavsky, D. *Emancipation and Adjustment.* New York: 1967.

Rutkowski, J. *Zarys dziejów gospodarczych Polski.* Poznań: 1923.

Rybarski, R. *Handel i polityka handlowa Polski w XVI-tym stuleciu.* 2 vols. Poznań: 1928; Warsaw: 1958.

Sadan, D. and H. Ormian, (eds.). *Zikhron Mordekhai Zev Braude.* Jerusalem: 1960.

Sadowski, J. N. *Pamiętnik Akademji Umiejętności.* Cracow: 1876.

Scharf, A. "Jews in Byzantium," *The World History of the Jewish People*, second series, Vol. II. New Brunswick: Rutgers University Press, 1966; pp. 49-68.

Scheffer-Boichorst, P. "Zur Geschichte der Syrer im Abendlande," *Mitteilungen des Institutes für österreichische Geschichtsforschung*, VI. 1885; pp. 521-550.

Schorr, M. *Die Hauptprivilegien der polnischen Judenschaft.* Vienna: 1917.

__________. "Organizacja Żydów w Polsce od najdawniejszych czasów aż do r. 1772," *Kwartalnik Historyczny*, XIII. 1899; pp. 482-520, 734-755.

__________. 'Zur Geschichte des Don Joseph Nassi," *Monatschrift für Geschichte und Wissenschaft des Judentums.* Vol. 41. 1897; pp. 169-177, 228-237.

__________. *Żydzi w Przemyślu do końca XVIII wieku.* Lwów: 1903.

Schtrigler, M. "Im Dr. I. Shiper be-Maydanek," *I. Shiper.* Ed. by Sh. Eidelberg. New York: 1966.

_________. *Maidanek.* Buenos Aires: 1947.

Schumpeter, J. *Ten Great Economists.* New York: 1965.

Seiden, D. "Konfektsye-industrye in Torne," *Torne.* Tel Aviv: 1954; pp. 235-239.

Seidman, H. "Ḥayyav shel Dr. I. Shiper Zal," *I. Shiper.* Ed. by Sh. Eidelberg. New York: 1966; pp. 55-64.

_________. *Togbukh fun varshever geto.* Buenos Aires, New York: 1947.

_________. *Yoman Geto Varsha.* Tel Aviv: 1946.

Shatzky, J. "Di ershte geshikhte fun yidishn teater; tsu Dr. Shiper's verk," *Filologishe Shriftn fun YIVO*, II. Wilno: 1928; pp. 215-264.

_________. "Di Yidn in Poyln fun 1772 biz 1914," *Di Yidn in Poyln.* New York: 1946.

_________. "Dr. I. Shiper (1884-1943)," *Zamlbikher*, No. 6. 1946; pp. 470-486.

_________. *Geshikhte fun Yidn in Varshe.* New York: Vol. I, 1947; Vol. II, 1948; Vol. III, 1953.

_________. "Shney Historyonim Kedoshim," *Metsuda*, II-IV. London: 1945; pp. 416-419.

Shazar, Sh. Z. "I. Shiper," in *I. Shiper.* Ed. by Sh. Eidelberg, New York: 1966.

Simonsen, D. "Les Marchands Juifs appelés 'Radanites'," *Revue des Etudes juives*, LIV. 1907; pp. 141-142.

Sokol, Sh. "I. Shiper," *Yidisher Kemfer*, XXI. New York: June 1943; pp. 10-11.

Sombart, W. "Der Anteil der Juden am Aufbau der modernen Volkswirtschaft," *Neue Rundschau*, XXI. 1910. Polish translation, *Żydzi a gospodarka społeczna* by A. W. and Z. K. Warsaw: 1911.

_________. *Die Juden und das Wirtschaftsleben.* Leipzig: 1911.

_________. *Der moderne Kapitalismus.* 2 vols. Munich-Leipzig: 1916-1917.

_________. *Jews and Modern Capitalism.* Glencoe, Ill.: 1951.

Spiegel, H. (ed.) "Schumpeter on Böhm-Bawerk," *The Development of Economic Thought*, (abridged edition). New York: 1964; pp. 369-380.

Sternberg, H. *Geschichte der Juden in Polen.* Leipzig: 1878.

Stobbe, O. *Die Juden in Deutschland während des Mittelalters.* Braunschweig: 1866.

Strauss, R. "The Jews in the Economic Evolution of Central Europe," *Jewish Social Studies*, III. 1941; pp. 15-40.

Streider, J. *Zur Genesis des modernen Kapitalismus.* Leipzig: 1905.

Strończyński, K. *Dawne monety polskie.* Piotrków: 1883.

Szczepanowski, St. *Nędza Galicji w cyfrach.* Lwów: 1888.

Szelągowski, A. *Najstarsze drogi z Polski na Wschód w okresie bizantyńskim i arabskim.* Cracow: 1909.

Szujski, J. *Odrodzenie i reformacya w Polsce.* Cracow: 1881.

Tartakover, A. "Darko shel I. Shiper be-Ḥeker ha-Kalkala ha-Yehudit," *I. Shiper.* Ed. by Sh. Eidelberg. New York: 1966; pp. 21-32.

Tawney, R. H. "Religion and the Rise of Capitalism," *The Development of Economic Thought.* Ed. by H. W. Spiegel. New York: 1964; pp. 17-30.

Tenenbaum, J. *Galitsye—mayn alte heym.* Buenos Aires: 1952.

__________. *Underground.* New York: 1952.

Theory and Practice of Historical Study: A Report of the Committee on Historiography. Social Science Research Council, Bulletin No. 54. New York: 1946.

Trani, Moses b. Joseph di. *She'elot u-Teshuvot ha-MaBIT.* Lwów: 1861; Brooklyn: 1960-1961.

Trevor-Roper, H. R. "A Fertile Error," *Commentary*, XII. July 1951; pp. 89-91.

Turkow, Z. *Fragmentn fun mayn lebn.* Buenos Aires: 1951.

Vambery, A. *Der Ursprung der Magyaren: Eine ethnologische Studie.* Leipzig: 1882.

Vogelstein, H. and P. Rieger. *Geschichte der Juden in Rom.* Vols. I-II. Berlin: 1895-1896.

Weber, M. *General Economic History.* New York: Collier Books Edition, 1966.

Weinreb, B. "Daniel Leibel," *Torne*. Tel Aviv: 1954; pp. 315-316.

Weinryb, B. D. "The Beginnings of East European Jewry in Legend and Historiography," *Studies and Essays in Honor of Abraham A. Newman.* Leiden: 1962; pp. 445-502.

_________. *The Jews of Poland: A Social and Economic History of the Jewish Community in Poland from 1100 to 1800.* Philadelphia: 1976.

Westberg, F. *Ibrahim ibn Jakub's Reisebericht über die Slavenlande aus dem Jahre 965.* Petersburg: 1898.

Wischnitzer, M. "On the Occasion of Schipper's Book about the Economic Life of Jews in Medieval Poland," (review). *Yevreyskaya Starina*, VI. 1913; pp. 133-137.

_________. "Dr. I. Schipper," *Historia Judaica*, VI. New York: 1944; pp. 98-100.

Wurtzel, E. "Funem yidishn arbeter kamf," *Torne.* Tel Aviv: 1954; pp. 667-669.

Zakrzewski, Z. "O brakteatach z napisami hebrajskimi," *Wiadomości numizmatyczno-archeologiczne*, I-IV. 1911-1913.

Zinberg, I. *Toledot Sifrut Yisrael.* 6 vols. Tel Aviv: 1959.

STATES RULED BY THE JAGIELLONS AT THE END OF THE REIGN OF CASIMIR JAGIELLO (1447-1492)

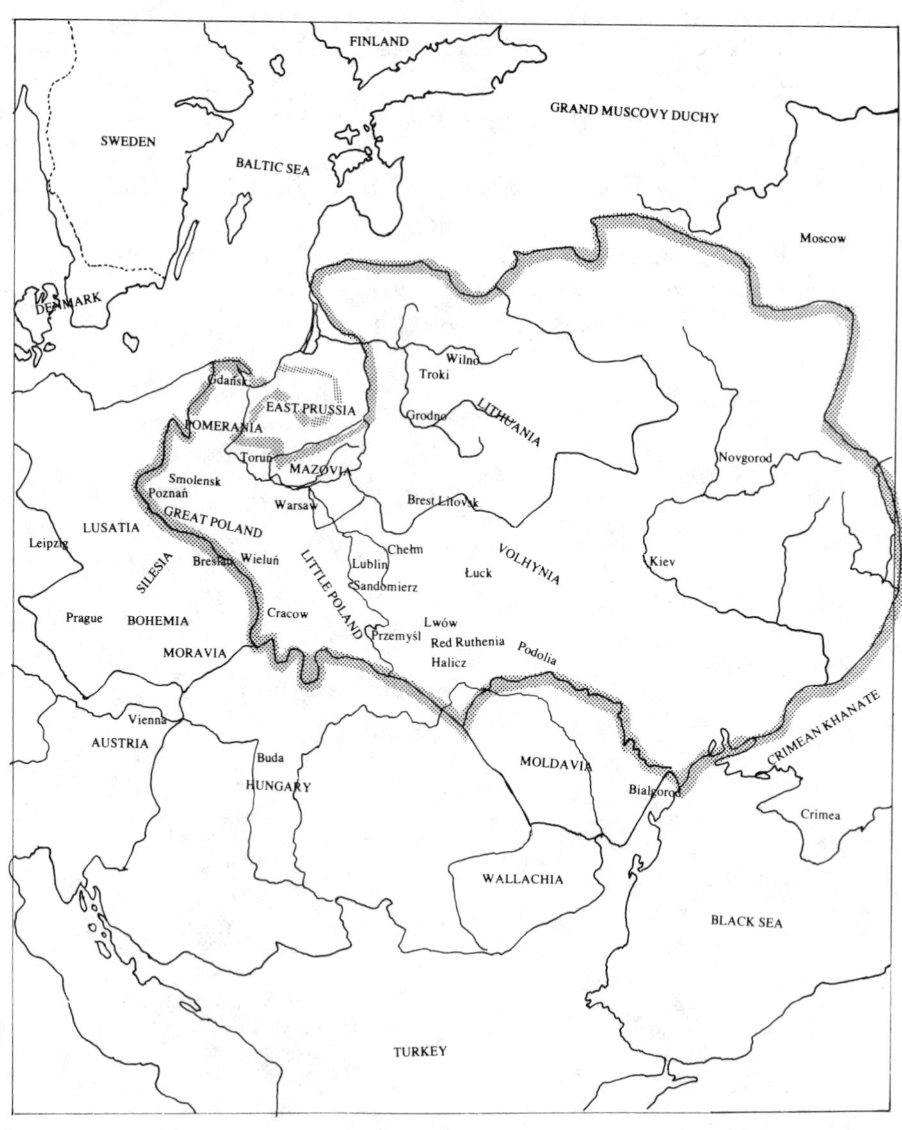

Index